D0812557

ALSO BY JOANNA RICHARDSON

Théophile Gautier: His Life and Times
Rachel
Sarah Bernhardt

Princess Mathilde

JOANNA RICHARDSON

CHARLES SCRIBNER'S SONS

New York

Copyright © 1969 Joanna Richardson

All rights reserved. No part of this book
may be reproduced in any form without the
permission of Charles Scribner's Sons.

920
M431N
132472

Printed in Great Britain
Library of Congress Catalog Card Number 70–75880

For
ENID STARKIE
to whom I owe my affection
for nineteenth-century France

Je veux laisser dans le cœur et dans l'esprit de ceux qui m'ont aimée une impression de vérité, de reconnaissance pour mes amis – c'est ma seule ambition.

Princess Mathilde to Ernest Lavisse

Contents

Illustrations

A*

The author and publishers are grateful to all of the copyright owners for permission to reproduce the pictures.

Foreword

There is no original Life of Princess Mathilde in English. The omission is remarkable, for Princess Mathilde was a woman of quite exceptional interest and distinction.

Through her father, Jerome, sometime King of Westphalia, and the youngest brother of Napoleon, she was a Bonaparte, the niece of the Emperor himself. Through her mother, Catherine of Wurtemberg, she was related to George III, and to the Czar of Russia. In a way, she synthesized the old order and the new. And since she so nearly married her cousin, Louis-Napoleon, since she very nearly became the Empress of the French, she remains a source of speculation. Speculation is, of course, not the biographer's province; but it may be said that while her private life affected history, history in turn affected her private life; and the private life of Princess Mathilde, a woman deprived of maternity, unable to find a man who deserved her love or her esteem, is itself an illuminating emotional and spiritual progress.

Princess Mathilde failed to be an Empress or to enjoy normal domesticity. She turned both failures into personal triumphs. Just as her uncle had crowned himself Emperor of the French, so she assumed an empire of her own: she created her own realm, within the Second Empire – a realm which lasted into the Third Republic. She made herself the benevolent sovereign of the world of scholarship and the arts. Disappointed in love and marriage, she found compensation in friendships: she made devoted friends of the men whose achievements adorned the age. It was in her salon at the rue de Courcelles (and, later, at the rue de Berry), it was in her château at Saint-Gratien, that decorations were demanded, sinecures bestowed, pensions and Chairs and Academic uniforms ensured. It was there that plays were first performed, sonnets were composed, novels read aloud, and music played,

The Court of the Tuileries was frivolous, ignorant of true distinction. Princess Mathilde recognized and fostered it.

For more than fifty years, from the beginning of the Second Empire, Frenchmen spoke of 'la princesse'. It was impossible that they should mean any other. They also spoke of 'la bonne princesse' – and this was not merely a compliment to royalty. Whatever her faults – and they were obvious – Princess Mathilde took a lifelong pleasure in benevolence. For all her personal disappointments, for all the more public tragedies she encountered, she remained affectionate and generous. She was, by her birth, involved in the history of France. She was, by her nature, a noble figure in French history. During the Empire, and during the thirty years she lived on in the Republic, she presided over a *salon* which the Goncourts called 'the true *salon* of the nineteenth century'. She brought the tradition of the *salon* to its highest point, its greatest brilliance. She gave imperial inspiration and faithful, strong affection. The affection was widely returned, and the inspiration remains a part of French civilization.

I should like to express my deep gratitude to Count Campello, who gave me access to the Primoli Papers. These include all the papers which Princess Mathilde bequeathed to her nephew, Joseph Primoli. I am very grateful to Professor Marcello Spaziani for introducing me to the Campello archives at Spoleto. I am much indebted to M. Claude Popelin, grandson of Claudius Popelin, who generously allowed me to use his family papers, and to M. Serge Grandjean, Conservateur au Musée du Louvre, who let me quote the Princess's letters to his grandparents, and has helped me frequently with his advice. I am grateful once again to M. and Mme Pierre Théophile Gautier, for their hospitality in Paris, and for much material for my book. I should like to record my gratitude to the late M. Émile Henriot, of the Académie-Française, who generously allowed me to use the letters of Théophile Gautier to Carlotta Grisi. I must also thank Dr Edwin Binney, Captain C. G. Gordon, Mr Harold Kurtz, Mme Loste, Mme M. Cordroc'h of the Départment des Manuscrits, Bibliothèque Nationale, and the staff of the British Museum Reading Room and Newspaper Library.

J.R.

London – Paris – Spoleto
June 1968.

Introduction

On 18 June 1815 the Battle of Waterloo ended the long war against Napoleon. On 13 July Napoleon addressed himself to the Prince Regent, 'the strongest, the stubbornest, and the most generous of my foes'; he asked to be given asylum in England.

It was hardly a request to be granted. England was too near France. The memory of the escape from Elba was still fresh in everyone's mind. As the Prime Minister told a colleague: 'The best place to imprison him would be a long way from Europe. The Cape of Good Hope or St Helena would be the most suitable place for the purpose.'

The genius of unrest was therefore sent to St Helena. The Emperor had ravaged Europe, and, for nearly fifteen years, he had tried to starve out England. Now, under the supervision of Sir Hudson Lowe, he spent his last six years on a tiny tropical island off the west coast of Africa.

The map of Europe was re-planned by the Congress of Vienna in 1814-15. In France, with the blessing of the Allied Powers, the Bourbons were restored. The dynasty had ended with the Revolution of 1789 – perhaps one should say with the execution of Louis XVI in 1793. Now it was restored in the person of his younger brother. Louis XVIII had entered Paris in triumph in 1814, when Napoleon had been exiled to Elba; he had hurried off to seek safety in Ghent during the Hundred Days. In 1815, he returned to France for the second time, to earn the title Louis Deux-fois-neuf.

Louis XVIII married a princess of Savoy, but he left no children; and when he died in 1824, his brother, the Comte d'Artois, became king as Charles X. The new king's anti-liberal, pro-Catholic policy led to the Revolution of July 1830, and the end of the rule of the elder branch of the Bourbons.

The last French king was Louis-Philippe of Orléans-Bourbon, the son of Philippe-Égalité, Duc d'Orléans. He belonged to a junior, collateral branch of the family. He came to the throne with the support of liberals and republicans, as a constitutional monarch.

As for the Bonapartes, they remained a potential danger. Until the reign of Louis-Philippe, no one cared to rescind the law of 12 January 1816. This law had made them into exiles for the foreseeable future, by depriving them of civil rights in France.

PART ONE

The First Exile

1820–40

'I was born in exile – civically dead – at Trieste, on 27 May 1820.'
So Princess Mathilde began her memoirs. She was the daughter of
Jerome, the ex-King of Westphalia, the youngest brother of
Napoleon. When Mathilde came into the world, the Emperor
was ending his prodigious life on St Helena, and the Bonapartes
were banned from France. 'Everyone,' Mathilde would write,
'knows about the events which made my family into so many
outcasts. My father, who had fought for France, who had been
among the last to shed his blood for her, saw himself rejected like
his brothers. He was robbed of his possessions, and his native
land was forbidden him.'[1] Since one of his possessions had been
the Kingdom of Westphalia, Jerome was now obliged to use the
derisory title of Prince de Montfort; and he was living far beyond
his straitened means, in the style which he felt befitting for a
Bonaparte and a former sovereign.

This extravagance was not surprising. Jerome had always been
irresponsible. Years ago, as a young naval officer, he had contracted a marriage with Elizabeth Paterson, the daughter of a
merchant in Boston, and there had been a son of this impulsive
and unsuitable alliance. Napoleon had had more appropriate plans
for his brother. He had commanded Jerome to leave his American
wife. The marriage had been declared invalid and Jerome had been
given a suitable consort: Princess Catherine of Wurtemberg.
Catherine's father, Frederick I of Wurtemberg, was at least a
nominal sovereign, and his sister had married Paul I of Russia.
Catherine's mother, by some irony, was a niece of George
III.

Catherine was undoubtedly Jerome's most precious asset. She
was regal, virtuous, and entirely devoted to him. She had refused
all suggestions that she should abandon him in exile. She had
brought domestic stability – as far as any wife could bring it –

into his feckless life. She had forgiven him, and she would always forgive him, for his numerous, ostentatious infidelities. She had given him a son, Jerome-Napoleon-Charles, in the summer of 1814; now she had presented him with a daughter.

Laetitia-Mathilde-Frédérique-Aloïssia-Élisabeth, who was born about seven o'clock on that May evening, thus inherited a double prestige. Indeed, her names proclaimed her remarkable ancestry and connections. Laetitia was the name of her paternal grand-mother, the Emperor's own mother, Madame Mère. Mathilde was the name of her mother's stepmother, Charlotte Augusta Matilda, daughter of George III and Princess of Great Britain and Ireland. Mathilde inherited the aura of the most illustrious parvenu family of modern times; she inherited (though she would always dismiss the fact) the dignity of a family which had known centuries of royalty.

Two Bonapartes, a brother and a sister of Jerome's, were asked to be godparents to Mathilde: Joseph, a former king of Spain, and Élisa, Grand Duchess of Tuscany. As soon as Mathilde had been christened, she was handed over to her nurse. She spent the next three years in Trieste. It was here, on 9 September 1822, that Napoleon-Joseph-Charles-Paul, her younger brother, was born.

Six months later, the décor of her childhood changed abruptly. The Allied Sovereigns gave Jerome permission to settle near his ageing mother in Rome. On 26 March 1823, accompanied by his family, by the Baroness de Reding, Mathilde's Swiss gover-ness, and by his secretary the Comte de Böhle, Jerome arrived at the palace in Rome which Madame Mère had temporarily put at his disposal.

The whole scattered Bonaparte family had reassembled round Madame Mère, a matriarch of almost classical character. When Jerome came to Rome, she was seventy-three, small and thin, with dark eyes full of fire. She was still unmistakably Corsican: indeed, Henry Fox, the future Lord Holland, said that she spoke French 'with great difficulty, and with a very strong vicious Italian accent ... The only thing that struck me about her as very peculiar is her smile, which ... appears extremely engaging.' Henry Fox was privileged to earn this 'extremely sweet and playful' smile;[2] for, in the eyes of her son, Madame Mère was an unsmiling figure:

A black merino dress, a turban in the Empire style: this was her sole and sober attire.

She never crossed the threshold of her palace except in a carriage, and a closed carriage; every day, from one till three, she would go out like this, and have herself driven into the Roman countryside. And there, in those solitudes where everything seemed dead, except for the memories of the past, she would walk alone . . .[3]

Her half-brother, Cardinal Fesch, spent the greater part of his time with her, arguing or dozing; she ate her meals with him, or ate alone. And every day, from four to six, announced by the old Chevalier de Colonna, her sons and daughters and daughters-in-law would visit her at the Palazzo Rinuccini.

Jerome did not miss a single visit: she kept great authority over him, and often reprimanded him, chiefly for his extravagance. Her rebukes were understandable, for the Bonapartes were far from rich. She herself had £3,000 a year, and saved, because she spent only half of it; all the other Bonapartes, said Hortense, the former Queen of Holland, lived 'by selling jewels and bits of old finery they have saved in the wreck, but this cannot last long.' Madame Mère wanted security for her sons, and this anxiety embittered her life.[4]

Jerome and his family must have been acutely aware of her bitterness. Everything about her palace in the Piazza Venezia was silent and severe,

submitted to unchanging rules and imbued with some mysterious aroma of the past. Everything, even the furniture, which had to be respected as one respects the habitual surroundings of the old, fascinated and astonished the little children; sometimes their natural turbulence would suddenly give way to fear, in the presence of this bereavement – for they felt, though they could not comprehend, its profundity.[5]

Every Sunday, after Mass, Mathilde and her younger brother would be taken to this sombre palace, where the rooms were cold and high, and there was hardly a light to be seen after sunset, and the old servants, dressed in black, were always sad and silent, constantly in the presence of mourning. It was a formidable experience. Half a century later, Mathilde still recalled the old Roman matron, dressed – she said – in brown, with a white bonnet.

She had small hands. I particularly remember their fineness and transparency, but her fingers were crabbed with age. She had with her Napoleon's nurse, old Saveria Robaglia, who always gave us biscuits . . . I remember her perfectly: she was rather hunched, and very small.

Mme Laetitia used to greet us politely, but without affection. Napoleon did not like kissing her; still less did he like to kiss the diaphanous, wrinkled hand which, on occasion, she held out to him. Her old face troubled him. This visit, during which she sometimes spun, used to last ten minutes.[6]

Mathilde was not allowed, for a moment, to forget her Bonaparte connections. Every Sunday, when she had paid her visit to Madame Mère, she would be taken to see her great-uncle Fesch, in the Falconieri palace on the banks of the Tiber. The walls were dark and hung with pictures, the rooms were very cold, and the Cardinal, small, rotund and lively, in his French *soutane*, impressed her by his love of the arts and by his devotion to France: whatever offers were made to him, he refused to abandon his title of Archbishop of Lyons and Primate of the Gauls.

When they had visited Great-uncle Fesch, the children would be taken, every Sunday, to see their Aunt Hortense, the daughter of the Empress Josephine. She was living apart from her remarkably difficult husband, Louis Bonaparte, the former King of Holland, now known as the Comte de Saint-Leu. She tried to maintain the reputation of a woman of feeling, and among her admirers were Isabey, the miniaturist, and Joseph Méry, Marseillais man of letters, and author of the epic poem *Napoléon en Égypte*. Mathilde and her brother used to visit the Palazzo Ruspoli with relief, for Hortense welcomed them eagerly, and she was always showing them baubles and trinkets which caught their imagination. When her son Louis-Napoleon was there, Mathilde's delight was complete. Louis-Napoleon was twelve years older than herself, and he had the prestige of age, but he played very amiably with her and Napoleon. When Louis came to the Montforts' palace, he exhilarated Mathilde by doing all that she did not dare to do: he was even mischievous during mass. 'Judging by his lack of piety during the service,' she would write of the future Napoleon III, 'one might have expected less religiosity from him when he ascended the throne.'[7]

When the Prince de Montfort first came to Rome, he was deeply

in debt; but that did not prevent him from buying a palace from
his brother Lucien, Prince of Canino. It was in the Palazzo
Nunez, 'certainly the best mounted and most princely looking
establishment in Rome',[8] that most of Mathilde's Roman
childhood was spent.

The Palazzo Nunez stood at the corner of the Via Condotti
and the Bocca di Leone. One floor was given up to reception
rooms, another to the apartments of Jerome and Catherine, and
the third was a summer 'penthouse', where Catherine used to
move at the end of April. This 'penthouse' was not much used,
however, for the Montforts nearly always spent the summer in
the country, generally in the March of Ancona. In 1826 Jerome
bought a seaside villa at Porto di Fermo, but politics decreed that
they spent only one summer there. The King of Naples could not
allow a Bonaparte so near his frontier.

The Montfort household, like the Palazzo Nunez, recalled
Jerome's vanished state. Catherine had a lady-in-waiting; Jerome
had an equerry and a secretary. Mathilde would in time have a
second governess as well as the Baroness de Reding. 'I shall not
list all my mother's ladies-in-waiting,' she wrote, blandly, in
her later years. 'They changed quite often . . . My father was the
most amiable of men, and he carried gallantry to the point of
imprudence. However, his equerry, Baron de Stoelting, was a
good scapegoat . . .'[9]

In this atmosphere of royalty, dynastic pride, and licence,
Mathilde was brought up with her younger brother. Indeed,
until she was seven and Napoleon was five, they shared a room;
and no doubt, in their small mahogany beds, as they talked to
one another after dark, they laid the foundation of their close
relationship. Mathilde would sometimes be exasperated by
Plon-Plon (as Napoleon was called from his nursery days), she
would criticize him, in public, with brutal frankness; but she
would never lose her affection for him. It would be the maternal
fondness of an elder sister, who understood his passions and
frustrations; it was tinged with a certain respect for his intelligence. No one denied that Plon-Plon had intelligence, though,
alas, he would often misapply it. 'There is so much gold in
him,' a friend wrote to Mathilde, 'that one must forgive him
for the alloy.'[10]

In 1827, when Plon-Plon was five, he was entrusted to tutors, and Mathilde, who was seven, had a governess. Strangely enough, the Emperor's niece was given an English governess, who not only stayed for four years, but won her affection; she was followed by an unsatisfactory French governess, whose reign was brief, and then, as Mathilde was nearly eleven, a series of masters took over her education.

I was an excellent pupil [she confessed, in her memoirs], I was full of self-respect, zealous and docile, and very devoted to my teachers. Napoleon was having his lessons with me at the time and I must admit that he was lazy and mischievous. All the same, he was my mother's favourite. She had had him at the age of forty-two. He was extemely like the Emperor Napoleon, which made him very happy, and very proud . . . As for me, I never had very much love from my mother, because I was a girl. She was rather quick with her hand. She had been brought up in the German fashion, and she decided to bring me up the same way. Had it not been for my father, who had quite different principles, she would have educated me according to the methods of the *ancien régime* . . .[11]

In later life, Mathilde still recalled 'the agonies of her childhood, . . . which made her unable to see her mother except as a torturer who was jealous of her.'[12] She had been forced to stand in a box, so that she would curtsey correctly. She had been compelled to wear stiff, high corsets; one day she had puffed herself out so as not to get them on, and her mother had thrashed her. Mathilde had a horror of pigeon and Plon-Plon detested veal, and they had been forced for months to eat pigeon and veal. They had begun by throwing the execrated food under the table, then they had changed plates with one another, and finally they had come to like what they were given.

Yet, looking back on her education from the vantage-point of her middle age, Mathilde would have to own that she and her brother had been educated with care; and, in a passage in her memoirs which is worth recalling, she would express her debt to her parents.

I must do this justice to my parents: I must admit that they gave us excellent principles. It was they who taught us to adore France, and to love liberty. It was they who taught us to respect the old, and to love every form of charity. Though we were princes and brought up as princes, there was never any room in our hearts for the spirit of caste, that vain, absurd egoism which makes one scorn all those who

are not nobly born. We were taught the value of diligence, the extreme importance of occupation. My father respected people who
worked; he often used to repeat the well-known saying: 'There are
no stupid occupations, there are just stupid people.' As for religion,
we were taught to believe in God, to hope in His goodness and to
respect all religious ceremonies. We were brought up simply, . . . but
we were healthy, and we were loved by everyone who knew us.[13]

Much of the credit for this balanced childhood, and for
Mathilde's own disposition, must be given to a member of the
household who had been in Catherine's service throughout the
exile. Madame de Reding was the widow of a Swiss baron; she
had lost her own child in infancy. She had watched over Mathilde
from her birth, and gradually she had come to love her as her
own daughter. It was inevitable that Mathilde, who received so
little affection from her mother, should respond to her maternal
governess. Her devotion to Madame de Reding began as the
love of a small, dependent child, it would remain unshaken
through all the vicissitudes of domestic life, all the changing
circumstances of politics. Mathilde would love Madame de
Reding as she could not love her own mother. She loved her
with all the warmth of her nature.

No-one was ever looked after by a more affectionate soul, a more
devoted being [she wrote, some twenty years after Madame de
Reding's death]. I loved her more than my mother, whom I hardly
knew. Her memory is a religion to me. My eyes grow wet with tears
whenever I think of her, and nothing has been able to lessen my regrets
for her. I have not taken any important decision, I have had no joy,
no grief in my life without thinking about her and trying to discover
what she [would have] felt, as I always did when she was alive. There
was never a secret between us; she was good and generous at heart,
strict in her principles, but gentle in her piety. I can truly say that I've
felt her loss more than any other.[14]

Mathilde's Roman childhood, so carefully recorded in her
memoirs, did not pass unobserved by the outside world. Henry
Fox used to visit the Palazzo Nunez. He observed the royal
etiquette, punctiliously kept at dinner-parties, and he enjoyed a
Carnival ball, at which Catherine did the honours 'with great
good-humour and dignity'.[15] The Montforts were also observed
by that lively woman of letters, Lady Blessington. She noted that
they gave *soirées* twice a week, and received 'all the foreigners of

distinction, several of the Roman nobles, and the Ambassador of
Russia and his attendants'.[16] Since Catherine was the first cousin
of Nicholas I, the Russian envoy paid her every respect. No one
in Rome was allowed to forget her two-fold royalty. She used
the Bonaparte liveries of dark green and gold, and every day she
drove out in her carriage with her children, Mme de Reding,
and her lady-in-waiting. Jerome de Montfort rode through Rome
attended by his chamberlain and by two or three others of his
suite.[17]

In the summer of 1828 Lady Blessington called on the
Montforts. They asked her questions about England, 'about which
they seemed to experience much interest.' The illusion of
domestic bliss was enhanced by the presence of 'two remarkably
fine children, a boy and a girl, with the preceptor of one, and the
governess of the other.' Both parents, Lady Blessington wrote,
'seemed gratified by our admiration of them.'[18]

It was a curious interview which she described in *The Idler in
Italy*. Catherine de Montfort expressed 'a strong desire to visit
England', but added, with regret: 'I am too nearly related to the
royal family of England to go there, situated as we are . . . My
children may perhaps visit it under more propitious circumstances.'[19] Yet the Princess who spoke so warmly of England
was married to the brother of Napoleon, and their palace had
become a museum devoted to the Emperor's memory. One room
was hung with engravings of all his battles, and Lady Blessington
noticed that 'three of the hats worn in battle, and sundry pairs
of gloves used on the same occasions, [were] placed in glass cases
beneath the engravings of the actions where they were worn!'[20]

Mathilde, who was never close to her mother, never shared her
affection for England: indeed, she would visit it only when
family duty demanded. She would conceive for England and the
English a lifelong and implacable aversion. England would
remain for her the country of Nelson and Wellington, of the
Prince Regent and Sir Hudson Lowe. In the palace of Madame
Mère, the palace of Cardinal Fesch, the palace of Queen Hortense,
in the Palazzo Nunez at the corner of the Via Condotti, she was
never unaware, for a moment, that she was the niece of
Napoleon.

In 1830 came the news of the July Revolution. Fifteen years after

Waterloo, the Bourbon Restoration was over. Charles x went into exile, and Catherine de Montfort told her children: 'At last you are going to be French.' Perhaps the Duc de Reichstadt would return to France and ascend his father's throne.

All the hopes of the Bonapartes were dashed when Louis-Philippe became the King of the French; but the Vatican had been disturbed by Jerome's intrigues and correspondence. Some said that the Pope ordered him to leave Rome; Mathilde ascribed the move to her father's prudence and to his own anxiety about the Roman government. Whatever the reason, Catherine's brother, William I of Wurtemberg, offered to take her elder son, Jerome, to Louisburg to finish his studies, and then to take him into his service. In the late summer of 1831, Mathilde learned that her parents would leave Rome before the winter, and settle in Florence.[21]

Only the most unresponsive could fail to be spellbound by the capital of Tuscany. Marguerite Blessington fell in love with the sheltering Apennines, the nearer vineyards and olive-groves, the Cascine which was to Florence what Hyde Park was to London (though in Hyde Park, perhaps, one might not find 'the abundance of pheasants and hares that run across the green glades'). Above all, it was delightful to sit on a terrace after sunset, 'enjoying the balmy air, unshawled and unpelissed'. The nights were delectable: 'The moon, reflected as in a mirror on the placid Arno; the spires and towers that rise at every side silvered with its rays, and the sounds of the guitar continually passing and repassing on the Lung-Arno, give an indescribable charm to them . . .'

It was a charm which Mathilde must have known in the last years of her childhood and the early years of her adolescence. In November 1831, when she was eleven and a half, her family settled at the Palazzo Seristori, on the banks of the Arno.

However, she was far from wasting her time in romantic daydreams: she worked extremely hard. She and Plon-Plon had most of their lessons together. There were few distractions. Twice a year, at most, they were taken to the theatre. In the summer, they went to the seaside at Leghorn. Their life was kept strictly separate from that of their parents; they had their meals apart, and went for walks with their tutor and governess. Mathilde, like many children, enjoyed the security of a well-filled life: the comfort of predictable routine. It was in Rome and Florence that she formed the attachment to organization and occupation which she would keep for the rest of her long existence. She was to practise this bourgeois virtue with all the diligence of a Wurtemberg and all the energy of a Bonaparte.

It was not, perhaps, surprising that her favourite subject was history; but she worked intensely at English and German, and she already showed a passion for drawing. As for music, she learnt the piano, the harp, and singing, and showed no disposition for any of them. Her speaking voice was musical, but she could not sing in tune. 'They say,' she wrote, complacently, 'that this is a sign of my race.'[2]

It was, however, at a concert that Joseph Méry, the friend of Aunt Hortense, recorded Napoleon's niece. Early in the 1830s, gathering material for his travel book, *Scènes de la Vie italienne*, Méry found himself in Florence, where the Prince de Montfort was having a concert in his new and splendid palace, the Palazzo Orlandini. Even in Florence, a city known for its dancing and its music, Jerome was famous for his entertainment. The art of entertaining was an art which he would teach his impressionable daughter. Indeed, Méry's comments on this evening in Florence were the kind of comments that visitors would make on Mathilde's own *salon*, many years later. In this palace where the arts were fostered, where politics were forgotten, 'there shone, like a diamond, young Princess Mathilde.'[3]

By the summer of 1833, Catherine de Montfort's health was causing her family some anxiety. July found her taking the baths at Battaglia.

My dear little Mathilde [wrote Jerome de Montfort on 6 July],
Your letter of the 27th is so well written that I am answering myself to tell you it has given me double pleasure. Kiss my dear Napoleon; but tell him that papa is cross that he is not working, and here I must reprove the good Alde for taking you to the theatre although Mr Topaz was not pleased with your work.
Mama stopped taking the waters for three days, we spent the time on a visit to Venice, today everyone is taking the waters again and on the 24th at the latest we shall be back in Florence from which we shall go to Leghorn and thence to Stuttgart. We have heard from Jerome, who is well and sends you his love, he is delighted at the thought of seeing you again & says that he is counting the days . . .[4]

On 1 September the Montforts finally set off for Stuttgart. On 17 September, after a journey of more than a fortnight, they reached the royal castle; and here the two eldest princesses, Marie and Sophie, the King of Wurtemberg's daughters by his second

marriage, took charge of Mathilde and Napoleon. Sophie, who
would be the wife of William III of Holland, conceived a lasting
affection for Mathilde. Mathilde, who was thirteen, no doubt
admired this elder cousin of fifteen; she loved her instantly for
her generosity, her poetic nature and warmth of heart. Drawn
together in their youth, they would remain devoted to each other
until Sophie died in 1877. Sophie was the only woman of her
own rank to be an intimate friend of Mathilde's. The isolation
imposed by their social status, the vicissitudes of their marriages,
the turbulence of international politics, would only bind them
closer to each other.

My God [wrote Sophie on 16 September 1836], it will be three
years ago tomorrow that I saw you for the first time, my dear Loko;
do you remember, you had a lilac grey dress, a straw hat, and your
grandmother's little earrings? . . . I shall never forget that moment.
It was upstairs, in those Rooms which I have only seen once since
then, when the Grand Duchess Helena was living there . . .[5]

It is *eight years* ago today that I saw you for the first time [added
Sophie, then Princess of Orange, on 17 September 1841]. You were
almost a child, then, but you already had that indefinable charm of
your own, you were a little embarrassed, we were excessively so . . .
I can still see dear Nanan [Madame de Reding] coming in, I can see
my aunt, & the pale & wan face of Napoleon. That was eight years
ago, and the weather was fine like it is today . . .[6]

When Mathilde was writing her memoirs, she came across
an album in which the cousins had written their farewells. On
4 October 1833, Sophie had written: 'Dear Mathilde, in finding
you I have found a friend for life. I know that, even when we're
apart, nothing will break the bond between our hearts.' After an
interval of forty years, Mathilde could add: 'She spoke the truth:
nothing has broken, or ever can break, the bond between our
hearts.'[7]

The return to Florence was dismal, largely because of Catherine's
condition. This only worsened during the next few months. The
doctors, who were anxious to shed responsibility, seized the
pretext of a cholera epidemic to advise her to go to Switzerland.

In April 1835, the family set out. Mathilde and Napoleon
travelled in a big berlin, with Mme de Reding and Mlle de

Malchus, their mother's lady-in-waiting. Their parents went on ahead in a coupé; behind them followed a carriage full of servants. After a week or so, they reached Geneva, where they stayed for a month; and it was here that Catherine became a helpless invalid. Jerome decided that they should winter in Lausanne, where the climate was usually mild. The family arrived there early in October.

It soon became evident that Lausanne would not restore Catherine's health. In November, the doctors announced that she had dropsy.

The illness had already proved fatal to several members of her family, and it was clear that she, too, would not survive. Jerome sent for his elder son, and, on 28 November, Mme de Reding took Mathilde and Napoleon to their mother. They knelt beside her bed, and she blessed them.

She died at half-past two next morning, 29 November 1835. Napoleon was thirteen, and Mathilde fifteen.[8]

Jerome was overwhelmed by the death of his wife. He mourned her good sense and gaiety, her nobleness of nature, her exceptional loyalty and devotion. She had accepted him, almost unknown; she had spent most of her marriage in exile, bearing him three children, forgiving him his extravagance, his financial straits, his bitterness and, above all, his unfaithfulness. He had brought little to the marriage but the glamour of his family, the derisory kingdom of Westphalia, and his own attractive, commanding person; she had brought the majesty inherited from generations of royalty, and she had brought the more solid virtues of domesticity and fidelity. Her younger son, Napoleon, was to be unmistakably Bonaparte. Mathilde was to show, throughout her life, the contrasting, complementary sides of her nature. She would show the panache, the energy, the unpredictable passion, the ardent love of glory, of the Bonapartes. She would be proud of her Bonaparte blood with a fanatical pride. Yet from her mother, whom she would recall with small affection, she would inherit her instinctive royalty, and her most endearing qualities: her almost bourgeois love of home, her integrity and her absolute faithfulness.

3

Catherine de Montfort was buried in the Wurtemberg family vault at Louisburg. When Queen Hortense heard of her death, she promptly sent Louis-Napoleon to Lausanne. He invited the Montforts to spend the rest of the winter at Arenenberg, his mother's château on the shores of Lake Constance. Jerome decided that Napoleon might go. Mathilde might spend a week there, before she visited her uncle, the King of Wurtemberg, at Stuttgart.

It was evident, even now, that Hortense was not merely offering hospitality to her nephew and niece. Louis-Napoleon was twenty-seven, and it seemed time that he married. He might well find a wife in Mathilde, and, now that her mother had died, Mathilde might be all the more inclined for domesticity. Her father would no doubt be delighted if she married a Bonaparte, and he would gladly shed the financial burden. In Catherine's lifetime, he had enjoyed a pension from Russia and another from the King of Wurtemberg. William of Wurtemberg had now reduced his allowance to twelve thousand francs a year for the education of Mathilde and Napoleon.[1]

Hortense had clearly made these points to her son before he went to Lausanne, for Louis-Napoleon no longer looked on Mathilde with a cousin's eyes. He had been sent to comfort the girl who had just lost her mother; he had also been instructed to consider the girl as a possible wife. He did not feel a *coup de foudre*.

Mathilde is charming [he reported to Hortense], but don't think that I'm in love with her. Not at all. I have quite a different feeling for her. If I weren't afraid of marriage, I should be glad to have her as my wife, but her visit to Stuttgart will spoil her. The King of Wurtemberg is extremely good to them all, he wants to treat her like a daughter, and you know that Courts are like coquettes: you always malign them, but you can't leave them once you have known them.[2]

Early in December, Jerome and his two younger children set out by coach across Switzerland, for Arenenberg. They spent their nights at different inns, and once, believing his daughter was asleep, Jerome had a long conversation with Mme de Reding. Mathilde, as it happened, was awake, and she heard every word.

The conversation was about me; my father said he wanted me to get married, he mentioned the difficulties there would be, but he spoke of the possibility of my marrying Prince Louis-Napoleon. As for the Baroness, she maintained that my cousin liked me very much, she had constantly found him gazing at me. She said if it only suited me, she was sure that it could easily be arranged.[3]

Two days later, the Montforts reached Constance, where Louis-Napoleon was waiting to escort them to Arenenberg. It was a kind of brick and timber châlet, Mathilde remembered, adorned with the pretentious title of château.

Hortense showed her infinite kindness. She gave her a room near her own, and every morning Mathilde would go to the bedroom hung with white muslin and rose-coloured cambric, where her aunt lay, smiling, in bed, and talked about Mathilde's future, 'so that putting together what she said and the conversation I'd heard between my father and Baroness de Reding, I concluded,' wrote Mathilde, 'that Queen Hortense had similar ideas.'[4]

Years later, Mathilde looked back with affection on her week at Arenenberg. No one else, she wrote, had her aunt's gift for creating a happy atmosphere around her.

Prince Louis was gay, unruly, a bit of a story-teller, and a little given to banter. He took a good deal of interest in us, &, without actually paying court to me, he showed a great preference for me. This did not worry me, quite the opposite. So I readily joined in our little flirtation.

For all these reasons, I was very sorry to leave my aunt. She had an indescribable charm. She would in fact have liked to keep me, but the King of Wurtemberg had insisted that I should spend the winter with him and his family, & my father felt obliged not to refuse him. Louis asked permission to keep Napoleon with him, and make him work. Permission was given. I set off, full of envy for my brother's fate . . . , escorted by my father & accompanied by Mme de Reding.[5]

At Stuttgart, Mathilde led the same life as her cousins, Marie and Sophie. She was enchanted to be treated as an adult, and allowed to wear a low-cut dress and short sleeves. She was not unaware, even now, of her powers of attraction. She knew the charm of her brown eyes, of the complexion so delicate that admirers could not distinguish a rose-petal from her cheek. The King of Wurtemberg, she observed, 'was clearly not insensible to my good graces. After dinner I sometimes played Pope Joan with him. He was a remarkably bad player.'⁶

While Mathilde strove to earn her uncle's approval, Sophie was seized by a passion for Lord William Russell, the English Ambassador: indeed, one day, when he was at the castle, she persuaded Mathilde to slip a note under his door. 'He picked it up,' Mathilde recorded. 'I don't know what could have been in it, but I don't imagine it was worth all those precautions.'⁷ As for Marie, she was flirting with Mathilde's brother, Jerome, now an engaging young man of twenty-one. 'What my cousins needed more than anything else,' wrote Mathilde, indulgently, 'was to put a little romance into their existence. That lasted until they were married.'⁸ Sophie would be the first to get married: she would become the wife of the Prince of Orange, the future William III of Holland. Her marriage would be largely ruined by her husband's infatuation for the celebrated Madame Musard. Marie of Wurtemberg would marry Count Alfred de Neipperg, the son of General Count Neipperg who, after Napoleon's death, had married the Empress Marie-Louise. 'Except for the name Neipperg, I think that the man would please you,' Sophie told Mathilde. 'He possesses every quality to make a woman happy.'⁹ Neipperg made Marie unhappy until a hunting accident ruined his physical and mental health and forced him to end his days in an asylum.

In the winter of 1835, Mathilde, like her cousins, needed 'a little romance' more than anything else. Hortense ensured that it was not forgotten. Letter after letter came from Arenenberg, making 'allusions & reflexions' which were not lost on the emotional young girl, 'and made me begin,' confessed Mathilde, 'to think seriously of Prince Louis'.¹⁰

On 7 April 1836, she returned to Arenenberg, where her father had preceded her, and Hortense received her 'with open arms. It was not long,' continued Mathilde, 'before she spoke to me about the plan for the marriage which had been arranged. My father gave his consent wholeheartedly.'[11]

In the four months of her absence, Mathilde seemed to have changed from an unassured adolescent into a self-possessed young girl. She had now recovered from any feeling of bereavement, and resumed her instinctive gaiety. Her Uncle Wurtemberg had paid her compliments on her looks, given her an interest in dress, made her aware that she was no longer a child, but a girl who drew men to her. The benign approval of the Court, and the enthusiasm of her cousins, had made Mathilde quite sure of her charm. Besides, she had had a long time in which to reflect on her future, on the romantic elder cousin she had known in Rome, the cousin who, said Mme de Reding, was already enamoured of her.

It was no wonder if, in his absence, Louis-Napoleon had taken an increasing part in Mathilde's imagination. She associated him with the Bonaparte legend, with the romantic décor of Arenenberg, with the charm and warmth and affection of Queen Hortense. Some people thought Louis-Napoleon was ugly and ungainly, but to Mathilde he was a Byronic figure: twelve years older than herself, practised, no doubt, in the ways of the world, imaginative, dreamy, slightly mysterious. Her father wanted the marriage, and so did her aunt; Mme de Reding said that it could easily be arranged if Mathilde were willing. She could not help but feel drawn towards it: to be willing, too.

And so, accompanied by the motherly Baroness de Reding, she returned to Arenenberg. At eight o'clock on the morning of Tuesday, 7 April 1836, Mademoiselle Valérie Masuyer, lady-in-waiting to Hortense, was informed that the visitors had arrived.[12]

Mlle Masuyer, unmarried, and rapidly approaching her thirty-ninth birthday, might not have been benign about romance; but even she confessed that Mathilde was 'a delightful creature'. Within the week, she and Hortense had agreed that Mathilde was the only wife for Louis-Napoleon. As for Jerome de Montfort, he so favoured the marriage that he bought Gottlieb, an old castle near Arenenberg, in which John Huss, the reformer, had been imprisoned. He planned to restore it and live in it, so that he could be near his married daughter. He and Hortense decided

that the marriage would take place in six months' time, when
Mathilde was sixteen and a half.

Mathilde, in her memoirs, many years later, declared that her
cousin had 'courted her assiduously'.[13] But it is hard to determine
the truth. They had lived together, as children, in Rome, they
knew each other well, and Louis-Napoleon, said Mathilde, 'had
always been like a brother'.[14] Perhaps he still felt more like a
brother than a future husband. Even now, if Mlle Masuyer is to
be trusted, he blew hot and cold, and the fact that his father had
not yet consented to the marriage did not increase his ardour.
He and his mother had both written to the Comte de Saint-Leu
for his permission, but there was no answer from Rome.

It was at this point that Mlle Masuyer became less tolerant, and
suddenly less sure of the romance. Perhaps she herself cherished
day-dreams about Louis-Napoleon. Perhaps she had exhausted
her sympathy for a girl who might have been her daughter: a
girl who might enjoy a life beyond her own possible aspirations.

She and the Prince were inseparable [she scratched away in her
diary]. He sat at her feet and went through all the antics of a man in
love. He told her a thousand pretty things which she could not understand, she hasn't enough heart . . . I thought bitterly that the Princess
will never understand him. She is coquettish, frivolous, and, Heaven
knows! he has all the opposite qualities. How much more he
deserves![15]

The innocent romance continued. Mathilde herself would
recall its almost childlike simplicity.

We played charades, and innocent little games, we kissed each
other as often as we could, sometimes furtively, when we could
escape the vigilance of my good Mme de Reding – to whom, more-
over, I recounted all my little coquetries. Louis and I used to rake the
paths in the park, Napoleon came too. He used to tease us and
tyrannize over us in our amusements, by threatening to disclose that
we sometimes kissed in front of him.[16]

Early in May it seemed quite clear to Mlle Masuyer that there
was an understanding between Mathilde and her cousin. Louis-
Napoleon seemed much in love. Mathilde appeared to be
unmistakably sure of her position. The assurance was apparently
more than Mlle Masuyer could bear, and she and Élisa, the other
lady-in-waiting, found solace in exchanging malicious gossip.

Mathilde, said Élisa, had made the advances according to plan. Mathilde was neither goodhearted nor affectionate. Mathilde, she added, had nothing but her appearance in her favour. Mathilde stuffed herself with cake between meals so that she could pine and starve at table.[17]

Jerome de Montfort was now tired of waiting for his brother's consent, and decided that they would go and see him. 'He took the pretext of making sure of his brother,' wrote Mathilde. 'But he was much more anxious to see his mistress again than to hasten my marriage. [He counted a good deal on me] to influence his brother's decision.'[18] Since Jerome was to take Mathilde away before her birthday, Louis-Napoleon celebrated it early. On 19 May he summoned singers from Ermatingen to row out on Lake Constance and serenade Mathilde as she sat with him in a boat on the peaceful waters. Even Mlle Masuyer grew mellow. 'The weather was superb, the air was gentle under the crescent moon, and surely these two young people will long remember this evening of happiness and love.'[19]

Two days later, with her father, Mathilde set off, in tears, from Arenenberg. Louis-Napoleon had given her a ring set with a turquoise forget-me-not, and a locket containing a curl of his hair. Mathilde had promised to have her portrait painted for him in Florence. They had sworn to write to each other under cover of their parents. He escorted her as far as Constance.

Jerome de Montfort, who had found Arenenberg excessively tedious, regained all his vivacity the moment they departed. In Florence, they went together to see the Comte de Saint-Leu. The former King of Holland was now so infirm that he could hardly walk, and one of his arms was paralysed. At first he only made lewd jokes at the idea of Mathilde's marriage to his son. It would be better for her, he said, if he married her himself, she would be happier with him than she would be with his wife. He spoke of Hortense in terms which Mathilde found detestable.[20]

Mathilde resumed her usual occupations; she practised the piano, and even the harp. Every day she visited her favourite Aunt Julie, the deserted wife of Joseph Bonaparte, the former King of Spain. She discussed all her plans with her, and Aunt Julie showed her maternal kindness. There was room for talk and speculation, and for kindness, too. At the end of August, there

were still no preparations for the marriage, although the engagement had been announced, and everyone concerned had given
their consent.

Mathilde could not understand the delay, and she asked her
aunt to make enquiries. Jerome was making certain financial
suggestions to his future son-in-law; he reminded him that he
still approved of the marriage. On 11 September Louis-Napoleon
wrote to his mother from Thun: 'I've told my uncle that I still
considered myself engaged, and that nothing could alter my
feelings. I also said that if he didn't think me rich enough for his
daughter, I should agree, regretfully, to wait until the spring,
when some of my mother's financial claims would have been
settled.'[21] On 3 October Louis-Napoleon wrote again to
Hortense: 'Do explain to my uncle why I can't return to Arenenberg at once; I hope you'll settle everything with him, and that
I'll soon have the happiness of marrying Mathilde.'[22]

It was at this point that Jerome paid a visit to his brother Joseph,
now living in London, and it was in London that he learned of
what was called the Strasbourg skirmish. Louis-Napoleon had
made a wild attempt to seize power in France and to restore the
Bonaparte dynasty. He had been arrested and exiled to America.

The news only reached Mathilde by public rumour; but, as she
would recall, 'we didn't need any more in order to understand
my cousin's negligence, or the delays in solemnizing the marriage.
I must be honest and say that, on this occasion, none of his family
took Prince Louis' part . . .' As for Jerome, he overwhelmed his
nephew with reproaches for his deceit: for daring to ask him for
Mathilde when he was meditating such an act of madness. He
forbade Mathilde to write to Louis-Napoleon or to Hortense.
He said that the marriage would henceforth be impossible.[23]

Neither Aunt Julie nor Mme de Reding, who had Mathilde's
best interests at heart, suggested that she might share her cousin's
exile. Even if they had done so, even if her father had considered
the possibility, only an overwhelming love could have driven
her to throw away her future. Mathilde felt no overwhelming
love. She maintained, in later years, that she had been more upset
by her anxiety for Louis-Napoleon than by her regret at her
broken engagement. The thought of the marriage had certainly
pleased her, but what she felt for her cousin was great friendship

rather than love. The marriage would not have rescued her from her false position; it might, on the contrary, have made it permanent. Louis-Napoleon's political agitations had already closed Italy to him, and only left her the prospect of spending her life at Arenenberg. 'I saw little pleasure in that,' she wrote. 'I foresaw a monotonous, almost cloistered life, while all my desires, all my ambitions led me to live in Paris, that marvellous Paris which they had described to me time and time again: Paris, the scene of the glory of the founder of our House, which was, for us, exiled from the cradle, the true Promised Land.'[24]

Louis-Napoleon considered the broken marriage with his usual fatalism, and yet with real and obvious regret. As he sailed to exile in America, he recalled the idyll at Arenenberg; and he wrote sadly to Hortense:

When I was coming back through the park, a few months ago, after seeing Mathilde on her way back to Florence, I found a tree that was shattered by the storm. I said to myself: our marriage will be shattered by fate ... The event which I vaguely imagined has come to pass. Have I exhausted ... all my share of happiness?[25]

~~4~~

During the summer of 1837, a notable statesman and historian arrived in Italy. At the age of forty, Adolphe Thiers was already the author of a massive standard work: *L'Histoire de la Révolution française*. As a political journalist, and one of the founders of the newspaper *Le National*, he had helped to bring about the July Revolution in 1830, and he was now a member of the Government and *persona grata* with Louis-Philippe. Thiers was preparing to write his second classic work, his *Histoire du consulat et de l'empire*, and he was anxious for assistance from the Emperor's brother; Jerome de Montfort, for his part, wanted a politician who might, perhaps, persuade Louis-Philippe to ease his financial strain and allow him to return to France.

In later life Mathilde set down her impression of Thiers. It can hardly be called a first impression, for it is strongly coloured by the political changes and the personal disappointments of many intervening years. It is a bitter, rather malicious impression, yet it contains an element of truth.

During the summer of 1837 [Mathilde recorded], M. Thiers came to Italy. It was then that I saw him for the first time. His wife was with him, and so was his sister-in-law, Mlle Félicie Dosne. Mme Thiers said that she was unwell. People claimed that she had had the tenderest affection for the maestro Bellini, and that her marriage with M. Thiers was far from satisfactory . . .

M. Thiers rented the Villa di Quarto, where he established himself with his wife and his sister-in-law. This political personage with his little toupet, his little hooked nose, his little spectacles, his little piping voice and his little figure, seemed to me very little for a great man . . .

The whole Thiers family came to dine in Florence with my father. M. Thiers paid us several visits . . . M. Thiers wrote several times to my father and to me on his return to France, and, until the advent of Napoleon III, we remained on terms.[1]

One of the subjects which Thiers discussed was a possible marriage between Mathilde and the Duc d'Orléans, the eldest son of Louis-Philippe. Privately, Thiers was well aware that there might be more than one political advantage in uniting the House of Bonaparte with the House of Orleans. Such a marriage would give glamour to an unattractive bourgeois monarchy, and it would lessen the danger of a Bonaparte restoration. If it were arranged, it would also give him lasting claims to the gratitude of both parties. No doubt Thiers kept such thoughts to himself, and emphasized to Jerome that the marriage would bring his family out of exile. Mathilde had not met the Duc d'Orléans, but the point seemed trivial: he was a highly presentable young man.

The project was proposed by Thiers (so Plon-Plon later told Mathilde), but he allowed it to be thought Jerome's suggestion. On 3 March 1838, he sent Jerome an entirely inexplicit letter from Paris, and spoke of 'a first overture on the subject which concerns you'. 'I think that papa had not said yes or no,' wrote Plon-Plon to his sister in 1886. 'I believe he suggested Princess Marie of Wurtemberg: he didn't want to annoy Thiers by a refusal because of our claims . . .'[2] Jerome contrived, indeed, to keep on the friendliest terms with Thiers; in mid July, from the Baths of Montecatini, where he was staying with Mathilde, he told him he thought of visiting his brother-in-law in Stuttgart, and he would certainly go through Milan so that he and his daughter might call on the Thiers family.[3] The journey to Stuttgart had to be abandoned; 'but we like to think,' wrote Jerome on 13 September, 'that Mme Thiers' health will allow her to accompany you to Florence; and if the Villa di Quarto doesn't seem too isolated for you, we should be very happy to see you there.'[4]

While Thiers had been ruminating about an Orleans marriage for Mathilde, while he had been expressing his wishes for her return from exile, a figure had appeared on the scene who seemed destined to solve every problem. In June 1838, accompanied by Jules Janin, the novelist, essayist and dramatic critic, Anatole Nikolaievitch Demidoff came to Florence.

Demidoff, who was twenty-five, was not a new acquaintance for Mathilde. Before 1828 (when he had settled in Florence with his father), she had seen him in Rome; and, though she was then

a child, she had not forgotten him, It was in fact difficult to forget
the Demidoff family. Old Demidoff had revivified Roman society
with his entertainments. He had had the villa of San Donato
built for him in Florence, and established a silk manufactory there.
Anatole had transformed the villa into a veritable palace, which
he sometimes inhabited. Fiercely handsome like the hero of a
romantic novel, and the inheritor of a fabulous fortune, he now
arrived in Florence with Janin. They asked if they might come
on St John's Day and see the illuminations, the processions and
rejoicings, from the Palazzo Orlandini.

Janin, like a true journalist, was not wasting his opportunities:
he was publishing his impressions of the journey in a series of
letters to the *Journal des Débats*. The letters would appear in book
form as *Voyage en Italie*.

In his letters home, Janin gave his impressions of Florence, and
of the Bonapartes who lived there in lamentable exile. His style
was purple, his feelings were heightened, for he wrote for
publication; but he drew a miniature of Mathilde at a vital
moment in her life.

In Prince Jerome's house we encountered, with keen emotion, a
fair young Bonaparte, rosy-cheeked, and without ambition, a
Bonaparte with no regret but that for her native land, a Bonaparte
as charming and inoffensive as the other had been mighty and
terrible . . .
What a misfortune that she is entombed like this beneath the great
name, a child who might simply be the niece of the King of Wurtemberg! And how France must regret this lustrous pearl fallen from the
imperial crown.![5]

This admiration was not merely destined to enliven the
Journal des Débats. Janin persuaded Demidoff to share it. During
his three weeks in Florence, Janin suggested to Demidoff that he
should marry Mathilde.[6]

The idea attracted Anatole. He was all too aware of his social
inferiority. His title, his uncountable riches, his *hôtel* in Paris, his
palace at San Donato, could not make him forget his origin.

His ancestor, Nikita Demiditch, had been a blacksmith at
Toula who had happened, by a freak of fate, to earn favour with
the Czar. The Czar, impressed by a pair of pistols which the
moujik had made, had given him his freedom and some land.

By some extraordinary chance, the fields, in the Ural region, were found to be rich in iron ore. Demiditch had transformed his smithy into a munitions factory, and provided the Russian troops with guns for their war with Sweden. The Czar had given him the title of Count Demidoff, which was later made hereditary. The Demidoffs had acquired further mines, and in some of them they found platinum and silver deposits.

Their wealth had become a legend, and yet they had never been accepted by society. Even Anatole's father, who had married a girl of good family, had found himself so ostracized that he had moved to Paris, where his ancestry would be unknown and his wealth would command respect. After his wife's death he had gone to Rome, but he had been expelled on account of the scandalous plays performed by his troupe of actors. He had then moved to Florence, where his *nouveau riche* extravagance was publicly enjoyed and privately despised by society.

Anatole, his elder son, had tried to perfect his education, and he had earned the entrée to literary and aristocratic circles in Paris. In 1837, with Janin and other friends, he had sailed up the Danube and visited Hungary, Wallachia and Moldavia; the journey was followed by others, and Anatole summed up his observations in two books with illustrations by Raffet. His account of his travels in Southern Russia would be his chief title to his election to the Institut de France in 1843.

However, in the summer of 1838, this intellectual triumph lay in the future; and Anatole remained well aware of his humiliating origins. Mathilde was the cousin of the Czar, she was related through her mother to most of the ruling families of Europe. She was also the niece of Napoleon. He saw that marriage to Mathilde would bring him unbelievable prestige.

Mathilde found Anatole distinguished. His swarthy face and dark moustache suggested fierce virility, and the thought of his turbulent private life added to his charm. He also had an *hôtel* in Paris, a fact which weighed heavily in his favour.

At first Jerome de Montfort refused to consider the marriage. He had an understandably low opinion of the Demidoffs, and he knew – as all Florence knew – about Anatole's absorbing liaison with Mme de Montault. However, when the Montault liaison was abruptly broken, Jerome could no longer deny the advantages of a son-in-law of unlimited wealth. He encouraged

B*

Mathilde. He also made financial demands of Anatole. Anatole rejected them, and the prospect of an immediate marriage was lost.

Such difficulties convinced Mathilde even more that she wanted to marry Anatole. She was much upset by the delay.

I had envisaged this marriage with pleasure, because it rescued me from the false position in which I found myself, and I was beginning to feel the burden of my situation. Just imagine a girl of eighteen living alone with a father who paid no attention to her whatever – a father ruled by his love of pleasure, sacrificing everything to his passions: money, time and consideration.[7]

Her situation had indeed become a burden to her. She felt isolated from the world; and the motherly devotion of Nanan – the Baroness de Reding – and the almost daily sympathy of Aunt Julie, were no substitutes for a sister's understanding. Mathilde greatly needed a girl of her own age in whom she could confide. There had, perhaps, been only two such confidantes in her life. One was her cousin, Sophie of Wurtemberg, but they saw one another all too rarely. The other was Hélène Villamil.

In the late 1830s Mathilde had delightedly welcomed the Villamils to Florence. Little is known of the family except that they were French and seemed to bring her closer to the country for which she longed with constant passion. Mme Villamil helped to satisfy her thirst for knowledge of Paris, and the two Villamil daughters became her intimate friends. When they eventually left for France, she begged them 'to consider Mathilde as another sister'.[8] In August 1838, in the weeks that followed Anatole's departure, she sent letter after letter to Hélène. She wrote as she spoke; and in these spontaneous, urgent, intimate letters she found relief.

All one can expect in this world is to be happy once, twice would be too much to ask of Providence [so she wrote on 2 August] . . .

I'm working hard at my painting, and they say I'm making progress . . .

I go to see my dearest Aunt Julie nearly every day, and my love and affection for her grow with every visit. I find that when I'm with her nothing sad and unhappy can touch me; to see this picture of virtue and resignation is for me a refuge from trouble; and then I know that she loves me as if I were her daughter, and that only makes me love her all the more . . .[9]

In this August of 1838 it seemed for a moment as if the monotony of daily life in Florence would be broken. Jerome thought of taking his daughter on a visit to Germany. Mathilde told Hélène that she might travel north, and Hélène at once assumed that father and daughter were coming back to France. On 9 August Mathilde was forced to disillusion her. The letter began in deplorable English, and it reflected a Byronic mood.

You did not understand me when I wrote that it was probable we would travel towards the north [explained Mathilde]. God knows how happy I would be to see my fatherland and to leave for ever these regions. It is always with the greatest pleasure that I remember all the details of Paris which the good Madame Villamil gave me so kindly; but all is illusion, my fate is to hear only the name of happiness; patience, time is passing and youth with it; perhaps in my old years shall I then enjoy more than in my young years. God abandons nobody, he will take care of me.[10]

Mathilde was apt to dramatize; and yet, for all the romanticism of her style, she was expressing real loneliness and despair; and, relapsing into French, she confided a clearly genuine unhappiness.

I was sober enough already, it's cruel to become more sober every day, I've aged, but I'm not yet broken. How stupid of me to tell you all this, you won't understand a thing; paper isn't discreet enough for anyone to entrust it with their heart and soul, but perhaps one day I'll tell you everything, for as you see hope never leaves me.

We shall direct our steps to cold Germany, then, towards the end of this month or at the beginning of September. I shall embark on the journey with pleasure, but as what I want never happens I shan't believe it until we are actually in the coach . . .

I'm drawing like a madwoman, I do nothing else all day and I've begun to do watercolours again. Thanks to my assurance, patience and perseverance, I'm getting on quite well . . .[11]

But nothing seemed to give Mathilde particular pleasure; two days later, she was again at her desk, to tell Hélène:

Yesterday evening, for the first time, I saw a tragedy. I couldn't say if it was entertaining or not . . . It was as good a way as any other of spending an evening . . .[12]

A few days later Jerome took his daughter to the Villa di Quarto, and there, with Nanan and the household, they remained in isolation. 'We have been completely alone in the country for the past week,' Mathilde lamented on 21 August.

I don't need to tell you that our solitude often makes me think of you, but it's when we have company that I miss you more and feel more isolated. I was so used to talking to you, exchanging glances with you, that I enjoyed myself a hundred times more than I do now. For now I have to be pleasant for hours on end without the happy prospect of telling people I love all the little bits of gossip which have so often amused us so much. Believe me you will find that I've aged . . .[13]

In the same letter, Mathilde announced that she and her father would soon be on the road to Como, to see Thiers and his family. But in spite of the Thiers' kindness she was apprehensive of the personal remarks that might be made. Thiers would doubtless be told of her projected marriage to Anatole, and she was dreading the public discussion of her future. It was perhaps as a safeguard that she now wrote in her lamentable English to Hélène (L.N., she called her); she still mistrusted the secrecy of a letter. She came as near as she could to making a confession.

It would be necessary for me to have some person to whom I could tell what I feel, what is the cause of my sorrows and sometimes of my happiness; you must understand me dear L.N., all the reasons you would find to explain my actual position would be wrong, a new event has taken place in my life, God shall assist me and let me hope it will succeed for my happiness, in your prayers recall my name L.N., and my gratitude for you shall be great . . .[14]

Mathilde did not record whether or not she was taken to visit Thiers; a month later, still from Quarto, she sent a letter to Hélène at Bayonne. Hélène Villamil, by the accident of her undistinguished birth, was enjoying the country that Mathilde had never seen, the country that she always longed to see. Would she ever see it? Her only chance of breaking out of exile seemed to be her marriage with Anatole; but the exile continued, and the marriage which promised her so much seemed to her unbearably uncertain.

Do you know what causes me such disgust with everything [she asked, on 20 September]? It's the uncertainty *of great happiness;* everything seems paltry to me unless it is related to my *hope*; and, like everyone who ardently longs for something, I torment

myself with the idea that it won't happen, though I have no reason to
think so. You understand all I'm saying, don't you? Though I'm very
young, I have had harsh experience of life, and that is what makes me
doubtful of happiness now . . .[15]

Fortunately Mathilde did not spend the winter in the isolation
of Quarto. Her next letter, sent from Florence two days after
Christmas, reflected a more animated scene. Her younger brother,
Plon-Plon, was now at the military academy in Louisburg, and
she missed exercising her maternal authority.

In losing my Nap: I have lost a brother who loves me to the point
of adoration, a brother over whom I hold sway, a friend with whom
I can talk of anything, who always understands me, a friend to whom
I could be of some service; the dear child was always at my heels . . .[16]

She found small consolation in the presence of her elder
brother, Jerome, now twenty-four and an officer in the West-
phalian service. Far from adoring his sister and waiting on her
every word, he showed a lofty unconcern which vexed her.
Jerome, she explained, in dudgeon,

is the young man in fashion, everyone wants him and contends for
him; as for him, he wants society and *high society*. A sister – what's an
unmarried sister? It's less than nothing, it only dreams about dresses,
you can't reason with it, and above all *it can't talk horses and railways*,
which are inexhaustible topics for the young man in fashion.[17]

Mathilde clearly found relief from her frustration in cynicism.
In her letters to Hélène she could assert the worldliness and
wisdom, the femininity and importance which her elder brother
denied her. Yet she herself was not as reluctant as might be
supposed to mingle with *le beau monde*. Florentine society was this
year particularly brilliant. The Poniatowskis were organizing
three charity performances of operas – Donizetti and Rossini –
at the theatre, and Mathilde was hoping to go; and, more important, an infallibly romantic figure had suddenly appeared upon the
scene.

I nearly forgot to tell you that I've heard and met the famous Liszt,
the celebrated pianist [she dashed off to Hélène]. He's a charming young
man, and he bears an astonishing likeness to the Emperor when he
came to Italy in '96, he's given several concerts which we've been to,
I am delighted and enchanted with him. He is a man of vast genius
and unexampled modesty: the other day he said to me, quite seriously:

'I promise you that I never sit down at the piano unless I'm told to, because I feel I must be very boring.' But can I give you a greater idea of his miraculous talent than by telling you that the Florentines have agreed to pay 15 pauls to hear him? Mme Mouravieff said to me very solemnly when she'd heard him: 'If I was young and pretty I'd go mad about him.' There's a beautiful woman with him, she's left her husband and 5 children, she's the Comtesse d'Agoult, I met her at Bartolini's where she's having her bust done like I am and I found her very pleasant. She is tall and very thin, she looks like the figure of Hunger, but her face is very interesting and above all very noble; of course her conduct is inexcusable and yet when you see her you cannot prevent yourself from being drawn to her . . . She has done very wrong, there's no doubt of that, but at least she has been carried away by genius, not by self-interest; and that makes her guilty but not contemptible.[18]

Florentine society had distinct advantages; and, as Mathilde would recall in her memoirs, with a certain complacency, she herself was popular in Florence. For all the cynicism and sadness in her letters to Hélène, she set out to make herself agreeable, and she enjoyed her popularity.

Yet Florentine society had all the disadvantages of being a closed society. To her, Aunt Julie and the faithful Nanan, the Demidoff marriage seemed to be a providential means of escape. 'As for me,' she wrote despondently in March 1839, 'if I could see myself in Paris, how happy I should be, my dearest dreams would be realized. Unhappiness could not touch me there; I long for my own country more than ever and perhaps it has never been further away . . .'[19] Her longing for marriage must have grown more acute when she thought of her cousin Sophie's approaching marriage to the Prince of Orange. 'Will you think of me on my wedding-day?' asked Sophie from Wurtemberg on 1 May. She added, with a gesture which showed the depth of her affection: 'Let me send you a flower from my wedding bouquet, & when you get married you can add it to your own.'[20]

In Stuttgart, the final touches were put to Sophie's abundant trousseau.[21] In Florence, the summer passed uneventfully. The vicissitudes of Mathilde's betrothal seemed to be unending. Sometimes Jerome de Montfort made unacceptable demands, sometimes Anatole ceded a point and rejected another, so that the marriage itself was always indefinitely postponed. On 10 March 1840, when certain points which had seemed to be settled were once again in question, Anatole withdrew his candidature.[22]

Then his decision was reversed. That August, two years after his visit with Janin, he arrived at last in Florence, determined to conclude negotiations. He was soon accepted as Mathilde's fiancé, and the marriage preparations began.

There were several delicate points, and one of them was the question of the mixed marriage, for Anatole belonged to the Greek Orthodox Church. However, the Archbishop of Florence was authorized to give the couple his nuptial benediction, and Mathilde and Anatole signed an agreement to bring up their children in the Catholic faith. The fact that the Greek synod made a similar demand did not embarrass Anatole. He presented his fiancée with the agreement written in Greek; neither of them could read it, Mathilde signed it in genuine ignorance, and the problem was solved.

There were, however, other problems. One was Jerome's insistence that the marriage should take place at the French Legation. Since the July Revolution of 1830, the Bonapartes were no longer deprived of civil rights, but they remained an exiled and potentially dangerous family, and the idea of solemnizing the marriage alarmed Monsieur Bellocq, Louis-Philippe's envoy to Tuscany. It needed the intervention of Anatole's friend, the Duc d'Orléans, to overcome the objections; and, ironically, it was Ferdinand-Philippe d'Orléans, who might have been her husband, who helped to arrange for Mathilde to be Mme Demidoff.

On 14 October the Duchesse de Dino reported that Anatole had asked for permission to announce his wife in Paris as Her Royal Highness the Princess de Montfort. Louis-Philippe had given his consent. Soon afterwards, the Duchess learned that the Grand Duke of Tuscany had created Anatole Prince of San Donato, 'giving him the name of his silk manufactory, and endowing him with the title of Excellency!' The marriage was, she said, a question of vanity for Anatole: he was embarking on it so as to be related to the King of Wurtemberg and the Czar of Russia. Neither sovereign welcomed the alliance. The marriage, she added, had been arranged on condition that Anatole paid the substantial debts of the Prince de Montfort.[23]

Jerome's financial position was certainly embarrassing. When

Mathilde asked him, now, about the fifty thousand francs which had been left to her by her aunt, Pauline Borghese, he confessed that he had spent the sum long ago. He did not even pay for her trousseau, and, in order to raise funds, he later made her buy back some of her mother's lace. He exploited Anatole's cult of the Bonapartes, and sold him the statues of Madame Mère and Napoleon for ten thousand francs apiece, and several family busts for four thousand francs each. He kept back a turquoise and diamond parure which Mathilde had inherited from the late Queen of Wurtemberg, and apparently he later sold it. He accepted a pension of twenty-five thousand francs from Mathilde from the day of her marriage, and he later sold Quarto, his country villa, to Anatole. As for the dowry of two hundred and ninety thousand francs which he had contracted to give his daughter, it remained a figment of his imagination.[24]

Mathilde was married to Anatole Demidoff at the Greek chapel in Florence on 1 November 1840. After this ceremony, they were married again in the Duomo, and a nuptial mass was said. Finally there was a great *déjeuner*, attended by several of Anatole's friends, the witnesses, and Mathilde's assembled family.

I had a low-cut dress of English lace [Mathilde would recall], with a veil in the same material, and when I made my appearance, wearing the pearl necklace which the Emperor Napoleon I had given to Queen Catherine, my mother, the necklace which M. Demidoff had bought back from my father, I was – and I can say so, now, because it's so long ago – a charming and beautiful bride. My wedding-presents and my trousseau had all come from Paris; nothing was wanting, indeed everything was there in abundance. I was overwhelmed with flowers, with compliments and poems and benedictions from Quarto to San Donato, and on my return. M. Demidoff seemed very much in love with me, and he showed that he was proud of me.[25]

In the fortress of Ham, where he was imprisoned for a second attempted *coup d'état*, Louis-Napoleon heard that Mathilde was married. It is reported that he wept, and said: 'This is the last and heaviest blow that fortune had in store for me.'[26] Caroline Murat, the niece of Mathilde, was to set the words down in her memoirs. 'It is possible,' she added, 'indeed very probable, that had my aunt been Empress of the French the Franco-Prussian War would never have taken place . . . She would have made an admirable Empress.'[27]

PART TWO

The Interregnum

1840–52

It had been decided that, when they had spent a few days at Quarto, 'the happy Tuscan couple, drunk with joy,'[1] would go to Rome, and then, by way of Naples and Florence, to Paris. The Bonaparte star was once again in the ascendant. Louis-Philippe, sure of his future, determined to acknowledge national glory, had sent his son, the Prince de Joinville, on a mission to St Helena. Joinville had been ordered to bring home the body of Napoleon. The Emperor had died on the island on 5 May 1821. On 17 December 1840, he would be brought to rest at the Invalides in Paris: to lie, as he had wished, on the banks of the Seine.

Mathilde had won her right to live in Paris. She had set her heart on being there when her uncle was triumphantly brought home. She was not to be there, and this was her first deception as Mme Demidoff. Ten days after their marriage, she and Anatole left for Rome. They had hardly arrived when he showed all the roughness of his Demiditch forebears, all the uncontrollable violence of his nature.

On 6 December the Duchesse de Dino recorded events in detail:

Apparently he had told the Greek priest that his children would all be brought up in the Greek religion, and he had told the Catholic authorities that they would be brought up in the Catholic faith. He also said, with his usual assurance, that one could buy anything from the Court of Rome, and that he had sent the Pope 100,000 francs for the dispensations he had obtained. Cardinal Lambruschini was indignant at this allegation, and published an article (everyone is quoting it) in the *Gazzetta romana*. The article ... proves quite decisively that M. Demidoff had paid nothing for his dispensations except the sum of 90 francs, the cost of sending them. The Russian Minister refused to treat on Demidoff's behalf with the Court of Rome, and Demidoff thereupon went round to insult him. After all these fine frolics, he had to leave Rome, and, if he has not died of rage, he is much embarrassed none the less.[2]

Mme d'Agoult, Mathilde's acquaintance, confirmed to Liszt that Rome had been scandalized. Jerome de Montfort was furious, Mathilde had grown thin and melancholy.[3] For Anatole had not merely disgraced himself and his wife; the Russian Minister, astounded by an altercation which had nearly led to violence, had reported the incident to St Petersburg. Anatole had been summoned there, and commanded, on pain of confiscation of his property, to give an explanation of his conduct.

In mid January 1841, Mathilde and Anatole set out on their journey. They reached Vienna to find it snowbound, and the penetrating cold, the sight of the endless tracts of white so depressed Mathilde that she could take no interest in the city, even though she was seeing it for the first time. As they went through Olmütz, where it was five degrees colder than in Vienna, Anatole, with complete composure, took Mathilde's fur wrap for himself. She made no comment, because his health was said to be indifferent.

They stopped at Cracow, the second city in Poland; it was little but a long unmade street piled with snow, ice and refuse, with wretched wooden houses on either side. After Cracow, they had to mount the carriages on sledges; the cold grew more and more intense, and between Cracow and Warsaw they had to dismount the carriages four times. Sometimes they put them on wheels to make their way through the slush, sometimes they put them on sledges to cross the ice. Several times they overturned, but nobody was hurt. It was a strange and lamentable honeymoon.

Warsaw was ice-bound: indeed Mathilde could hardly tell if the Vistula was a river or a street. As they went on, the wind cut to their bones, but luckily at every post-house they found a big stove, ready lit, and hot water for making tea. There was no food to be bought, but they had brought a few provisions: frozen meat, preserves and bouillon cubes. At last, after three particularly strenuous days, they came to Egyptan, a village on the Russian frontier.

They spent the night there, at a little inn, to let the customs officials examine their luggage. By some coincidence, which

Mathilde would recall in her old age, a barrel-organ outside the inn was playing *J'irai revoir ma Normandie*.[4]

Two days later they set out again, across a vast lunar landscape where the monotony of the snow was broken, here and there, by a cluster of sombre pines. The night before they reached St Petersburg, the postilion fell, frozen, on the road. Mathilde, in her memoirs, did not explain whether he had fainted or died. At last, on 14 March, after eight weeks' travelling, they reached the capital of the Russian empire.

Mathilde had been married for four months, and she must already have questioned the wisdom of her decision. Anatole was not only violent, he was entirely selfish, and he was too preoccupied, now, to pay her the least attention. However, they established themselves in his palace on the Nevski Prospect, and Mathilde prepared to use all the influence of kinship, all her personal charm, to avert disgrace for her husband.

On the Sunday after her arrival, the Grand Duchess Helena presented her to Nicholas I. Mathilde was dressed entirely in white; she wore a low-cut dress, and a little white lace head-dress ornamented with miniature roses. She also wore pearls: no doubt the necklace which Napoleon had given to her mother. It reminded her of her all-conquering lineage.

Behind the Grand Duchess Helena, a figure like a great shadow advanced towards her. As an elderly woman she would still remember the expression, both gentle and commanding, in the Czar's eyes. She would still recall his imperial bearing, the sense of energy and determination, the feeling of omnipotence, which he inspired. He was the perfect incarnation of the absolute monarch.

Nicholas I embraced her, and made a comment in Russian to his sister-in-law. Mathilde learned afterwards that he had referred to his son's fiancée, the Princess of Darmstadt. He had said bluntly: 'Here is someone who would have suited us much better.' Looking back on the incident, Mathilde would reflect: 'I was destined to suit other people, and to miss my own chance.'

On 9 March the French Ambassador, Prosper de Barante, wrote to Guizot: 'The one topic of conversation is Princess Mathilde's grace, charm and perfect manners.' On 1 May, the St Petersburg gazette announced Anatole's reintegration into active service, and the restoration of his title of Gentleman of the Chamber. Everyone noticed the Czar's respect and affection for Mathilde, and he made it clear that he had pardoned Anatole for her sake.

Anatole bitterly resented the triumph of his wife. He saw that, despite his dazzling marriage, he would have no future in St Petersburg. As for Mathilde, she still longed for Paris with all her Bonaparte passion: a passion only intensified by her disastrous honeymoon. In June, at a private audience, she asked the Czar for permission to spend the winter in Paris with Anatole. Nicholas I expressed a certain apprehension, for he wondered what new follies Anatole might perpetrate; however, he agreed, with regret, that Anatole might go with her. 'You will not be happy with Demidoff,' he said, 'but, whatever happens, you will always find me on your side.'[5]

The Demidoffs entered France through Strasbourg. As she crossed the border, Mathilde Bonaparte, the Emperor's niece, saw her first French soldier. At that moment of relief, vast pride and exaltation, she stopped her carriage, leapt out, and embraced him.

On 17 August 1841, at seven in the evening, after a childhood and a youth which had seemed an endless age of waiting, Mathilde entered Paris. Her husband's *hôtel* in the rue Saint-Dominique-Saint-Germain seemed to her like a palace in a fairy-tale.

She would have liked to go at once and make her pilgrimage.

But I contented myself [she recalled] with going to gaze at the silhouette of the Hôtel des Invalides, its cupola looming vast in the darkness. I came back very agitated, and hardly slept that night, I was beside myself with joy at being at last in Paris: Paris, the object of my dreams since I had been conscious of my being.

Next day, after *déjeuner*, we went to see the Emperor's tomb.[6]

From the Invalides, she and Anatole went to the Place Vendôme to visit her uncle, Prince Paul of Wurtemberg. He was living in a handsome apartment with his mistress, Lady Wittingham, and their daughter. He welcomed Mathilde delightedly; and she often came back to the Place Vendôme to talk to this frank and upright and highly intelligent man.

She recorded some of her other visits with a touch of cynicism. Mme Thiers, for example, 'always had a sullen look, she hardly spoke at all and she often slept after dinner.'[1] As for the Duchesse d'Albuféra, Mathilde suspected that she received her from curiosity as much as affection. At the Duchesse d'Albuféra's she met the Comte de Delaborde, Monsieur Rambuteau, the Préfet de la Seine, and Sainte-Beuve, who was already renowned as the literary critic on the *Revue de Paris* and the *Revue des Deux Mondes*. Mathilde soon detected from their conversation that they considered themselves superior. 'I except Monsieur de Rambuteau,' she added, thirty years later. 'These gentlemen more or less admitted him into their circle because of the thousand little favours he could do for them. But between Mr Ste Beuve and Mr de Laborde . . . there was anxiety to outshine and outclass each other. It seemed to me rather difficult and dangerous ground if one had wanted to compete with them.'[2]

All through August she visited the monuments of Paris, and, at last, she went to Versailles.

The railway journey was a novelty for me – I was young, and ardent, and impatient to see everything, and the time seemed to go very slowly . . . At last we reached Versailles, the magnificent Palace stretched out before me . . . I felt I was exploring sacred ground . . . I went back there several times before I left for Dieppe, where I was to go sea-bathing in September.[3]

She and Anatole spent a month at Dieppe, where Mathilde watched a performance of *La Tour de Nesle*. It was only nine years since Dumas' grim historical drama had been seen for the first time. Mathilde shared the Romantic, melodramatic tastes of the age. 'That horrible drama delighted me,' she confessed as a middle-aged woman, 'and it was one of the best evenings I can remember spending at the theatre.'[4]

They came back to Paris for the winter, and the invitations began to pour in.[5] One evening, in December, accompanied by the Duchesse d'Albuféra, the widow of Napoleon's Maréchal Suchet, Mathilde went up the great staircase at the Tuileries. Her heart was beating hard as she reached the *salon* and saw the big, round, lamplit table, where Queen Marie-Amelie was sitting. Marie-Amelie was wearing a bonnet kept in place by diamond clips, and she was grave and dignified. Round her were clustered the princesses, no doubt drawn by curiosity to see Napoleon's niece.

An usher announced '*La Duchesse* d'Albuféra' [Mathilde remembered], and everyone turned towards us. The Queen half rose, took the Maréchale's hand, and turned to me, and said: 'You are welcome here, Madame.' She indicated a chair for me between herself and an old lady with a shrewd and smiling air, telling her my name, Princess Mathilde. The old lady gave me her hand, she was Mme Adelaide – after a few minutes the King appeared at the door of the salon with Monsieur Molé, whom I knew.[6]

Louis-Philippe was a massive man; his somewhat elongated head, surmounted by a toupet, emerged from a stiff collar and the numerous folds of a black cravat, and under his cutaway coat he wore a waistcoat embroidered with silver flowers. 'He hurried up to me, with a smile,' continued Mathilde. 'He was toying with the trinkets on his watch-chain, and he made a very gracious but extremely confused remark to which I just replied with a curtsey. Monsieur Molé then intervened and said to the King: "Doesn't Your Majesty think the Princess is like Napoleon?" "Yes, I do," said the King. "She's the pink-and-white Bonaparte Janin told us about." '[7]

Perhaps, at this point, when she wrote her memoirs, Mathilde allowed herself a little licence. By that time she was middle-aged, unhappy, and uncertain of herself; perhaps it gave her

confidence to recall the phrase from Janin's book and attribute it
to the King. Perhaps it gave her a certain solace to dwell on her
youthful triumph.

Her memories of other people were not always kind; and her
portrait of the Duchesse d'Orléans, the daughter-in-law of Louis-
Philippe, was brutal. Soon after her visit to the Tuileries, Mathilde
was invited to visit the Orléans at the Pavillon Marsan.

I ordered a high-necked dress in white watered silk [she remembered],
and I wore a sky-blue velvet hat – blue was always a colour that suited
me very well. The Duc d'Orléans, in uniform, received us in the great
salon . . . After a moment or two the Duchesse d'Orléans appeared.
She wore a white satin hat and a velvet dress. I saw a bony, ungloved
hand with red joints; she curtseyed to me, asked me to sit beside her
in the coupé, and studied me with visible . . . curiosity. The Duc
d'Orléans made all the conversation, seeking occasions to say something nice to me. He thought that I was pretty, and she was vexed;
I had made an effort. He led us back as far as the ante-room, declaring
his admiration for my family and saying that he would always be
glad to be agreeable to me. As for her, she gave me a curtsey stiff and
starched like the rest of her . . .

I have never seen a more sullen face . . .; and the whole of my visit
I was saying to myself what a pity that such a charming Prince should
have married such an uncharming Princess.[8]

It was a bitter picture, drawn some thirty years after the event;
and yet, perhaps, the bitterness was understandable. It was the
Duc d'Orléans, this most delightful of princes, whom Thiers had
once suggested as a possible husband for Mathilde.

By now it was clear that the Demidoff marriage was a disaster.
Mathilde felt increasing anxiety about her husband. He had
resented the fact that he owed his imperial pardon to her personal
influence with the Czar. He now resented her princely relations,
her easy conversation, her scorn for money – which was his one
claim to distinction. Sometimes, in his wild attempts to make a
good impression, he boasted of his wealth. Monsieur de Salvandy
met the Demidoffs at the Duchesse Decazes'. People were discussing the current story that Rachel, the actress, had sold herself
to Dr Véron, the publicist, for two hundred thousand francs.
Anatole exclaimed at once: 'You see the power of money!' The
guests could not help glancing at Mathilde.[9]

At one moment Anatole would behave 'in the tenderest and indeed most respectful way to his wife'. They would both speak of their 'supreme happiness'.[10] The next moment they would quarrel violently. Their marriage became a series of scenes and reconciliations. Perhaps it was to escape from such precarious intimacy that they entertained and went out so much.

Their passport to France had nearly expired; at the end of May they had to start for Russia. Once again, in St Petersburg, the Czar showed his affection for Mathilde. Their mutual admiration exacerbated Anatole. He knew that the Czar looked on him with aversion, he felt perpetually humiliated, he lost his thin veneer of good manners. He was also losing his love for Mathilde: all that remained of it was his sensuality. It was said that he beat her, and that he was unfaithful to her with Princess Schouwaloff. Sophie of Orange seems to have learned something of Mathilde's misery. 'I do not wholly understand the reasons for your torments,' she wrote on 25 June 1842, 'but what I have heard of them has made me tremble for you! What anguish you must have suffered! . . .'[11]

By the spring of 1843, Mathilde had decided to leave St Petersburg, and she had explained her position in a private audience with the Czar.

I explained to His Majesty, once and for all, my position in general, and Anatole's, and I told him that I wanted to go. *He* showed a kindness and affability which were beyond all expectation. *He* talked to me for a long time with the most perfect friendliness. The result is that in the meantime we are granted six months' leave, that *He* completely understands my difficult position, that *He* has nothing but praise for the way in which I have dealt with it, and that whenever I come back to Russia *He* will be delighted to see me. As for Anatole, *He* made this remark: 'I never forbid a husband to escort his wife.'[12]

On the journey back to Florence, Anatole was ill; there was such a sore on one of his fingers that they consulted a doctor. He spoke of having the finger amputated, but they decided to get the opinion of other specialists before they resorted to such a drastic measure.

Early in July they reached the San Donato palace. It stood near the Porta al Prato, behind the Cascine. It had onion domes, in the Russian style, greenhouses, stables, a riding-school, a theatre and a private chapel. The profits from the silkworm nursery, which was hidden by the tall trees of the park, were enough to maintain the ornamental buildings. It was more like a principality than a palace.

Mathilde was enchanted with San Donato, but she was increasingly concerned about Anatole's health. His finger had now become gangrenous, and he suffered from other ailments, too. Dr Zanetti was summoned; he diagnosed that a certain disease, which had seemed to be checked at the time of the marriage, had now flared up again. Mathilde, in her innocence, did not know about venereal disease, and Zanetti felt obliged to ask Aunt Julie to explain matters to her. Aunt Julie was appalled to learn the truth about Anatole, and terrified at the thought that her niece was living with a tainted man. She sent for her at once. Mathilde remembered Anatole's visits to Princess Schouwaloff, and the mysterious rumours that had circulated about her. Now she understood everything.

She still remained too proud to reveal her dissensions with Anatole. She was not deeply religious, but she was faithful by nature, and marriage seemed to her a binding contract; besides, she could not bear the thought of living alone. And so, in 1844, she and Anatole were still accepted as the richest and happiest couple in Florence. Their Thursday evening receptions were dazzling. 'We couldn't be gayer,' wrote Mathilde to her old friend Mme Villamil, in January 1845. 'We dance a great deal every Thursday at home at San Donato, which has become a magical place . . . Nanan sends her kindest remembrances. Anatole sends his best wishes.'[1]

The façade of the marriage remained intact; but the moment that Mathilde and Anatole were left alone together, they grew bitter with rancour and suspicion. Anatole was now becoming extremely irascible, and seemed to prefer his small apartment in Florence to the luxuries of San Donato. So it was that Mathilde discovered a new and serious cause of dissension: his liaison with Valentine de Dino.

She had accepted his infidelity with Princess Schouwaloff because she had thought it just a passing fancy, but she had no illusions about the importance of this new love-affair. Anatole had never been able to forget Valentine de Dino. When, in 1838, she had married Talleyrand's nephew, he had been distraught at losing her. His own engagement and marriage had put her briefly out of his mind, but, on his first return from Russia, he had met her again in Paris, and he had once again fallen under her spell. She had now come to settle in Florence. The Duc de Dino took no offence at this ostentatious liaison.

Anatole was infatuated with Valentine de Dino, and he longed to rid himself of the obligation to live with his wife. When Mathilde tried to reason with him, he said he had never kept a mistress for more than three years, and he did not see why he should keep her longer. Soon afterwards he proposed an arrangement that they should both have their freedom, and she should have as many love-affairs as she wished, but no children. Mathilde rejected the offer. He tried to force her to take a lover, so that he could find her guilty and make his own conditions. He arranged for the servants to let a Monsieur de Meryem into her room to seduce her. Mme de Reding learned of the trap, and warned Mathilde in time.[2]

Mathilde remained in an unremitting nightmare. She could not live with 'this Cossack who was rotten to the marrow, whose very contact brought the risk of gangrene': this husband whom she found one day making love to another man;[3] and yet she continued to bear his insults and to act, still, as his nominal wife.

Her only escape lay, now, in painting. She took it up again, and she worked in a studio in Florence. One afternoon in 1845, when she was visiting the Convent of San Salvi, she noticed a young man copying Andrea del Sarto's *The Last Supper*. Possibly she heard him speak, and knew that he was French. Certainly her interest was roused, and she had him introduced to her. He was Ernest Hébert, a student at the French School in Rome. He was twenty-seven.

Hébert came into her life at a moment when she thought she could only fill it with work or friendship. He was sensitive, sincere and romantic, and, in an alien Florence, he brought her a reminiscence of France. It is said that he became the first of her lovers; and, indeed, in his fifties, when at last he was thinking of marriage, he told her: 'I'm horribly difficult about intelligence, feeling, figure, hands, shoulders, feet &c. Not to mention fits of passion, black jealousies and slanders, none of which I can do without any more. Whose fault is that?'[4]

The liaison – if such it was – did not last for long. Mathilde soon discovered that her need of love was greater than her need of him; and she was too honest to feign a passion. She had, in fact, already met the man to whom she was overwhelmingly attracted. She had met him in the Place Vendôme, for his brother-in-law had married the illegitimate daughter of Prince Paul of Wurtemberg. Now he appeared in Florence, escorting the Comte de Chambord, the Legitimist Pretender to the French throne. They were making a grand tour of Italy, and the Comte expressed a wish to see the Demidoff collections.

At San Donato, against a background of purple velvet curtains, standing by Canova's busts of Napoleon and Madame Mère, Mathilde renewed her acquaintance with Alfred-Émilien, Comte de Nieuwerkerke.

Nieuwerkerke was thirty-four, the son of a cavalry captain, Charles O'Hara de Nieuwerkerke, who had been a gentleman of the bedchamber to Charles x. He owed his official title to his grandfather, the illegitimate son of a minor *stadtholder*, and he owed his unofficial title, 'le beau Batave', to his Dutch ancestry and to his astonishing good looks. He was over six feet tall, with a full, fair beard; his high forehead gave an impression of nobility. The expression in his eyes suggested a lion at rest. He was separated from his wife, the former Mlle de Vassan, on grounds of incompatibility; and the knowledge of an unfortunate past only added to his attractions. His manners were suave, and he understood how to pay compliments (he knew something of courts, for he had been a page to Charles x). He was also a sculptor: he had produced some simple works under the guidance of Marochetti; and this success – which he had made much of – spared him further efforts. For art was less important to him than a certain elegance in his style of living, a moral licence in his life as an artist.[1]

While Anatole showed his art collections to the Comte de Chambord, Nieuwerkerke turned to Mathilde. No one knew better than he did how to talk of spiritual kinship. Mathilde was twenty-five, unhappy, impressionable and innocent: she would always keep her simplicity. Nieuwerkerke was physically drawn to her, dazzled by the aura of the Bonapartes; she could not fail to fall in love with him. Their meeting had finally broken her marriage.

Soon after this momentous meeting, the strains of the marriage were abruptly publicized. One summer night, at a fancy-dress ball at San Donato, where Anatole was escorting the Duchesse de Dino, Mathilde made her entrance as Diana the Huntress. She was clad in a tiger skin, and she carried a quiverful of arrows. She was so beautiful that she was greeted with general applause. She could not resist a scornful word to her husband's mistress. Anatole, in fury, slapped her face.

Soon afterwards, she received a further humiliation. Jerome de Montfort called on her to ask her to take a most degrading step. He was yet again in debt, and only Anatole could rescue him from a lamentable future. Mathilde could not bear the thought of approaching her husband, but finally she agreed to speak to him. Anatole was immovable; and, desperate to save the Bonaparte honour, she threw herself impulsively at his feet. Anatole rang for the footmen, and cried: 'There, you see, Napoleon's niece has thrown herself at my feet to get me to give money to her father.'[2]

On 20 December, the Czar arrived in Florence. He was on his way back from Palermo, where he had left the Czarina gravely ill. He had a long conversation with Prince Paul of Wurtemberg, who happened to be staying in the city; and, by the time he reached San Donato, he knew the truth about his niece's marriage. He said to her, with bluff affection: 'You don't know what a scoundrel you married.' Mathilde replied evasively: 'Your Majesty shows little generosity in speaking of my husband.' 'My poor child,' answered Nicholas, 'you will learn one day, and then you will come to me for support. You can always count on my real interest.'[3]

In March 1846, after the usual carnival celebrations, Mathilde left Florence with Anatole to spend the spring in Paris. Valentine de Dino had preceded them there, and took possession of him on his arrival. This time Mathilde had reached the limit of her tolerance. Among her papers is the draft of the petition which, presumably, she sent the Czar.

Sire,

I come to beg Your Majesty's august protection on the gravest and most important occasion of my life.

For six years of marriage, during which I have struggled to fulfil all my duties, I have been the object of every humiliation, every insult, every kind of ill-treatment which a woman may experience.

I have always hesitated to lay my complaint at Your Majesty's feet, because I felt that I must not complain until the cup was about to overflow.

This was the only reason which prevented me from opening my

heart to Your Majesty when you were passing through Florence. I still
wanted to wait, though I no longer hoped for anything.

Today, Sire, I come to ask Your Majesty to put an end to my
sufferings by separating me from a man who has no further right to
my esteem or to my affection . . .[4]

The Czar summoned Anatole to Russia. Mathilde and Anatole
left Paris in July, but this time Mathilde stopped in Holland. At
Het Loo, in the company of Sophie, Princess of Orange, she
waited for Nicholas 1 to grant her her freedom.

She waited a little while at Het Loo, but no message came from
Russia. She went back to Paris in despair at the thought that
Anatole might join her there. She had hesitated for years to leave
him, for she had only asked, like her Wurtemberg mother, to be
a devoted wife. Now she marvelled at the patience she had shown,
she had no time for indecision, or for social pretence. Thiers
advised her to be more cautious, because the separation was not
yet definite; but Mathilde had no time for discretion. She was
transfigured by her passion for Nieukerke, as she called him. She
decided to live in the rue de Courcelles in a small *hôtel* which he
had found her.

The Faubourg Saint-Germain had not yet decided what
attitude they should adopt towards her, but Mme Adelaide, the
King's sister, still showed affection for 'the little Florentine bird',
as she called her, and Queen Marie-Amelie enjoyed her company.
The Duc de Nemours invited her to his receptions at the Pavillon
de Marsan, and the Duc d'Aumale showed his open admiration;
he was not only a soldier, but something of a scholar, and he had
a genuine taste for the arts. He taught Mathilde the charm of
intellectual conversation.

Mathilde often went to the Place Vendôme, where her uncle's
liaison with Lady Wittingham suggested what her own liaison
with Nieuwerkerke might be. Prince Paul was fond of his niece,
and he wanted her to be happy. He had had the courage to break
his own marriage and impose his mistress on society, but he had
been quite sure of his happiness. He wondered if Mathilde could
be as certain of hers. 'Nieuwerkerke is a good fellow,' he said later
to the Austrian diplomat, Count Apponyi. 'I can understand that
my niece loves him, especially after her brute of a husband; but
her love-affair should have been discreet.' And he added: 'Nieu-

The parents of
Princess Mathilde:
Jerome and Catherine Bonaparte,
King and Queen of Westphalia,
later Prince and Princess
de Montfort.
From a painting by Kinson.

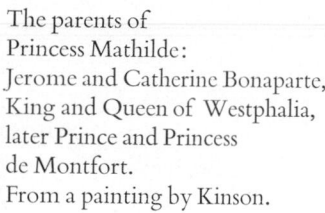

(*Above*) Louis-Napoleon, the future
Napoleon III, at about
the time of his engagement
to Mathilde.

(*Left*) Mathilde in 1836, at the time
of her engagement to
Louis-Napoleon.

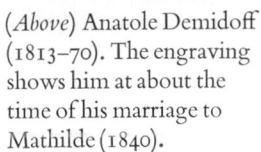

(*Above*) Anatole Demidoff (1813–70). The engraving shows him at about the time of his marriage to Mathilde (1840).

(*Above right*) Mathilde at about the time of her marriage. From a sketch by Eugène Lami.

(*Right*) Alfred-Emilien, Comte de Nieuwerkerke, Directeur-Général des Musées Impériaux. From a drawing by Ingres.

werkerke likes compromising women, he has always liked it; Nieuwerkerke has more vanity than most.'[5] He had had occasion to observe *le beau Batave*. He was not sure of his fidelity, even of his feelings for Mathilde.

It was difficult to counsel prudence to a woman in love; but one day Prince Paul called Mathilde urgently to the Place Vendôme, and advised her to leave Paris, in case Anatole should suddenly arrive. Mathilde replied that she had asked the Czar for help and protection, but she had had no answer. She could not leave Paris, for she had no money of her own. Prince Paul then told her that there was only one way to protect herself: she should bide her time in a convent.

Suddenly she understood how imprudent she had been to move into the rue de Courcelles, and to receive Nieuwerkerke, before the Czar himself had given judgment. It was from the Convent des Dames Augustines that she wrote to Thiers on 17 September.

As you see, I have made a grave decision. Until the situation changes, I've take refuge here, away from the intrigues and observations of the world.

For the past week I've been more or less locked up: confined to a very small room, very bare and plain, and strictly abstaining from meat three times a week.

All this is only while I'm waiting . . . I was told that it is usual in France for people in my situation to appear to withdraw a little from the world . . . Whatever happens, I shan't go back . . .

One thing is certain: henceforward I shall only have myself to depend on. It's very bold of me, isn't it, to dare so much? But confidence is a necessary virtue on the important occasions of one's life . . .[6]

She continued to wait for the Czar's decision. 'And what is your great Emperor doing?' Thiers asked, impatiently, in October. 'Can't he give better proof than he does of his love for beautiful princesses? I assure you that if I had his power I should behave quite differently to beautiful women ill-treated by their husbands. I should be a model autocrat, and I should make you the happiest of the oppressed . . . No one loves you more than I do.'[7]

Late that year, the Czar of All the Russias gave Mathilde her freedom. Her separation was arranged, she was to keep her jewels, and she was also to receive an annuity of two hundred

c

thousand francs. Though she gave her father an allowance of thirty-nine thousand francs a year, such wealth was enormous. Anatole was forbidden to return to Paris, and Mathilde welcomed Nieuwerkerke to 10, rue de Courcelles.

During the year 1847, Mathilde lived in tranquillity. All that remained of her marriage was the princely annuity which she would receive for the rest of her life. Her tainted, brutal husband had gone, and in his place was one of the handsomest, most charming men of his age.

If Mathilde had been hard-headed, she would already have lost her trust in human relationships: she had seen love turn to hatred, and intimacy scorned and destroyed. But she was not hard by nature, and she would never be sophisticated; she remained simple, trusting, and fiercely loyal. She expected to find a similar simplicity and trust, a comparable loyalty, in others. She was infatuated by Nieuwerkerke; she assumed fidelity in Jove.

Nieuwerkerke not only roused and satisfied her physical passion; he brought the world of the arts to the rue de Courcelles. He helped her to establish her *salon*. He seemed to fulfil every aspiration. In May her elder brother, Jerome, died at the early age of thirty-two. But Jerome had never been close to her like Plon-Plon, and his death in Florence, of a bone disease, hardly ruffled the smoothness of her existence. Political life, like domestic life, assumed a new serenity. Louis-Napoleon, who had escaped from Ham, wrote to Plon-Plon from London that he had admired her behaviour at the time of her retreat to the convent. Louis-Philippe and his family continued to show her affection, and Mathilde was fond of visiting Neuilly and the Tuileries. There was a comfortable bourgeois security, a sense of family life, which warmed the daughter of Catherine of Wurtemberg; she appreciated the middle-class virtues, she respected an ordered existence. After the revolution of 1848 she asked Sophie of Orange: 'Who will give me back my Neuilly?'

Mathilde was genuinely shocked by the February Revolution.

Profoundly Bonaparte though she was, she was filled with regret by the abdication of Louis-Philippe, and by the proclamation of the Second Republic. She was ashamed at the ingratitude of France to a king who had brought the country calm and prosperity. She mistrusted the proletariat, she did not want to believe that in France – as elsewhere in Europe in this year of revolutions – the people had grown aware of their strength. When, later in 1848, the country elected the Constituent Assembly, when universal suffrage for men was used in France for the first time, no doubt she waited apprehensively. She was astonished when four *départements* elected Louis-Napoleon.

Since his last abortive *coup-d'état*, his imprisonment at Ham, she had lost all political faith in him. He had seemed a hopeless theorist, an impractical dreamer who was incapable of changing destiny. The events of June 1848 began to unsettle her convictions. In September, when she was bathing at Dieppe, her latent Bonaparte hopes were suddenly roused. She learnt that he had arrived in Paris, and that he meant to stand for the Presidency.

She took the Paris train at once, and went to the Hôtel du Rhin, where he was staying. She had not seen him since the day in May 1836 when he had escorted her from Arenenberg. She was then sixteen, and engaged to him, Now, more than twelve years later, she had known a broken engagement and a disastrous marriage; she was twenty-eight, and he was forty. 'I think,' said an observer, 'that he is five foot rather than five foot one; he has a long nose, . . . a head too big for his body, brown hair, thick moustaches, and a brown beard . . .'[1]

Society was quick to assume that the old romance would be resumed. Mathilde was free of her husband, and Louis-Napoleon might surely be persuaded to discard Miss Howard, his English mistress, in favour of a splendid dynastic marriage. No doubt there was some trace of emotion, some recollection of Arenenberg, in the minds of both of them. But those who implied a more profound feeling, a more precise aspiration, had little understanding of Mathilde. She could not leave Nieuwerkerke and the rue de Courcelles for an impassible, unpredictable, unattractive cousin.

Yet while she felt no romantic love for Louis-Napoleon, she recognized that he brought a new and sudden hope for the dynasty. All her worship for her uncle, all the legend she had absorbed in the presence of Madame Mère, all her childhood in Rome, all her oldest, deepest instincts led her to support him in his latest bid for power. Before she left the Hôtel du Rhin, she had promised him her help. Soon afterwards she pawned her jewels and gave him the sum she had promised. She also assembled, in her *salon*, everyone who might serve his cause. 'When Louis-Napoleon arrived in Paris in 1848,' remembered Marshal Canrobert, 'he knew no one in the capital. He had left France at the age of eight and had come back twice a prisoner with a gendarme on either side . . . He was almost ignorant of French customs, and he hardly knew how French people lived. It was his cousin who brought him all the celebrities of the country.'[2] On 10 October, Marshal Castellane said that everyone at the rue de Courcelles believed that Louis-Napoleon would be President.[3] On 2 December, Mathilde presented Castellane to her cousin. 'I told him,' reported the Marshal, 'that his chances were increasing every day.'[4] 'Please give Louis all my good wishes, they are very sincere,' wrote Sophie to Mathilde. 'If he succeeds, I've promised a crucifix to the Catholic Church at Loo. God bless you all.'[5]

Louis-Napoleon's Press campaign had been skilful, his promises of social reform and the prestige of his name almost ensured his election. On 10 December he sent in his candidature for the Presidency, against Cavaignac, Lamartine and Ledru-Rollin. That evening Thiers and his mother-in-law, Mme Dosne, dined with him for the first time at the rue de Courcelles. It was, as Mme Dosne observed, a remarkable dinner. Mathilde had brought together a former minister of Louis-Philippe, and the Bonaparte pretender who, thanks to the fall of Louis-Philippe, was now to be the President of the Republic.

Louis-Napoleon was elected by an immense majority. He was to stay in office for ten years, during which his power over the Senate and the Legislative Assembly was to be virtually unlimited. On 17 December he left his campaign headquarters at the Hôtel du Rhin, and rode in triumph to the Élysée.

Jerome de Montfort, the only surviving brother of Napoleon, was appointed President of the Senate and given a magnificent allowance. He took up residence at the Hôtel des Invalides; and, at the age of sixty-four, he began at last to enjoy legitimate prosperity. Plon-Plon joined him; he had been elected a member of the Constituent Assembly, and he aired his radical opinions. 'He goes on as usual without warning,' Madame Dosne reported in trepidation. 'In this he is like his sister, Princess Mathilde, but she behaves more gracefully because she is a woman, and a little more modestly since she has become enamoured of M. de Nieuwerkerke . . .'[6]

However, within a week of her cousin's arrival at the Élysée, Mathilde had thrown all modesty to the winds. She was determined that Nieuwerkerke should be made Directeur des Beaux-Arts. Thiers warned her that she would do herself harm: she would bring down a hail of satires on herself and on her family. But Mathilde would only listen to the dictates of her passion, she addressed herself directly to ministers, 'and I should be very astonished,' recorded Mme Dosne, 'if they did not succumb to the solicitations of this beautiful woman'.[7] Mme Dosne was very astonished: M. de Malleville, the Minister of the Interior, did not only refuse Mathilde's demand, he refused it when it was repeated by the new President of the Republic. Mathilde appears to have blamed Thiers for the rebuff. On 30 December a chastened Mme Dosne recorded:

M. Thiers has always been extremely kind to Princess Mathilde Demidoff; he secured her return to France a few years ago, he had wanted to marry her to the Duc d'Orléans, which the prince and the King didn't want, and now she is saying a thousand things against him. She is pushed into it by M. de Nieuwerkerke, who is raging and storming because he was not made Directeur des Beaux-Arts! It is most shameful for a man to compromise a woman as much as this, and in so interested a fashion.[8]

Madame Dosne deplored the blatant influence of Nieuwerkerke on a woman so clearly entitled to respect. In spite of all the gossip, she remained admiringly fond of Mathilde. She had known her as a lonely young girl, chafing at her exile in Italy, she knew how she had suffered in her marriage. When she saw her, now, at the Hôtel de Ville, glittering with the Demidoff diamonds, she felt all her old affection and admiration. And yet a note of disapproval crept into Mme Dosne's account of the evening. Demidoff, she continued, had been ordered by the Czar to give Mathilde an annuity, jewels, and other advantages, not to mention her absolute freedom, of which she makes full use. She was accorded princely honours at the Hôtel de Ville. A private room, equipped with armchairs, had been set aside for her and her little court . . . The Comte de Nieuwerkerke was enjoying the glory of his princess, and endeavouring to publicize his passion just as if he had been in a private drawing-room.[9]

In May 1849 Comte Rodolphe Apponyi, the Austrian attaché, wrote in his journal what others had long feared and foreseen. For all her independence of character, for all her Bonaparte pride, despite her status as the first woman in France, Mathilde was ruled by Nieuwerkerke. 'He has established a tyrannical system of pressure against the poor princess,' wrote Apponyi. 'He has become the absolute master in her house.'[10]

Late in the spring of 1850, Marshal Canrobert dined at the Élysée. Mathilde was there 'in all her glowing beauty, doing the honours with perfect grace and dignity'.[1] She had now dropped the name Demidoff, and was always addressed as 'Your Highness'. Mme Dosne had grown waspish, and said that she wanted to be a princess of the blood;[2] but it was clear to many observers that the Presidency was moving towards a life-prorogation and the Empire.

Mathilde now welcomed a widening circle of friends to the rue de Courcelles. Among the newcomers were Prosper Mérimée, the novelist, Jules Sandeau, the dramatist, and Émile de Girardin, the founder of the cheap Press, the pre-eminent publicist of the age. Girardin came with his wife, Delphine, who wrote wittily under the pseudonym of Le Vicomte de Launay, and was known among men of letters as the Tenth Muse. Mathilde had not forgotten the figures who had charmed her life in Florence, and 'more than once the Abbé Liszt came with the Comtesse d'Agoult, who claimed literary recognition'.[3] On 28 January 1851 Apponyi went to a crowded rue de Courcelles, where the Duke of Brunswick was said to be wearing three million francs' worth of diamonds.[4]

Marshal Canrobert was touched by the welcome he received from Mathilde.

She is one of the noble figures of our age [he would recall], and on her admirably regular countenance she wears the mask of the Caesars. Her mind is fashioned exactly like her uncle's, all of a piece; she has never understood abstractions which cannot be applied . . . But there are no intellectual efforts which she does not admire, no great and noble things in which she does not take an interest. She always acts according to her heart and her feelings, without worrying about what people will say or think of her.[5]

One of her heartfelt wishes had already been granted. In 1849 the President had finally yielded to her insistence, dismissed the honest and capable M. Jeanron, and appointed Nieuwerkerke Directeur-général des Musées.

It is the memoirs of Viel-Castel which give the most continuous impression of Mathilde at this moment in her life. Comte Horace de Viel-Castel was a subordinate of Nieuwerkerke: a ferret-like official from the Louvre. He was aristocratic, civilized, and embittered by an unhappy marriage, and his uncharitable journals record all the gossip and all the sins of the age. Mathilde did not escape his criticism.[6] He deplored her 'Napoleonatry', her stubbornness and quick temper, he lamented her lack of sophistication, her inability to appreciate character. But, as he wrote, 'you cannot know her if you are to be her enemy'.[7]

On the evening of 1 March, after a brief illness, Mme de Reding suddenly died. She had never left Mathilde, except for the momentous journey to Russia. Mme de Reding was seventy-three, but her death was still unexpected. On the evening after the funeral, Viel-Castel found Mathilde in black, unable to speak of anything else, unable, sometimes, to restrain her tears. Her face revealed her desolation. He was drawn to her by such honesty of feeling. 'The death of the Baroness de Reding leaves her very alone, I don't see anyone near her who can take the place of her old friend . . .'[8]

There was no one; a week later, she wrote: 'The loss I have suffered is all the more cruel because it is irreparable. I never dared to think of it, I knew it would hurt so much.'[9]

Whatever her inner feelings, Mathilde concealed them; and Viel-Castel continued to record her full social life. She took him in a party to see *Manon Lescaut* at the Gymnase, she took him to see Verdi's *Ernani* from the President's box at the Italiens. She invited him to dinner with Lord Hertford and Mérimée, with the President's half-brother, Morny, and his mistress, Mme Le Hon; she invited him to a *soirée* at the rue de Courcelles. The garden was illuminated with coloured lanterns, and a dragoon band, among the trees, played incidental music. Among the guests was the President of the Republic.[10]

That summer Mathilde at last rented from the Marquis de Custine the château which she had admired for the past two years:

C*

the château of Saint-Gratien, near Enghien.[11] She kept a room for
Viel-Castel, and every summer week-end, at Saint-Gratien, he
amassed material for his memoirs. 'I see all kinds of people there,'
he explained. 'I often hear conversations which are not strange
(what *is* strange, nowadays?) but curious.'[12]

Early in July, the President visited Saint-Gratien. He did not
seem preoccupied; and yet it was clear that he had his plans, and
that he did not doubt his destiny. In April, still impassible, he had
told Mathilde that her *hôtel* in Paris would be too small for her
in 1852.[13]

On the night of 1 December 1851, while the National Assembly
was guarded by the loyal Colonel Espinasse, Louis-Napoleon
dissolved it and assumed full powers. On 2 December Paris
learned that he had made himself President for ten years. On 4
January it was announced that the currency would bear his
effigy. It was just a matter of time till the Empire was restored.

Soon afterwards, Mathilde's pride in her cousin was suddenly
shaken. Early in January she heard that he was contemplating a
decree which deprived the Orleans of their possessions. She
immediately recognized the influence of Persigny: he had long
insisted that this was the only way to destroy the Orleanist party.
Louis-Napoleon still hesitated: perhaps the confiscation would
only make the Orleanists into fervent opponents of the régime.
Perhaps he allowed himself to remember that it was Louis-
Philippe who had brought back Napoleon's body from St
Helena. Perhaps he reflected that Louis-Philippe had twice
spared his own life; a less tolerant sovereign would certainly have
had him executed after the Strasbourg skirmish of 1836, or after
the abortive *coup d'état* of Boulogne in 1840.

Morny and Rouher tried to dissuade Louis-Napoleon from an
act which would be both immoral and unwise. Mathilde, who
had known such kindness from the Orleans family, was horrified;
she went to see her cousin, to make a personal appeal. Persigny's
influence was stronger than that of the liberals, and on 22 January
the Orleans family were deprived of all their possessions, which
went to increase the funds of the State. 'I am *desolate* at this
extreme decision,' Sophie wrote to Mathilde. 'The papers say
you intervened in vain.'[14] Mathilde had not only intervened: she
sent a severe rebuke to her cousin.

She could not, however, desert him at his first political blunder, and she continued to go to the Élysée. In February, admiring her appearance at a ball, Apponyi noticed that she was wearing a diamond eagle in her hair.[15] This was only one of many indications of the future. A few days later, Napoleon's birthday, 15 August, was decreed as a national holiday. In May, from the balcony of the École Militaire, Mathilde saw her cousin restore the imperial flags, surmounted by their gilt eagles, to the French army.[16] In a patriotic gesture, designed to ensure his popularity, Louis-Napoleon announced the creation of a museum for the possessions of French sovereigns; he also decreed that the Louvre would be completed and joined to the Tuileries. In October he went to Amboise. The Emir Abd-el-Kader, who had fought the French in Algeria, had been imprisoned at Amboise by the Orleans. Louis-Napoleon gave him his freedom. Abd-el-Kader duly moved to Paris with his wives, and in November Viel-Castel observed him at 10, rue de Courcelles: grave and handsome, with dark olive eyes and an ebony-black beard. 'He was all in white,' noted Viel-Castel, 'only his slippers were green.'[17]

Soon afterwards Mathilde gave her first reception at 24, rue de Courcelles: the *hôtel* where, ten years earlier, Queen Christina of Spain had lived with the Duc de Rienzarès. The *hôtel* was Louis XVI in style, with a large courtyard in front. There were gardens on two sides, one giving on to the rue de Courcelles, the other continuing as a terrace along the boulevard Haussmann. The *hôtel* itself was far more splendid than the one in the same street where Mathilde had lived since the end of her marriage. Louis-Napoleon himself had given her the *hôtel* which would be among the most famous of the age.

He was gay and amicable when, on 23 November, he attended her inaugural *soirée*. No doubt he already felt assured of the result of the plebiscite by which, two days earlier, he had offered to restore the Empire. On the evening of 1 December, the Senate, the Corps Législatif, and the Conseil d'État went in procession to Saint-Cloud, where he was waiting. There, by the overwhelming vote of the people of France, they told him that he was Emperor.

PART THREE

The Second Empire

1852–70

◈ I I ◈

The Second Empire came into being by nearly eight million votes against a quarter of a million.[1] On 2 December 1852, the forty-seventh anniversary of Napoleon's victory at Austerlitz, it was proclaimed at the Hôtel de Ville in Paris, and Napoleon III rode into his capital through the Arc de Triomphe.

That afternoon, Mathilde proudly watched him review the troops at the Carrousel. She and her brother and father were to bear the title of Imperial Highness; Jerome de Montfort – known again as King Jerome – was to have a million francs a year and a residence at the Palais-Royal. Napoleon was to receive three hundred thousand francs and the other half of the Palais-Royal. She herself was to have two hundred thousand francs a year in addition to her Demidoff annuity.[2]

On 18 December, while the guns fired in salute, the new Emperor, with a mounted escort, arrived for the first of the *séries* at Compiègne. These imperial house-parties were to become a feature of social life in the Second Empire. 'My dear cousin,' the Emperor told Mathilde, 'until there is an empress, you are the first lady and you will always be on my right hand.'[3] On this occasion, Mathilde remained first lady of the Empire; 'but one thing seems certain,' Henri Bouchot would write in *Les Élégances du Second Empire*, 'and that is the presence of Mme de Montijo and her ravishing daughter.'[4] By an irony which she was unlikely ever to forget, Mathilde herself had presented Mlle de Montijo to her cousin.

She had first met Eugénie, she remembered, at her uncle Wurtemberg's in the Place Vendôme, in September 1845. Eugénie had been sitting at a lansquenet table. Mathilde had thought her beautiful.

Her skin was very white and matt, her red hair seemed even redder

since the colour was not then in fashion. She had a slender waist, and
an ample bosom; she was distinguished-looking, though she had a
very pronounced foreign air. She was also free in manner, with a
decisive tone in conversation, full of spirit, like a woman well
accustomed to homage from men.[5]

Eugénie was not drawn to Mathilde, but in 1849 she had begun
to frequent the rue de Courcelles.[6] It was in this *salon*, where she
professed to be extremely bored, that she was presented to
Louis-Napoleon; and, after that first presentation, she had often
met him there. She was not unaware of the attractions of an
unmarried head of state, a Bonaparte who might well be an
Emperor.[7] Mathilde had assumed that Eugénie would readily be
Miss Howard's successor. She had underestimated Eugénie's
ambition, her pride, and her strength of will. By November
1852, on the eve of the Second Empire, Louis-Napoleon had
eyes for no one else,[8] and Eugénie was waiting for the throne.

On 22 January 1853, the Emperor announced his engagement.
For 'reasons of state,' he advanced the date of the wedding by a
month, and the civil marriage was arranged for 29 January, at
the Tuileries; there was to be a nuptial mass at Notre-Dame next
day. Preparations were hurriedly made. Mathilde, ever anxious
to help her friends, wanted Viollet-le-Duc and Lassus to decorate
the cathedral. 'I should be glad to do something for them,' she
wrote to Mérimée. 'Chevreau is the person to speak to (he's the
secretary-general at the Ministry of the Interior). Come and see
me tomorrow. We'll talk to him.'[9] Viollet-le-Duc and Lassus
were entrusted with the task.

At eight o'clock on the evening of Saturday, 29 January, the
civil marriage was performed in the Salle des Maréchaux at the
Tuileries. It was the Empress's first official appearance in public,
and she 'looked charming and distinguished with her rose-
coloured dress and her set of pearls. As she had wind of the
opposition to her marriage, she was very nervous,' Mathilde
remembered. 'She took my hand, and did not want to leave me.
When she reached the Salle des Maréchaux and had to precede
me, she was visibly moved . . .' Mme de Montijo, the Empress's
mother, had a nervous tic of shaking her head. She was 'grotesque
with agitation.'[10]

Next day the nuptial mass was said; and then, recalled Mathilde, we came back from Notre-Dame to the Tuileries, there were embraces and congratulations, and then the Empress went to change her clothes to go to Saint-Cloud where she was to stay privately with her husband; she came back very animated, dressed in ruby velvet with furs . . . We saw her climb into a carriage . . . which took her to her new residence. The ladies-in-waiting and household followed. We all went home, tired and sad at heart; we felt that we were losing the Emperor.[11]

Some thirty years later, Maxime du Camp, the journalist and novelist, maintained that he had dined at the rue de Courcelles on the evening after the wedding.

One could feel the vendetta [he wrote], and the gossip was going hot and strong. The Princess was outraged; this marriage made her subordinate and relegated her to the second rank . . . Red-faced, purple-faced, spattering her talk with Italian, which was always a sign of anger with her, she tried to joke as she described the various phases of the wedding ceremony . . .[12]

By the time he wrote his memoirs, Maxime du Camp had left the rue de Courcelles under a cloud, and he sacrificed accuracy to malice. It is doubtful whether Mathilde regretted that she had not married her cousin. She herself insisted that she felt no regret, and no envy.

I was the only woman in the family, politically speaking [so she wrote], until that day I had been in the front rank; I made my *examen de conscience* with rigorous honesty, & I declare that I felt no jealousy whatever. I could have had a similar fortune in 1850. There was a question of my obtaining my divorce so that I could marry the President of the Republic. I refused outright, for I preferred the situation I had to the quite exceptional one which I was offered. I did so without any hesitation, & without the least regret. I could not have forfeited my independence when I felt that my heart was not involved. I have congratulated myself on my decision.[13]

Mathilde wanted Nieuwerkerke, and she wanted her freedom. She wanted to rule an empire of her own. She wanted to complete her cousin's reign by ruling over the realm of art and intellect which the Tuileries so little understood.

She did not choose her rôle to earn admiration from posterity. She chose the part instinctively, and she chose it out of patriotism. Fortune had smiled upon her, and all that was most distinguished in France must share the imperial favour which she enjoyed.

৩ 12 ৫

In the early years of the Second Empire, Paris already showed the vivacity and brilliance which would be associated with the age of Napoleon III. The sedate, domestic court of Louis-Philippe had now been succeeded by an Imperial Court distinguished by rigorous etiquette and by an almost unbridled love of pleasure. The Emperor was the 'topmost tinsel star on the Christmas tree of Parisian gallantry', and the permissive atmosphere at Court naturally spread throughout the capital. 'In our day', wrote Viel-Castel in 1853, 'people only live by their senses, and they deny themselves nothing that may satisfy their whims . . .'[1]

Entertaining was lavish and frequent. There were the *séries* at Compiègne, the entertainments at Saint-Cloud, the receptions at the Tuileries. On Shrove Tuesday, 1857, Mathilde gave a ball without specifying the dress that her guests should wear. The Empress assumed she should wear fancy-dress, and made her entrance as 'Night beneath her shadowy veils, starred with a milky way of diamonds'. She found her hostess in evening dress, 'without the slightest suspicion of disguise'. No doubt, as Mme Baroche suggested, Mathilde regreted her error, 'and went into her pretty conservatory to tell her troubles to the flowering shrubs.'[2]

The Government departments vied in hospitality with the Imperial family. At a ball at the Corps Législatif in 1853, Mérimée recorded Mathilde 'wearing a diamond pointed crown in the style of Semiramis, which caused a stir'.[3] When Maximilian of Bavaria visited Paris in 1857, Paris gave him a ball at the Hôtel de Ville and he opened it with Mathilde. No doubt Maximilian was more gallant than the young hereditary Grand Duke of Tuscany, who invited her to waltz at Compiègne. 'Don't worry,' she said, 'it's no pleasure for you to dance with a woman of my age.' The Duke replied: 'If I do, of course, it's only out of duty.'[4]

While Mathilde danced with visiting potentates, foreign envoys made their way to the rue de Courcelles: the Minister of the Two Sicilies, the Sardinian Minister, the Austrian Ambassador, and the entire Abyssinian mission in their native dress. Mathilde herself was known to dine at the Russian Embassy, and she attended the more spectacular embassy balls, like the Turkish ball of 1855, which brought together a host of names from the *Almanach de Gotha*. She was not too imperial to enjoy the fancy-dress parties and masked balls which were all the rage, and no doubt she would have liked to attend the celebrated *redoutes* which were given by her admirer, the director of the Comédie-Française, the handsome, ubiquitous socialite Arsène Houssaye.

Her own theatrical tastes were simple. She liked the full-blooded melodramas of Dumas *père* and the solid moral dramas of François Ponsard and Émile Augier, the pillars of the *école du bon sens*. She also enjoyed the popular songs of Gustave Nadaud, and it was at the rue de Courcelles, to his infinite embarrassment, that Nadaud met Napoleon III and was asked to sing *Pandore, ou les Deux Gendarmes*. Nadaud had already been summonsed on account of this work of doubtful taste, and he had been forbidden to sing it. He now professed that he had forgotten it. The Emperor insisted. Nadaud was obliged to sing it, and the Emperor laughed till he cried. He immediately raised the ban on the song.[5]

Sometimes, however, benevolence went astray at the rue de Courcelles. Alfred de Musset was invited twice, and on both occasions he was drunk.

One evening it was at a dinner given in his honour. They waited for him for an hour, and, when they sat down at table, they saw him emerging from the far end of the *salons*. He stumbled along, and, catching sight of his empty chair, he fell into it without a word. A sign was made to the servants not to give him any drink, and he didn't eat or drink anything throughout dinner. Then he went upstairs and sobered down, but the spell was broken.

Another time, he was going to read his *cantate d'Auguste* [sic], and Gounod was playing the piano, when Musset collapsed and fell asleep in the middle of the reading . . . He used to get drunk on a mixture of beer and brandy . . .[6]

In 1857 Mathilde invited Dumas *fils* to be presented to the Emperor. The author of *La Dame aux camélias* had the gross discourtesy to refuse her invitation, and to accept, independently, the decoration which she had wanted to give him. It was some years before Mathilde forgave him for the insult.[7] Edmond About was scarcely more civil. A brilliant young journalist, and the author of *Le Roi des montagnes*, he often came to the rue de Courcelles. Early in 1858, Mathilde prepared a surprise for him: he was, without his knowledge, appointed chevalier de la Légion-d'honneur. After a dinner-party one evening, Persigny asked him to shut his eyes; About obeyed, and the Minister prepared to pin on the decoration. As he did so, he enquired: 'What would you like to be?' About, too vain to assume that he might begin with the lowest grade of the order, replied: 'Officier de la Légion-d'honneur.'[8]

However, Mathilde was not content with giving About the decoration: she encouraged him to write for the theatre, and in 1859 she agreed to sponsor his drama *Gaëtana*. 'Thank you, Madame, for the hospitality which you graciously promise my play,' About wrote to her in November. 'It will be very honoured to make its entry into the world under the auspices of Your Highness and her friends. If it succeeds with you, I don't care about the public in the rue de Richelieu, I shall be content . . .'[9]

Gaëtana was, in fact, booed in the rue de Richelieu by students who resented imperial patronage. For the first time, but not the last, Mathilde was made aware that some were hostile to Notre Dame des Arts. As for About, his conceit was finally to bar him from her *salon*. One evening, as he paid court to her, he noticed Nieuwerkerke's evident disapproval. 'Jealous old man!' said About. Mathilde rang for his carriage.[10]

But though there were occasional mishaps, though there was occasional hostility, Mathilde had already begun to establish a *salon* of renown. Dumas *père*, a huge, vital egoist, entertained and sometimes vexed her guests with his monologues and his presumption. 'Just call me Dumas,' he told Mathilde. 'I've worked for years for that.'[11] Mérimée was already writing to Viollet-le-Duc, now the Emperor's architect: 'Our Princess has asked me to dinner on Wednesday. I expect she's asked you too. Would you come and fetch me?'[12] In 1855, Saint-Saëns, who was still in his twenties, thanked Mathilde for her encouragement by dedicating to her his *Sérénade* for piano, organ and violin. In January 1856 it was duly performed in her salon in the presence of Auber, the venerable composer and head of the Paris Conservatoire. Saint-Saëns himself played the organ, and enjoyed a brilliant success.[13] And it was to Mathilde that Gounod, the future composer of *Faust*, owed his first triumph in the theatre. He had written a comic opera, *Le Médecin malgré lui*, which was based on the play by Molière. Fould, the Minister of State, refused to let it be performed on the grounds that it infringed the rights of the Comédie-Française. Mathilde insisted that the ban was raised, and on Molière's birthday, 15 January 1858, the work – which was dedicated to her – was staged at the Théâtre-Lyrique. It had a hundred consecutive performances. 'I am sure,' Gounod told Mathilde, thirty-three years later, 'that your jewels are out-numbered by memories like this.' Writing in 1891, he had reason to address her as his 'constant, sure, devoted friend.'[14]

In February 1853, Comte de Hübner, the Austrian Ambassador, said that the guests at the *salon* formed a world apart. 'Except for the ministers' wives,' he noted, 'there are hardly any Frenchwomen; but there are many foreigners, especially Italians and Poles, more or less involved in some or other conspiracy.'[15]

Hübner saw the rue de Courcelles through the eyes of a diplomat. Viel-Castel continued to observe it as a vehement social critic. In his cynicism he observed what Mathilde was too inno-cent, too tolerant, too infatuated with Nieuwerkerke to notice. He saw her all too susceptible to flattery from schemers who would disown her the moment that fortune ceased to smile on her. Nor did she seem to understand how much the Emperor and Empress deplored her ostentatious liaison. To Viel-Castel it was evident that the imperial displeasure would be translated into deeds and words; he was apprehensive of the day. But Mathilde and Nieuwerkerke remained blind to all omens. They settled at the Pavillon de Breteuil, on the Saint-Cloud estate, where Nieuwerkerke played the master of the house with vulgar bravado. Mathilde herself was no more discreet: she spoke of Nieuwerkerke as a wife would speak of her husband.

And, for the moment, it seemed as if the apprehensions of Viel-Castel were unjustified. On 19 November, Nieuwerkerke was elected to the Académie des Beaux-Arts. The diarist greeted the news with a burst of indignation and some irrelevant comments on Nieuwerkerke's undistinguished origins.

His father, a poor cavalry captain, was very lucky to marry one of my cousins, Mlle de Vassan, a rich heiress who brought him an income of 60,000 francs. The Dutch nobility think nothing of the so-called nobility of the Nieuwerkerkes. Émilien . . . is more of a careerist than an artist. Art has only been a means to him . . . Nieuwerkerke likes brilliance, show, appearance, in a word he has too many little vanities ever to be a serious man. He is preoccupied with his waistcoat buttons, his shirt buttons, the lapis-lazuli buttons which he puts on his gaiters in summer, with his watch-chain, his suit, etc. He likes dress, and the first thing he thought of after his election was his new uniform . . .

Nieuwerkerke told me that with this election he hoped to be a Councillor of State before long, and that in four or five years the Emperor would probably make him a Senator. If things go on like this, no doubt the nation will make him Emperor ten years hence.[16]

Viel-Castel nearly always wrote with bitterness, but at times he came near the truth. It was sad that a woman of character and distinction should be so infatuated with this superbly handsome, hollow man. Mathilde herself was now fulfilling one of her imperial obligations: spending a few days at Fontainebleau. She wrote lovingly to Nieuwerkerke of her loneliness at Court. She told him how she longed to come home to her familiar surroundings, her habits, and even her sins. Nieuwerkerke received the letter on 25 November, and read certain passages to Viel-Castel. Suddenly he broke off his reading and turned to his servant: 'Tell M. Moissenet to write to Mlle Mignerot that I am expecting her at noon.' And, as Viel-Castel recalled:

The servant went away smiling, Moissenet wrote, smiling, and the commissionnaire, smiling, took the letter to Mlle Mignerot, for everyone knows that she comes to the Louvre to sleep with M. le Directeur-général des Musées, Intendant des Beaux-Arts de la Maison de l'Empereur, Membre de l'Institut.

It is a few minutes before noon . . . In two hours, Nieuwerkerke will answer the Princess. Poor Princess![17]

It was now eight years since Nieuwerkerke had come to San Donato, and paid court to the niece of Napoleon. It was seven years since she had received him at the rue de Courcelles. She was still in love with him, but perhaps, even now, she had lost her illusions of his fidelity. Years later she told a friend: 'He loved me for perhaps three weeks, he was unfaithful to me after two months. As I am proud, and a king's daughter, I didn't want to look ridiculous, and I tried to set an example of extra-marital fidelity. I was ashamed, you see.'[18] Nieuwerkerke had given her perfect happiness, as long as she had believed in his fidelity; even when she knew that he was unfaithful, she chose to share his favours rather than lose him. 'The great passions of which posterity may speak,' wrote Viel-Castel, 'the passions which for many reasons create the most effect, are sometimes very wretched when one sees them from the wings of the theatre . . . Nieuwerkerke, I regret to say, has neither passion nor anything which resembles it for the Princess.'[19]

In December, 1853, a month after Viel-Castel had recorded this reliable opinion, the commission was announced for the coming International Exhibition in Paris. Nieuwerkerke had not been appointed, and Mathilde told Fould that she considered this as a personal insult,

that all over Europe people would say that he hadn't been put on the list because he was her lover; that she didn't mean to be treated like this; that she had no need of the government and she had enough to live on without the miserable pittance of 200,000 francs that she was given; and, another thing, that if at the instigation of her black-guard father and brother, she wasn't treated properly, she'd go and live in a country [Russia] where the sovereign showed her considera-tion and treated her as one of his family.

Go and tell all that to the Emperor, she added, or else I'll go and tell him myself, more bluntly.[20]

১৩২

In politics, as in love, Mathilde was guided by passion and prejudice. She did not pause to assess or consider, she refused to doubt, her heart had already dictated her position. For politics, like love, were to her a question of loyalty, and her loyalties remained unshakable. They had the simplicity of a child's.

It was easy to observe that she herself was half Corsican, half German. She was illuminated by love of France. Her patriotism transcended political parties and régimes, she was French years before she set foot in France, intensely French till the last day of her life. However, with her passion for France, her idolatry for her uncle, there went a stubborn antipathy to England. Only three times in a life which lasted over eighty years is she known to have crossed the Channel; and on two of these occasions she went to attend the funeral of a relation. Her antipathy to England was not based on personal knowledge; it was, quite simply, based on the facts of Waterloo and St Helena. Mathilde had no knowledge whatever of English civilization; she had a schoolgirl's command of the written language, she is not recorded to have spoken it, or to have read any work in English literature. English politics were, to her, permanently alien, and she flatly refused to understand them. At the age of forty-five, she attended the *première* of Ponsard's *Le Lion amoureux*. When the old émigré in the play suggested seeking refuge with the English, Mathilde booed from the imperial box, where she sat with the Emperor and Empress. 'I was pleased with myself,' she said later. 'I can still burn with patriotism.'[1]

It was again a personal if somewhat selective memory which made Mathilde wholeheartedly pro-Russian. She chose to forget her uncle's retreat from Moscow, she chose to forget her own disastrous marriage, and she chose to remember the kindness which the Czar had shown her. Just as she identified England with

Wellington and Hudson Lowe, so she identified Russia with Nicholas I. The magnificent despot, the admiring and benevolent cousin who had rescued her from Anatole, deserved her unthinking political loyalty.

Early in 1854, on the eve of the Crimean War, she wrote to him, regretting the tension between France and Russia; and late in February, when Viel-Castel was dining at the rue de Courcelles, the Russian Consul-general brought his reply. Nicholas I declared that he was touched by her affection, and that she could be sure of his own. 'Princess Mathilde is always very Russian,' noted the diarist, 'and alas she is not discreet enough about it.'[2]

Far from practising discretion, Mathilde believed herself to be charged with a mission of peace, and she exerted influence to make the thought of war unpopular. When, in March, England and France declared war on Russia, she largely blamed the Empress: it was Eugénie, so she said, who had dragged the Emperor into war. No doubt it satisfied his need for prestige. She made no effort to hide her own political sympathies: she intensified her correspondence with the Czar and the Grand Duchess Helena, and she often read news from Russia to her guests. One thought, above all, enraged her. 'The Princess has little vision in politics,' decided Viel-Castel in September. 'She cannot forgive the Emperor for the English alliance, she would prefer alliance with Russia. She's against everything that happens in England or comes from the English . . .'[3]

The more pro-English Paris became, the more Mathilde showed her Russian sympathies. While the allied armies entrenched themselves round Sebastopol, Mathilde sent Nicholas I her particularly affectionate good wishes. 'I hope that God will grant these wishes,' Nicholas replied, 'by ending an unnecessary war . . . If those on whom peace depends desire it as honestly as I do, it is easy for them now to give the benefit to humanity.'[4]

This letter only intensified Mathilde's anger at hostilities. She expressed her pity for Napoleon III. She maintained that he was influenced by the English, who were jealous of his supremacy in the Mediterranean. She reproached Eugénie for taking a foolish pride in her husband's crusade, and when the Emperor threatened to go in person to Sebastopol and to make Eugénie Regent, Mathilde predicted the fall of the Empire. The Emperor was far from touched by such solicitude: he was understandably indig-

nant, and he ceased to talk politics with her at all. On 22 February
1855, Viel-Castel recorded that she had just received yet another
letter from Russia. 'We do indeed live in singular times,' added
Viel-Castel, 'when the Emperor's own cousin is corresponding
with the Czar, with whom we are at war . . .'[5]

A few days later, on 3 March, Mathilde learned of the death of
Nicholas 1, and decided, in spite of the war, to go into mourning.
The Empress took this gesture as an affront, though the Emperor
showed more liberality, and allowed her to attend a memorial
service.[6] Mathilde sent a letter of condolence to the new Czar,
Alexander II, and he replied with assurances of affection. Viel-
Castel declared that she was more flattered to be the cousin of
Alexander II than the cousin of Napoleon III. 'The Princess is
happy with this letter; she, an Imperial Highness of France, is
proud of the friendship and protection of our enemy.'[7] She was
indeed happy; she dashed off a letter to Sophie, now Queen of
Holland, telling her about the Czar's reply. 'It gives me pleasure,'
answered Sophie. 'It proves that people are just. I don't think it's
impossible to come to an understanding with him.'[8]

Such behaviour alienated Mathilde from the Tuileries, but it
did not change her affection for Napoleon III; and the Emperor
seems to have understood that for all her violent personal opinions,
all her diplomatic liberties, nothing would impair her fidelity to
France.

On 16 March 1856, Paris reverberated with a hundred-and-one-
guns salute. The Empress had given birth to a son. As Viel-Castel
made his way that evening to the rue de Courcelles, he did not
expect to hear much praise of Eugénie. Mathilde disliked her and
hardly troubled to hide her dislike. It was, he thought, unfortunate that the imperial family was divided by jealousy and not
even held together by interest.[9]

Perhaps, in the first years of her marriage, Eugénie would have
welcomed a warmer relationship with her cousin. Among
Mathilde's papers is a note which probably belongs to the mid
1850s: 'I am horribly vexed with you,' writes the Empress, 'for
treating me with such ceremony, because you know how fond I
am of you.'[10] She sent Mathilde two dresses to choose from: 'I've
waited till the evening, so that you can see them by artificial
light.'[11] When Mathilde, in a generous moment, presented her

with a sausage, Eugénie answered gratefully: 'Thank you a million times for the magnificent Sausage; I was particularly touched that you should have remembered my *passion* for them.'[12]

But whatever their early attempts at friendship, friendship seemed to be impossible. Eugénie was frivolous ('Marie-Antoinette at the Bal Mabille');[13] Mathilde was interested in the arts. Eugénie was fiercely Catholic; Mathilde believed in charity, but she had small time for outward observances. Eugénie was cold and superficial; Mathilde was passionate. Eugénie was a parvenue, and Mathilde was a princess. Eugénie, above all, was a foreigner, and Mathilde was French to the depths of her being. And so she was not resentful, now, or jealous or malicious at the birth of the Emperor's son and heir. 'She spoke very well of the Empress and the Prince,' said Viel-Castel. 'She rejoices in the birth of this child, and sees him as a pledge of confidence in the future.'[14]

In time she came to love the Prince Imperial not only as the heir to the throne, but as a child of character and charm. She delighted in giving him the pleasures which she might have given to her own children: in giving him the warmth which he could not get from his mother or find in the formal atmosphere of the Court. He was to be an only child, isolated from birth, he was delicate and always conscious of his position. His mother looked on him as an heir; Mathilde came to look on him as a lonely human being. She wrote to him, and signed herself 'the most loyal and devoted of aunts.'[15] She chose presents for him with elaborate care. On his thirteenth birthday she gave him a veloci-pede; and that evening, at the Tuileries, elated by champagne, when he drank to the Emperor and Empress, the French Army, the Imperial Navy and the Garde mobile, he remembered 'Michaux, the inventor of velocipedes, and accorded him an honourable mention.'[16] Mathilde entertained for her nephew and gave him his freedom at the rue de Courcelles. Once, at a children's fancy-dress ball, he left his shoes under the table. His mother frowned; Mathilde laughed heartily.[17] She gaily reported Loulou's *bons mots*; Mme Baroche declared that she 'adored him'.[18]

Probably she would have liked to have children of her own. She could hardly have wanted a child by Anatole, once she learned of his venereal disease, but she was young enough to have had a child by Nieuwerkerke. The possible loss of her Demidoff income, the question of illegitimacy, would hardly have deterred a rich princess who loved her lover with passion and proclaimed her long liaison with extravagant pride. Perhaps she was afraid of the effect which her pregnancy might have on a man who was far from faithful; perhaps she could not have a child, and disguised her regrets in coarse comments. ('Children!' she cried at the end of her life. 'I'd rather start a hundred than finish one.')[19] Edmond de Goncourt told her, frankly, that her love of dogs was merely a childless woman's compensation, and Mathilde denied it, vehemently.[20] Perhaps she was honest; and yet perhaps she protested too much.

In October 1849, Mathilde had fallen in love with Saint-Gratien.
The château stood on the outskirts of the village of the same
name. It had been built during the First Empire by the Comte de
Luçay, who was then the Prefect of the Palace; tradition said
that he had built it to provide a view for Queen Hortense, in the
nearby château de Saint-Leu, a gesture which prompted Napoleon
himself to attend the inaugural festivities. This dynastic memory
was not lost on Mathilde; besides, Saint-Gratien possessed a
second link with history. In the grounds was a small pavilion
which had once belonged to Nicolas Catinat, Marshal of France,
one of the great captains of the reign of Louis xiv.[1]

The estate of Saint-Gratien bordered on the lake of Enghien;
it was not far from the spa itself, and in the background rose the
wooded hills of Montmorency. It had all the comfortable
pleasures of the country and, which was most important, it was
only thirty kilometres from Paris.

Mathilde had decided one afternoon in 1849 that Saint-
Gratien should be hers. It belonged to the Marquis de Custine,
and, since 1851, when he had let it to her for the summer, the
Marquis had been anxious to sell it to her. He had originally
asked an exorbitant price, but, by 1853, he had modified his
demands, and in 1854 Mathilde had entered the château as
proprietor. Henceforward she would live there for six months
every year, until she died.

Gradually, piece by piece, she bought back much of the old
estate, until she had a park which extended for well over seventy
acres. Then, intent on perfecting her décor, she invited Baron
Haussmann to Saint-Gratien. The planner of Second Empire
Paris came with the landscape gardener who had transformed the
Bois de Boulogne; and, accustomed to taking drastic measures,
they advised her to begin by felling all the trees – including the

magnificent cedar of Lebanon. She thanked them politely for
their help. The centennial trees remained one of the glories of
Saint-Gratien.[2]

The visitor to Mathilde's estate would go up the little avenue
which led to the main entrance: to the massive gates, painted
Bonaparte green. Behind these gates, behind the high walls, the
vulgar world was all at once forgotten, and he found himself in
the vast, silent park. On the right was the lodge, and on the left
was the Pavillon de Catinat. Here and there, in the distance,
statues stood out white against the trees; and, at the end of the
drive, announced by Minton vases of scarlet geraniums, stood the
château: a big square house which gave the illusion of great size,
a simple house with a blue-and-white china frieze along the wall,
and a wing, with a terrace above it, on each side.[3]

On the right of the entrance hall was the library, on the left
were the stairs. Facing the visitor was the big salon, hung with
green flowered chintz, where the guests sat in the evening.[4] It
was in this salon, on Sunday mornings, that the visitors from
Paris assembled with the house-guests, and, on the stroke of
eleven, Mathilde – Notre-Dame de Saint-Gratien – came to greet
them. The salon led to the famous verandah; and a guest declared,
at the end of the century, that the glazed verandahs at the rue de
Courcelles and Saint-Gratien were models of their kind: they
had not been bettered for fifty years.[5] From the verandah, where
the gay Japanese awning softened the light, across the steps which
were flanked by two bronze eagles, the guests looked out across
the lawns towards the wooded hills.

And in the great calm, unbroken by any noise from the outside
world, in this slightly contrived, artificial world, a world made for
social life, a great peace emanated from everything, a feeling of ease,
luxurious and yet normal life, a settled life which had lasted for years
and would, it seemed, last all eternity.[6]

The rooms upstairs confirmed Mathilde's simple domestic
tastes. The bedrooms were homely, with bright-coloured
cretonnes and mahogany furniture. Her own apartments,
streaming with light, were cluttered with knick-knacks and
little cupboards. Her bedroom, which led out on to a terrace,
was hung with a grey chintz patterned with birds and flowers; on
one side it looked on to the lake, on the other on to the hills of

Montmorency. The mirrors reflected bunches of roses from the estate, and fresh roses were brought nearly every day. A private staircase led from Mathilde's apartments to the studio where, amid the welter of palm trees, divans, dog-baskets, tables and desks, she studied painting every afternoon with Eugène Giraud. Giraud was a close friend of hers, and, in a sense, he belonged to the surroundings. He was no Court painter, but a Bohemian artist, married to an actress from the Comédie-Française.

'There are châteaux near Paris which are more luxuriously furnished than Saint-Gratien,' Émile de Girardin wrote at the height of the Empire. 'But there may not be another which is furnished with such taste. Everything there is simple, but everything is convenient, it is English comfort enhanced by a touch of French style . . .'[7] Girardin's encomium appeared in *Enghien et ses environs:* a guide-book published in 1862; and, in the tone of a courtier, the author recalled how the village of Saint-Gratien owed its prosperity to *la bonne princesse*. It was to her, he said, that the *commune* owed the rebuilding of the church, the *mairie* and the school, which were just outside the estate, 'for if the princess is an artist, the artist is a princess. In fact, all her activities, all her works, are marked by this dual nature, which makes her a person both influential and charming.'[8]

By the time that Girardin sang the praises of Saint-Gratien, most of the significant men in France were aware of the trains to Sannois from Saint-Lazare and the hourly trains to Enghien (ten minutes from Saint-Gratien) from the Gare du Nord.[9]

From time to time, with no thought for propriety or for her position, Mathilde talked arrant nonsense about the Vatican. Whatever her powers of conversation (at her best, she was remarkable), she possessed no powers of argument: in discussion she showed the logic and the petulance of a child. Her tirades against the Vatican owed much to the fact that the Empress was violently ultramontane, in favour of the temporal power of the Pope; in attacking the Pope, Mathilde was attacking Eugénie.[1]

It would, however, have been a mistake to assume that she was irreligious: she had, in fact, a religion of her own. Mathilde's religion did not exclude superstition: she is said to have been superstitious about dates and numbers, and about Offenbach's evil eye; and, late in life, in the concourse of a Paris railway station, she insisted on touching a hunchback's hump, because it was said to bring luck.[2] Her superstition was said to owe something to her Corsican origin, her cynicism may have been derived from her atheist father. But her genuine piety owed something to her Protestant mother, whose religious integrity she respected. Though Mathilde ate meat on Fridays, she always provided fish for her scrupulous guests.[3] She kept a crucifix and a picture of the Virgin by her bed, and every night she said her prayers by them.[4] She laid the foundation-stone of the new church at Saint-Gratien, and she contributed generously to its building. She had her stall at Saint-Gratien, just as in Paris she had her *prie-dieu* at Saint-Philippe-du-Roule: an elegant *prie-dieu* in petit point embroidered with Bonaparte violets and bees.[5]

Perhaps Mathilde attended services as an obligation imposed on her by her imperial status; but she practised the Christian virtue of charity, and those who saw her making a collection in church saw only the most obvious sign of her benevolence. Most of her good deeds would remain unknown were they not recorded in

The salon at the rue de Courcelles.
From a painting by Charles Giraud, 1859.

The *jardin d'hiver* at the rue de Berry. The bust of Napoleon dominated
the scene, like the *genius loci*.

Mathilde, from the portrait by Ernest Hébert, 1867.

'The bearing reveals the race: it has an indefinable
air of sovereignty.' Sainte-Beuve's description of
Mathilde was realized by Carpeaux's bust (1862).

the letters and memoirs of her friends. She did not merely lend her name to charitable causes. In the early days of the Empire she undertook a massive social task, and she continued to fulfil it until the day she died.

It was in 1853 that the Abbé Moret, of Saint Philippe-du-Roule, took a little house in the passage Sainte-Marie-du-Roule as a home for deformed and incurable girls. The demand for entrance proved so great that the following year he took a larger house in the rue de Plaisance. The charity's resources grew from fourteen thousand francs in 1853 to fifty thousand in 1855, because Mathilde had taken it under her protection. In January 1855, through her influence, the government declared the work a public utility, and the Asile Mathilde, as it was called, was organized with a director-general, an administrative council and legal council; it was staffed by sisters of Saint-Vincent-de-Paul. Mathilde bought ground at Neuilly, and a new building was erected for three hundred boarders. In 1864 the Archbishop of Paris consecrated the chapel. By 1870 all loans had been repaid, a regular income was assured, and an annual lottery, organized by Mathilde herself, brought in additional funds. Frédéric Masson, the Bonaparte historian, wrote fairly: 'If her words were sometimes free, her faith remained intact . . . She preferred deeds to prayers, and the Incurables were her deed.'[6]

The Asile Mathilde allowed its patron to display some of her finest qualities: her piety and goodness of heart, her belief in work and usefulness, and her Bonaparte powers of organization. Mathilde was in many ways an extremely feminine woman, but she had a decisiveness, a natural authority, an energy and a driving sense of purpose which were almost masculine virtues. A generation later, she might have fought for the emancipation of women; as it was, she must often have felt frustrated. Her womanhood allowed her small scope to show her powers of command, and yet her imperial status, her royal relations and friends seemed to give her an opportunity to exert an influence on events.

From time to time, Sophie of Holland, who was devoted to the Bonapartes, asked Mathilde to take political action. 'The Duchesse d'Orléans, that tireless *intriguer*, is constantly getting advice from King Leopold,' she had informed her in April 1849. 'She is communicating with him all the time. Do tell the

President & then destroy my letter.'[7] In the autumn of 1852, Sophie had written more urgently:

The horizon is growing darker and darker & I'm beginning to think there will be war. Like you, I have little interest in the Turks . . .

Wouldn't you be tempted to arrange a meeting with the Grand Duchess Marie [the Duchess of Leuchtenberg, the daughter of Czar Nicholas I]? What about Cologne? If you did, I'd come as a third. Perhaps your visit would do good, for, after all, it's *She* who has the most intelligence & the most influence on her father.[8]

Mathilde would have liked her kinship and understanding with the Czar to help avert the war in the Crimea. She was not alone in thinking the hostilities quite unnecessary. After the war was over, she wanted to create an understanding between the new Czar and Napoleon III. Nineteenth-century politics were largely a matter of personal understanding between sovereigns; she felt that she might bring her two cousins together. In September 1856 she went to visit her uncle William of Wurtemberg, on the pretext of celebrating his seventy-fifth birthday. At her request, he came to Biarritz the following month and suggested to the Emperor that they should meet Alexander II at Stuttgart. Unfortunately the proposal was not pursued.

However, Mathilde did not abandon her active interest in politics; and she often discussed the state of the country with the liberals who came to see her. Viel-Castel claimed that she received anonymous letters from London, giving her details of socialist plans, and that she acknowledged them in *The Times*.[9] It is difficult to substantiate this particular claim, but many politicians came to her *salon*, and a French naval officer, Commandant de la Roncière Le Noury, visiting the rue de Courcelles in January 1857, lamented the number of foreign visitors. 'There were about eighty Italians, seventy Russians and some forty French', he told his wife. 'It was the exception to hear a few words of French spoken . . . This sort of thing makes me indignant. I'm too French to live in France . . .'[10]

The presence of eighty Italians at the rue de Courcelles was hardly surprising. Mathilde recalled her childhood in Trieste and Rome and Florence, and the happy retrospect made her warmly pro-Italian. She wholeheartedly encouraged the idea of Italian unity; she supported Victor-Emmanuel, King of Piedmont, and the policy of his minister, Count Cavour. The rue de Courcelles, as she said herself, became the headquarters of the pro-Italian politicians. 'The Italian question has always been the touchstone by which I recognized the real supporters of the Empire,' Mathilde wrote in her memoirs, 'and I have rarely been mistaken. The Empress was all imbued with Gothic ideas about divine right, and she would have liked to impose her old-fashioned nonsenses on the Empire. She reacted with all her might against the Italian policy.'[11] Where Italy was concerned, Eugénie considered Mathilde an enemy; 'and she was right,' continued Mathilde. 'I deplored her intrusion into politics, and found her tendencies invidious. I could not conceive how she let herself thwart the Emperor in everything and sow mistrust in his path.'[12] In May 1857, at the great ball at the Ministère de la Marine, Mathilde toured the rooms on the arm of the Grand Duke Constantine of Russia. This was not only to proclaim her Russian sympathies, but to vex the Empress, who had pointedly failed to invite her to the family dinner-parties which she gave for the Grand Duke at the Tuileries. Behind Mathilde and Constantine came the Comtesse de Castiglione, also on the arm of a Russian.[13]

La Castiglione had been sent cold-bloodedly, by her cousin, Count Cavour, to rouse the Emperor's sympathy for Italy. There was some uncertainty about her date of birth, but she was at most twenty-two, and many connoisseurs considered her to be the most beautiful woman of her time. She had not found it difficult to seduce Napoleon III. Mathilde now made a point of chaperoning the Emperor's mistress. When the Minister of Marine refused to invite her to this particular ball, Mathilde had demanded an invitation for her. She asked Giraud to paint her portrait; she invited her, with her complaisant husband, to dine at the rue de Courcelles. La Castiglione repaid such attentions – according to Viel-Castel – by granting her favours to Nieuwerkerke.[14]

In her passion for the Italian cause, Mathilde had earnest discussions with such liberals as La Guéronnière and Girardin. Viel-Castel, at Saint-Gratien, found himself dining with the Sardinian Ambassador, and, later, with Benedetti, the director of the political section at the Ministry of Foreign Affairs. In July 1858 the Emperor and Cavour ratified the treaty of Plombières, and arranged the marriage between Prince Napoleon – who was thirty-six – and Princess Clotilde, the sixteen-year-old daughter of Victor-Emmanuel.

Napoleon and Clotilde were married in Turin on 30 January 1859. On 3 February, Mathilde and her father went to Fontainebleau to meet them. Eight days later, Sophie of Holland warned Mathilde:

If Clotilde has an Austrian complexion, beware of one thing: she will never show open opposition, she will hardly ever express an opinion, she will be very careful in her observations, and she will remain unapproachable. I know the race. They have a wall of brass in front of them . . . For them, *isolation* is *grandeur*.[15]

Within the month, even Mathilde was deploring her brother's impossible treatment of his wife. Clotilde was still stupefied by his behaviour. 'He won't have *déjeuner* with her,' noted Viel-Castel 'and he doesn't see her during the day. He has forbidden her to come and find him, and if she has something to tell him, she has to write it . . .' Napoleon spent his days with Girardin and people said that he had already gone back to his mistress.[16] Yet though Mathilde showed scant approval for Napoleon, she does not seem to have made any effort to sympathize with his wife. Perhaps she watched her sister-in-law with political mistrust. Perhaps she felt her lack of humanity. 'As for Clotilde,' wrote Sophie, 'her own father Victor-Emmanuel told the Empress-Mother of Russia: "When I parted from my daughter, I wept, but the child herself did not weep!" What a heart for a girl of sixteen!'[17] Clotilde was devout, and she would use devotion as her one escape from her hopeless marriage; Mathilde did not appreciate her unhappiness or her nobility. Clotilde's fervent piety, her dowdiness, her lack of intellectual vitality, were foreign to her, and she could see no compensating virtues. When Clotilde left after a visit to Saint-Gratien, Mathilde said with relief: 'Now that the children have gone to bed, let's enjoy ourselves!'[18]

As for the political union which the marriage had confirmed, it gave Mathilde increasing anxiety. She had longed for the war that would unite Italy; now she had information about the strength of the Austrian forces, and she was afraid that the French troops would be utterly overwhelmed. The Papal Nuncio told her at a dinner at the Tuileries that a war would only profit the revolutionaries; he said that the Pope would be ready to come to an agreement with the King of Piedmont, and he maintained that Austria would give up Lombardy if she were offered compensation. Mathilde raised the matter at once with the Emperor, but he was too involved with Cavour to retreat. Lord Cowley, the British Ambassador, and Count Hübner, the Austrian envoy, tried in vain to keep the peace. On 23 April came the ultimatum which began the Italian campaign. 'As the Empress was made Regent,' Mathilde recorded, acidly, 'she was not violently opposed to the war. Who does not remember the Emperor's triumphant departure to join the army?'[19]

Espinasse and Canrobert, who were both friends of Mathilde, were given important commands, and she expected to see them push the Austrians back to Vienna. The victories of Magenta and Solferino made it look as if she was right. In June, General Fleury sent her effusive praise of the Emperor's conduct in the campaign.[20] Within a month, distressed by the bloodshed, and afraid of Prussian intervention, the Emperor broke off hostilities and signed the premature peace of Villafranca. Victor-Emmanuel had hoped to conquer the whole of Italy; Napoleon III would only consolidate the small advantages already gained.

Two years later, by 'spontaneous action', Tuscany and Emilia rejected their princes in order to be allied to Piedmont. The Pontifical Army, unable to check Garibaldi's troops, fell back on Rome. The Kingdom of Italy was created. Mathilde's delight was so obvious that the curé of Saint-Gratien expatiated one Sunday at High Mass on the spirit of persecution of those in power against the Vicar of Christ. Mathilde immediately left the church, followed by the whole congregation.[21]

The new decade opened in Paris with a frenzy of entertaining. 'We are in the Parisian paradise or the Parisian hell,' declared a writer in *L'Artiste* on 1 February. 'Every night since 1 January has been spent in festivities, spectacles, concerts and dances. It's a constant coming-and-going, a ceaseless merry-go-round, a perpetual volcano. They are dancing at Court, they are acting comedies at Prince Napoleon's, they are singing everywhere, except at the Opera. I'm wrong, they're singing at the Opera, too. At Princess Mathilde's they're talking. It's the last of the *salons*. But there has never been more than one *salon* in France.'[1]

Mathilde herself was drawn inescapably into the social vortex. She received Vefyk Effendi, the Ambassador of the Sultan of Turkey. She received Mr Faulkner, the new envoy from the United States. She gave audiences to the Ministers of Hanover and the Dominican Republic. And, at the Duchess of Alba's ball, she created a sensation.

Fifteen years earlier, as a young wife, she had spellbound the guests at San Donato by appearing as Diana the Huntress. Now, when she was nearly forty, and an Imperial Highness, she appeared at a society ball as a Nubian woman. Mérimée confessed that the dress had been 'much too accurate'.[2] Mme Baroche found the disguise more artistic than flattering, for Mathilde had not only painted her body brown, she had painted a blue tattoo-mark on her forehead. 'She must have been mortified,' added Mme Baroche, 'when the Emperor caught sight of her and burst into peals of laughter.'[3] Lord Malmesbury learned of the episode with the horror that might be expected from a former British Foreign Secretary: 'Her dress was of the scantiest, very *décolletée* . . . The drapery behind was transparent, which she was probably not aware of, as she had not dyed her skin in that particular place, and the effect was awful.'[4]

Twenty-four years later, Lord Malmesbury published the comment in his *Memoirs of an ex-Minister*; and there, to his acute embarrassment, it was read by Mathilde.

Mylord [goes the draft of her reply],

I have in front of me a book entitled *Memoirs of an ex-Minister* (*1807–1869*) by Lord Malmesbury; on page 307 I find a paragraph about myself.

It is neither true nor courteous. Although I was a Princess, I had enough honest friends during the Empire of Napoleon III not to let me do something unseemly, and to stop me in time, had the need arisen.

The costume which I wore at the Duchess of Alba's ball was that of a fellah. The dress was high-necked and had a train, it was in brown wool, and my face was hidden by a yatchmak [sic]; the dress was not slit anywhere, and it had sleeves. I have as witnesses HM the Empress Eugénie and Mr Ernest Hébert, Director of the École de Rome; they could, if need be, testify to the truth of what I say.

I do not have the honour of knowing you, but that cannot explain your malicious paragraph.

You did not see me as you describe me; and to credit me, gratuitously, like this, with unbecoming and unseemly conduct is unworthy of a gentleman.

I enclose a photograph of my costume.

I beg you to accept, Mylord, my most distinguished regards.

MATHILDE.[5]

Lord Malmesbury sent his apologies, and confessed that he had not re-read his diary when it was prepared for the printer.[6]

On 24 June 1860, at the age of seventy-five, Jerome de Montfort – King Jerome – died at Villegenis, his château near Meudon. His daughter-in-law, Clotilde, and his mistress, Mme de Plancy, had struggled to persuade him to receive the last sacraments. Jerome had received them, but, as Plon-Plon said: 'Mme de Plancy makes my father think of heaven, but it is the heaven of her bed.'[7] Mathilde was not greatly saddened by the loss of the spend-thrift father who had virtually sold her to Demidoff, and had passed his life in a series of liaisons.

The last brother of Napoleon lay in state at the Palais-Royal. On 3 July he was buried with an imperial sense of occasion. Next day, Mathilde heard the terms of the will which he had signed in 1852. As he had threatened, he had strongly favoured Plon-Plon,

who already had a million francs a year on the civil list. Mathilde
was enraged by the injustice – and all the more enraged as until
1850 her father and brother had lived on the pension which she
had given them.[8]

She demanded justice from the Emperor. Napoleon III was
hesitant to make a decision. Mathilde told Sophie of Holland of
her griefs. 'Your letter makes me sad,' answered Sophie. 'Don't
talk against *Him*. He has so many enemies already, so few friends!
For myself, I see a general conspiracy around him, that's why he
gives in to the people who shout loudest.'[9] At last, on 22 November, it was announced that the Emperor gave Mathilde a new
annual grant of three hundred thousand francs. Her total income
from Demidoff and imperial sources was now seven hundred
thousand. As Viel-Castel observed, it was 'enough for her to
maintain a worthy appearance'.[10]

Ever since he had become an habitué of the rue de Courcelles,
Viel-Castel had deplored the rest of the company who assembled
there. His criticisms were so constant over the years that perhaps
they contained an element of truth. Perhaps indeed Mathilde was
too often influenced by the unscrupulous, by the parasites and the
social climbers. If so, it was regrettable; for if she was deprived
for a time of her mediocre acquaintances, she rapidly became
herself again: 'in other words, charming, intelligent and good'.[11]

There were times when she considered that friends presumed
too much on her bounty. Saint-Saëns was one who overstepped
the mark. Mathilde had often helped him. She had secured him
exemption from service in the Garde nationale on the grounds
that he was organist at the Madeleine, she had invited him to the
rue de Courcelles as her pianist-in-ordinary. In 1861 his ballet,
Une nuit de Cléopâtre, and his suggestion for an opera, *Macbeth*,
were both rejected by the Opéra. He saw Mathilde as his last
resource, and she was asked to intervene in his favour. She dismissed the demand at once. 'What, isn't he content? He plays the
organ at the Madeleine and the piano for me; isn't that enough?'[12]
And when it was hinted that another composer would be happy
to become an Officier de la Légion-d'honneur, Mathilde replied
with graceful finality. She slipped a rose into his buttonhole, and
told him: 'There's the rose. You are still too young for the
rosette.'[13]

However, in May 1861, anxious to find a sinecure which would relieve him of some of his journalism, Théophile Gautier asked Mathilde to forward a petition to the Emperor. 'Your letter is being forwarded with a word from me,' she answered, 'which will ensure that it reaches its destination directly. I shall believe that I have some talent [as an artist], since you've been kind enough to address a charming poem to me. I am going to punish you for always being a poet by sending a little watercolour I painted for you.'[14]

La Fellah was the first of the poems which Gautier wrote for Mathilde. It had been suggested by *Une Fellah*, one of the four watercolours which she showed this year at the Salon.[15] When he reviewed the Salon in *Le Moniteur universel*, Gautier devoted nearly half an article to her work.[16]

It was their common interest in art which drew the artist-princess to the pre-eminent art critic of the time. When Mathilde sent Gautier the 'little watercolour', *L'Esclave noir*, and Gautier sent her his poem, *La Fellah*, they established the loving friendship which he perfectly defined as *L'amitié voluptueuse*.[17]

It is in fact doubtful whether Mathilde and Gautier could enjoy a serious conversation about art. In art, as in politics, Mathilde was led by personal prejudice: she admired the work of Eugène Giraud, because he was her friend, she refused to recognize the power of Delacroix, largely because Nieuwerkerke condemned him.[18] At Saint-Gratien, there was a salon of paintings which showed all Mathilde's anxiety to help her friends, and all the permutations of bad taste over twenty years.[19] At the rue de Courcelles, the magnificent collection of pictures was largely chosen by her advisers.[20] But if Mathilde lacked natural taste and an open mind, if she lacked real responsiveness and an inquiring intellect, she had at least a genuine and lifelong enthusiasm for painting. She practised the art with diligence, and she enjoyed the feeling that perhaps it made her someone in her own right. She felt an instinctive *camaraderie* with artists and sculptors, she liked to talk studio slang and to feel that she belonged to this Bohemian yet professional world.

Gautier was not only a link with the world of the arts. He was the Court poet of the rue de Courcelles. He was, indeed, the first poet of stature to become an habitué of the *salon*. Mathilde was not a romantic woman in the 1830 sense of the word, she was not

D*

a natural reader of poetry; she was endowed with commonsense rather than imagination. But she was feminine enough to be proud of her own accredited poet; and, if she failed to understand poetry, she perfectly understood the man who wrote it. Gautier, the journalist, longed for acceptance as a poet. At the rue de Courcelles, at Saint-Gratien, he was given his imperial licence. He was applauded by an admiring *salon*, encouraged and inspired by a handsome and still desirable woman who had all the Bonaparte magic about her. Mathilde was devoted to Gautier. She was flattered and proud to have the author of *Émaux et Camées* at her command; and no title was dearer to Gautier than the unique and well-deserved title of *le poète mathildien.*

The 1860s, the great decade of her *salon*, brought Mathilde's devoted friendship with Gautier. The year 1861 also brought the real beginning of a complex relationship which was one of the most significant in her life.

It was in 1841, soon after her arrival in Paris, that she had met Sainte-Beuve for the first time, at the house of the Duchesse d'Albuféra.[1] She had disliked his ostentatious cleverness, his determination to shine in conversation. She had also disliked his novel *Volupté*; and to her the mere appearance of the writer had explained the unhealthy impression of his work.[2] Mathilde herself was inclined to find people ugly if she did not like them, but most women would have found Sainte-Beuve repellent. 'He was ugly, small and short, his hair was red and thin, his cheeks were pink. He had a big paunch, and his hands were rather small, but not well shaped. His eyes were a rather deep blue, and, under his bushy eyebrows, they gave him a certain slyness of expression.'[3] He was not made to charm Anatole's wife, an abundantly healthy woman of twenty-one.

In the twenty years that had passed since that first meeting, Sainte-Beuve and Mathilde had changed. Sainte-Beuve had become the lion of *Le Constitutionnel* and, more recently, of *Le Moniteur universel*. His *Lundis*, his Monday *causeries* on literature, had established him as a scholar with an astonishing range of erudition, and as a master of re-creative criticism. At fifty-seven, he was a magisterial figure in French intellectual life. Mathilde had always liked older men: indeed, she confessed that she could be taken with a man of fifty. She found young men callow, she preferred mature men who could talk. Now she was no longer a girl on her first visit to Paris: she was a woman of forty-one, anxious to gather intellectuals about her, anxious – perhaps unconsciously – to find a man of eminence whom she could revere

for the distinction of his mind. For the first time, she had found
one.

It was through her brother, a loyal friend of Sainte-Beuve's,
that she met him again, once or twice, at the Palais-Royal; and,
this time, she was not disconcerted by his cleverness, or deterred
by his unfortunate physique. 'He was rather clumsy in his manner,'
she noted, 'but he liked the company of women, he always
knew how to be pleasing and polite to some, attentive to
others . . .'[4] Mathilde had touched on one of his gifts: even among
Frenchmen, Sainte-Beuve was remarkable for his understanding
of women. His appearance might suggest that his successes lay in
the library rather than the boudoir; but in fact the library had
enriched his appreciation of women, given him comprehension
as well as flair. 'He was encouraging in conversation,' Mathilde
confirmed in her memoirs, 'he didn't lecture, he left you time to
answer, and he seemed to appreciate you.'[5] She was delighted by
such appreciation.

She could not fail to be delighted by his conversation: it was
so brilliant that it blinded people to his person, and it enthralled
the most sophisticated and the most difficult.

He knew that his conversation had the power to fascinate, and he
used it like a prodigal man who knew he had an everlasting fortune . . .
But he was not one of those tyrants who enthrone themselves in an
armchair and take possession of a conversation . . . He talked, and he
wanted you to respond . . .[6]

In the summer of 1861, Mathilde urged Sainte-Beuve to leave
the heat and bustle of Paris and to refresh himself at Saint-
Gratien. He accepted her invitation.[7] He would have been less
than human if he had not taken pride in this intimate friendship
with a princess.

For the friendship soon assumed a delightful freedom of
manner. 'You put us at our ease,' Sainte-Beuve explained, 'you
let us think aloud in your presence, and that is one of the charming things about you. Don't be surprised if we take advantage of
it.'[8] When he failed to pay a Sunday visit to the rue de Courcelles,
Mathilde was desolate;[9] when he suggested that she might dine
with him in the rue du Montparnasse, she replied: 'It's good of
you to want me.'[10] When he published a *Lundi* on the mystic
writer Mme Swetchine, Mathilde exclaimed: 'What wit and

grace you show! . . . Forgive me all my weaknesses: especially the weakness of thinking myself important enough to judge other people and send you my bad writing.'[11]

In March 1862, she gave a ball at the rue de Courcelles, and the Emperor took a holiday from politics and talked literature with the author of the *Lundis*.[12] 'Two more days,' Mathilde wrote eagerly to Sainte-Beuve on 14 June, 'and I shall have the pleasure of seeing you.'[13] And again, in July: 'Which day are you coming this week? Tell me, . . . so that I can enjoy it in advance.'[14] That month, when she could not go and see him because of a feverish cold, Sainte-Beuve declared that he could not be deprived of the promised favour. 'There is now a fair copy of the portrait,' he added, 'and it awaits comparison without flinching – but not without a certain trepidation.'[15]

The portrait in question was the portrait of Mathilde which he had written for the *Galerie Bonaparte*: a collection of biographies and verbal portraits to be published by Glaeser. This portrait of Mathilde was later reprinted in the *Causeries du lundi*. It was a worthy companion-piece to the bust which Carpeaux sculpted this year: it presented Mathilde in her prime, at the height of her Bonaparte splendour.

The head, so nobly set, so proudly held, stands out from a splendid, dazzling bust, from matt white shoulders worthy of marble. The hands, the finest in the world, are simply those of the family. It is one of the remarkable features of the Bonapartes, this fineness of the hands . . . The bearing reveals the race: it has an indefinable air of sovereignty, of a woman in full possession of life.

The character is simple, straightforward. Nothing is in shadow. Violets hide themselves in the grass; eaglets like the sun . . .[16]

The portrait was shrewd and designed to flatter. Mathilde was so enchanted with it that, regardless of etiquette, she called on Sainte-Beuve to thank him. The day after her visit, she composed the companion portrait: a vignette of the critic in the rue du Montparnasse. It was written on an impulse, written with verve, perception and affection. It revealed the writer as much as her subject: it proved her a sound observer of human nature.

In a corner of Paris, there is a street less frequented than the rest; I was given an invitation to 11, rue Mont-Parnasse, and I accepted it with great pleasure. I have kept the most delightful memory of my visit yesterday. I discovered a charming little nest: fragrant, tranquil, not too brightly lit. I found a long room and a big table laden with books, paper, pens; not an inkstain anywhere. In the midst of all this dwells an eminent mind, subtle, caustic, stimulating, indulgent out of goodness of heart and from experience of life; smiling at every kind of malice, finding it everywhere; accessible to everyone, but keeping his preferences; a philosopher in the manner of the ancient Greeks, whom he greatly resembles in outward form; a believer without religion, a philosopher with reasons for indignation, a seeker out of curiosity; in fact a mind which understands all minds, explains all minds, and has the rare good fortune to have just the necessary passion to remain fair and impartial.

How, then, can I not be proud to have occupied this man's attention for several hours?[17]

Sainte-Beuve, in turn, was delighted, and urged Mathilde to take up her pen every time she felt so inspired.

They grew still closer to each other. Mathilde sent him a carpet, and he thanked her in fulsome style. She enquired if the week would pass without a visit from him, and he promised to come and bring her an advance copy of Renan's pamphlet on the Chair of Hebrew at the Collège de France. Renan had given public lectures on the part played by the Jews in the history of civilization, and the Government had suspended them as unorthodox. Mathilde was glad to be at the centre of the intellectual scene, and told Sainte-Beuve she was anxious to meet 'M. Renan, that enigmatic spirit, . . . because he must deserve the praise you give him'.[18] Sainte-Beuve replied that Renan would be glad to come to Saint-Gratien. He had already presented Gavarni, for she admired his lithographs and his caricatures. Gavarni had found her 'devilishly seductive'.[19] Now Sainte-Beuve was able to tell her: 'You've conquered M. Renan; he didn't say so in the same terms as Gavarni, but he felt the same . . .'[20]

Mathilde found Renan unprepossessing, but she was conquered by his conversation. Some years afterwards she drew his portrait.

Mr Renan. Very difficult to describe exactly. He is short and fat, slovenly in appearance, anyway careless in his dress. He has thick features. He has a proud look, though he doesn't open his eyes very wide. He usually crosses his hands on his stomach. He never gets carried away or even heated in discussion. He rarely discusses things. When he doesn't agree with you, he generally acquiesces and says: 'That's possible.' A kind of concession which doesn't warm up the conversation and shows that he has a certain disdain of contradictions. All the same he has an indefinable charm, the same as his writing. One doesn't always agree with him, but one is always seduced by his thoughts and his expression . . .[21]

The *salon* which Viel-Castel had deprecated was now assuming extraordinary brilliance. On 16 August 1862, nine days after Renan had been presented, the Goncourts dined at Saint-Gratien for the first time. Edmond was forty, phlegmatic and serious; Jules was thirty-one, volatile, and obviously the spoilt younger brother. They had already published studies in French history, and part of their work on eighteenth-century art, and for the past eleven years they had been keeping the diary in which, by some astonishing fusion of sympathies and beliefs, they spoke with a single voice. Vain, fastidious, critical, and bewildered by Mathilde's sudden invitation, they arrived at Saint-Gratien. They observed Mathilde with uncompromising eyes, and decided that she looked like a courtesan past her prime. Nieuwerkerke, 'un joli beau vieux garçon', with gentle eyes and gentler voice, was clearly the master of the house; but he charmed them by his solicitous manner. The dinner was mediocre, the conversation was spattered with studio slang, and free, they thought, like a conversation with a demi-mondaine. Mathilde fulminated against Baron Haussmann, who had taken a substantial piece of her garden in the rue de Courcelles for one of his boulevards. The Goncourts were not impressed by the evening.[22]

132472

About a fortnight later, Mathilde left for Italy. She had recently acquired a villa at Belgirate, on Lake Maggiore; and, warmly welcomed by the Italians, she had spent some weeks there the previous year. But it was clear that no foreign villa, whatever the splendour of its situation, whatever the comfort it offered, would satisfy her. She had found no charm, the previous year, on the shores of Lake Maggiore;[23] and now, in the autumn of 1862, she was again overcome by nostalgia for France. 'Here I am, settled on the shores of the most beautiful lake in the world,' she told Sainte-Beuve on 13 September.

The sunshine is brilliant, the warm air gives you a sense of well-being, your body seems to disappear and to lose awareness of its existence.

In spite of that my thoughts go out to Paris, at every moment I want news of all the people I've left behind: particularly of you.

I can't tell you how much I value the proofs of sympathy you give me. The delightful habit of seeing you every week is one of the greatest pleasures of my life. And so on Wednesdays and Saturdays (the days you chose for your visit) I always look back towards a past which I hope to begin again on my return . . .

Give me credit for my good intention to write as legibly as possible – if I haven't succeeded as well as I'd like, I know I'm dealing with an indulgent master.[24]

It is clear from this letter that Mathilde's relationship with Sainte-Beuve was now a relationship of some complexity. Mathilde was not an intellectual, and she found it impossible merely to admire Sainte-Beuve for his intellectual eminence. She was a warm, possessive woman, and her admiration had led her to be emotionally drawn to him.

Sainte-Beuve could not go beyond the limits of devoted friendship.

Princess [he replied],

. . . There's an unpleasant word I don't want but don't dare to cross out in your charming letter, the word *proof* of sympathy: it's more than that, and it deserves to be called by a quite different name . . . My life is so restricted, my future is so brief, my present is so occupied, that I dare not let my thoughts dwell and wander at will on what in other times would have been a theme for long reverie and habitual sweetness. But I am doing something simpler and more within my reach, I am enjoying it as long as I can in reality: I'm seeing you and growing accustomed to what I just allow myself to find pleasant and full of charm.

Princess, I can only offer you my gratitude and loyal affection . . .[25]

One of Mathilde's main reasons for visiting Belgirate had been her determination to show herself pro-Italian. It was no doubt as a gesture of support for Victor-Emmanuel that she impulsively went to Turin for the marriage of his daughter, Maria-Pia, to the King of Portugal.

Mathilde, who showed such public interest in Italian politics, was not happy about the situation in France. She had no delusions about the solidity of the Empire. On 16 September, a banquet was given in Brussels, that permanent centre of opposition, to mark the publication of Hugo's novel, *Les Misérables*. Victor Hugo had done much to bring Louis-Napoleon on to the political scene; but he had turned against the Prince-President when he received no offer of high office. When the Second Empire was founded, he had gone into exile; and he had refused to come home when an amnesty would have made it possible, saying that he would only return when liberty returned.

In September 1862 the Brussels banquet proved a fine occasion for voicing opposition to the Empire; a complete account of it was published as a pamphlet, and Sainte-Beuve sent Mathilde a copy.

Ask someone to read it to you [he wrote]. They have no idea of this in the rarefied, gilded atmosphere of Compiègne. Well, the young people whom they haven't troubled to rally to them will read these things and they'll be fired by them . . . You will think me very gloomy and pessimistic, Princess; but I am one of those who look at the weather every morning.[26]

Mathilde read the pamphlet and she felt sombre, too. 'I'm not so worried about enemies in general,' she answered, 'as about the complete lack of friends.'[27]

The correspondence flew between the rue de Courcelles and the rue du Montparnasse, and the visits continued to be exchanged. A few days later, explaining that she had asked some eminent man to dinner, Mathilde told Sainte-Beuve: 'I expect you to come and take your place beside me.'[28] 'I used to go and spend two hours with him every Sunday,' she recalled as an elderly woman, 'and I looked forward to my Sunday as if I had a rendezvous with a handsome young man . . . On Wednesdays he was the soul of my *dîner des bêtes*, as it used to be called at the Tuileries . . . He was a wonderful conductor, and he made everybody play their part.'[29] She was proud of his friendship; she also recognized that no one could help her better in her self-appointed task: to bring the intelligentsia closer to the sources of power.[30]

By the end of 1862, Sainte-Beuve already occupied a unique position at the rue de Courcelles. He was perhaps the only man whose intellect Mathilde respected, whose counsel she would take. His knowledge of literature and, indeed, of the human heart seemed so profound and wide that it set him apart from the rest of those she knew. Beside him, the Goncourts must have seemed narrow, Gautier superficial, and Renan lacking in human understanding. Sainte-Beuve seemed to stand above the world of social climbers and place-seekers, of politicians without ideals and statesmen without vision.

She could not cease to show her admiration. She thought of him living his simple life in his modest house, and sent him mandarines. They had been introduced into France at the beginning of the century, but they were still rarely eaten; and Sainte-Beuve sent his thanks in academic style: 'I have received the golden apples, the mandarines which I'd never eaten before . . . My ignorance is only equalled by your kindness.'[31] Within a fortnight, on the pretext of the New Year, Mathilde sent him a clock. The clock was followed by a counterpane which she had embroidered. 'Oh, it's too much, I protest, Princess!' cried Sainte-Beuve on 1 January. 'That's what you call not playing fairly, that's cheating.'[32] Soon afterwards he wrote again, thanking her for her presents to his servants.[33] 'I'm longing to see you again by my fireside,' she told him, the same month. 'That's where I enjoy you, your mind and conversation at my ease – and I don't lose or waste a bit of it.'[34]

The Emperor ushered in the New Year by presenting Mathilde with a statuette of Napoleon;[1] and 1863 began in a dazzling spin of activity. Mrs Moulton, the American singer and socialite, recorded Mathilde at the first ball of the season at the Tuileries, dancing in the *quadrille d'honneur* with the Prince of Wales.[2] Mathilde invited the Emperor and Empress to the rue de Courcelles, where a halberdier stood on guard in the ante-room, and Bressant and Madeleine Brohan gave a performance of Musset's proverb: *Il faut qu'une porte soit ouverte ou fermée.*[3] Among the 'few elect' who were invited were the Goncourts. As usual, they found some cause for vexation. 'Flaubert is there, beside us . . . We are almost the only three not to be decorated.'[4]

And so, beside the Goncourts, on 21 January 1863, Flaubert appeared for the first time at the rue de Courcelles.[5] Mathilde had read and re-read *Madame Bovary* soon after its publication in 1857; and she had delighted in its true portrayal of provincial life. She had found it harder to appreciate *Salammbô*, which had appeared in 1862; but *Salammbô* had brought Flaubert into fashion, the Empress had wanted to meet him, and so she had invited him this evening. 'Flaubert came early,' she recalled. 'I had no trouble in recognizing him, for I had heard a good deal about him.'[6] He was massive and robust, with fine blue eyes, a large drooping moustache and long hair (Mathilde thought it slightly too long). He was carefully groomed, and distinctly benign. This evening marked the beginning of a steadfast friendship.

A week later, dining with this princess who was 'fundamentally stupid and unintelligent like a woman,' the Goncourts met 'a scientist by the name of Pasteur.'[7] Pasteur was proud to know Mathilde; and, in time, he was grateful for her friendship and her moral support. Some years later, the École Normale affair was the talk of Paris. A pupil by the name of Lallier had been asked to leave, and Pasteur, the administrator, was said to have expelled him. Pasteur insisted that the decision had been made unanimously, and legally, by himself and the two directors of studies. *La Presse* declared that the statement 'did not lessen his errors'.[8] Pasteur believed that the whole affair had been contrived to discredit him, and he wrote to Mathilde to clear his name.[9]

Mathilde admired Pasteur's integrity; she assured him of her goodwill, and she invited him to the rue de Courcelles. She showed such an interest in his work that he asked her to an evening lecture at the Sorbonne.

In 1863, Mathilde already illuminated the lives of writers and intellectuals. Mérimée's social agility enabled him to be favoured both at the Tuileries and at the rue de Courcelles, and with Mérimée she had established a vivacious friendship. Since his health was indifferent, Mérimée lived in the South, at Cannes, and their conversation was largely carried on by correspondence. Mathilde was bewildered by this versatile man who was archaeologist, novelist and amateur artist; but she enjoyed his wit and erudition, and she plainly appreciated his letters. Mérimée was not averse to gossip (he often regaled her with anecdotes of the Empress); he also gratified Mathilde by addressing her as an artist, or, as some would say, an artist-highness. He showed her a nicely judged professional respect, and an appreciative deference. She promised him lessons in watercolours, and he sat for her in the studio at Saint-Gratien; the watercolour portrait flattered him and strengthened their friendship. 'I have reason to be proud of such a success,' he told her, 'but I am even prouder that Your Highness should not think me unworthy of an intimacy which ... it would be my ambition to cultivate ...'[11] Compelled to live in exile from Paris, he cultivated the intimacy none the less. 'I address myself to Your Highness as the devout address themselves to the Madonna, to ask a miracle. To tell the truth, I don't demand so much. But I am persuaded that Your Highness is so good that she will send me some news of the world and ensure me a good day with a few lines in her hand.'[12]

She was indeed good, and for her friends she would do anything. 'Everything for those you love; nothing for those who do not love you.' Sainte-Beuve admired her guiding principle.

Her friendship was sometimes severely tested. Since the autumn of 1862, Viel-Castel had been in disgrace. He had published an article in *La France* which Mathilde had taken to be a malicious impression of her *salon*.[13] Since then, according to Viel-Castel, the rue de Courcelles had ostracized him, and Nieuwerkerke, his superior at the Louvre, had been icy to him.[14] Now, on 11 March 1863, in another article in *La France*, Viel-Castel questioned Nieuwerkerke's rules for the exhibition of contemporary art. Next day, Nieuwerkerke dismissed him from the Louvre.

My dear Viel-Castel [Mathilde wrote to him],
I'm very sorry about the step which has been taken against you, but I must admit that, when I read your article on the Exhibition, I thought you'd found a pretext to leave the administration of the Museums . . .
I deplore it all, believe me, for everybody's sake, and the more so because I believed that you were entirely one of us.[15]

Viel-Castel replied that he was indeed a *mathildien*, and that he had not attacked administrative measures, he had simply made some observations about a rule that was going to be revised.

My dear Viel-Castel [answered Mathilde],
Either I cannot read, or you are strangely unaware of the significance of your words . . .
I promise you there's no bitterness in the decision taken against you: it's a necessity which you've provoked yourself. Don't make it impossible for those who take an interest in you to arrange some useful compensation . . .[16]

Late in April there was still no sign of 'useful compensation'. Viel-Castel relieved his feelings in violent criticism of Nieuwerkerke: his sinecures, his wealth, his meanness, his lack of discretion. He condemned the rue de Courcelles.[17] He attacked Mathilde herself for her lack of religion, he attacked Sainte-Beuve, 'that fat rotund journalist, who looks like a plucked ortolan.'[18]

For months Viel-Castel continued to rage. Late in August 1864, he made his final entry in his black books.[19] Three months later, he died of cancer. In 1883, when his memoirs were published, someone asked Nieuwerkerke why Viel-Castel had really been dismissed. Nierwerkerke said that the article in *La France* had been a pretext. Viel-Castel had in fact been dismissed for stealing from the Louvre.[20]

For all their bitterness, their violence, their scabrous gossip, the memoirs of Viel-Castel leave a certain sense of truth; perhaps, at times, they come nearer to reality than the encomiums of flatterers. And from the very fierceness and violence rises one distinct impression: Viel-Castel was enamoured of Mathilde. All his criticisms were made when she failed to attain the ideals he had set for her; all his violence was directed against those who exploited her, who led her astray. In 1854, on the eve of his fifty-second birthday, Mathilde had slipped the ribbon of the Légion-d'honneur through his buttonhole, and said to him: 'Now kiss me!' 'It seems I was very gauche when I kissed her,' he recorded, 'and I was as awkward as a boy.'[21]

In the spring and early summer of 1863, while Viel-Castel had been fulminating in his notebooks, Mathilde had not wasted her time in regrets. She invited Velati, the blind mandoline virtuoso, to make his début at the rue de Courcelles. Faithful to her friends, she attended the sixth performance of Augier's *Le Mariage d'Olympe*, and the revival of Gautier's *Giselle* ('Her Imperial Highness,' said *La Presse*, 'repeatedly gave the signal for the applause').[1] She made her annual collection for the Asile Mathilde at Saint-Philippe-du-Roule,[2] she attended a memorial service at the Tuileries on the forty-second anniversary of Napoleon's death.[3] She had a one-act opera performed in her salon.[4] She inspired Gavarni to fall in love with her.[5] She asked Sainte-Beuve to present Taine to her ('I am delighted to know the people whom you admire').[6] She received the Duc de Brabant, the future Leopold II of the Belgians; she received the King of Portugal and the Prince of Orange, the son of Sophie of Holland.[7] She dined at Girardin's with Morny, Boitelle, the Prefect of Police, and Paul de Saint-Victor, the critic;[8] and she invited herself to dine with Sainte-Beuve. The dinner took place on 3 June, just before she left Paris for the summer, and she asked him to Saint-Gratien the next week.[9]

She had also asked Sainte-Beuve if she might attend the Magny dinners. These fortnightly Monday dinners had begun the previous November at the restaurant Magny in the rue Contrescarpe-Dauphine, and they drew a constellation of artists and intellectuals. Sainte-Beuve was disconcerted by Mathilde's request – perhaps the presence of a woman, an Imperial Highness, would change the nature of the gatherings. Mathilde recognized that she had gone too far. 'I saw by your expression that you were doubtful,' she confessed. 'You're right, I suppose I must be content with being nice to these Gentlemen in my own house, though I cramp their style rather more than it's cramped at Magny's.'[10] Sainte-Beuve suggested, tactfully, that he would bring the guests she wanted to the rue de Courcelles. *Le dîner des bêtes* would become *le Magny impérial*.

Mathilde's devotion to Sainte-Beuve remained intense and constant. 'One doesn't always resist one's impulses,' she told him, 'and I yield very readily to the one that draws me towards you.'[11] In July, she asked him to Saint-Gratien again, but he pleaded a bad knee and asked to postpone the visit 'which is the joy and recompense of my week'.[12] Perhaps he did not like to leave his familiar surroundings. She offered him the Pavillon de Catinat, and suggested that he brought his household with him. Sainte-Beuve accepted, but – said the Goncourts – the women of his household opposed him.[13] He stayed in his sitting-room in Paris, overlooking his bleak little Trappist garden, but he kept a plaster bust of Mathilde on his table;[14] and, by correspondence, he continued their conversation.

Mathilde was far from seeking rest at Saint-Gratien. She toured the new thermal establishment at Enghien,[15] and she called on the old Academician Pierre Lebrun, on his country estate at Provins. Lebrun, who was seventy-eight, had survived more than one change of dynasty: encouraged by Napoleon I, he had been in charge of the Imprimerie Royale under Louis-Philippe: he was now a Senator under Napoleon III. 'I've tried to make M. de Sainte-Beuve regret not coming as much as possible,' Mathilde explained to Lebrun after her visit. 'But I think him lost for ever for any kind of locomotion. Nowadays it is only his mind that travels; his body stays behind on the bank.'[16]

In the same letter, she told Lebrun that she would soon be sending him her portrait of the Duc de Lesdiguières. This watercolour copy of the Rigaud portrait had just been exhibited at the Salon, and it had brought her public acclaim. Émile Cantrel had declared in *L'Artiste* that it might be signed by Rigaud himself.[17] Paul de Saint-Victor, in *La Presse*, had discussed Mathilde in the same breath as Winterhalter.[18]

It was sad that Mathilde, who painted with such diligence, who delighted in the company of artists, who wanted to give her patronage to the world of the arts, should have let her personal feelings sway her judgment. For years she had been fighting for Nieuwerkerke's advancement in the administration of the fine arts. It had been a long, determined struggle against her family. Among her correspondence is a note dated simply '22 June', in which her cousin had explained his problems:

My dear Mathilde,
I'm very sorry to tell you that after much hesitation I am obliged to refuse you the position you asked for your protégé. But I find such resistance *on every side* that I cannot follow the dictate of my heart which would be to do everything I could to please you. As an example, I'm sending you an extract from Napoleon's letter . . .

My dear Louis [Plon-Plon had written],
Yesterday evening I was assured, though I cannot believe it, that the Minister of the Interior was to propose a Mr de *Neuwerkerke* for some or other place in the Fine Arts! I cannot give you many details in writing, but I do not want *to lose a minute* in telling you that such a nomination would be a *scandal* for our family, and especially *for me, I beg you to prevent it.*[19]

In 1849, despite such uncomfortable opposition, the Prince-President – as he then was – had kept his promise to Mathilde, and appointed Nieuwerkerke Directeur-général des Musées.[20] Now, on 29 June 1863, as Emperor, almost certainly at her instigation, Louis-Napoleon created the post of Surintendant des Beaux-Arts in his honour. *L'Artiste* declared that the appointment was warmly welcomed. 'The director of museums, the sculptor of so many well-known works, the intelligent, benevolent man of the world, . . . had every claim to the high position . . .'[21]

Perhaps Arsène Houssaye or Paul de Saint-Victor had made the comment to please Mathilde. At the end of the century, in his *Souvenirs*, Maxime du Camp declared that Nieuwerkerke had always been suspect to the world of the fine arts, and that they had never accepted him as a colleague. Indeed, Du Camp doubted if Nieuwerkerke had the qualifications for his post. It was Nieuwerkerke, he recalled, who bought a modern terracotta as a sixteenth-century work by Benivieni. (He was later reported as saying that if the bust was modern, so much the better: he would pay another fifteen thousand francs for another work that was as good.)[22] The Surintendant des Beaux-Arts committed graver errors: he interfered with the constitution of the École des Beaux-Arts; and, at Mérimée's instigation, he allowed Viollet-le-Duc

to be appointed titular professor of art and aesthetics. The
Emperor's architect had his qualifications, but the appointment
strongly suggested Imperial favouritism. Nieuwerkerke was
aware of the fact. Inviting Sainte-Beuve to the inaugural lecture,
he suggested 'you would do well to come armed'.[23] Sainte-
Beuve replied that he would bring his umbrella.[24] Accompanied
by Gautier, Sainte-Beuve and Mérimée, Nieuwerkerke tried to
instal the new professor. Viollet-le-Duc had only risen to his feet
when the students began to pelt him with eggs. After half an
hour, the platform party were obliged to retreat to Nieuwerkerke's apartments at the Louvre. They were followed across
the Pont des Arts by a mob of students. One group was singing
the first line of the air in *William Tell*: 'O Ciel! tu sais si Mathilde
m'est chère!' A second group was answering with a parody:
'À sa Mathilde, ô ciel qu'il coûte cher!' Mathilde herself was
outraged, and declared that her reputation had been dragged in
the gutter.[25]

As an administrator, Nieuwerkerke was indifferent, irresponsible, even disastrous; as a sculptor he had produced very little in
the years before his appointment. But then, as a pamphleteer
observed: 'He does not aim at masterpieces, and he has never
achieved much – at least in art . . . He does not care about
posterity, the present is enough for him. He is a handsome man,
over six feet tall . . .'[26] Women had been ineluctibly dazzled by
his physical splendour; men had found his manner prepossessing.
Banville – in a moment of extraordinary hyperbole – declared
that in Nieuwerkerke 'universal knowledge, lively Parisian wit
and elegant benevolence are strangely allied with energetic power
of feature and the massive stature of the gentleman of ancient
times . . . He has been just what he should have been: a great
lord among artists, governing his states of the Louvre . . .'[27]
Arsène Houssaye added, at the end of the century: 'Nature had
given him one of the finest of human forms, and so the Louvre
of Masterpieces will not for a long while be so well represented.
There was not one of the Cent-Gardes who could have stood up
to him . . .'[28] Artists were dazzled when Nieuwerkerke received
them at the Louvre by the light of flambeaux. A Second Empire
journalist expressed the hope that the Frenchmen of the future
would learn the art of salutation and withdrawing from the
presence like Nieuwerkerke.[29] Charles Jalabert, the painter, was

flattered when Nieuwerkerke, 'particularly gracious', showed him the art treasures at the rue de Courcelles.[30] The incident was eloquent: it underlined the fact that the Surintendant des Beaux-Arts was, above all, the *amant en titre* of the Emperor's cousin.

Nieuwerkerke's aesthetic sense was sometimes singularly poor. He had failed to appreciate Delacroix, and – which was more regrettable – he had led Mathilde to share his views. When Delacroix died, in this summer of 1863, she sent no carriage to the funeral. Jules Sandeau was shocked and disappointed. 'No carriage from Princess Mathilde, who prides herself on loving and cultivating the arts. It is true that [Delacroix] was only a great man, a great artist, a great painter, the greatest painter of our time . . .'[31]

Mathilde more than once showed deplorable lack of judgment: not only in painting, but in literature. This September, the death of Alfred de Vigny left a vacancy among the Immortals. Sainte-Beuve apparently persuaded her that Camille Doucet should be a candidate. Mathilde at once campaigned for Doucet, a dramatist now virtually forgotten.[32]

Yet it is perhaps unfair to wish that Mathilde had shown a more advanced taste, a more reliable, considered judgment. She was not an intellectual, she was a warm-hearted woman impelled by her benevolence, and understandably swayed by Nieuwerkerke and by Sainte-Beuve. And, if she was not intellectual, she was at least determined to school herself for her functions as Notre Dame des Arts. In October she asked Sainte-Beuve to find her a history master; and he finally chose Jules Zeller, the history professor at the École Polytechnique. In December Zeller began his lessons at the rue de Courcelles.[33]

The Press continued to record Mathilde's unremitting interest in the cultural life of the time. On 27 February 1864, she gave a dinner for the Emperor and Empress, and afterwards, in the great salon, Coquelin and Mlle Emma Fleury first performed Banville's comedy, *La Revanche de Scapin*.[34] Two days later, with the rest of the Imperial Family, Mathilde attended the première of George Sand's *Le Marquis de Villemer*. The play was a triumph, and, after the tumultuous curtain-calls, she went to the greenroom to shake the author's hand.[35] On 7 March, as the friend of Dumas *fils*, she

watched the *première* of *L'Ami des femmes*.[36] On 27 March, at the
rue de Courcelles, Gounod himself sang excerpts from his new
opera, *Mireille*.[37] Three days later, with Plon-Plon and his wife,
Mathilde took the train to Rouen, and visited the Hôtel de Ville,
the museum, the library, and the church of Saint-Ouen.[38] On
10 April, 'in the very imperial theatre of Madame la Princesse
Mathilde,' Madeleine Brohan, Worms and Bressant gave the
first performance of a comedy by the remarkably gifted Duc de
Morny. 'The audience that evening [said *L'Artiste*] included
MM. Théophile Gautier, Émile Augier, Arsène Houssaye, Sainte-
Beuve, Émile de Girardin, Alexandre Dumas . . ., in fact everyone
from the Princess's Sundays.'[39]

One never knew who might attend her Sundays. One evening
in May, it was the Japanese mission who had been in conference
at the Ministry of Foreign Affairs.[40] As *La Presse* observed:

> The artist-highness *reunites* rather than *receives*; she reunites all those
> who are separated outside the rue de Courcelles. She reunites the
> painters and critics, the poets and the ministers, the Academicians and
> the candidates . . . The *reunions* of the rue de Courcelles . . . will
> remain celebrated in the memoirs of the time.[41]

The artist-highness had two exhibits in the current Salon. One
of them was a copy of Chardin's portrait of Mme Lenoir. 'What
a marvel of art and life!' cried Saint-Victor.[42] Charles Clément
pointed out in *Le Journal des Débats* that the painting belonged to
Sainte-Beuve, and 'it could find no better home than with the
most refined of our critics'.[43] Sainte-Beuve was delighted. 'Here
I am, prouder than ever,' he told Mathilde. In a letter which must
have elated her, he added that he was glad to have it 'as a master-
piece of talent, and as a monument and token of an affection
which gives life all its worth'.[44]

Madame Lenoir was not the only subject of their correspondence. On 1 June the Renan affair had burst on Paris. Renan's
lectures on the Jews had already been suspended as unorthodox.
Now, after the publication of *La Vie de Jésus*, his chair at the
Collège de France was itself suppressed; he was made assistant
curator and sub-director of the department of manuscripts at the
Bibliothèque Impériale. Mathilde saw this move as a conciliating
gesture by the Minister of Public Instruction. 'My opinion is,'
she told Sainte-Beuve, 'that M. Duruy wanted to spare M.

Renan, and that M. Renan won't spare anything at all; he didn't even spare Christ!'[45] Renan refused the second appointment, and claimed to keep the first. But it was the Emperor who decided the appointments; on 11 June a decree from Fontainebleau revoked Renan's nomination to the Bibliothèque Impériale, and relieved him of his functions at the Collège de France.

Sainte-Beuve deplored the whole affair, and said it had been mishandled from the beginning. In October Renan left for Syria and the Levant, to prepare for the second volume of *Les Origines du Christianisme*; before he wrote *Les Apôtres*, he needed to visit the places best known to St Paul. He bore no apparent resentment for the past; but on the eve of his departure he asked to come and pay his respects to Mathilde. Under a dictatorial and at times oppressive régime, she and her brother showed a refreshing belief in free thought.[46]

Her liberalism took many forms. For all his political vagaries, she still showed her affection for Thiers. 'I've always believed,' he had written to her, 'that one could keep both opinions and affections, and I'm very glad that Your Imperial Highness lets me keep my respectful affection for her, the affection I have felt for so many years . . .'[47] Now, in 1864, at her request, he sent her a photograph of himself – no doubt for the album in which she kept the photographs of her guests.[48]

Mathilde did not only show her liberalism in her friendships. English visitors to Compiègne had been 'struck by the freedom in conversation and manners of the Court, which is most remarkable in Princess Mathilde. Their forgetfulness of all *convenances* is quite incredible'.[49] Lord Malmesbury's observation indicated the chasm between the Court of Victoria and the Court of Napoleon III; and certainly Mathilde's behaviour would have astonished any English princess. One day, at Compiègne, she greeted General Gallifet with the words: 'I'm told that you're a bounder!' 'All I ask,' said the General, 'is to prove it to Your Highness.'[50] Mathilde was delighted by the audacity. Late one night at Saint-Gratien, she dismissed a guest: 'And now let's go to bed.' He gallantly expressed the wish that he might obey her. 'My dear, you'd be cheated,' said Mathilde, 'there's no night service here.'[51]

Her freedom of speech was not vulgar, it was simply natural, and Mathilde was the most natural of women. Her eyes were frank, her laugh was heartfelt, her speech was honest and spontaneous. Her lack of inhibition – just as much as her stately bearing – announced the distinction of her birth. She was fascinated by love: at dessert, declared the Goncourts, the conversation always turned to love. She questioned Gavarni, she questioned Sainte-Beuve, she lamented that she had no vice, she insisted that if she had her youth again, she would enjoy all the licence that she had denied herself. No one who knew Mathilde could believe her: she was much too conscious of her dignity, she was much too faithful by nature. But, like many women who are sexually conventional, she found release and pleasure in verbal licence. She was exhilarated by free speech.

Sometimes, in anger or excitement, she would speak too freely, and she would speak to a worthless confidant. She had entrusted Viel-Castel with countless observations on the Emperor and Empress and on her controversial, promiscuous brother. She showed small discretion when she talked politics, and Mme Dosne declared at the time of the Austro-Prussian War, in 1866, that Mathilde had cried: 'Perish the Austrians, and the Prussians, too!' It was, as she said, an unfortunate outburst from a princess who should have shown peaceful inclinations.[52] But Mathilde's outbursts were short-lived; and she was not treacherous or malicious. She had a strong temper, but she felt no hatred. The Goncourts found themselves refreshed by her primitive simplicity; she cast a healthy atmosphere around her. Jean-Philippe Worth, the couturier's son, said that her greatest charms were her good-nature and simplicity.[53]

Her good-nature and simplicity were indeed endearing. She revelled in eating *bouillabaisse* with Charles Giraud, of the Institut, when he gave her a Provençal dinner: she joined wholeheartedly in the 'rather garlicky gaiety around her'.[54] She charmed the Goncourts by bursting into their dining-room, unexpectedly, and taking a spoonful of jam from the pot. 'Ah,' cried one of the brothers, 'if the Duchesse d'Angoulême could have seen you!'[55] 'When something annoys the Princess,' said Gautier, 'she actually says: "What a bore"!' If Louis xiv or Mme de Maintenon heard those words, they would faint. And Gautier went further:

It would be a mistake to think that there's a great difference between the Princess's *salon* and the *salons* of the *haute bicherie*. At . . . Mme d'Estourbey's, for example, I find the same society as I do here: Prince Napoleon, Taine, Sainte-Beuve, etc. There are the same scents from Houbigant and Lubin, the same dresses from Worth and Mme Roger ... It's only that the one is anxious to appear the great lady which she's not, and the grace of the other consists in exactly the opposite: in making one forget her rank.[56]

At the rue de Courcelles, at Saint-Gratien (which was 'as gay as a merry song by Béranger'), the vivacity and freedom recalled those of art students in Montmartre. A pamphleteer felt obliged to say that Mathilde was 'a thousand times better than her reputation'. But if people could criticize her freedom of manner, they could not reproach her for any serious fault. 'Her devotion and her kindness, like her frankness, hardly know any limits.'[57] She did not only give her friendship to the conventional: she had welcomed Cham, who showed as much wit in his conversation as in his caricatures; it was said that she encouraged Nadar, the photographer and cartoonist, who was obsessed by a passion for ballooning. Mathilde, said the pamphleteer, had made a generous contribution towards the cost of his balloon, *le Géant*, though she had never climbed into the basket. She had wisely not risked her life, but the money she had given had profited – and would profit – French science.[58]

Now, on the last day of July 1864, she joined the crowd who had come to Enghien to see Godard make his ascent in his fire-balloon. It was a glittering high summer day, and that evening the lake was covered with barges festooned with coloured lights. 'It was a real Venetian festival ... on the shores of this Lake Como, twenty-five minutes from Paris.'[59] July and August brought a stream of visitors to Saint-Gratien: Sainte-Beuve and Augier and Girardin came for a literary dinner; Girardin returned to dine with Gautier. Paul de Musset, the poet's brother, arrived with his wife, and the thoughtful Mme de Musset brought Mathilde 'a charming little green frog in a glass jar'.[60] On 14 August, the eve of the Fête Napoléon, the park at Saint-Gratien was opened to the public, and there was a handsome firework display. The house-guests bathed in the lake before *déjeuner*, and used Mathilde's latest acquisition, 'a kind of bathing-machine which stays on the surface of the water and can be directed wherever you want'.[61] Mathilde's young nephew, Joseph Primoli, remembered that they nicknamed her dogs, *ces*

chères demoiselles: Chine was called Blanche du Louvre, because
she was white and belonged to Nieuwerkerke; Miss was called
la Vicomtesse de Saint-Gratien, 'because she and Saint-Gratien
are Aunt Mathilde's two favourite things'.[62]

But Mathilde remained a serious person. This August, on
behalf of the Empress, she gave the prizes at the Maison impériale
Napoléon at Saint-Denis, and she made one of her few recorded
speeches. In her address to the pupils, on the eve of their holiday,
she laid down some of the principles which should guide their
lives. They were principles which she inherited, no doubt, from
her Wurtemberg mother; they would have earned approval
from Queen Victoria. They were certainly the principles which
guided Mathilde every day.

I hope that this freedom you enjoy for the next few weeks will not
be a cause of idleness and laziness. Beware of these two enemies: they
tarnish life and fill it with boredom, weariness and danger.

However barren it may seem to begin a task, never be discouraged.
With perseverance you will come to like what today appears a needless
and uninteresting enterprise . . .[63]

As *La Presse* observed soon afterwards: 'No woman of high rank
has more right than Princess Mathilde to attack idleness and
laziness, to say they *tarnish* life, for no woman leads a busier
existence.'[64]

Even if Mathilde had been of an idle disposition, her status would
have allowed her little leisure. In August, while her brother was
away and her pious sister-in-law was in retreat, she was obliged
to play her part in the state visit of the King of Spain. She resented
the idea of leaving Saint-Gratien, even for a few days. 'I'm
irritated and almost sullen at the thought of having my peace
disturbed by the arrival of this Spanish Bourbon. These festivities
have no attraction for me,' she assured Sainte-Beuve, 'unless they
are an occasion for seeing my friends . . . I shall see a great many
people, and I'll be terribly bored.'[65] On 17 August, she added,
with resignation: 'I get into harness this evening. I'm bad-
tempered and tired in advance! The King is a cretin . . . He
prefers money to everything. He's a Bourbon, and that explains
it all . . . I regret my Wednesday.'[66] And in a moment of vexation
she wrote to Lebrun:

I feel great antipathy for the Emperor's guest, first because he's a Bourbon, and then because he is said to be stupid and ill-natured. Kings are only bearable when they are handsome and intelligent, superior to the rest of mankind; even a mediocre king is an odious being, out of place. True merit must prevail over high position, and excuse it, otherwise it creates hatred and envy.[67]

In her letter to Lebrun, Mathilde touched on an ambition which she had had at heart for some time. She was determined that Sainte-Beuve should be a Senator. She had recently sung his praises to the Emperor yet again; and the Emperor 'had spoken of him as never before. Shall I manage to get him appointed at once?' Mathilde asked Lebrun. 'I want it so much that, as I'm still capable of illusions, I hope to see him a Senator before the end of the year. I should consider that justice, and an honour for the Senate.' Lebrun broached the subject, tactfully, with Sainte-Beuve himself; but Sainte-Beuve could not fail to recognize the source of the suggestion. 'I have always avoided . . . talking to you, openly, about these things,' he told Mathilde, 'and I'll say only one thing now: that the way of life which would please me most would be the one which gave me the honour and happiness of seeing you more often.'[68]

Sainte-Beuve was not appointed a Senator, and his rejection seemed to him like a rejection of literature. He thought that the Emperor, who could have made the appointment, had slighted him. 'As far as the master is concerned, he has alienated me personally. In future I shall not accept anything from him. I was your candidate, Princess, but I should have been his.'[69] 'As for the Senate affair, which I have so much at heart,' replied Mathilde, 'it's something certain and promised for the first occasion. Only one thing worries me, and that is that, having failed this time, you could have thought that I had other irons in the fire. I am completely loyal and I tell you *no*. I only spoke for you.'[70] She saw that, for all his philosophy, Sainte-Beuve was embittered, and this worried her, because it made her think that he did not completely trust her. 'There are times,' she told Lebrun, 'when I hate mankind; I see that one can do no good, however one may try. I have less courage because I have less time before me.'[71]

It was the letter of a disappointed woman. Perhaps Mathilde was coming to have a new sense of values. She expressed no pleasure in the fact that Nieuwerkerke had just been appointed to the Senate.[72]

E

On 26 January 1865, Monseigneur Darboy, the Archbishop of
Paris, consecrated the new buildings of the Asile Mathilde at
Neuilly; three hundred incurable girls could now be given shelter
and occupation. The Asile Mathilde was a monument to the
charity of *la bonne princesse*: a lasting and magnificent proof of her
determination to do good. Mathilde herself delivered a speech at
the ceremony, 'in her golden voice';[1] she had submitted the text
to Sainte-Beuve for comment and correction.[2]

She was constantly trying to cement their relationship: not
only impulsive gifts, by generous *étrennes* (she had sent him a table
and lamp for the New Year), but by requests for advice, by a rain
of little notes in which she talked literature and discussed their
friends. Ardent and vigorous herself, she did not always understand the problems of those who suffered from ill-health. Sainte-
Beuve was far from well; and on 30 January he told her that he
must reduce his social life for the three or four years of mental
vigour which remained to him. He intended to refuse all formal
dinner-parties, and he would have to publicize his visits to the
rue de Courcelles as little as possible.[3]

Mathilde took the letter as a warning that she herself might see
less of Sainte-Beuve, and she wrote to him with acute anxiety.
'I've acquired the habit of seeing you, I delight in it, I depend on
your heart and mind. Oh, if you took it all away, I should be so
unhappy!'[4] 'Of course I have every intention of coming to-
morrow,' he replied. 'It never entered my mind to deprive myself
of my one day a week, but I certainly can't allow myself any
other.'[5] Mathilde still professed to think him hard. Perhaps she
genuinely did, perhaps she merely needed an assurance of his
affection.

Princess, don't tell me I seem so hard [he answered]. How could I be hard about something which has been one of my sweetest dreams and enchantments?

. . . I've entered the last phase of my life, I must now accept it, and I am trying to do so as hard as I can . . .

This is what I venture to explain with candour and trust – not to Your Highness, but to a friend . . . I have never been more aware how much I value what binds us to you for ever – those of us whom you have once distinguished and honoured by your kindness.[6]

But Sainte-Beuve continued to be unwell, to conserve his limited energy, and Mathilde continued to be afraid that she would lose his company. She could not bear the thought of losing her Wednesday evenings with him: they had become her weekly festivals. On 21 March she had a letter from him which she read with apprehension: indeed, with such emotion that she did not understand what he said. She dashed off a reply at once:

I'm desolate that you don't want to go on seeing me . . . You make me feel the whole burden of your indifference . . .

For the past two years, when you've come and dined here every Wednesday, I have tried hard to invite only the people you like . . . I thought I was doing what you wanted . . . Now you tell me you won't come and dine, you're denying yourself a distraction and you're denying me a great pleasure . . . I don't have the pretension to call myself your friend – but I'm really devoted to you, and I know only one way to soothe your cares, and that is to have the company of the people you love, the people whom you know love you in return. But I'm not complaining any more since your decision is final – you've been preparing me for it for three months. I'm profoundly unhappy, and I hope you haven't completely forgotten me . . .[7]

Sainte-Beuve was troubled by such an outburst. 'Your letter worries me,' he wrote. 'I see by your last words that there's still a little misunderstanding . . . One day, soon, you'll let me explain myself more clearly . . . And then there won't be any shadow of doubt about my feelings or my behaviour . . .'[8]

Mathilde, who showed such intensity in her relationship with Sainte-Beuve, continued to live her daily life with vigour. She visited the Gobelins factory, where she listened to a chemistry lecture; she went to the races, attended the annual charity sermon on behalf of the Asile Mathilde, she admired the cashmere and crêpes-de-chine at La Colonie des Indes, in the rue de Rivoli, she attended a family dinner at the Élysée. And then – for Sainte-Beuve had explained himself, and the crisis had passed – she dined at 11, rue du Montparnasse. In the intervals she painted busily. *La Petite Revue* recalled how a visitor to an art exhibition had asked to see a picture by Gérôme. 'I don't know where Prince Jerome's picture is,' answered the attendant, 'but I can show you one by Princess Mathilde.'[9]

La Petite Revue also announced that Mathilde would review the Salon in *La Vie parisienne*: the articles would be written, it said, 'with an eagle's quill, cut by *la bonne princesse*'.[10] The statement seems implausible; but *la bonne princesse* showed two water-colours in the Salon, and this year the jury awarded her one of the forty medals. Mathilde was overjoyed, and thought of mounting the medal as a brooch; but she did not want to deprive another artist of recognition and she replaced it by an equivalent. This year, by her grace and favour, there were forty-one medals.[11]

It was a bemedalled Princess who invited Mrs Moulton, the American socialite and singer, to entertain her guests in the winter garden (the famous winter garden which the Goncourts dismissed as a bric-à-brac exhibition in a virgin forest). On this particular evening in 1865 the palm trees and banana trees sheltered a remarkable company. As Mrs Moulton remembered:

Rossini was, as a great exception, present . . . When the Princess asked him to accompany me, saying that she desired so much to hear me sing, he could not well refuse to be amiable, and sat down to the piano with a good enough grace . . . I was amused at his gala dress for royalty: a much-too-big redingote, a white tie tied a good deal to one side, and only one wig [sic] . . .

Gounod played most enchantingly some selections from *Roméo et Juliette*, the opera he has just composed . . . Princess Mathilde asked me to sing again . . . Auber offered to accompany me in the *Song of the Djinns*, from his new opera . . .

This was a great occasion, seeing and hearing Rossini, Gounod and Auber at the same time . . . I wonder I had the courage to sing before them. Among the guests was an Indian Nabob dressed in all his orientals, who in himself would have been sufficient attraction for a whole evening . . . I asked him, by way of saying something, how many children he had. He answered, 'Quite a few, milady.'

'What does Your Highness call a few?' I asked.

'Well, I think about forty,' he replied.[12]

April brought Mathilde a new occasion to show her affectionate interest in the arts. Gavarni, whose work she so admired, whose devotion she enjoyed, was threatened with eviction from his house at Auteuil, because of plans to build a viaduct. He was too ill to go in person to the Emperor, even if an audience were granted: but he asked the Goncourts to enlist help from Mathilde. She said he should write to the Emperor, and demand that the City of Paris should buy his property at his own valuation. She herself would give his letter to the Emperor, with her warm support.[13] Gavarni hesitated.

My dear Gavarni [insisted Jules de Goncourt],
The Princess has just been talking to us. She needs to know *positively* and *precisely* what you want. We told her you wanted 500,000 francs . . . She is ready to demand these 500,000 francs for you, ready to join her brother in getting them – and you are completely at liberty to approach him.
So there you are. Now try to make these two influences work together . . .[14]

Alas, Gavarni was evicted and his house was destroyed; the episode darkened the last years of his life.

However, April brought Mathilde the triumph which was closest to her heart. On the 28th of the month, by imperial decree, Sainte-Beuve was granted the dignity of Senator.

The honour was so clearly her personal achievement that the Minister concerned sent her the official letter so that she could give it to Sainte-Beuve. The failure of October only intensified his delight. 'My joy is very great,' he wrote, 'and . . . you know quite well whom I want to thank in this first fine rapture.'[15] Mathilde had triumphantly written to Taine, and told him the news. 'All literature is honoured,' he answered, 'and therefore grateful to you, for you double the worth of favours by the manner in which you do them. We amateurs of style and form are greatly concerned with manner; we are aware of yours, and we can't help loving you. There, the word is out! But is there another?'[16]

Sainte-Beuve had material reason for gratitude: he earned fifteen hundred francs a year from *Le Constitutionnel*, and his elevation to the Senate would bring him a regular income of thirty thousand. As a journalist observed, 'it was not a bad situation for an old bachelor'.[17] And yet Sainte-Beuve surely spoke the truth when he told Mathilde that, coming from her, the official letter had twofold grace. 'That was another of your *works of art*, Princess, a living work of art which will only live to thank you and to love you.'[18]

The Goncourts spent the mid-August week-end at Saint-Gratien. They recorded Mathilde as a simple, passionate woman who was far from fulfilled. As they went by boat round Lake Enghien, she was bickering with Nieuwerkerke about the women he greeted *en passant*; and when they passed some woman on shore, breast-feeding her child, Mathilde burst into indignation. 'Maternity,' they noted, 'always makes the Princess angry. She was born to be a devoted mother, and she's reduced to mothering her dogs.'[19] The Goncourts touched the depths of her nature. Mathilde was passionate, like her father, but she was also domestic, like her mother. She had made a disastrous marriage, she had failed to have children, and she was aware – like all the world – of Nieuwerkerke's infidelities. Now, at the age of forty-five, she burned with regrets, she had no human being to whom she could give her whole affection.

She was forced to put her emotion into countless friendships, to devote her energy to the rôle of Notre Dame des Arts; and, when she came back from her tour of the lake, on that August day, two of her protégés had arrived at Saint-Gratien. Protais and Boulanger, the artists, had just been awarded the Légion-d'honneur, and they sat on either side of her at dinner. She herself – as she always did with her friends and candidates – pinned the coveted crosses to their lapels. One of the Goncourts mentioned that Flaubert had not been decorated. 'If I'd only known,' she said, 'I'd have asked for it directly.'[20]

As they drove back to Sannois to catch the Paris train, the Goncourts pondered their impressions; and they found themselves affectionate, touched, benign.

We were judging the Princess. We decided that people are severe and exacting for someone of her rank, and that few bourgeoises would show such good-nature and kindness. We found the Princess more attentive to her guests, treating them with more delicate distinction, than almost any woman of the world we have so far met. We thought of the freedom of manner, the thoughtfulness, the charming brusqueness, the vivid, passionate talk, the artistic language which never minces matters, the slashing at everything, the mixture of masculinity and little feminine touches, this collection of faults and virtues, marked with the stamp of our time, all new and unknown in an Imperial Highness, which make this woman the type of the nineteenth-century princess, a kind of Marguerite de Navarre in the skin of a Napoleon.[21]

From time to time the Goncourts catch the fundamental features of a character, they suddenly present a person in a phrase which seems instinctively written and agrees with the instincts of the reader. In a moment of truth, they had recognized Mathilde's frustrated maternal instincts; in another moment of truth, they noted her strange mixture of masculinity and femininity. She had indeed a commanding manner, and one can almost date it from the beginning of the Second Empire. It was as if she had cultivated a Bonaparte style of behaviour which she felt in keeping with her status. It was as if she had imitated what she imagined had been her uncle's manner, a characteristic of her dynasty. And perhaps she cultivated her imperious attitude all the more to hide her disappointments as a woman.

But while her commanding manner dated from the early 1850s, she was intensely feminine all her life; and if she fought for her friends like a general of the Grande Armée, she bound them to her by delicate, thoughtful gestures which could only come from a warm-hearted woman. One morning, Gautier was seen without a dressing-gown, taking an early stroll at Saint-Gratien. Soon afterwards, blue flannel robes, in the Turkish style so dear to him, were issued to all the guests. These gandouras became a sort of nocturnal uniform at Saint-Gratien.[22] 'You are Notre Dame de Saint-Gratien,' wrote Sainte-Beuve this autumn, 'you know how to suit your kindness to every situation and every need.'[23]

Since the end of August, Mathilde and Sainte-Beuve had been campaigning for Charles Robin, the anatomist, professor at the École de Médecine. Sainte-Beuve was anxious to see him elected to the Académie des Sciences, and on 26 August he had asked Mathilde to get the vote of Chevreul, the chemist.[24] Chevreul would not commit himself, and on 5 September Mathilde wrote to the faithful Lebrun: 'I'd be so glad if you'd speak to him in favour of M. Robin. It would give me the greatest pleasure. You won't refuse me, will you?'[25] Lebrun could not refuse. 'You know all my respectful sympathy for the Princess,' replied Chevreul. 'If it could be greater, it would be greater because of her persistence in obliging a man like M. Robin . . . If there were a vacancy in the medical section, I should vote twice rather than once for M. Robin, but the vacancy is in the zoological section . . .'[26]

Mathilde was certainly persistent. She had just sent Pasteur a note about his article on Lavoisier; but no doubt she had an additional motive in asking him to dinner. In November Sainte-Beuve approached him, and intimated again that Mathilde took an interest in the candidate. Pasteur replied that he was drawn to Robin by the thought that Claude Bernard, the physiologist, supported him. 'I don't want to take any notice of another patron who is treacherously suggested in your letter, because my philosophy is *entirely one of feeling*, and might well falter . . .'[27]

Early in 1866, by thirty votes to twenty, Robin was elected to the Académie des Sciences.[28]

There was one more cause which Mathilde supported in 1865. In artistic circles, it was the *cause célèbre* of the year, for it summarized the whole question of imperial patronage. In April, at the rue de Courcelles, a constellation of men of letters had heard Lockroy, the dramatist, read *Henriette Maréchal*, the new play by the Goncourts. 'They listened attentively, they applauded warmly,' noted *L'Illustration*. 'But as for *Henriette* – that's the title of the play – will it be performed?'[29]

The Goncourts must have wondered, themselves; for they felt they were pursued by malevolent Fate. Their first novel had appeared on the morning after the *coup d'état* of 1851; it had therefore been doomed to failure, and it was withdrawn. Soon afterwards they had been prosecuted – but acquitted – for quoting licentious verses in an article. Now, in an age of harsh and sometimes ludicrous censorship, when Flaubert and Baudelaire had been accused of *outrages aux mœurs* in their masterpieces, they were offering an audacious study of modern life for the stage. But Mathilde was fond of the Goncourts, and she meant to help them. At her insistence, *Henriette Maréchal* was accepted by the Comédie-Française.

Mathilde remained apprehensive about its reception; and 'I

am like you,' wrote Flaubert, 'I am in agony about *Mlle Henriette*.'[30] It was a mediocre play, but its dramatic merit had become of incidental importance. By December, when it was to be performed, its imperial patronage was no secret, and the *première* promised to be another *bataille d'Hernani*. However, while the Hugolian battle had been a clash between Classical and Romantic, a violent but literary affair, the Goncourts' battle was to have little relevance to literature. 'Either MM. de Goncourts' play is immoral or it is not,' wrote Henri Rochefort, the political journalist. 'If it's immoral, then august patronage is fostering dissolute and corrupting works.'[31] On 5 December, the day of the first performance, Pipe-en-Bois, the notorious leader of claques, summoned a number of students to hiss the play. It had become a symbol of a resented régime.

Just after midnight, Got, the actor, recorded in his diary: 'I have never seen a play so outrageously sent up . . . Did the illustrious Pipe-en-Bois really resent that it had been accepted or acted under so-called pressure from Princess Mathilde? Very well. But the authors and actors had at least the right to be heard'.[32] A few days later, Pipe-en-Bois himself published a pamphlet on the episode: 'Well, I think it's sad to see what our fathers called favouritism . . . perpetuated today in the cause of dramatic art. One cannot have anything striking performed on the Paris stage unless one is the friend of Monsieur or Madame Maecenas'.[33]

Mathilde herself had gone home from the Français with her hands still burning from her militant, affectionate applause. She was exasperated, and well aware that she had been the object of the abuse. 'How brave you were!' cried Flaubert. 'All literature should be grateful to you!'[34] The voice of literature was drowned by the strident cries of politics. *Henriette Maréchal* had brought down on Mathilde all the accumulated resentment and hatred of the régime. She received anonymous letters, assuring her that her *hôtel* would be gutted, and that 'all her lovers' would be hanged. 'All her lovers?' enquired the Goncourts. 'We have now been going to her *salon* for three years; we are not unobservant, and the devil take us if we have seen any one of us called upon to deceive Nieuwerkerke!'[35] *Henriette Maréchal* was withdrawn after six performances; but by 21 December the *Gazette de France* had published four articles on the subject, *L'Avenir national* five or six, and *La France* a leading article directed against the play

E*

and the liberalism of the rue de Courcelles.[36] The Goncourts were
more than ever convinced that Fate was against them.

Their first impression of Mathilde, three years earlier, had been
brutal.[37] They had decided that her *salon* bore no comparison
with the great *salons* of the past. Mathilde was a modern woman,
and her *salon* was modern, too, and, 'nowadays, one has no right
to be demanding'.[38] The criticism was doubtless inspired by the
Goncourts' love of the eighteenth century, but it was curiously
stupid to blame Napoleon's niece for not being a creature of the
Régence.

But the Goncourts were already flattered by her interest in
them, and they were intrigued by the contradictions in her
character. They were touched to find that she liked men of talent,
even when she failed to understand them; they noticed, approv-
ingly, that she was bored with boredom. Gradually, they had
begun to record her with delicacy and affection. They noticed
how it always needed a day or two, after absence, to enter her
intimacy again, 'to find the caress of her words again, the *dear*
instead of *Monsieur*'.[39] They were touched when she thought of
wearing a dress which they had admired. 'The Princess was kind,
caressing, enveloping us with affectionate gentleness, as she can
do when she chooses . . .'[40] 'The Princess affectionate, *spirituelle*
as she is on her good days . . . She has returned to her Paris
amiability.'[41] Whatever their intellectual reservations, the
Goncourts were drawn, inescapably, by her femininity and her
touching kindness. As Edmond wrote: 'The Caesarean socialism
of the Empire, the Government's hostility towards us . . . always
prevented my brother and me from being Imperialists; but the
open, tender and delicate friendship of the woman who happened, by chance, to be a princess, made us *Mathildistes* –
Mathildistes both affectionate and devoted.'[42]

On 23 January 1866, Mathilde attended the opening of the Corps Législatif at the Louvre. She was probably in no mood for the splendour – for Nieuwerkerke, grand in scarlet, and a broad blue ribbon, for the leviathan Cent-Gardes on duty round the dais.[1] A few days earlier, Sainte-Beuve had had an operation; indeed, that morning the doctors were meeting at the rue du Montparnasse. 'Your note has arrived in the middle of the doctors' consultation,' he scribbled to her at ten o'clock, 'so I'm waiting before I send the messenger back. Ricord will vouch for the invalid, in spite of the pain . . . Oh, the Wednesdays!' Five days later he mentioned a possible date for her visit; it would, he said, give him the patience he still needed. Not until late in February did he finally invite himself to dinner.[2]

On 4 March, at his suggestion, George Sand called at the rue de Courcelles. Mathilde had long ago earned her gratitude. In 1861, when she had competed for the Grand Prix of the Académie-Française, Mathilde had persuaded the Emperor to offer her an equivalent award in case the Académie rejected her. George Sand did not receive the Grand Prix, and she proudly refused the consolation prize, but she had been touched by the gesture.[3] Mathilde now found her 'pleasant, simple, even affectionate . . . She is dining with me on Friday', she told Sainte-Beuve on 6 March. 'Wouldn't you like to come too? I do hope you will, because you know it's going to be a very small party so that she can feel completely free.'[4] The small party, which was organized with such goodwill and tact, was far from a success. Gautier constantly exchanged ridiculous jokes with Flaubert, and Mme Sand sat in bewildered silence. But she returned to the rue de Courcelles. She was warmed by Mathilde's warmth of heart; she was touched by her enquiries after her health. 'I thank Your Imperial Highness a thousand times for thinking of me. I'm much better and I'm leaving for Nohant. I am yours with all, *all* my heart.'[5] 'I shall come and dine with you on Wednesday,' she added in May 1868. ' . . . Very happy to see you again and to express all my devoted affection for Your Highness.'[6]

Mathilde turned instinctively to women of intelligence and achievement. Noble birth was not enough to impress the niece of Napoleon. Society women were accorded little but a polite relationship. Foolish and pretentious women were sometimes briskly treated. Mme Camille Doucet, wrote Mathilde, 'is an utter fool. Avid to make her presence felt, aiming at an aristocratic manner. It was she, one day, who pursed her lips and refined her voice and asked me if princesses had the same emotions as other women. To which I replied I knew nothing about it, since I was not a princess by divine right.'[7]

Fleury and Sonolet, discussing Mathilde's *salon* in the sixties, recalled that the women were discreetly dressed, and rarely belonged to the purely social world. They were more or less associated with art or literature.[8] This was true of the *salon* in any decade. Mathilde had entertained the first Mme de Girardin (Delphine Gay, the charming, accomplished woman of letters).[9] She invited Rachel's sister, the actress Dinah Félix, to stay at Saint-Gratien.[10] She was sympathetic to Mme Octave Feuillet ('how often,' remembered Mme Feuillet, 'she let me tell her my troubles, and how often she soothed them!').[11] She was very fond of Mme Strauss: the daughter of the composer Halévy, the wife of Bizet and, later, of Strauss, the barrister.[12] But women of such character were rare; and in 1862 Mathilde complained to the Goncourts of the remarkable decline of women since the eighteenth century,

and her regret at being unable to find a woman interested in artistic things, in literary news, a woman with interests which, if not masculine, were at least educated or original . . . She was ready to receive all the intelligent women of the day: 'Mlle Rachel, good God, of course I should have received her! But the women one sees, there isn't one you can talk to. Look, if a woman came in, now, I'd have to change the conversation at once.'[13]

Mathilde herself continued to earn the title of Notre Dame des Arts. On 17 March 1866, she attended the *première* of Augier's *La Contagion*; next day a Feuillet comedy was performed in her salon. Gautier lent his diamond sparkle to her dinner-parties, Flaubert dined again with *ma Princesse*, who watched benignly as he indulged in paradox and wild hyperbole, and declared his horror of the bourgeois. ('I could never make him clearly define what he meant by that word, I'm sure it just meant everything that displeased him.')[14] May brought Mathilde's annual fête for the Emperor; the garden glowed with electric light, like some midsummer night's dream, and here and there the foliage stood out with theatrical brightness against the sky. In the background, through the windows, the chandeliers lit up the purple hangings; and, here and there, a patch of black was slashed in two by scarlet: by the ribbon of a Grand Cross of the Légion-d'honneur.[15]

The Légion-d'honneur. Mathilde was still determined that Flaubert should receive it; and she had asked Victor Duruy, the Minister of Public Instruction, to recommend him to the Emperor. The Minister replied: 'I am glad to be able to comply with the wishes of Your Imperial Highness.'[16] Mathilde dashed off a note to Sainte-Beuve: 'Flaubert and Taine have been decorated. I'm delighted.'[17]

The author of *Madame Bovary* was as gratified as his own Monsieur Homais by this official recognition. 'I don't doubt M. Duruy's goodwill,' he wrote to Mathilde, 'but I imagine that someone else helped, just a little, to put the idea into his head? And so the red ribbon is more than a favour, it's almost a memento. I had no need of that to think often about Princess Mathilde.'[18] In a gesture of pride and affection, she promised to give him the cross; and, as Flaubert said, the gift meant more to him than the honour. 'For the honour is shared by many, but the gift is not! And I don't know what to say and how to thank you.'[19]

The letter was addressed to Mathilde at Belgirate, near Milan. On 22 August she had left Saint-Gratien for a holiday at her Italian villa. She had wanted Flaubert to spend September with her – 'but the novel,' he wrote to his niece, 'the novel which I'm longing to take up again – oh, my God, what would have become of it?'[20] He chose to work on *L'Éducation sentimentale*, but the Seine outside his windows made him dream of Lake Maggiore. 'I journey there in my imagination, Princess, and I lay myself at your feet.'[21]

Mathilde had also asked Sainte-Beuve to come to Belgirate, but he could not face the long journey. Indeed, he wrote to her,

every poetic instinct, every prospect and gleam of the future must now have vanished for me, since this journey with you did not even tempt me. One must resign oneself and, above all, know oneself. My powers are what I feel them to be, not what they seem . . .
I expect that . . . there will be some fine evenings on the terraces at Belgirate, and that they will not be inferior to what one imagines the *Hexamerons* and *Decamerons* to have been. Send me a foretaste of them in a note, Princess, and deign to believe that I am present in spirit.[22]

He hardly needed to ask for a note; she wrote to him almost daily. On 13 September, disturbed by signs of hostility to the Second Empire, she burst into criticism of the Swiss:

For the moment they show their hatred of France by selling a multitude of pamphlets, which differ from each other only in title; they insult the Emperor and his family, even his friends, in the most scurrilous way. On board the steamer which brought us from Geneva to Lausanne, several hawkers came up to us to show us the libellous little brochures. I was revolted, and I couldn't burst out as I wanted, more than once I had tears in my eyes . . .[23]

It was a disturbing experience; but even Sainte-Beuve, pre-occupied by ill-health, must have smiled as he read on:

Do tell me if you know M. Barbier, the author of the *Ïambes*. Yesterday, when I came back from my outing, I found him sitting on a bench, waiting for me, to ask me to give him his fare back to Paris. I was a little surprised by this casual introduction, but I did as he asked. The man seemed to have no prejudices to me.[22]

Mathilde, who castigated Taine for the phrase 'the unfortunate Hudson Lowe,' had clearly not read the *Ïambes*, particularly *L'Idole* in which Barbier had denounced Napoleon. Indeed, Sainte-Beuve could not believe that Barbier would have dared to ask favours from her. He assumed that the visitor had been some brash impostor.

Mathilde had, it seems, intended to stay at Belgirate until the end of September; but the thought of Saint-Gratien was too strong. By 20 September, to her 'infinite pleasure', she was back among her floral chintzes.

I spent twenty-four days in Italy, in the sun [she told Lebrun], and

I'm glad to be home again, a wandering life is not at all to my taste . . .

Italy is calm, undisturbed, a little surprised by its freedom. France and its Emperor are very popular there, except among the journalists, who are always the sad members of society . . .

If Italy only had a man of action, what could not be done with that noble country? Cavour has a handsome statue in a big square in Milan, and that's all . . .

I have seen M. de Sainte-Beuve again, and I found him gay and well.[25]

I thought that M. de Sainte-Beuve would go to Lake Como with you [replied Lebrun]; he has no taste for travelling, but the travelling would have been incidental, and he would have acquired a taste for it in your company. He has buried himself in Port-Royal, he tells me. He's certainly right to make the work as complete as possible . . .

Now that Italy possesses all that war can give her, the hardest thing remains to be done. It needs more than a large country and twenty-five million inhabitants to make a great nation. It needs more than the statue of Cavour; as you say, it needs *a man* . . .[26]

Mathilde had not lost her childhood love of Italy; and she was soon rewarded for a political sympathy which was even stronger. The Czarina sent her the Grand Cordon of the Order of St Catherine, with the star in diamonds.[27] Mathilde received it, one suspects, with a touch of melancholy. She had not forgotten that Nicholas I would have liked her to marry his son; had circumstances been different, she herself might now have been sharing the throne of All the Russias. 'So this woman who was talking to us has missed two imperial crowns!' the Goncourts wrote in October. 'And on certain days of sadness, it must come back to her, and the shadow of the crowns which have brushed against her must pass across her brow.'[28]

In her heart of hearts she was unhappy; her constant occupation, her hatred of idleness, sometimes hid her emptiness, her profound disappointment. On 1 October the Goncourts recorded her outburst against 'empty' women, whose only occupation was their children. 'All this occupation with creatures who give you no return!' 'Look, Princess,' said Eugène Giraud, with the boldness of an old friend: 'You like dogs because you haven't got children. You miss it.' Mathilde burst out: 'Stop talking about children! You always have to come down to their level, go stupid and talk baby-talk. Children stunt your intel-

ligence.' And then, illogically, she tried to relate her emotions
to her own childhood. 'I've got more philosophical ideas about
education . . . Perhaps that's because of the way I was brought up.
My mother didn't love me, you see. She used to annoy dear old
Madame de Reding by saying: "I'd give all my children for
Fifi's finger!" Fifi was my father . . .'[29] Catherine de Montfort
had not been a loving mother; but her coldness did not explain
the fact that Mathilde had strong maternal instincts, that she had
funds of affection she could not give.

She relieved her feelings in cynicism and anger; and, as always,
she turned to benevolence. She invited Flaubert's friend Louis
Bouilhet to Saint-Gratien, and on 29 October she took a large
party to the Odéon for the first performance of his play, *La
Conjuration d'Amboise*.[30] A few days later, on her Wednesday,
Flaubert himself was moved by the grateful thought of the rue
de Courcelles. 'Your usual guests must be with you. I join them
in spirit, and I am not among those who rejoice the least in your
return.'[31]

So the year drew to an end in Paris. The correspondent of *La
Presse*, stationed in the Bois de Boulogne, watched the sprightly
Auber spanking past in his victoria, and Mirès the banker and
Arsène Houssaye, the ubiquitous socialite, bowling by in their
'little coupés and fancy carriages'. The swans and ducks disported
themselves on the turbid yellow lake, and the leaves fell from the
chestnut trees.[32] *La Presse* further reported that Mathilde and her
sister-in-law, 'accompanied by a senator and several other people
of distinction', had explored one of the wonders of modern Paris:
the main sewer. They had gone down the steps which led to it
from the place de la Madeleine, and followed it as far as the steps
which came out by Notre-Dame-de-Lorette. Their Imperial
Highnesses had then taken a carriage to the place du Châtelet,
where they went down to the sewer a second time 'and followed
it by boat as far as Asnières'.[33]

Three days later, Mathilde set out on a more salubrious
expedition, and left to join the fourth *série* at Compiègne.[34]

The Emperor was preoccupied by the Prussian problem. Only a few months earlier, at the Battle of Sadowa, the Prussians had defeated the Austrians overwhelmingly, and the balance of power in Europe had been changed. France was now acutely aware of a highly-trained militaristic nation across the Rhine, and of a Prussian statesman called Otto von Bismarck, who was bent on the unification and triumph of Germany. It was clear that France would not tolerate this growing Prussian supremacy. Sooner or later there would be a conflict.

However, there was no French general to match von Moltke, there was no French statesman to match Bismarck; and, at the time of the Austro-Prussian War, the French army had been in no condition to undertake a campaign against Prussia. Napoleon III had doubtless decided that, for want of military triumphs, the Parisians' goodwill depended very largely on his ability to entertain them. This was one of the reasons why he had chosen to hold an International Exhibition in Paris in 1867.

He opened the Exhibition on 1 April.

Mathilde was fascinated by the Exhibition. She went to it with Flaubert,[1] and she went again with Silvestre de Sacy, who was weary but exhilarated.[2] 'I greatly envied M. de Sacy,' Lebrun informed Mathilde. 'He said the Exhibition was very fine, but he still admired you more than anything. I should probably have been of the same opinion.'[3]

The Exhibition was enticing; and since most of the sovereigns of Europe, their heirs and ministers, chose to come to Paris, social life was dazzling and intense. On 17 May 'two thousand hearts beat happily' at a ball at the British Embassy.[4] On 29 May, Mrs Moulton sent home a dazed account of the ball at the Austrian Embassy, where a ballroom had been built in the garden, and hung with pink and lilac satin. As the Emperor and Empress made their entrance, 'the famous Johann Strauss, brought from Vienna, . . . struck up the *Blue Danube*, heard for the first time in Paris.'[5]

Mrs Moulton had an evident weakness for figures from the *Almanach de Gotha*, but she charted social life with useful precision. Yet, as the summer wore on, even she had a surfeit of society. 'There are so many kings and princes here,' she added, wearily. The King of Prussia had now arrived with the colossal Bismarck, who 'clanked his sword on the pavement, quite indifferent to the stare of wondering Frenchmen'. Prince Umberto of Italy looked small beside such a giant. The Khedive of Egypt, the Shah of Persia, the ex-Queen of Spain, and other sovereigns were all, said Mrs Moulton, 'flitting about'. They were followed, early in June, by the Czar of Russia.

On 4 June, at the gala performance at the Opéra, *La Vie parisienne* observed 'the kind, intelligent face of Princess Mathilde, a diadem of diamonds on her brown hair'.[6] A few days later came a military review at Longchamp; and then, in the second week in June, came the imperial ball.

It would be difficult to describe the prodigious appearance of the Tuileries garden last night [said *La Presse* on 12 June]. Long garlands of light in white glass globes, thirty thousand gas lamps illuminating the private garden . . .

Dancing began at eleven o'clock, under the masterly bâton of Strauss, and it continued until three o'clock in the morning.

The following afternoon, at the floating harbour at the Exhibition, Mathilde boarded the Khedive's dahabiah; twelve Nubians, in state uniforms, rowed her down the river to Saint-Cloud, where they gave her a concert of native music.[7]

It was a gay, original summer. Count Bismarck went to see Hortense Schneider in *La Grande Duchesse de Gérolstein*, and he 'laughed heartily at the scene where General Boum plans his campaign'.[8] Mathilde and the Empress, for once indulging similar tastes, chose 'a ravishing variety of plain and figured dresses' at *La Malle des Indes*, an Exhibition boutique for Indian silks; and among Mathilde's dresses there was one, said *La Vie parisienne*, 'at which there must be an outburst of admiration. It has a white ground, with a figured pattern of rosebuds and ears of corn, broken at regular intervals by a poppy-coloured line. It is an adorable marriage of poppy red and white, a miracle of coquetry and grace . . .'[9] It was perhaps in this notable dress that Mathilde attended the farewell dinner for the King of Prussia.

The *élan* of the Exhibition bore society forward, brilliant and carefree, until 1 July. That morning, while the Exhibition awards were being distributed at the Palais de l'Industrie, the news was circulating that Maximilian, Emperor of Mexico, had been shot at Queretaro.[10]

Maximilian was the brother of the Emperor Franz-Joseph of Austria. In 1864, under pressure from Napoleon III and Eugénie, he had accepted the imperial crown of Mexico. In the early days of his reign, he had been supported by a French army; but the troops had recently been withdrawn, and the least perceptive observer must have foreseen that the Mexican Empire was doomed to collapse. Now Maximilian had been shot, and his wife had been driven insane by disaster. They had been the victims of French political ambitions: of an uncompromising Empress and of an ailing Emperor with *folie de grandeur*, who lacked the moral courage and, now, the health, to command events.

Mathilde looked at her cousin's reign with increasing apprehension and despondency. No doubt she saw the significance of Maximilian's death; certainly she was aware of the growing threat across the Rhine. She had never been pro-Austrian. She could not approve of the invaders of Italy – she could not forget the disloyalty of Napoleon's Marie-Louise, the imprisonment and death of l'Aiglon at Schönbrunn. But since the Prussian victory at Sadowa she had sometimes felt it would be wise for Austria and Italy to form a strong alliance which might intimidate Bismarck. 'Bismarck knows no faith or law,' Sophie of Holland told her. 'He deserves to be chastised.'[11]

Soon after the opening of the Exhibition, Sophie wrote more urgently: 'I ask myself in terror where we are going. We are threatened and enfolded by the hate and greed of that mighty Prussia. She has no principles and she has no faith . . .'[12]

Mathilde had no doubt been glad, in July, to escape her *sovereign fatigues* (the phrase was Flaubert's), and to return to Saint-Gratien. Guiding the Goncourts round the rooms she kept for her friends, she told them she had only had one pleasure, the pleasure of living among those she loved. If she had wanted, so she said, she could have done remarkable things, built magnificent châteaux, 'but she much preferred her chintz with her friends sitting on it'.[1] The Goncourts almost certainly recorded the words verbatim: they were words which came from her heart. Mathilde did not want Compiègne; she much preferred the comfortable country house where she led her regular, placid life. Her household reflected her kindly nature. She was good to her servants, and they loved her devotedly. Most of them remained in her service for twenty or thirty years, and they were still in her service when they died. Julie, her *femme-de-chambre*, was the wife of Eugène Devaux, her *maître-d'hôtel*, and she was with Mathilde for forty years. Despite the imperial atmosphere that hung, inescapably, about Saint-Gratien, it remained above all a home.

One of those who recalled Saint-Gratien most clearly, in this particular summer and autumn, was a *collégien* of sixteen, Joseph Primoli. He was the eldest son of Pietro Primoli and Charlotte Bonaparte (the granddaughter of Joseph, King of Spain). He was therefore only distantly related to Mathilde; but, from his adolescence, he adored this kind, gay, warmly affectionate aunt, and Mathilde was drawn to Gégé, as she called him: to this vivacious, sympathetic, and remarkably mature young boy.

To Gégé, who was on holiday from the fashionable Collège Rollin, Saint-Gratien appeared like a dream.[2] On 1 September 1867, he recorded life there with precision. 'At 7 o'clock, the château stirs, the green shutters open, the valets sweep and dust; the gardeners water the shrubs, and change the flowers in the vases. At 11 o'clock they ring the first bell for *déjeuner*, at 11.15 they ring the second . . .'³ And so the familiar, comforting, unchanging routine began.

The previous evening Taine had come to take leave of Mathilde before he joined his sister in the country. Gégé had noted his mannerisms, recalled his conversation, and assessed his character with a sharpness which the Goncourts would have respected.

Mr Taine is not much more than 38 [he was 39], but he wants to seem older: he is quite tall and rather thin but he doesn't hold himself well; his head is a real German head, pale and fair, his expression is gentle and intelligent, his face is interesting and aristocratic, his blue eyes are full of kindness as well as fire, but unfortunately, in spite of the blue spectacles he wears, they are squinting. He possesses the charm of speech to such a degree that one hardly notices this slight infirmity. He was very witty – perhaps too witty; I think he listens to his own conversation. When you hear him it's like deciphering a manuscript: first he says something clever, in an unstudied form; then comes the correction, he repeats the same idea, but more clearly; gradually the idea emerges into broad daylight . . .

His greatest pleasure, so he says, is to go and shut himself up in an old monastery, and there continually re-read his two favourite poems: *Iphigénie en Tauride*, by Goethe, and a romance in verse by Miss B. Browning [sic], *Aurora Leigh*.

As for French poets, the only one he knows and appreciates is Musset . . . He goes so far as to find only one line in Racine, one of the most insignificant: 'La fille de Minos et de Pasiphaé.'⁴

The time did not pass entirely in such destructive monologues. Gautier arrived to spend a fortnight at Saint-Gratien. The poet who enchanted Mathilde enchanted her nephew, too.

He's certainly the pleasantest man I've ever met [wrote Gégé]. He has all the qualities of the great genius without his arrogance . . . I've heard him talk clothes with women, and turn philosophers into poets. He is a master of the art of conversation, and – while he sometimes delights in toying with the fan of paradox, which he does with incredible dexterity – he expresses sound new ideas in poetic and original forms . . .

But wit is the least of his qualities; he has feeling and excessive delicacy . . . How does this almost wild exterior hide a susceptibility which even the heroine of a novel doesn't possess? He has a fine head, and I think he still keeps some claim to masculine beauty . . . His hair is still hanging down his neck, but a few threads of silver mingle with the jet locks; his eyes are still black, but the fire has gone out in them as it does in the eyes of a vanquished lion . . .⁵

One morning Gautier and his admirer took an early stroll in the park. Slowly, solemnly, leaning on his gold-handled cane, *le poète mathildien* paced the paths of Saint-Gratien. He was maturing a sonnet. He recited the first four lines; by the time they returned to the point of departure, the second quatrain was finished. Then the *déjeuner* bell interrupted their walk, and they saw Mathilde coming to meet them. As they walked towards her, Gautier improvised the final tercets; and, kissing her hand, he greeted her with one of the dozen sonnets which would be his published tribute to his princess.⁶

It was at Sainte-Beuve's suggestion that Mathilde herself drew Gautier's portrait.

He was a man of middle height with a broad, long torso and short legs; he had the head of a southerner, a monocle to correct his short sight; he wore his hair long, curling on his neck, a relic of the Romantic of 1830. His expression was kind, though a little sleepy, his glance calm, without vivacity, like his gestures and his whole manner. In private he often sat on the floor, cross-legged, a cigar between his lips: you might have taken him for an oriental.⁷

So it was, years later, that Gégé remembered him at Saint-Gratien: saw him, again, at the feet of Mathilde, 'gathering up the lines of poetry which seemed to be born under her magic glance, and making them into sonnets'.⁸

'If I don't come this Wednesday,' Gautier once told her, 'don't think I'm dead as the newspapers suggest, I've been very unwell for two or three days, that's all. I hope to write you many more sonnets yet.'⁹ It was perhaps in answer that Mathilde wrote: 'Come back quickly. My Wednesdays are dull and colourless without you.'¹⁰

Some of Mathilde's relationships were less happy this year. It was probably in 1867 that she ended her friendship with Émile de Girardin.

The pre-eminent publicist of the century was ruthless, vigorous, self-made. For years he had paid court to the Imperial Highness whose château at Saint-Gratien was so near his villa on Lake

Enghien, whose receptions at the rue de Courcelles were a social necessity for the ambitious. He had asked her to be godmother to his daughter, Clotilde. His letters had reflected more than affection: they suggested what Gautier called *l'amitié voluptueuse*.

'I am not "men",' he had told Mathilde in 1862, 'I am a man, and there is only *one* woman for whom I should happily give my life . . . Where everything is significant, nothing is forgotten. I had not forgotten. My respectful adoration.'[11] Even Mathilde, who was accustomed to gallantry, must have believed in Girardin's devotion; and among her papers she chose to keep a page in his microscopic hand, described as a page from an unpublished novel. It is difficult not to read it as an indirect declaration of love:

She knew that he loved her. He had told her so, just once, once only! A second time would have added nothing to the first, and would have detracted from it. Never, never had he repeated it to her. She was all the more sure of his worship for her, for he did not love her, he adored her. Between him and Her he kept the distance which lies between Earth and Heaven. It was a kind of oath to live and die for Her that he had religiously put into her hands – the most royally beautiful hands which the divine moulder had ever moulded. Although he kept in the shadows, kept aside, She knew, without seeking it, that his timid glance always sought her, and, without thinking of it, she knew that his constant thought never left her. The certainty of being loved had changed into such transparent trust that he read Her thoughts, and . . .[12]

It was hard, in fact, for Mathilde to trust Girardin. In 1866 she told him that she hated politics, for she never knew whom she could rely on. He had answered, gallantly, that she must not say such things, for he would be obliged to quit politics as a proof of his 'respectful passion'.[13] But Girardin had no intention of quitting politics; and his politics were strangely at variance with his professed adoration for this ardently Bonaparte princess. In March 1867 Mathilde had asked Sainte-Beuve why Girardin was attacking the Emperor and his government with such fury. 'How ignoble men are!' she added. 'And what courage one needs not to scorn them and have a horror of them . . . If he goes on like this, I shall turn my back on him.'[14] Five days later she told Sainte-Beuve: 'Believe me, the government has no reason to reproach itself, as far as Mr de Girardin is concerned – except for having given him the chance to attack it by establishing *the freedom* [of the Press]. Mr de Girardin has no more moral sense in politics than he has in his private life.'[15]

She kept no letters from Girardin after 1866. As his views became increasingly anti-imperial, she must in fact have turned her back on him.

More than once, in the eventful year of the Exhibition, Mathilde found men ignoble. The Goncourts, strolling with her at Saint-Gratien on 5 August, heard a bitter outburst against the ingratitude of Eugène Fromentin.[16]

Fromentin was artist, novelist, travel-writer and critic. He had been a frequent visitor to the rue de Courcelles, where he delighted in meeting famous colleagues, and in recommending deserving friends to Mathilde. Now, at the International Exhibition, Hébert had been proposed for a first-class medal in painting, and she had warmly supported his candidature. Hébert had not received the medal, and someone had persuaded her that Fromentin and his friends on the jury had been responsible for the rejection: that they had opposed Millet to Hébert. Posterity might not find it hard to choose between the two artists; but Mathilde looked on Hébert with particular affection. She could only see his failure as an act of injustice, both to him and to herself.

All her life she suffered from this inability to distinguish between the personal and the professional; all her life she refused to accept that her friends should not succeed, and that her patronage should be disregarded. She was apt to consider the failures of her friends as insults to herself; and she constantly made a mistake which was far more serious: she assumed that those who came to her *salon* would accept her views. If they could not bring themselves to do so from aesthetic or intellectual conviction, then they should do so as a moral obligation, as a gesture of unity and loyalty. There came a point when Mathilde considered her friends' behaviour as a matter of integrity; and they, in their own integrity, maintained their different but well-considered opinions.

Fromentin was an admirer and a friend of Hébert's, and he had in fact voted for him. Throughout the unfortunate affair they remained on good terms. But Mathilde was angry and stubborn and refused to let Fromentin explain. The affair grew increasingly complex and bitter, and she brusquely forbade the 'culprit' to enter her salon. Some years later, he returned to favour (and he returned at a time when some of her friends were anxious to leave her). But in 1867 he was punished for his behaviour by the postponement of his promotion in the Légion-d'honneur.[17] He did not become an Officier until 1869.[18]

The year did not pass without honour for Hébert. At Saint-Gratien, Mathilde was sitting to him for a portrait which caught the Wurtemberg stateliness of her middle age. One evening, in the salon, Nieuwerkerke offered him the post of Director of the École française de Rome.

Hébert went to the Villa Médicis. He asked Mathilde to keep him 'just a little footstool' at her feet.[19] And, from time to time, he reminded her of his 'deep and more than devoted attachment',[20] of 'all the tender feelings which go through my heart like burning arrows when I think of you'.[21] Mathilde had given him a photograph of his portrait of her; and 'I have the little photograph on my table, constantly in front of me,' he told her, 'and I often look into those eyes which are as changeable as the sea. You can understand how upset I'd be if I brought the dark cloud of anger into them.'[22]

Mathilde insisted that he should not express his true feelings for her; but, unchangeably feminine, she felt acute resentment when he later married Mlle Gaby d'Uckermann, who was forty years younger than himself. She is said to have asked the new Mme Hébert: 'How could you marry that old fogy?' Gaby Hébert answered simply: 'Genius has no age.' She soon came to love Mathilde, none the less.[23]

Fromentin was forced to wait for his rosette; but Mathilde was determined that the Goncourts should receive the scarlet ribbon to which every man with ambition aspired. The brothers were not averse to it: years ago, at the rue de Courcelles, they had gloomily observed that they and Flaubert were the only guests without the decoration. Flaubert had now received it. In 1865 the Goncourts had learned, with gratitude, that Mathilde had asked the Emperor to honour them.[24] Either the news had been incorrect, or the Emperor had changed his mind, for now, in 1867, *la bonne princesse* still needed to ask for the cross. She remained apprehensive. Like Sainte-Beuve, she wondered if the honour would come in time, and if it would come twofold.

Early in September Mathilde was obliged to tell the Goncourts that Edmond was decorated. 'And like all the pleasures of life,' the brothers wrote in their *Journal*, 'this one comes incomplete, and he who is honoured suffers from it . . .'[25] Flaubert tactfully sent Edmond a double length of ribbon; half of it was to be kept for the day when Jules could wear it.

It was no doubt through the influence of Mathilde that Théophile Gautier *fils* found himself a sous-préfet by the end of the year and then chief of the Press department at the Ministry of the Interior;[26] and late in October Judith Gautier, married to the disastrous Catulle Mendès, called on Sainte-Beuve to talk of Mathilde's benevolence, and to ask how it could be used to help her husband. Sainte-Beuve reported the conversation to Notre Dame des Arts.[27] Mathilde secured a pension for Mendès, and arranged for Judith to write for *Le Moniteur universel*.[28]

Mathilde's New Year present to Sainte-Beuve was a majestic armchair: it was, he assured her, not so much an invalid's chair as a working chair, for he still hoped to write. He found his work increasingly difficult, and, as January wore on, he often thought of the more informal moments at the rue de Courcelles: of Zeller's history lessons, and the mornings spent in talking in the studio. In February he told Mathilde that he thought of her, above all, in the tedium and privation imposed on him. In March, when he heard that she planned to call, he waited eagerly for the tête-à-tête: he had so many questions to ask, so much to hear, he was so anxious 'to pick up every thread of the past . . .'[1] She sent him a photograph of herself, and he kept it on the mantelpiece in a room which, so he said, had come to resemble a temple to a goddess. He needed consolation: in the summer La Presse observed that 'it was only by an incredible effort of will that he recently took part in the discussions of the august assembly [the Senate]'. In July the paper reported that he had recently suffered a grave relapse, and he was still obliged to stay at home.[2]

It was a genuine sadness which Flaubert noticed in one of Mathilde's letters; and he was disturbed, for she was usually robust in spirit.[3]

There was more than one reason for her depression. One evening in May, while Nieuwerkerke was away in Spain,[4] the Goncourts heard Dumas fils maintain that all sentiment depended on digestion; he enlarged on the theme with verve, and they supported him with enthusiasm. And then, they said, 'the Princess uttered cries of horror. It was as if someone were tearing away what she cares about most of all – her illusions, the kind of ideal that she likes to form not only of people but of things.'[5]

It was another of the moments when the brothers touched the underlying truth. Mathilde was desperately anxious to keep illusions. She had always sought for the absolute, and she would always seek it. If she could not find it, she had at least to believe that she had done so. Practical, decisive and commanding, she still needed a certain illusion to protect her against reality. In July, at Saint-Gratien, the Goncourts analysed her behaviour, and, probably, they touched the truth again.

For some months we have noticed the Princess's sanguine out-bursts, her fits of anger with anyone and everyone, about no matter what, her brutal violence and almost imbecile coarseness in con-tradiction. It seems to spring from some secret anxiety which she is trying to repress. Does she feel the Empire is collapsing? Does she suspect that Nieuwerkerke is roving?[6]

The Goncourts' observations were endorsed by Mérimée, who was sitting to her for his portrait. 'It seems to me that she's beginning to take a sad view of life,' he noted in September. 'I think she has some reason to complain of one of her friends, who is no more faithful than he need be.'[7]

Soon afterwards Gégé Primoli recorded in his diary:

I've spent a month at Saint-Gratien, the month of September . . . My aunt was sadder this year: she feels she's growing old, and she finds herself alone . . .
. . . For twenty years [sic] she has been, so to speak, morality itself in her immorality . . . She has sacrificed everything to the man she loves: her honour, her friends, and her beliefs, and now that he has had every advancement which she could procure him, he is turning from her.[8]

It seemed as if Mathilde's unhappiness, her loneliness and growing disillusionment, drew Gégé closer to her. He felt a filial affection for her; but, at seventeen, absorbed in his own imaginings, romantic and bewildered, he was also more than a little in love with her. This October, in the diary which was his companion and confidant, he wrote:

I spent Sunday at Saint-Gratien with my aunt Mathilde . . .
Oh, I do love her, because when I think about her the tears come into my eyes and a strange tremor runs through my body . . . My ideal is composed of Her and my mother . . . When I read, it is always the two of them who assume the likeness of the heroine . . . that is my dearest dream, the one in which I cradle myself before I go to sleep.

If she had only had a passable husband, I am sure that M. would have been the most virtuous of all women . . . No, it had to be as it is, the other was impossible, for then perfection would have dwelt on earth, God would have been jealous, He would have called Her back to Him.

This is how I imagine the enchantresses of Antiquity and the Saints of Christianity to have been . . .

And yet how happy her loving soul, her loyal heart would easily have been if she could have leant nobly on a husband's arm and given her other hand to a child! Oh, a child! . . . A child of hers! How she would have kissed it, adored it, spoilt it! . . . She wouldn't have had the time to love anyone else! . . . When she sinks into these unhappy dreams, the tears must surely come into her eyes . . . She has come to have a horror of marriage and husbands, she says she wouldn't want to have children . . .

Really, if she was younger, and I was older, I should think myself in love with her . . .

What's the use of falling in love? I'm so happy as I am: I love my mother so![9]

As the Goncourts had suggested, Mathilde was increasingly apprehensive about the future of the Second Empire. She was also aware that, at forty-eight, she had long lost all charm for Nieuwerkerke. Twenty-three years earlier, she had seen him as the absolute she had been seeking. She had wanted a complete and durable relationship. Nieuwerkerke had never sought for such a liaison, he was incapable of fidelity. Mathilde was wholehearted; he preferred to satisfy his pride with an endless series of conquests. At Compiègne, 'pleasantly conscious and flattered', he had called Mrs Moulton's attention to some of his former mistresses round the dinner-table.[10]

All Paris talked of the love-affairs of le Surintendant des Beaux-Arts. For many years Mathilde had been hurt and humiliated by the public scandal; she was hurt, above all, because she had tried to set an example of fidelity, because – like her mother – she was single-minded. Now she was still an idealist, and she was still faithful. She could not bear to lose Nieuwerkerke, even when she knew that she was in love with an illusion.

She felt affection, every degree of love, with intensity. Eugène Giraud and his son, on their return from the Basses-Pyrénées, excused themselves from a visit to Saint-Gratien because they were tired from their long journey. When Mathilde suspected that they had spent the evening at a theatre, she was so hurt, so angry, that the Goncourts wrote: 'One feels what rich and warm and jealous passion she puts into loving those she loves.'[11] She invited Flaubert to spend a week at Saint-Gratien, and showed him such touching attention that if he had followed his own instincts, 'I should,' he wrote, 'have stayed with you indefinitely'.[12] Mérimée, flattered by his portrait, declared that she had shown him 'perfect kindness'.[13] Gautier, caressed by *l'amitié voluptueuse*, blossomed into enormous eloquence.[14]

The inspiration was momentary. Gautier's health was worsening. In March he had had a heart attack, which left its effect upon him; it had been followed by another early in April. Ill-health had increased his despondency; and, lying in a boat on the Lake of Enghien, he asked the Goncourts why it was that a gifted man, a man with many friends, a man without enemies, should not be a Senator or an Academician or even be granted a museum sinecure. If he were ill for a fortnight, he said, his household would just survive; if he were ill for six weeks, he would have to enter a poorhouse.[15]

Mathilde, too, was anxious about his future. The previous year she had tried to have him made librarian at the Élysée, but the Emperor had chosen to do away with the post, 'which was only a pretext for giving Ponsard a pension'.[16] Mathilde was now all the more disturbed about her poet's future as the coming change of administration at *Le Moniteur universel* made his livelihood problematical. 'It's so difficult to open ones purse for those one would like to help, if they are in Gautier's position,' she explained to Sainte-Beuve in October, 'I want your advice on how to set about it. I'd thought of giving him the title of my librarian so that I could attach six thousand francs to the post. But wouldn't that be ridiculous? Tell me honestly. And would he accept it?'[17] Sainte-Beuve answered promptly: 'I don't see why Théo shouldn't be your *reader* and *librarian* with privileges and emoluments.'[18] Mathilde wrote to the Emperor, asking for his sanction; he replied, from Biarritz, with untroubled suavity: 'I am charmed that you should make M. Théophile Gautier your librarian. I'd have been happy to give him such a place if I had had a vacancy myself.'[19]

It only remained for Mathilde to ask Gautier to Saint-Gratien and tell him of her project. She scribbled off her invitation. But Gautier was suffering from gout;[20] and in Mathilde's mind a new difficulty arose: perhaps he would be too proud to accept the sinecure. 'What do you think?' she asked Sainte-Beuve. 'Should I wait or should I write to him? If you see him, couldn't you touch upon it? . . . I should have thought it needed less diplomacy to give people pleasure.'[21]

It took one more diplomatic move, which was made by Sainte-Beuve. Within the next few days, Gautier came to see him, and 'Uncle' Beuve took the initiative. Gautier, he told Mathilde,

> had no inkling of the affair . . . I told him everything; there wasn't a moment's hesitation, but an outburst of natural gratitude both for the benefit and for the delicacy with which you bestowed it.
>
> All the imperial government's debt to Théo has now been paid, thanks be to you, Princess; it remains for the Académie to acquit the debt of literature to one of the most charming of our writers.[22]

On 27 October, Paul Dalloz, the editor of *Le Moniteur universel*, wrote to thank Mathilde for her gesture. 'I cannot tell you the delight with which this nomination was greeted; it will be the same throughout the world of letters.'[23] It was, perhaps, true, as *La Presse* observed, that Gautier had become 'a librarian without a library.'[24] But Mathilde was not disturbed by the paradox.

She was delighted when, a few days later, Sainte-Beuve announced that the Académie might soon have a chance to pay its debt. Empis, the dramatist, was dying, and his death would leave a vacancy among the Immortals. 'We're thinking of our dear Théo,' wrote Sainte-Beuve on 9 November. 'You will have to use your diplomacy; I shall do all I can.'[25] She answered: 'If he was elected to the Institut, . . . I should be doubly happy.'[26]

Late in December, Pongerville, a notably tedious Immortal, was invited to dine at the rue du Montparnasse; and there Sainte-Beuve and Mathilde used all the powers of flattery they possessed, to ensure his Academic vote.[27]

On 1 January 1869 *Le Moniteur universel* became independent, and ceased to be the official newspaper of the Empire; *Le Journal officiel* was established as the recognized organ of the régime.

Sainte-Beuve had agreed to write for *Le Moniteur universel* on the expiry of his contract with *Le Constitutionnel*. This change in the position of *Le Moniteur* would have released him from his contract, but he considered himself to be morally bound to Dalloz; besides, he did not want to enrol himself under the official banner of Eugène Rouher. He had therefore sent Dalloz an article. However, Dalloz asked him to suppress a criticism of Monseigneur Dupanloup, the Bishop of Orleans: it had, he said, shocked a clerical associate. On 31 December 1868 Sainte-Beuve replied: 'I withdraw the article, and I am resigning, at the same time.'¹ Offended by this *lèse-majesté*, by this chicken-hearted gesture from a so-called independent editor, he decided to write for *Le Temps*.

His decision to leave *Le Moniteur* can have been no surprise to Mathilde. He himself had told her, the previous summer, that no one had troubled to ask his advice about the prospective changes, and he would therefore have no ties with the new administration. 'I shan't desert anyone,' he had explained, 'but I shall go where I please . . .'² But if Mathilde understood why he left *Le Moniteur universel*, she could not accept his decision to contribute to *Le Temps*, a paper she thought hostile to the Empire. Sainte-Beuve was not only her counsellor and friend; he was also her Senator.

Mathilde never found it easy to understand compromise, or to comprehend the delicate, complex motives of behaviour. As Sainte-Beuve himself had pointed out, shades of meaning did not exist for her. Simple by nature, she saw black and white, she drew no line between personal and professional loyalties. If Sainte-Beuve was her friend, if she had earned his devotion, she considered that she had rights over his work. She did not see his change to *Le Temps* as a move to keep his freedom of expression, maintain his intellectual integrity. She did not pause to think what sort of articles he would write. Intensely emotional, she considered his action as a personal betrayal.

On Sunday, 3 January, while the whole Press was proclaiming that Sainte-Beuve would write for *Le Temps*, Mathilde paid her usual Sunday visit to 11, rue du Montparnasse. Sainte-Beuve was suffering from the prostate trouble which had kept him in pain since the previous year; but he was still illuminated by conversation. In the little house, next to a girls' boarding-school, in the white-and-gold sitting-room overlooking the *petit jardin de curé*, they talked together for an hour, and they did not mention his decision.[3]

Next day, 4 January 1869, Sainte-Beuve's first article appeared in *Le Temps*. That day, against all custom, Mathilde returned to the rue du Montparnasse.

The rumble of the carriage at the door was so familiar [recalled Troubat, the critic's secretary], that Princess Mathilde was announced in Sainte-Beuve's study before she had actually appeared.

M. Edmond Scherer [of *Le Temps*] was visiting Sainte-Beuve. When her name was mentioned, he took his leave.

I went down to the salon with him.

'Do you think she's come to take him away from us?' asked Scherer.

'Don't worry,' I replied, 'he'll hold firm.'

A few moments later, Sainte-Beuve sent for me to go upstairs.

'Keep Her Highness company,' he said.

His face was twisted, he was in such pain . . .

Princess Mathilde stood arguing, and gestulating with her muff. She looked like the portraits of Napoleon 1 in anger.

'It's my brother and I,' the Princess went on, 'who had M. Sainte-Beuve made a Senator . . .'

'I don't see how he's proved unworthy,' I said. 'The Empire has a Left and a Right . . . He's said so himself in the Senate . . . He can't go with M. Rouher . . .'

'M. Sainte-Beuve was a vassal of the Empire.'

I was no more bold than usual, I was not less civil than I should be with someone of her rank, for whom Sainte-Beuve's household had every regard; but, at the word *vassal*, I cried:

'There are no vassals any more, there are only citizens . . .'

The argument grew general. We were both raising our voices higher and higher.

'Well, Troubat,' said Sainte-Beuve, abruptly opening the door, 'it seems to me you're talking rather loudly . . .'

I was glad to go.

She went soon afterwards, slamming the doors behind her. I repeated the word *vassal* to Sainte-Beuve. He went white, and said to me:

'They will see if I'm a vassal.'[4]

The Goncourts saw Sainte-Beuve next day; he seemed tired, preoccupied and sad. On Wednesday they reported it at the rue de Courcelles. Mathilde said nothing, but led them into the salon where she held her private conversations. And there she burst out that she would never see Sainte-Beuve again, she had quarrelled with the Empress over him, she had showered him with presents, she had spoken to the Emperor on his behalf the last time she went to Compiègne. And what had she asked of him? She had not asked him to renounce a conviction, she had just asked him not to sign a contract with *Le Temps*, and, on behalf of Rouher, she had offered him everything. He could have been on *La Liberté* with Girardin, that was still possible, it was his world. 'But with our personal enemies, with *Le Temps*, where they insult us every day!' Mathilde was breathless, choking with anger, clutching her embroidered corsage, beating her breasts with it, at moments she could not speak for emotion. And, shaking one of the brothers by the lapels, as if she wanted to drive in her indignation, she said: 'Look, Goncourt, it's ignoble, isn't it?' She took a few steps, twitching the train of her white silk dress behind her on the carpet, and came back to him. 'I'm not talking about the princess,' she cried, 'it's the woman, the woman! . . . I've had dinner with him . . . I've sat on the chair that Mme Rattazzi had sat on . . . And I told him when I went: "But your house is a brothel, a filthy place, and I've come here for you . . ." Oh, I was hard! And I said to him: "What are you? An impotent old man! You can't even attend to your personal needs . . . What ambitions could you still have, then? . . . Listen, I wish you'd died last year, you would at least have left me the memory of a friend!"'[5]

'What are you? An impotent old man!' At that moment, when she lost control, Mathilde touched a cardinal point in her relationship with Sainte-Beuve.

Though she was to have only two serious liaisons in her life, Mathilde profoundly needed her *amitiés voluptueuses*. She needed to know – particularly as she was middle-aged – that men were aware of her femininity. She constantly needed to be admired; and, as she had not enjoyed a normal domestic life, as she was hurt by Nieuwerkerke's endless infidelities, she had to be reassured all the more that she was desirable.

It is impossible to think that she could have felt physically attracted to Sainte-Beuve. He was short and pallid, his bald head was ringed by a fringe of sandy hair, his health was indifferent for most of the time she knew him, and his sexual prowess was so small that he had to take his pathetic pleasures with women of the lowest degree. Was he even capable of love? She had once ventured to ask him, and his answer had shown little self-esteem. When you were ugly and middle-aged, Sainte-Beuve had replied, there was no chance of love; you had to content yourself with charity and tolerance. It was the secret grief of his life that he had not been a handsome hussar. Mathilde had smiled at his naïveté, but no doubt she had recognized the truth of the confession.[6] Sainte-Beuve had once loved Adèle Hugo, the wife of the poet. He was now incapable of love, he could not give it and he did not expect it. He was an incomplete man, and his incompleteness disturbed and disappointed Mathilde. 'You see,' she would explain to Gégé Primoli, years later, 'between an incomplete man like him and a woman like me, there will always be something missing, there will always be things that cannot be explained.'[7]

For though she could hardly want to know Sainte-Beuve as a lover, she probably wanted him to desire her, or at least to show an emotional interest in her. She admired him with an admiration which she felt for no one else in her circle. Gautier, Flaubert, Edmond de Goncourt, Renan, Taine: she talked literature with them all, but Sainte-Beuve alone was her mentor. From Sainte-Beuve alone she accepted guidance, took praise and criticism like a pupil ('I know I'm dealing with an indulgent master').[8] It was Sainte-Beuve who had chosen Zeller as her history professor, Sainte-Beuve who had told her what to read and criticized her speeches. Once or twice, as a gesture, he had asked her advice, but the real relationship was clear.

He had not only been her literary guide, he had been – as he said – her solicitor-general: he had been her vigilant adviser in philanthropy. He had helped her in her self-appointed task: helped her to bring the intelligentsia closer to the sources of power. He had encouraged her to do good, told her where to show charity, and expressed his appreciation of her work. She was benevolent by nature, she had always wanted to do good, but she had also wanted to please him.

From her admiration for his mind, her pleasure in his advice, she had come to be dependent on him; and, since he lived in Paris, she had grown accustomed to frequent visits and frequent correspondence. She usually answered his notes within twenty-four hours, sometimes she had written twice in a day. Working with him, she had come to feel close to him; she had grown possessive and vulnerable. When he deferred his visits through ill-health, she had been quick to assume that he was tired of her *salon*. When he attempted to explain, his graceful, gallant letters had merely added to the confusion. Her own impulsive, eager notes only strengthen the conviction that the relationship was deeper and more complex, more frustrating and, perhaps, more essential to her than any other relationship in her *salon*. That was why, when she broke with Sainte-Beuve, she did so with all the violence of her nature. As Flaubert guessed, she had been touched to the heart.

A fortnight after the Monday meeting, on 17 January, Sainte-Beuve himself, in bewilderment, had tried to restore the relationship.

Princess,

A fortnight has passed.

I have sought, and searched myself in vain, I cannot find that I have done any personal wrong to Your Highness.

You have accustomed me, Princess, to a quite different friendship – a friendship so different that I can only consider the Monday meeting as an extraordinary accident, something that came not from you, but from another.

As for me, I have left the marker at the Sunday visit. For me the book was shut at half-past five that evening. Will there ever come a day when it opens again?

I know what I owe to so much kindness, so many memories, so many offers of friendship – a friendship the signs of which surround me and will always be about me. I have found it hard to recover from the astonishment which overcame me on Monday – but that will pass. Everything that went before remains and will remain. In this at least I shall keep the faith which I so often lack: even when I can no longer hope, I shall still be waiting, and an inner voice will murmur in the very depths of my being: *No, it is impossible!*

I lay at your feet, Princess, my respectful, unchangeable affection.[9]

Mathilde replied next day:

I, too, told myself it was impossible: the man who refused me so stubbornly was not the man I had known and loved and so often consulted, the man whose ready and conciliating spirit had so greatly helped me. The vivacity you seemed to reproach me for was only an effect of the shock I felt, as a friend, at your refusal . . . I've had to be silent and resign the place I thought I should occupy for ever. When I came to see you I didn't come to demand some or other concession, I came to ask you not to tie yourself by contract to our enemies. I assured you that we had nothing to do with M. Dalloz' refusal to publish your article in his paper, I expressed the hope that one day we should see you come back to *Le Journal officiel*, indicating and *choosing* yourself which position would suit you best. You refused everything, you didn't want to hear anything, and it is no use saying that it isn't going over to the enemy to publish one or more articles in a hostile paper, the public doesn't judge things like that. Today the very people who have won you over are celebrating their victory and our defeat. However that may be, I am deeply afflicted by it all. I send you my good wishes for your health and for your satisfaction in all things, and I hope for a better future.[10]

The letter was blunt and unforgiving, but it showed the intensity of her feeling; it was the letter of a woman who was angry, and, above all, hurt. As time passed, Mathilde came to understand that her indignation had been excessive, that her hurts had not been serious. She regretted her haste and violence, she was concerned by reports of Sainte-Beuve's failing health. She missed his conversation and, perhaps, at some crisis in her life, she needed his advice.

In April, three months after her visit to the rue du Montparnasse, she sent an emissary to him to suggest reconciliation. Sainte-Beuve replied that he had embarked on *Le Temps*, and that he had gone too far away to disembark again at Saint-Gratien.[11]

ᴓ26ᴒ

On 26 April, Mérimée arrived in Paris from Cannes; he had come partly to vote for Gautier at the Académie-Française. He was greeted by a note from Mathilde; and 'as soon as I feel strong enough,' he answered, 'I'll come and lay my respectful homage at Your Highness's feet'.[1] Gautier, who called on him the day after his arrival, made a more cheerful comment on his health; Mérimée had been cured of galloping bronchitis by taking glasses of brandy every hour, alternating with cups of hot soup. 'Thanks to this treatment, the pulse which was 135 has come down again to 75, and the invalid is well; there's one vote assured for me.'[2]

Another certain vote was that of Sainte-Beuve, who, ill as he was, had determined to make the journey from the rue du Montparnasse.

He has made his plans to go to the Académie in three stages [Gautier explained to Carlotta Grisi]. First he will have his hair cut at a hairdresser's some way from his house, then he will have a bath a bit further on; finally he will lunch at Magny's, and go with his secretary, Troubat, to the Institut, where he will arrive about two o'clock. I myself shall be at Pingard's – he's the usher at the Académie, and he'll let me know the votes as and when the nominations come in. Oh, what a bother it all is, how much simpler it would be just to live with those one loves! But when you're caught up in the apparatus, you have to come out the other end, not too flattened if you can help it.[3]

So Mathilde's poet reluctantly stood for election as one of the Forty. He had wearily paid the calls which etiquette demanded: visited each Academician to canvass his vote. He found formality tedious, and he was well aware that the retrograde Immortals still considered him the Romantic which he had been thirty-nine years earlier. They had not forgotten the now legendary pink doublet he had flaunted at the *première* of *Hernani*; they had not forgotten him as the author of the equivocal *Mademoiselle de Maupin*. He had since written a trio of outstanding travel books, the ballet *Giselle*, the poems of *Émaux et Camées*. He was the master among art critics, the awe-inspiring contributor to *Le Journal officiel*. He was fifty-eight, an *officier de la Légion-d'honneur*. But his Romantic past remained against him.

So, too, did his irrepressible nature. On the evening before the election, the Goncourts found him at the rue de Courcelles, talking to an Academician, the scrupulously correct Silvestre de Sacy, and describing his love for a panther-woman he had seen at a fair.

Next day, eager to see him triumph, Mathilde drove to the Institut; and there she learned of his defeat. In choosing Auguste Barbier, the author of *Ïambes*, the Academicians had deliberately insulted the Empire. In rejecting Gautier, the protégé of Mathilde, they had made their dislike of the Empire doubly clear.

Writing to Carlotta Grisi a few days afterwards, Gautier recorded Mathilde's reaction. 'She was so furious when she heard, that she wept with rage and called the Academicians "pigs"! Which may not be very imperial, but is certainly very feminine . . . Believe me,' added Gautier, to his lifelong Egeria, 'my Academic failure really leaves me quite indifferent.'[4]

Mathilde had been ambitious, determined and impassioned; she must have felt exasperated by Gautier's impassibility. And yet, within an hour or two of his Academic defeat, she found herself applauding his minor triumph at the rue de Courcelles.

That evening, 29 April, she was to give her annual reception for the Emperor's birthday. Two hundred guests had been invited. Mme Agar and Mlle Bernhardt were to perform François Coppée's recent success from the Odéon: his one-act poetic drama, *Le Passant*. Then – a bold stroke – there was to be a recitation of Hugo's ode: *Le Retour des cendres de Napoléon*. Mathilde was anxious to end with a new and more personal work, and she had asked her poet for some verse.

Gautier had at first refused 'to play a guitar after a Beethoven symphony'. Mathilde did not share his worship of Hugo, and she was naturally vexed by his refusal. A diplomatic guest recalled that Napoleon III – who had then been a prisoner at Ham – had written a noble passage of prose on the return of Napoleon's body. Perhaps it might be turned into verse. The passage was found; and, as Gautier explained:

It was interesting to see the same subject treated by the poet and the Emperor, one from the point of view of glory, the other from that of a member of the family. The *soirée* was to be on Thursday, and it was then Tuesday evening . . . However, I told the Princess not to worry. On Wednesday morning I went off to the Bois de Boulogne . . . I came home with half the piece, got dressed, took a carriage and set off for the Jardin des Plantes, where I finished my work, gazing vacantly at the lions and bears, the elephants and buffaloes. Next day, when *Le Passant* had been performed and Victor Hugo's ode had been recited, Agar began my stanzas . . . It was a triumph. The Emperor came and thanked me; he said he was proud and happy to see his prose translated into such fine verse, he did not know he was so great a poet . . . So people could see, by this success, which counterbalanced my defeat, that I was not an ass, as *MM. les académiciens* might have suggested. The good princess was a little consoled.[5]

The Goncourts were not consoled. They were no lovers of the Empire, and they regretted that Gautier should have let himself be so publicly compromised; they maintained that the Emperor and Empress hardly thanked him for his poetry.[6]

Coppée did not see his play. Threatened with pneumonia, he had been forced to winter in the South. But he sent Mathilde a copy of *Le Passant* with a dedicatory sonnet. Soon afterwards, still a timid young clerk from the Ministry of War, wearing his first tail coat, he was presented to her. He remained her friend for some forty years, and he was beside her when she died.[7]

Early in June, at the Gare de Lyon, Mathilde greeted one of her oldest, most intimate friends, Sophie of the Netherlands. Soon afterwards, the Emperor gave a state dinner for the Queen at the Tuileries, and a cast from the Odéon again performed *Le Passant*.[8]

Sophie had earned this attention from Napoleon III; her correspondence with Mathilde had for years reflected her affectionate admiration for him, and she had tried, when she could, to smooth his political path. She had shown a patriotism that was much more French than Dutch.

If Sophie had earned the Emperor's gratitude for her love of France, she had long ago earned Mathilde's sympathy for her personal unhappiness. In 1840 she had married William, Prince of Orange; her marriage had been calamitous from the start, and the birth of children had failed to retrieve it. William III – as he became in 1849 – had fallen under the spell of a courtesan, Mme Musard, and only wanted to discard his family. 'He has given her everything he could give her,' Sophie told Mathilde. 'He has stripped his palace of all its handsome furniture, he has given her the diamonds inherited from our grandmother. Everything, everything! and my children have nothing . . . I have given half my Dutch income to him, so as to keep [my son] Alex with me, and now, as Queen of the Netherlands, I have 18,000 florins . . .'[9]

And so, while Madame Musard wore a dress embroidered with three thousand pearls at her dinner for the Prince de Chimay, the Queen of the Netherlands arrived in Paris in 1869 dressed in unrelieved black grenadine.[10]

Soon after Sophie's visit that June, Mathilde returned to Saint-Gratien, where, throughout the summer, she received a series of visitors: the Viceroy of Egypt, the inevitable Goncourts, Mérimée and his doctor, and Gautier. They were no doubt already entertained by a new figure in the household. In July, Mathilde had appointed the Baronne de Galbois as her reader.[11]

Marie de Galbois was the daughter of Colonel de Galbois. She was forty-one, prudish, unpunctual and assertive. She had a long, sharp nose and straight fair hair. 'Pigeon-chested, pigeon-brained,' added an ungenerous observer. But, whatever her shortcomings, for twenty-seven years, until her death in 1896, Mme de Galbois gave Mathilde unshakable loyalty; and she earned her own immortality from the Goncourts and from Proust.

She earned it for a naïveté which would have pleased Molière. She was the very prototype of the ingénue. In her philosophic moments, she spoke of the beginning and the end of the world as the Alma and the Omega. In her human moments, she readily settled personal problems. One day, when Mathilde was regretting that she must give a young couple separate rooms; 'What does it matter?' asked the Baroness, with an air of authority. 'My father never entered my mother's room, I know.'[12]

F*

'Nieuwerkerke likes to compromise women, he has always liked it. Nieuwerkerke has more vanity than most.'[1] So Prince Paul of Wurtemberg had observed to Count Apponyi, at the beginning of Mathilde's liaison.

The judgment was fair. For twenty-three years Nieuwerkerke had compromised Mathilde. He could hardly have made their liaison more public. Mathilde had not corrected him; as Napoleon's niece, as the Emperor's cousin, as an Imperial Highness, she had appreciated a dominant man: a man so full of self-conceit that he ignored her titles and considered her simply as a woman. Sometimes, in her relationships, she had longed for equality, she had wanted to be human and not a goddess. After the first weeks of their liaison, Nieuwerkerke had treated her with complete familiarity. He had taught her – and the Bonapartes were a passionate race – the power of physical passion; and since he had come into her life with absolute precision, 'after the horrible affair with Demidoff': since he had really made her aware of love, since he had aroused her emotions and given her, for two decades, some semblance of domesticity, she loved him ardently.

It was deplorable that she wasted her devotion on him. Had she met a man of suitable birth and character and distinction, had she divorced Demidoff to marry him, she would have been an exemplary wife. But she had refused to divorce Anatole on the eve of the Empire: she had preferred her liaison with Nieuwerkerke to marriage with Louis-Napoleon. And Nieuwerkerke had determined that Mathilde would make his career.

In 1849 he had duly been appointed Directeur-général des Musées; in 1853 he had been elected to the Académie des Beaux-Arts. In 1856 he was made Commandeur de la Légion-d'honneur, in 1859 he was appointed Chamberlain to the Emperor. He became a Member of the Institut. Stars and ribbons were showered upon him. In 1863 he became Grand Officier de la Légion-d'honneur, and he was made Surintendant des Beaux-Arts. The Emperor had created the title for him.[2]

Two places are vacant in the Senate, to whom will they be granted [Viel-Castel had enquired, that October]? Will Nieuwerkerke put himself forward again? Mme de Nieuwerkerke is very ill after a third paralytic attack which has left her mouth all twisted; Dr le Helloco, her doctor, told me the day before yesterday that she is lost.

From time to time Nieuwerkerke goes to his cousin de Gouy's place near Compiègne, where Mme de Nieuwerkerke is living, to see if she is ripening nicely for death, if she is definitely disposed to quit this life; the day she leaves this world, nothing more will stand between Nieuwerkerke and the title of husband of Princess Mathilde except the apoplectic Demidoff, already senile and bereft of speech.

Nieuwerkerke is persuaded that, given the deaths of Mme de Nieuwerkerke and Demidoff, the Emperor would admit him into his family; he told me so, some years ago. If that happened, he would only have to get himself the title of *Highness*, and his mission on this *base* earth would be accomplished.[3]

Nieuwerkerke became a Senator; but late in 1868 his brilliant comet had begun to fall. A rumour circulated that he was gravely ill; and though the rumour was contradicted when he attended a first night at the Gymnase,[4] soon afterwards certain papers announced that he was partly paralysed.[5] *Le Gaulois* launched an attack on him for dereliction of duty. There had been a fire in the apartments of Troplong, the President of the Senate; and two pictures from the national collection, which happened to be there, had been destroyed. There were also some twenty Flemish paintings from the Louvre adorning Nieuwerkerke's club, le Cercle Impérial. The Surintendant des Beaux-Arts seemed to show no sense of responsibility.

The pictures at Troplong's had not in fact come from the Louvre, and they had not been in Nieuwerkerke's care; but it was more difficult to refute the other charge, that of making private use of public treasures. Nieuwerkerke explained that the Flemish paintings had been given a temporary home while certain alterations were made at the museum. The work was now nearly finished, and the pictures would soon be shown in the Salle des États. This official statement, strangely enough, was made at the annual general meeting of le Cercle Impérial. It still did not justify the fact that the Flemish pictures had adorned the walls of the club for three years.[6]

Throughout the first weeks of 1869, the Press attacks on Nieuwerkerke continued. On 7 February, in the *Chronique des Arts et de la Curiosité*, a critic pointed out that the Louvre was gravely endangered by the fodder stocks and gaslit stables underneath the picture galleries. The following week the same writer professed astonishment that so little work had been done on the catalogue of the museum. In another article he expressed anxiety about the fate of some drawings. 'Good God!' wrote the Goncourts. 'Nieuwerkerke may be reproached for a good many things, but what is underlying all these attacks? . . . It's always envy (and at this moment a terrible amount of envy) – envy, the crude and simple envy of the *petite bourgeoisie*, a cowardly, almost savage envy of a handsome man who is also a count, and fortunate, and has been the lover of great ladies: a man with a big position and big emoluments!'[7] The Goncourts refused to consider that the public might resent a careerist who grew fat on public money and showed very little care for his work. In their journal they lamented the cruelty of the Press, the war against this modern martyr, 'the St Sebastian of the smaller papers'.[8] On 17 February, at the rue de Courcelles, they sensed an unpleasant bitterness in the conversation; people were discussing the libels and insults which were published, morning and evening, in the Press. Mathilde herself kept on repeating that Nieuwerkerke should have answered his detractors. 'But Princess,' he said, 'I cannot answer an accusation of theft!'[9]

A month or so later, on 24 March, Nieuwerkerke told the Goncourts that he was looking for a plot of land. He wanted to build a house for his *objets d'art*, a house he could live in if he left the Louvre, about as far away as the parc Monceau. He spoke of a forty-thousand-franc house, and assured them that an architect could build him something at that price which would last for twenty years. 'Besides,' he added, 'I want a house which doesn't attract attention, everything must be inside . . . In time of revolution, it mustn't have anything which marks it out.' The Goncourts were astonished; and, for once, they criticized him. They considered that when a man had enjoyed all the benefits of a régime, it was a point of honour to risk its fall.[10]

By March 1869, Nieuwerkerke was already expecting some reverse in his fortunes; by the summer he clearly saw that there was nothing more to be gained. Demidoff remained paralysed and on the verge of death; but even if death removed Demidoff and Mme de Nieuwerkerke, he would not think of marriage to Mathilde. There was no reason to tie himself to a woman whom he had loved some twenty-four years ago.

The Goncourts, constantly aware of the emotional climate, watched Mathilde at the end of August 1869. It seemed to them that she was disturbed by some tumult within herself. When Nieuwerkerke slapped one of her dogs, she grew hysterical; at dinner she suddenly felt sick and rushed from the table. She was tired of her enthusiasms, tired of her work, tired even of her painting; and in this physical and moral crisis the diarists detected something tender, melancholy, loving, as if she were rather tempted by a last flirtation.[11]

And some in her circle, aware that she and Nieuwerkerke were parting, aware of this new freedom, this new tenderness, may have felt a new freedom and tenderness in their turn. Dumas *fils* was one of them; and in a letter of explanation he sent her in September, there is a strong hint of a friendship, an *amitié voluptueuse*, which, with encouragement, might have turned to love.

> 16 September 1869.
>
> I will allow myself to observe to Your Highness that it was I who wrote to her last: very briefly, it is true, yet none the less to tell Her that I loved Her with all my heart. Such a letter needed no answer, of course, since that is what I always write and you have no further objections to make to it; unless that is one of the points on which we disagree. If you don't want me to love you, Princess, say so; I don't promise to obey you, but I shan't mention it to you any more.
>
> As for the famous points, the black points (as they say in politics) on which we disagree, I know that they exist only in your imagination. If I have sometimes let myself develop certain radical and absolute theories about women in Your Highness's presence, that is because I consider Her as being beyond discussion by the frankness, openness and valour of her life. If I thought you were like the other women I talk about so freely, I shouldn't speak to you about my devotion or my affection; I shouldn't speak to you about anything; I should foster our relationship with the banalities that will do for any woman, I'd

drink your iced lemonade this Sunday, I'd leave my name on your birthday and New Year's Day, and that would be all. If, at my age, knowing what I know about life, about things and people, having known you for several years, expecting nothing of you, and having explained myself to you as I've done on a hundred questions concerning women: if I still tell you, again and again, that I love you, it is because I love you very sincerely and very loyally and as you must be loved when you are you and I am myself. Perhaps I was a little too quick; perhaps I seemed to want to enter your intimate life too abruptly, and to want to take places which have long been properly filled. All the same, you made a slight movement of withdrawal, very visible, and as if to say: a little patience, *young man*; you don't come in like that and I don't need you as much as you seem to think. And so I withdrew into myself a little, and I was silent, after I had sent you my last profession of faith and summed it up in these very simple words: I love you with all my heart.

That, Princess, to tell you the whole truth, is the cause of my silence, and even of my incivility, because it is uncivil to go through Paris and not to come and see you. I didn't want to impose myself on you, and as you had let me understand that one had to wait for a vacancy and that you didn't want to create a new post, I have waited. It was fortunate that I did, because I've received your nice letter of this morning.

And so, at the end of the month, before I leave for Burgundy, between one arrival platform and another, I shall ask your permission to come and dine at Saint-Gratien, with your old friends – as a supernumary.

Madame Dumas and Mlle Colette [our daughter] are very touched by Your Highness's kind remembrances, they ask me to assure Her of their most affectionate feelings – and I, Princess,

I love you with all my heart.

A. DUMAS *fils*.[12]

In November, when Mathilde had gone back to Paris for the winter, Nieuwerkerke's absence became public news; and in December Mérimée, in Cannes, read in the Press that there had been a break.[13] 'People send me all sorts of gossip,' he told Viollet-le-Duc. 'The Surintendant is said to be in love and very cruel to our friend in the rue de Courcelles.'[14]

Gégé Primoli said that Mathilde's physical relationship with Nieuwerkerke had ended some years earlier.[15] If this is true, she was almost unbelievably innocent to think that he would want to marry her. And yet, long after the event, Gégé also said that Mathilde had really thought that she would legitimise the liaison. It had needed Nieuwerkerke to destroy her illusions, to say he had promised marriage to a young girl. He had told her so one evening, without warning, and she had thought she must be going mad. She wanted a witness of this revelation, a proof that this illusion was reality, and they had gone together to see Giraud. Nieuwerkerke professed not to know that Mathilde was still in love with him. 'I don't understand,' he told Giraud, 'why the Princess doesn't want my *tendresse transformée*.' 'What use would she have for your transformed tenderness?' Giraud enquired. Nieuwerkerke found his behaviour quite natural. He wanted to exchange her worn-out love for that of a young girl whom he respected. He dared to tell her so. As soon as she understood, she turned him out of Saint-Gratien. 'And I remember,' wrote Gégé, 'how she told me about it, . . . and added this feminine touch: "And he had to go on foot across the fields, because I didn't order a carriage for him." '[16]

Gradually her anger subsided. Giraud told her that Nieuwerkerke was desperately afraid that he would lose all his official functions. Mathilde decided that he might come to dinner twice a week, on the evenings when she had company, but that if he ever attempted to talk to her in private, she would give him his public dismissal. Nieuwerkerke accepted her terms.[17]

It was difficult to know if Mathilde had acted from compassion, or because she wanted to hide Nieuwerkerke's desertion from the world. Perhaps she hoped to cure herself of love by making him appear more despicable; perhaps she sought revenge, perhaps she cherished some vague hope of his return.[18]

Whatever the truth, she could not feign indifference. Gégé went with her to the Gymnase to see *Fernande*, the new play by Sardou. It presented so many parallels with her own situation that she sobbed aloud, and in the third act she had to leave the theatre.[19] Twenty-one years later, she wrote: 'From 1846 to 1869, God knows I was deceived. And finally I was abandoned.'[20]

'It is ten o'clock at night. The Princess had migraine and had to go to bed very early, so everyone dispersed at half-past nine.'[1] It was 19 August 1869; and François Coppée's letter to his mother reflected the unhappiness at Saint-Gratien. Yet the fact that he was staying at Saint-Gratien at this moment was itself a tribute to Mathilde. She did not allow her personal desolation to cloud her friendships. Forty years later, in his *Souvenirs d'un Parisien*, Coppée could still write: 'Those few weeks in the summer of 1869 . . . remain among the happiest of my youth.'[2]

Mathilde felt maternal solicitude for this gentle, sallow poet of twenty-seven, who looked so like the young Bonaparte on his return from Egypt. Coppée, on the threshold of his literary career, was hampered by ill-health, and she was determined to ensure his physical well-being and his success. On his return from Amélie-les-Bains, where he had spent the winter, she had invited him to Saint-Gratien.

Coppée, like many other urban intellectuals, resented relaxation, even when he knew that it was necessary. He found it hard to adapt himself to the tempo of country-house life. He wanted stimulus and privacy, he wanted his comfort, and his freedom from social obligations.[3] In fact he showed the selfishness and complexity of the creative artist; and, looking back on Saint-Gratien in his *Souvenirs*, recalling that he had been only one of many guests, each with their pride, complexity and distinction, he marvelled at the tact of Mathilde.

In the summer of 1869, his own resentments had been lulled asleep, and in his hours of privacy, soothed by the security and comfort, he had begun to write a play, *Deux Douleurs*.[4] In his hours of sociability, he watched his imperial hostess, happy to be surrounded by men of letters, artists and scholars, 'always ready to please them and help them, always ready to learn. She often listened, rarely spoke, and then it was only when necessary; and then she would throw the essential word into the conversation: often amusing and picturesque, never spiteful or commonplace, always full of sense and truth.'[5] (It was just as well that Coppée did not read her later comment on himself: 'Has managed his affairs very well, and known how to cultivate useful contacts. His verse is always honest, but not gripping.')[6]

August passed by peacefully for Coppée, at Saint-Gratien. Gautier, who had recently presented him to Mathilde, arrived to spend a few days at the château; and one afternoon, as the guests were strolling in the park with their hostess, Flaubert arrived. Flaubert's letters faintly reflect a picture of himself at Saint-Gratien; Coppée, in his *Souvenirs*, gave a first impression of Flaubert which was vivid, and absolutely convincing.

... Before his name had been pronounced, I was struck by the appearance of this giant with the apoplectic complexion and the moustaches of a Mongolian warrior, very dressed up, with a certain magnificence, and even a suspicion of a shirt-frill. When he had greeted the Princess, he put his top-hat on again, a shining, broad-brimmed hat, and as he walked his sparkling patent shoes squeaked in the grass.

Gustave Flaubert had been exceedingly handsome in his youth, and he had kept certain dandyish habits of dress since the days when his appearance had caused a sensation in the theatre at Rouen. As I saw him in 1869, ravaged by prolonged ill-health, and by huge excesses of wakeful nights and work, he still had his nobility. Nothing was loftier than the way he held his head – it was the bearing of the Romantics; one could still perceive the fineness of his features in his florid, swollen face. His countenance was adorned by the most triumphant pair of moustaches, and illumined by his big blue eyes, full of honesty and courage, the eyes of a Norman of the Conquest; and, on his half-denuded head, his long, dishevelled, greying locks went wild with a quite Merovingian wildness. Gustave Flaubert, as he grew old, was no longer handsome, but he was still superb.

That evening, in the Princess's summer residence, on the steps of the verandah, watching a magnificent summer sunset, I had the joy of a long talk with Gustave Flaubert; and, after the first words had been exchanged, he spoke to me – with what verve, what familiar eloquence! – of what he loved best in the word, of style.

He soon told me his famous formula:

'I don't know if a phrase is good until it's gone through my *gueuloir*!'

And, joining example to precept, he promptly declaimed one or two.

Those who have not heard Flaubert, with a vigour of speech and an amplitude of gesture worthy of Frédérick Lemaître, *gueuler* (there is no other word) a sentence from Bossuet or Chateaubriand, will never know what happiness a man can find in literary admiration.[7]

Coppée was concerned with his health; Flaubert was still oppressed by the recent death of his friend, Louis Bouilhet. Both of them found strength in Mathilde. Coppée, who was young enough to have been her son, gave her his affection and admiration. Flaubert, who was only a year younger than Mathilde, felt more complex, more profound emotions.

He felt the admiration which any man might feel for the princess, dressed by Worth, holding court in the rue de Courcelles, for the Bonaparte châtelaine of Saint-Gratien. He was stirred by the thought of living, from time to time, in an imperial world, he was moved when Mathilde insisted that he should read her his latest novel ('*She* has time to hear me, the Princess!').[8] He was touched by her constant care for his health, the presents she used to send him: an Indian knife, a watercolour which she herself had painted, and a copy of her bust by Carpeaux. ('It is like a continual smile in my solitude, a benediction hovering over me.')[9] He was flattered when Mathilde wanted his photograph; and he was perpetually delighted by the conversations, literary and political, gossiping and personal, which she carried on by letter (even though her writing recalled 'those great Turkish ladies who let us see their splendid eyes through gauze'). Mathilde brought a tonic, affectionate air into the solitude of his study at Croisset; she had the radiance of a princess, and the gentle, determined solicitude of a mother. She was so consistently kind to him, that Flaubert could only feel affection; she was so feminine, so unattainable that he could only be enamoured of her.

The fact that her imperial status removed any physical danger was, perhaps, important in Flaubert's eyes; for he was not an ardent lover of women. Despite his liaison with Louise Colet, despite his long devotion to Élisa Schlésinger, his deepest attachments were probably for men; and, like many men with a homosexual strain in their nature, he liked maternal women. Mme Colet was thirteen years older than himself; and Mme Schlésinger, who remained a potent dream, portrayed in *L'Éducation senti-mentale*, was, in all probability, never his mistress. He had first seen her on a beach, breast-feeding her child.[10]

Mathilde was another hieratic and maternal figure; and, at the same time, she had the spell of a mistress beyond desiring, beyond possessing. Flaubert's love for her was complex, it had to remain unrequited; it was somehow symbolized by his promise to be at the station at Rouen, when her train passed through, on its way to Paris.

And yet, it seems, he longed to declare his love for her. One evening, in the 1860s, when he was her guest at Saint-Gratien, he asked her for a private audience. The evening was recalled by Gégé Primoli; he saw Flaubert in the character of Mathô, the warrior-hero of his own *Salammbô*. Mathilde herself had told Gégé how, at eleven o'clock, she had dismissed her guests, ordered the servants not to put out the lights, and settled down again to her embroidery.

The door half-opened; Mathô came in furtively, more like a timid schoolboy than a conquering hero. With a mistrustful glance round the room, he assured himself that all the guests had gone . . . Then he slipped between the table and the sofa, and sat down on a buttoned armchair beside the Princess. Silently, he watched her at work – and it was indeed a picture worthy of an artist or a poet: this imperial profile bent over the embroidery under the pink light of the lamp. He gazed at the neck as smooth as a column, and at the pearl which was trembling on the lobe of her ear; he gazed at the famous shoulders, so often celebrated, which emerged from the shot-silver burnous, he gazed at the fairy fingers as they coursed across the canvas, making the flowers blossom . . .

The Princess felt this burning look as it passed across her neck, her shoulders, and her hand, and . . . she waited . . . For a long moment there was silence, and then, provoked by these eyes which were fixed upon her, she suddenly looked up:

'Well? What have you got to tell me that's so confidential and urgent? We're alone, as you asked, and I'm perfectly ready to listen . . .'

Imagine her surprise when she saw him turn very red and then very pale! The most diverse expressions crossed his face: fear, anguish, terror, despair . . . He stammered some incoherent sounds, then he rose precipitately, made for the door and ran . . .[11]

On 20 February 1865, in an autograph album, Flaubert wrote: 'Women will never know how timid men are.'[12]

In August 1869, while Coppée was convalescent, and Flaubert was weighed down by his bereavement, the Goncourts were struggling to emerge from profound depression. They were suffering from overwork, from their own hypersensitive natures, and Jules was trying to ward off mental instability.

He had become so vulnerable to noise that it affected him like physical violence. Dr Le Helloco, Mathilde's doctor, had tried in vain to cure his nervous state, and in October the Goncourts escaped to Trouville.

They found no peace there. Driven from Trouville by a plague of yelling children, the two distraught brothers asked to stay at the Pavillon de Catinat. Mathilde agreed readily. They arrived on 1 November, *le Jour des morts*. Mathilde had just presented some bells to the local church, and the curé rang the bells for two days.[13]

While the Goncourts had been enduring Trouville, Gautier was making his slow, reluctant way to Egypt. He had been asked by the Khedive to attend the opening of the Suez Canal; and the eager traveller of earlier years, the author of *Voyage en Espagne* and *Voyage en Italie* was now, at fifty-eight, unwilling to go far afield. 'Princess,' he wrote, 'I'm grieved to think that the honour of being watched from the top of the Pyramids by forty centuries and a half will cost me eight Wednesdays with Your Imperial Highness. It's really very expensive . . .'[14]

Soon after he sailed from Marseilles, he slipped on the steps between-decks on the *Moeris*, dislocated his shoulder and cracked a bone in his arm. Demoralized by his accident, by his sling, by enforced inactivity, by the thought of the journey still to come, he became increasingly miserable. The moment he reached his destination, he sent Mathilde a letter which recorded his hypochondria, and suggested something of her own understanding.

Princess,

Here I am at last in Cairo, as well as can be expected in my condition. I'm afraid I'm plaguing you with my letters in the most tedious way, but . . . I have the arrant presumption to count you among the three or four people who care about me . . .

I am staying at Shepheard's Hotel, Esbekieh Square, Cairo, Egypt, and I don't need to tell Your Highness the request implied in this very detailed, largely written and entirely legible address.[15]

Before Mathilde replied, there occurred an event which reduced Gautier's complaints to their true proportions.

Since the day when she had gone to the rue du Montparnasse, and hurled her violent insults at Sainte-Beuve, Mathilde had had time to reconsider her precipitate action. In April she had sent Charles Edmond to arrange a reconciliation, but Sainte-Beuve had refused to be reconciled. Now, on 11 October, Dr Gosselin, the surgeon from La Charité, operated on the 'huge abscess' on Sainte-Beuve's prostate gland. Sainte-Beuve bore the operation bravely, but he was exhausted. 'We are between hope and fear,' reported his old friend Dr Veyne, 'but fear is the stronger.'[16]

Mathilde forgot any hurt to her pride, and telegraphed to Troubat, the critic's secretary, for news. Dr Veyne dictated a purely medical answer. Mathilde acknowledged it by sending a telegram to Sainte-Beuve himself. 'So you wrote to her?' Sainte-Beuve asked Troubat. Troubat replied that she had asked for news, and that Veyne had said it was his duty to send it. Sainte-Beuve smiled. 'That's typical of Veyne – he is always chivalrous!' He dictated a long telegram in answer.[17]

The nine months' silence had been broken. The book which had shut was open once again. Mathilde sent an emissary: the history professor whom Sainte-Beuve had chosen for her. Zeller brought a letter from her; and it was Zeller, sitting by the austere iron bed, who took down the faint reply:

Princess,
 . . . It is a profound satisfaction to have found again what one had ceased to believe in. Respect and affection.
SAINTE-BEUVE.[18]

Someone guided his hand as he signed. He died at half-past one next morning, Wednesday, 13 October.[19]

Mathilde was surprised by the intensity of her regrets. Ten days later, she told Lebrun: 'I didn't think [his death] would move me so. I'm glad he went with the knowledge of my real affection . . . I shall always treasure the thought of our friendship.'[20] She had planned to give his bust to the town of Boulogne, where he was born.[21]

Yet, even now, the friendship created a final disturbance. In the same breath, she told Lebrun that she wanted all her letters to Sainte-Beuve to be returned. Sainte-Beuve himself had agreed that they should be given to her; but Mathilde, impulsive as ever, did not wait to receive them: she brought an immediate action against his heirs. Troubat was understandably angered; but Sainte-Beuve's own wishes were respected, and her letters were returned in exchange for his own. Mathilde did not, as *Le Gaulois* had feared, need to bind the letters in *peau de chagrin*; and when she tried, through Flaubert, to buy back her watercolour of Mme Lenoir, Troubat gave it to her.[22]

On 2 January 1870, by Imperial decree, the young deputy
Maurice Richard was appointed Minister for the Fine Arts.
The appointment was clearly a political gesture. Émile Ollivier
had come to power, and the new liberal government were
determined to prevent plurality of functions: they had separated
the Ministry of Fine Arts from the Ministry of the Imperial
Household. Marshal Vaillant, at the Emperor's wish, took the
latter office. Maurice Richard was appointed to the newly-
created Ministry in gratitude for his service in the Chambre des
Députés. He had been Ollivier's associate and adviser throughout
the recent political crisis, and Ollivier had to find a portfolio for a
loyal colleague. Mérimée wrote eloquently: 'I don't know M.
Richard . . . He won't find it hard to do better than his pre-
decessor.'[1]

It was perhaps through Mathilde's good graces that Nieuwerkerke had not been relieved of all his functions. When the
Ollivier Ministry was formed, she had written to the Emperor;
she had, she said, heard that Nieuwerkerke was to be dismissed.
She asked the Emperor not to increase her unhappiness by
making her the cause of Nieuwerkerke's misfortune.[2]

Nieuwerkerke was not completely disgraced; but it seemed
that criticism had finally had effect. Le Sénateur Surintendant
des Beaux-Arts was now merely Surintendant des Musées
Impériaux. At the age of fifty-nine, he had become subordinate
to a Député twenty years his junior, a man who was young
enough to have been his son. The *buen retiro* near the Parc
Monceau, which he had dreamed of less than a year ago, the little
house which the Goncourts had considered with surprise and
disapproval, had become a necessity. Nieuwerkerke, it is said,
'bore his semi-disgrace with great dignity. He left the Louvre,
and retired like a philosopher to the small *hôtel* he had built

himself . . . There, in the big hall on the second floor, where the walls were hung with arms and armour, he received his visitors with perfect grace.'[3] For some, even this decline and fall were not adequate retribution. *La Presse* complained that Nieuwerkerke had been given a new post. 'Everyone thought that the ex-Surintendant des Beaux-Arts would cease to be concerned with the museums, and content himself with his salary as a Senator.'[4]

For many people, Nieuwerkerke's demotion was over-shadowed by the news which came only three days later, that Baron Haussmann had been compelled to resign the office of Préfet de la Seine, which he had held for nearly seventeen years. He had recently presented the City of Paris with a deficit of some thirty million pounds sterling: a larger sum than the National Debt of Belgium or Bavaria. 'France still has her Napoleon,' remarked *The Times*, 'but Paris has lost her Emperor.'[5]

On 9 January, Mathilde gave her first Sunday of the season. Her reception seemed to mark the end of an era. For there, with the steadfast Flaubert, listening to the duet from Rossini's *Barber of Seville*, were Haussmann and Nieuwerkerke.[6] And there, very probably, to emphasize Nieuwerkerke's fall from power, was Claudius Popelin, Mathilde's new lover.[7]

Popelin was forty-four. He had been born at 22, rue Beaurepaire, in Paris, on 2 November 1825. His father, Antoine Popelin, had set out from Burgundy to make his fortune in the metropolis, and he had established a highly successful concern, Le Charbon de Paris. Antoine Popelin had married a childhood friend from Burgundy, Philiberte Ducarre, who later founded a Parisian fashion house. Claudius may have inherited his artistic sense from his mother.[8] He came of bourgeois stock, and he had a bourgeois nature: solid, loyal, domestic, sometimes boldly romantic, but occasionally lacking in refinement.

Popelin was erudite, well versed in anthropology, in archaeology and heraldry. Though he was a generation older than the Parnassian poets, he had come to know them well, and he had contributed to *Le Parnasse contemporain*, the anthology which gave the group their name. His own poetry was carefully wrought, though rarely distinguished; but it had brought him the friendship of Heredia. In 1866 his book *L'Émail des Peintres* had opened with a sonnet by Gautier.

Three years later, Popelin had enlarged this work into his manual on the enameller's art, *Les Vieux arts du feu*; for he was the perfect Parnassian, he was both a poet and a craftsman. A pupil of Ary Scheffer, he had devoted himself for years to reviving the forgotten art of the enameller. It had been the glory of Limoges, and now, in the Second Empire, it enjoyed a brief renaissance. Popelin had exhibited more than once at the Salon. In 1865, he had won a medal in the paintings and drawings section: in 1869, at the distribution of awards to exhibitors, he had received the cross of Chevalier de la Légion-d'honneur.[9]

His progress had not gone unobserved. He had been noted, acidly, by the Goncourts: 'Claudius Popelin, the enameller, a favour-currier everywhere, an artist who has grown rich and stayed bitter; a worn, nervous face, a dry, repugnant, contra-dictory manner of speaking . . .'[10] The portrait was doubtless exaggerated, but a world of difference lay between the ex-Surintendant des Beaux-Arts and the earnest painter of allegories, who enamelled a plaque of the Emperor flanked by figures of Strength and Temperance.[11] Nieuwerkerke had been an imperial lover, superbly at home in the rue de Courcelles.[12] Popelin, too, was tall and bearded, but his features were plebeian, and his manner was grateful and deferent. When he was decorated, one of the Goncourts wrote that he had won his cross 'through a thousand little mean acts; the ones I know suggest the ones I suspect'.[13] The observation had been made at about the time of the break with Nieuwerkerke. Perhaps the diarists had already noticed a sign of a new interest.

A few years earlier, Mathilde would not have considered Popelin as a lover. She had needed a suitable prince consort. Now she was nearly fifty, and, though Mérimée insisted that she looked younger, a less affectionate observer said that she had been ageing visibly for some years. 'Princess Mathilde,' wrote a pamphleteer, 'has only the position and the title of a princess, and she bears a remarkable likeness to a bourgeoise of the rue Notre-Dame de Nazareth.'[14]

Mathilde herself was acutely conscious of advancing age: so conscious of it that, one day, she set down her thoughts on the art of growing old.

I should be glad if my experience was not wasted for the women who read these lines. I should be glad if they could find them useful . . . in the very difficult passage from youth to middle age. I should like them to look without apprehension and terror at the moment when they are reduced to the rôle of *good women*.

I address myself to those women who wake up one fine morning, and see the change in themselves. They weep, they grow desolate, . . . their self-confidence disappears, and they are overwhelmed by despair . . .

It is at this moment that a new life should begin, a life full of thoughtfulness and compassion . . . *L'amitié voluptueuse* – to quote Th. Gautier's charming phrase – must replace the love that one can no longer inspire . . .[15]

In 1869, Mathilde could no longer inspire a Nieuwerkerke. She was forced to ask less of men, to be grateful for less; and she was grateful for Popelin's loyalty. As Gégé Primoli recalled:

> There was an artist with azure eyes and a sharply pointed blond beard, a veritable prince of the Florentine renaissance . . . He had adored her for twelve years . . . He felt like an earthworm enamoured of a star . . .
>
> Every new work he published was to him a pretext for laying his devotion at the Princess's feet. He had his book superbly bound, set an exquisite enamel in the binding, and, on the first page, he wrote a sonnet in the depths of which he buried his timid homage, which the great lady confused with all the rest . . . She saw no man except the man she loved.
>
> And so he contented himself with following her from afar, . . . and the day when she found herself deceived, betrayed and abandoned, he emerged from his obscurity and held out his hand.[16]

It was a time when both of them needed solace and affection. In April 1858, Popelin had married Marie-Thérèse Anquetil. They had had a son, Gustave, the following year. In February 1869, at the age of thirty-two, Marie-Thérèse died of cancer.[17] Popelin wrote to tell Mathilde, for she had 'taken an interest in the cruel sufferings of my dear, brave wife . . . It is one steadfast, honest soul the less on this earth where they are rare,' wrote Popelin. 'I am left almost alone in this world, with a poor little child, and my grief is beyond expression.'[18]

Three months later, on Mathilde's forty-ninth birthday, Popelin declared that 'when a great Princess is so good, so sincere & so charming, that a man who is more free than a king, & quite as proud, has no dearer wish than to live at her feet, every year adds to her grace and makes the sweet vassalage closer and more precious'.[19]

Now, on 5 January 1870, the Goncourts recorded:

It certainly looks as if it has happened; and Claudius Popelin, who is always at the Princess's feet, seems to want to proclaim to the world, like an ill-bred man, that he has replaced the Surintendant.

Poor Princess! Instead of ending her life with Nieuwerkerke, a liaison which seemed rather like a marriage, instead of resolving to condemn herself to widowhood, she is going, in her fiftieth year, to present a spectacle which is saddening for her friends and ridiculous to everyone else: the spectacle of a passion for a man devoid of talent, for this enameller, this fabricator of little cut-out cardboard Napoleons, for this man who is physically awry . . .[20]

The Goncourts, who were both devoted to Mathilde, were unlikely to be kind about her lovers. Like Viel-Castel, they wanted her to play the ideal part they had chosen for her. Her liaison with Popelin offended their historic sense, their aesthetic sensibility.

Mathilde was much more human than the Goncourts would allow; no doubt, with her sense of social distinction, she recognized that Popelin was inadequate. But she needed consolation for Nieuwerkerke. She needed what, perhaps, Nieuwerkerke had never given her: genuine admiration and affection.

⁓ 30 ⁏

The year 1870 brought, all too soon, a warning that the Empire was insecure. In January there was a violent quarrel between two Corsican papers, *La Revanche* and *L'Avenir*, and there was an imminent prospect of a duel between Tommasi, a journalist on *La Revanche*, and Prince Pierre Bonaparte, son of Lucien, Prince of Canino, who had defended Napoleon's memory in *L'Avenir*. A journalist called Paschal Grousset took up the cause of *La Revanche*, and insulted the prince in *La Marseillaise*. The prince, who was one of the wildest of the Bonapartes, immediately challenged Henri Rochefort, the editor of *La Marseillaise*, 'because he would not stoop to challenge one of his hacks'. Grousset sent two witnesses to the prince's house at Auteuil: Ivan Salmon, known as Victor Noir, and Ulrich de Fonvielle. There was a heated altercation, the prince fired several revolver shots at his visitors, and killed Victor Noir.

There was no doubt that Victor Noir was a scurrilous journalist, and that he had provoked the prince to action, but his death at the age of twenty made him a martyr, and his funeral next day was a rallying-point for Republican extremists. The cortège set out from his house at Neuilly for the cemetery at Auteuil; and Gautier, who also lived at Neuilly, sent a sombre account of events to Carlotta Grisi in Switzerland.

I'm worried [he ended] about the fate of the Imperial Family. They have been so good to me, and, should there be a reverse, they would be massacred without pity. I don't believe that any concession would disarm the party that calls itself irreconcilable. If it were granted all the freedoms of England, America, Belgium and Switzerland, it would continue its agitations, because it wants, purely and simply, the fall of the Napoleonic dynasty. That hardly makes the situation comfortable. The Princess keeps her admirable serenity. Her face shows no anxiety and maintains its usual cheerfulness.[1]

In fact Mathilde was bitterly conscious of the opposition to the Empire. She had been born in exile, she had been banned from France until her marriage; she was well aware of the fickleness of French politics, the desertion that followed failure, the cruelty that was shown to those who had lost their power. In the peaceful, domestic days of Louis-Philippe, she had probably felt much more confident of the future than she had ever done in her cousin's reign.

Pierre Bonaparte was acquitted by the High Court of Justice, and he retired to the Ardennes; and the Second Empire continued to glitter with diamanté splendour. In January, at a Tuileries ball, a journalist observed that the cold collation was set out on wax bases modelled in the shapes of roses, camellias and narcissi.[2] The imperial salads were made with asparagus tips and sliced truffles. The consumption of champagne reached a total which *La Presse* did not dare to publish.[3]

In January and February there were family dinners at the palace; and to Gégé Primoli, invited for the first time, Mathilde stood out for her honesty and her simplicity: she was like a page of Molière which had somehow strayed into a comedy by Marivaux.[4] The Empress declared she would take more interest in a man who had crossed Africa than she would in a man who wrote poetry. 'Well, I shouldn't!' cried Mathilde. 'We are the two extremes,' said Eugénie. 'You're the town mouse and I'm the country mouse. I'm the carrier pigeon, and you're the homing dove.'[5]

Mathilde, still interested in poetry, had Coppée appointed assistant librarian at the Senate,[6] and Coppée, nursing his health at Pau, learned that the papers were announcing the *soirée* at the rue de Courcelles at which his new one-act drama would be performed.[7] He had written *Deux Douleurs* last summer, at Saint-Gratien; now, in March, it was presented before the Emperor and Empress.[8]

Soon afterwards, Mathilde went with Gégé Primoli to see Eugène Sue's *Mathilde*. The drama was based on the novel which he had published the year after her marriage, and when he created the villain, Count Lugarto, Sue had no doubt had Demidoff in mind.[9] There was a close resemblance between the

Prince of San Donato and this brutal half-caste, the son of a negress. Mathilde herself could not have missed the significance of his soliloquy: 'I wanted to be a nobleman, I bought a name and a title . . . Oh, nothing is impossible with five million a year . . .'[10]

It was in April 1870 that the Porte-Saint-Martin revived the play which had first been performed there in 1842. The revival coincided – deliberately, perhaps – with the sale of the San Donato Collection. On 22 March the first of six sales had been held in Paris to dispose of the treasures from the palace. On 28 April the last *objets d'art* changed hands.[11] Next day, 'as if something within him had broken at the last stroke of the auctioneer's hammer,' Anatole Demidoff died.[12]

He was only fifty-seven, but he had looked much older.

Bent and broken, perpetually chewing sweets, he had seemed to sleep in his invariable stage-box. He had seemed to watch without seeing, silent, sad, lugubrious, . . . and every night it was the same. One used to see him at the theatre, every day that God gave him, sometimes at one, and sometimes at another, always silent and as if he was lost in profound decrepitude.[13]

Le Moniteur universel announced that he had died from a cold which he had caught at the Théâtre-Français.[14] The *Daily Telegraph* said he had died, 'rather suddenly, of congestion of the liver.'[15] An unidentified French paper, describing how he lay in his Paris *hôtel* in a bedroom 'literally hung' with jewelled icons, said that 'the fatal illness was a simple pulmonary congestion'.[16] The truth was probably more unpleasant. Fourteen years earlier, in his journal, Dr Prosper Ménière had noted: 'He is now forty-four, and he looks as if he was sixty. He's had the beginning of a cerebral lesion, with half his body paralysed . . .' Demidoff had probably died of his old venereal disease.[17]

The funeral service was held on 21 May at the Russian church in the rue Daru. Demidoff was buried at Père-Lachaise. Mathilde was represented at his funeral by the officers of her household.[18]

On his death, she had cancelled her Sunday receptions for May, and *Le Moniteur universel* announced that she had gone into mourning. But she could hardly regret the death of the husband who had brought her pain and humiliation, the husband whom she had not seen for twenty-five years.

On the day of Demidoff's funeral, in the Salle des États at the

Louvre, a deputation from the Corps Législatif presented the Emperor with the result of the plebiscite of 8 May an: overwhelming vote of confidence in the Second Empire. Mathilde stood on the dais, with the rest of the Imperial Family.[19] The day of her husband's funeral was the day of her cousin's triumph.

She was certainly distressed by another death which occurred soon afterwards. It had been clear for many months that Jules de Goncourt was suffering from venereal disease, and that it had affected his mind. Once, last summer, at *déjeuner*, when Mathilde praised a Jewish scholar, Jules had been overcome by an 'unhealthy irritation which I can no longer master'; he had burst out: 'Well, Princess, be a Jewess!' Silence had followed. The guests turned pale. Jules had regretted his outburst at once, and after *déjeuner* he had apologised to Mathilde. His tears fell on her hands as he kissed them. Mathilde, affected by his emotion, had taken him in her arms.[20]

But the 'unhealthy irritation', the nervous state had continued; and Jules had suffered from bouts of melancholy so acute that they almost amounted to madness. He had been so obsessed by noise that 'the sound of a barrel-organ, the voice of a street singer, even the tinkle of a bell were enough to hurt him . . .'[21] And Gégé Primoli recorded how, after dinner at the rue de Courcelles, as Mathilde was working at her tapestry, Jules had suddenly kissed her forehead, and tittered like an idiot. She had said nothing, but she was near to tears, and Edmond was openly weeping. It was the last time that he brought his brother to see her.[22]

Now, on 20 June 1870, at the age of thirty-nine, Jules de Goncourt died insane. 'I am sick at heart when I think of your grief,' Mathilde wrote to Edmond, 'I am really distressed by the thought of your solitude, of your life cut in two . . . I'm not making any suggestions, but you know my house is yours; come when you want, for as long as you want . . .'[23]

Next day Jules was buried at the Cimetière Montmartre. The cortège took the road which had so often led the Goncourts to the rue de Courcelles. Gautier, who had hurried back from Switzerland for the funeral, dined that evening at Saint-Gratien. 'We talked about Goncourt all the time,' he told Carlotta Grisi, 'and I came back at one in the morning.'[24]

It was a suitable farewell. Edmond, writing to thank him for his return from Geneva, told him: 'Your thought-stirring conversation was one of [Jules'] great delights. Last year at Saint-Gratien it gave him his final hours of happiness.' And Edmond added bitterly: 'After all he died of his profession as a stylist, and, as you expressed it so well at a dinner last autumn, a little because of the greyness of life in the nineteenth century.'[25]

Life, which had seemed grey to Jules de Goncourt, grew darker in the month after his death.

Early in July, Count Bismarck advanced a Hohenzollern candidate, Prince Leopold of Sigmaringen, to fill the vacant throne of Spain. France expressed such violent alarm at this threatened act of 'encirclement' that the candidate was promptly withdrawn. But France needed war; ever since Sadowa she had been aware of the Prussian challenge to her grandeur. No French government could idly watch while Prussia united Germany under her, and the Press began to stir up warlike feeling. The Emperor was sixty-two and in lamentable health; he had no wish for war. Nor had Émile Ollivier, who had recently come to power. But the Emperor was being pushed by his Foreign Minister, the Duc de Gramont (who was still smarting from Bismarck's comment: 'The stupidest man in Europe'); he was also being pushed towards war by the Empress, who declared that their son would not reign unless they retrieved the misfortune of Sadowa.

Gramont now assumed a hectoring tone towards Prussia. It was not enough that she had withdrawn her candidate, she must be humbled for her presumption. He therefore cabled Count Benedetti, the Ambassador in Berlin, to keep the crisis hot. William I of Prussia, who was taking the waters at Ems, received Benedetti on 13 July with the greatest courtesy, and assured him that no one wanted war less than he did. He considered the unification of Germany his grandson's task, not his own. But, while the Emperor was being pushed by Gramont, the King was being pushed by Bismarck. On his momentous visit to Paris in 1867, Bismarck had observed that the French Army was pitiably unprepared for modern warfare; and he had diligently trained a massive, modern army of his own. He had long since decided

G

that war with France would cement the German federation. The pretext had to be carefully chosen, for it had to be one that showed France in the most unfavourable light. Now that France was insisting on further diplomatic victories, trying to humble Prussian pride, and showing quite unnecessary belligerence, Bismarck decided that the time had come. At Ems, the King had been irritated by Benedetti's insistence on a guarantee that the Hohenzollern candidature would not arise again. He declined to give such a guarantee, and refused Benedetti's request for a further audience. A telegram describing his refusal was then despatched to Bismarck in Berlin. Bismarck sharpened the tone, and stated that the King had 'refused to receive the Ambassador again, and he had had the latter informed by the adjutant on duty that His Majesty had no further communication to make'. Bismarck sent his version of the Ems Telegram to the Berlin Press and to every capital in Europe.

Even with Bismarck's editing, the Ems Telegram was hardly a *casus belli*; but it was enough to entice Napoleon III into the trap.

I am rusticating at Saint-Gratien [so Gautier told Carlotta Grisi on 14 July] . . . In the morning, after I've drunk my soup, I go and row on the lake until *déjeuner*, which makes my arm strong and supple and my breathing easier. After *déjeuner* we smoke and chat and stroll a bit in the park, then the princess goes into her studio and begins to paint as if her life depended on it . . . At six o'clock the guests from Paris arrive with news from the city, where there is now considerable agitation. Will there or will there not be war with Prussia? I know absolutely nothing about it, though Mme Benedetti, the wife of the French Ambassador in Berlin, is staying here, and I'm dining every day with the cousin of Augustus. They are both as silent as sphinxes. All the same, the princess seems to believe that peace won't be disturbed. The students marched down the boulevards yesterday with banners, crying: 'À Berlin, à Berlin!' to the tune of *Les Lampions*, which you heard in 1848. But I hope it will all end like Shakespeare's comedy *Much Ado About Nothing*.[1]

Next day, Friday, 15 July, the Senate was crowded when, at 2.20 p.m., the session opened. Canrobert, who had so distinguished himself in the Crimea, Duruy, who had left his mark on the educational system, Haussmann, who had transformed the capital, were among those who assembled to hear the Government's declaration. It was Nieuwerkerke who moved that the declaration should be read.

The Minister for Foreign Affairs then gave the official account of the talks at Ems between the King of Prussia and Benedetti. 'We have done everything,' he said, 'to avoid a war, we shall prepare to fight the war which is offered to us. We shall leave to each his due responsibility.'[2]

At half-past nine that night the Emperor presided over a council of ministers at Saint-Cloud. At midnight the ministers left the palace. 'It is war!' declared *Le Moniteur universel*. 'God save France!'[3]

Next morning, at Tromsoe, in Norway, on board his yacht the *Jérôme-Napoléon*, Prince Napoleon had the telegram which announced the declaration of war. Some time ago he had warned the Emperor that an unsuccessful war would mean the end of the dynasty. Now he showed the telegram to Renan, who was with him, and said: 'They're mad – but this is their final folly.'[4] He abandoned his expedition to Archangel, and sailed at once for France, and he landed at Calais within the week. On 28 July, with the Emperor and the Prince Imperial, a boy of fourteen, he left Saint-Cloud, to join the Rhine army headquarters at Metz.[5]

Eugénie had seen her husband and son to the train; she bade her son farewell, and exhorted him to do his duty. An eye-witness said that the Emperor answered: 'We shall all do our duty.' Then the train had left, and Eugénie had returned to Saint-Cloud to pray for France.[6] Clotilde was with her, pious as always, strong with moral courage. Mathilde was not there; and the Prince Imperial, who had visited Clotilde the previous evening, had not paid a visit to Saint-Gratien.

Mathilde had not wanted war with Prussia. Canrobert and Pelissier had told her of the appalling state of the French army, she saw the disorderly regiments entraining for the frontier, she knew of the urgent and unsatisfied demands for arms and clothing which reached the Ministry of War every day. At the Tuileries, she had found Eugénie urging the Emperor to assume command of the armies, so that MacMahon would take orders from him. Mathilde must have been astounded at Eugénie's arrogance and stupidity. The Emperor, with only book knowledge and the brief Italian campaign behind him, was being urged to command a Marshal of France. The Emperor, who was in such pain from gallstones that he was hardly able to sit his horse, was being forced to direct a campaign which needed the tactical genius of the great Napoleon in his prime.

Eugénie had urged her husband on; Mathilde had burst out in protest, and told her cousin, bluntly, that he was unfit to command. No doubt she warned him that he would lose both war and dynasty; and, very probably, aware of Eugénie's influence, her eagerness for this needless war, her apparent determination to lose it, her obstinate, deplorable thirst for glory, Mathilde had expressed all her latent and accumulated scorn. The Emperor, fatalistic as ever, left to command his army. It is probable that Eugénie forbade her son to go to Saint-Gratien, and that Mathilde refused to comfort her for encouraging predictable disaster.

Within two days of the Emperor's arrival at Metz, Eugénie had a letter in which he told her of the confusion and chaos, the lack of co-ordination and supplies. The first necessity of his strategy was to launch an attack across the Rhine – but now it was out of the question. On 2 August he announced a slight advance at Saarbrücken. On 6 August the armies of MacMahon and Frossard were beaten at Forbach and Froeschwiller. Soon after ten o'clock that night a telegram arrived at Saint-Cloud. It began: 'Our troops are in full retreat. Nothing must be thought of now except the defence of the capital.' At thirty-five minutes past twelve Eugénie sent a telegram to Mathilde: 'I have bad news from the Emperor. The army is in retreat. I am returning to Paris to call a cabinet meeting.'[7]

The council of ministers met at the Tuileries at three o'clock that morning. Émile Ollivier, who knew that his ministry was threatened, spoke in favour of a *coup-d'état*; Eugénie, who had most of the Ministers on her side, demanded the strictest collaboration between the Crown, the government and the Chambers. Ollivier insisted that the Emperor should return at once to Paris; Eugénie said that he must not come back under the shadow of defeat. She recalled Parliament for 9 August, and when, as expected, the government fell, she asked the Comte de Palikao to form a new Ministry. Palikao had led the successful Chinese expedition of 1860; he now submitted a drastic programme to put Paris in a state of preparedness, and obtained overwhelming support from the Chamber.

On 9 August Marshal Baraguay d'Hilliers, commanding the Paris army, resigned his post. Eugénie had tried in vain to dissuade him. Only Mathilde, who was a friend of his, might persuade him to stay. Eugénie summoned Mathilde to Paris. Two hours later, Mathilde was there. She drove to the Marshal's *hôtel* in the Place Vendôme. But Baraguay d'Hilliers was jealous of Palikao, who was now both Prime Minister and Minister for War; he had also been wounded by what he thought the Empress's lack of confidence in himself. No arguments could move him. Mathilde rose and faced him: 'You are a coward. You took advantage of the Empire as long as it prospered, and now that its luck has turned you desert it.'[8]

One Sunday, some years later, Baraguay d'Hilliers ventured to present himself in her salon. She looked him in the face, and said: 'Get out!' He tried to laugh off her injunction; but she rose and cut him short with an even clearer: 'Get out!'[9]

On 10 August 1870, the day after the Marshal's resignation, Edmond de Goncourt went to Saint-Gratien. It was a Wednesday, the day when Mathilde usually welcomed the elect. He found that she was in Paris, 'to be nearer the news'. Only the presence of Zeller prevented her from being alone with the servants. 'One can already feel emptiness spreading, very slowly, almost furtively, through the imperial household.'[10]

Gautier was not deserting her. It was from Saint-Gratien, two days later, that he wrote to Carlotta Grisi:

You couldn't imagine a more anxious, more enervating time. One is exhausted, unable to think, unable to work. For want of real news, the most absurd rumours, coming from God knows where, are spreading through the city and causing inconceivable panic and madness. I should never have thought such demoralization possible. All political parties are agitating, hoping to triumph in the disorder, and they're arguing as if the Prussians weren't marching on Paris ... I am rooted here – any absence would look like flight – waiting for events which no one can foresee. What does the future hold? At this very moment, perhaps, they're fighting and our destiny is being decided ...[11]

In Paris destiny had been anticipated: early that month the preparations for the Fête Napoléon had been cancelled, and the great imperial crown, hoisted to the top of the Arc de Triomphe, was brought down.[12]

All the blood that France possesses she will give; it will not flow in vain [Gautier told Carlotta, on 14 August]. That is why I'm staying here. And then I belong to the Emperor's household, and it would be a shabby deed to leave just at the moment when wretches and madmen are yelling for his fall . . .[13]

He offered to stay in Paris if his presence was a help or comfort to Mathilde. It was she herself who dissuaded him. 'I know your devotion, I rely on it, but it's no use here, and I'd be glad to see you go to Switzerland with your daughter . . . I need the security of knowing that those I love are safe.'[14]

On 31 August, Rear-admiral La Roncière Le Noury wrote indignantly to his wife that Mathilde was going to leave France. He was exasperated by such desertion.[15] Yet it is hard to know what other decision she could have taken. Prussian troops were now a few hours from Paris. At best, Mathilde might find herself in a beleaguered capital: detested by the populace, who blamed the Bonapartes for every defeat and humiliation. If – and it must have seemed certain, now – the dynasty should fall, if some domestic revolution occurred, Parisians would show no grace to the Imperial Family. It was less than eighty years since the executions of Louis xvi and Marie-Antoinette.

In fact, the rapid and disastrous course of the war, the sudden appalling glimpse of the future had left Mathilde in a state of stupefaction. On the last day of August, Goncourt found her dazed with fear. At the rue de Courcelles, the curtains had been taken down, as if for some grotesque, protracted holiday. Round the dinner table sat Eugène Giraud, Popelin, and Zeller who, an age ago, had been recommended as a history master; now the patronage of Sainte-Beuve, of Mathilde, had borne its latest fruits, and he was the new rector of the University of Strasbourg. Zeller's career alone symbolized the national disaster: the guests commiserated with each other on the bombardment of Strasbourg, and the burning of the priceless manuscripts.[16]

After dinner that night, Mathilde complained of the smell of tobacco, and all the smokers retired to the ante-room: all except Popelin, who installed himself in the centre of the salon, and blew smoke-rings, ostentatiously, from his cigar. Goncourt observed him with fastidious, deprecating eyes; he watched as Nieuwerkerke arrived, and Popelin greeted him. But palace revolutions suddenly seemed trivial. At that last Wednesday in the rue de Courcelles, there was only one thought, one preoccupation.

Three days later, on Saturday, 3 September, the news reached Paris. The Emperor, debilitated by gallstones and prostate trouble, worn by the fatigues and trials of the campaign, had surrendered with his army at Sedan.

On 4 September, the fall of the Empire and the Bonaparte dynasty was decreed, and the French Republic was proclaimed. At half-past three the tricolour was hauled down from the Pavillon de l'Horloge at the Tuileries. The street signs in the rue du Dix-Décembre were duly smashed, and someone replaced them by notice-boards hurriedly inscribed 'rue du Quatre-Septembre'.[17]

PART FOUR

The Second Exile

1870-71

⊰ 32 ⊱

On the evening of 3 September, on the insistence of her friends, Mathilde had left Paris. She was accompanied by Eugène Giraud, by Eugène Devaux, her *maître-d'hôtel*, and by his wife, Julie, who was her *femme de chambre*. A young lieutenant in the Garde Mobile, the Marquis Nicolas de Faletans, put Mathilde on the train, and he took advantage of his uniform to help her.[1] Popelin was not with her. A day or two earlier, he had taken his son, a child of eleven, to Puys, near Dieppe, where Dumas *fils* had a châlet; he had entrusted him to the Dumas family.[2]

Mathilde stopped at Rouen; she expected to spend the night there before she went to Dieppe, where Dumas *fils* had promised to find accommodation for her. At midnight (so she later told Gégé Primoli), Dumas *fils* had arrived to say that the republic had been declared, and that she should turn back at once towards Belgium. Some cases had been seized at Dieppe, and were thought to be hers, and this error might put people on the alert.[3]

It is hard to determine the truth of the episode of Dieppe. It is only certain that Popelin had left Gustave at Puys, and that he decided to join Mathilde.[4] Eighteen years later, in a distasteful passage in his diary, Gégé Primoli suggested that Popelin had joined her out of duty. 'P. considered their respective situations. He was still young, a widower, rich and good-looking, while the poor woman would be old in a few years' time . . .' (Popelin was in fact forty-five, and Mathilde was fifty.)

He understood, he confessed to me [Primoli continued], that, left to herself – she was so demented at seeing her family exiled, her house sacked [sic], her friends all scattered – she would be capable of anything. She was alone, there must be a man to control her: he resolved to be this man, the man who must devote himself to her, body and soul, and never leave her. He did not hesitate. He sacrificed his life, his independence, his museum [sic], his country and his son to her – and

he left with Her. She did not want it. 'Everyone,' he told me, 'understood the decision which I had imposed on myself, and everyone was
grateful to me.'[5]

It would be pleasant to think that Popelin had chosen, out of
love, to follow his mistress. Apart from the fact that he had left
Gustave in the care of the Dumas, it is hard to see what 'sacrifice'
he made at that moment of national turmoil. It is difficult to
believe that on the fall of the Empire, when the Prussians were
advancing towards Paris, he really paused to consider his prospects
of *un beau mariage*, the social liabilities of a middle-aged princess.

Whatever the reason which impelled him, Popelin seems to
have joined Mathilde at Dieppe. Gustave said, long afterwards,
that they had ordered a carriage and left for Gounod's villa; it
was in the composer's carriage (so he thought he'd been told)
that they drove to a local railway station, and caught the train for
Rouen. From Rouen they had made their way to Valenciennes
and Mons. Gustave's account was written fifty-six years after the
event.[6] Twelve years after the event, Popelin himself gave a
detailed statement to Edmond de Goncourt; but there is no confirmation for it, and it conflicts in places with his son's.[7] It also
differs from the account which Mathilde herself gave Primoli a
few days after her escape from France.

She crossed the frontier with only a trunk of linen between her,
her lady [in-waiting] and her *femmes de chambre* [sic], and she stopped
at the first Belgian town she came to: at Mons. She had no trouble
with the French authorities, as she had a Belgian passport and a Dutch
one which her cousin the Queen of the Netherlands had given her.
The pictures had been rolled up and were still in Paris, some of her
jewels had been sent to the bank in London, and the other things had
stayed at Saint-Gratien, exposed to the Prussians, and in the *hôtel* in
the rue de Courcelles where the Republic had affixed their seals. And
so there was not a word of truth in the infamous libel about the
73 trunks she was taking with her . . .[8]

It was a time for emotional and irrational speculation; and the
story of the trunks occupied the Press for some days. On Sunday,
4 September, so *La Vigie de Dieppe* assured its readers, a story had
spread like wildfire through the town: Mathilde had arrived in
Dieppe with forty or fifty million francs in boxes. The *Journal de
Rouen* put the sum at fifty-one million.[9] *The Times* recorded,
without question: 'Princess Mathilde, as you know, was arrested

on Sunday afternoon at Puys, near Dieppe, and her luggage, amounting to no less than 62 packages, was taken into custody.'[10] Next day the paper added that she had been released and taken to the frontier.[11] *L'Indépendance belge* explained that she had been arrested just as she was embarking for Newhaven, and that her sixty-two pieces of luggage were already on board the packet.[12] On 9 September it insisted that she had been arrested because her luggage contained the imperial correspondence which the Press had promised would be published. On the night of Saturday, 3 September, after the news of Sedan had reached the capital, this correspondence (the paper said) had been sent from the Tuileries to the rue de Courcelles. It was packed in crates which bore the address of one of her valets.[13] Small wonder that on 9 September Gautier wrote to his younger daughter from Paris: 'I still don't know for certain whether the good princess was arrested or not. I'm going to the *hôtel* to find out.'[14]

On 6 September, Dumas *fils* addressed himself to the editor of his local paper:

Sir,
I read in yesterday's *Journal de Rouen* that boxes belonging to Princess Mathilde, containing 51 million francs, had been seized at Dieppe.
For more than ten years I have had the honour of being received by Princess Mathilde; I have come to know her, and I can say this:
I do not know if the boxes which were seized did contain 51 million in gold or silver. I don't believe they did. People who have 51 million francs to send abroad aren't stupid enough to put them into boxes, because they know that no porter could carry luggage as heavy as that. But if the boxes . . . did contain anything that France could claim, I am sure that those boxes did not belong to Princess Mathilde. If the Princess has gone abroad, you can be sure, Sir, that she has left this country much, and that she has stolen nothing from it. Nobody who knew her well will not be prepared, as I am, to guarantee her loyal and disinterested conduct.[15]

The *Journal de Rouen* simply added: 'The day after the arrival of the luggage and the millions, another train, also from Dieppe, brought several other crates which had been among the Princess's luggage. These contained a number of very important pictures, which had vanished from the collections at the Louvre.'[16]

This time Dumas *fils* wrote to the *Vigie de Dieppe*:

Sir,

Would you kindly give me the hospitality of your columns? I want to finish with the ridiculous rumours once and for all . . .

The *Journal de Rouen* and various Paris papers have announced that Princess Mathilde was arrested at my house, at Puys, near Dieppe; that the authorities had seized luggage which contained enormous sums of money, diamonds, and pictures stolen from the Louvre. All this is completely untrue. Princess Mathilde did not come to Puys, she was never arrested; she left France by crossing the Belgian frontier. As for the luggage which was seized, it contained no gold or diamonds or valuables or pictures, and it did not belong to her.

I challenge anyone to prove the contrary.[17]

While the *Vigie de Dieppe* published Dumas' letter, the *Journal de Rouen* refused to withdraw its accusation. On 8 September Dumas *fils* wrote to the editor again:

If it is proved that Princess Mathilde took – or even wanted to take – anything whatever out of France . . . which has not long been known to be her own property, acquired with her own money, I ask to be accused with her as her accomplice. If the allegation is false, all I ask of your good faith, which has been imposed on, is that you should publish in your paper the pure and simple statement that you were ill informed.[18]

Dear friend [wrote Dumas *fils* to Popelin, soon afterwards],

You didn't say in your messages where and if one could write to you. Your letter to your son seemed to say that it was at Mons. At all events, I'm writing to you there. The Dieppe affair has created a hell of a fuss. Yesterday I was still said to be concealing eleven pearl necklaces of Princess Mathilde's. The *Journal de Rouen* said that she was carrying off 51 million francs just when the Prussians, etc. etc. . . . These personal items of news will give you an idea of what the public news must be . . . Greetings to Giraud, whose son arrived here the day before yesterday, all anxious because he had read that the Princess had been arrested. He left reassured. De Faltan [sic] has been here, too, having wrested from the Prefect of Police the order that whatever authorities detained the Princess, they should hand her over to him, and that he was entrusted with taking her to the frontier. A very nice boy, very ardent and very brave. There's the news. It was time I came back to Puys to reply to the libels and to [soothe] the anxieties of friends. I've written to Flaubert.[19]

Flaubert was not content with letters. He went next day to Puys to hear an exact account of events.

Princess [he wrote],

I think of you, continually. The anxieties which I know you feel become mine – and the idleness I languish in is unbearable!

[Popelin] writes to me this morning that you're regaining hope. Everyone's like you. It seems to me that the wind's about to change, people have more confidence.

You must be overwhelmed by everything that people round you are saying! – and for that, too, you have my deepest sympathy.

I spend my life waiting for news.

What heartens me is that nobody is thinking of Peace. If the Prussians get as far as Paris, it will be formidable. The whole of France will stand there. May she be annihilated rather than humbled. But we shall conquer them, and we shall force them back across the Rhine. The most peaceful bourgeois like myself are quite determined to be killed rather than submit.

Who would have said that, six months ago?

Whatever happens, another world will begin – and I feel too old to bow to new ways.

Now that I have recovered from the first shock, I feel more settled. I've even begun to work again – for otherwise I should have gone mad with rage.

Write to me when you have nothing better to do. I kiss your hands, and I am more than ever yours, Princess, more than ever yours.[20]

In Gégé Primoli's notebook, *Politique et Voyages, 1870,* he recorded, on 12 September, how he had gone to Belgium partly in the hope of finding Mathilde. To his great surprise and pleasure he heard that she was at Mons, an hour from Brussels, and he sent a telegram to Mme de Galbois at the Hôtel de la Couronne. The answer came immediately: an invitation to *déjeuner* next day.

Gégé and his mother were duly ushered into a little dining-room at the Hôtel de la Couronne, where they found Eugène, the faithful *maître-d'hôtel.* Soon afterwards Alexandrine, one of Mathilde's *femmes de chambre,* came to say that Madame would like to see Monsieur Joseph. She found it hard, noticed Gégé, to say 'Madame' instead of 'Her Imperial Highness'. He went up to room 21 on the second floor, and there he heard the familiar yapping of two little dogs, and there he found Mathilde. She was wearing deep mourning, and she was crying. She had, she said, foreseen everything; she had not shared the fanatical enthusiasm for the Ollivier government: she had known that the liberal régime would mean the end of the Empire. She had openly disapproved of the war and of the Prince Imperial's joining the army.

As she lamented Saint-Gratien, the furniture she had collected, piece by piece, her sunlit bedroom, her terrace, Gégé glanced round the hotel room with its narrow white bed. He saw that Mathilde had not brought her sheets, only a single pillowcase trimmed with lace. On the table where she usually dined were a few books: *La robe de Nessus*, by Amédée Achard, and *L'Ensorcelée*, by Barbey d'Aurevilly. There were a porphyry matchbox, some letters, and a pin-cushion in the shape of an imperial crown, which was sewn with pearls. By the delftware basin on the washstand stood an open dressing-case: the contents, made of gold and marked with her cypher, were spread out on a walnut dressing-table. There was a little jewel-case partly hidden under a shawl. Gégé was moved by the contrast between grandeur and crudity.

With all the ardour of his nineteen years, he offered to spend his life in her service. Mathilde was no doubt touched, but she refused the sacrifice. He and his mother begged her to come to Italy; but she had never been drawn to Belgirate, and Rome seemed too far away. Belgium was almost France, and she wanted to wait there, on the frontier, for the Siege of Paris to end.[21]

She wrote to the Emperor, and told him that she meant to visit him at Wilhelmshohe,[22] but it was less than a fortnight since Sedan, and he had no wish for emotional scenes. He said he was touched by her intention, but he preferred to remain alone with the people who shared his captivity. 'If the present conditions continue,' he added, 'then I hope I may count on your visit . . . The Empress is now in England, and I want her to stay there for some time.'[23] Mathilde considered his answer 'as cold as if he was still at the Tuileries'.[24]

33

She herself could have suffered no more agonizing hell than a second exile. She had been born in Trieste, in exile; she had spent her childhood in Rome and Florence, in Wurtemberg and Switzerland, in exile. Paris had always been to her, 'exiled from the cradle, the true Promised Land'. She had passed her early years longing to go home – to the home which she had never seen, but to which she was drawn by all her instincts as a Bonaparte. 'All my desires, all my ambitions, led me to live in Paris.' She had married Anatole Demidoff partly because he could take her to live in 'that marvellous Paris, the scene of the glory of the founder of our House'.[1] Paris had meant the Bonaparte legend, her uncle buried in the Invalides. Now it also meant the familiar brilliance of the Second Empire.

When she left France, she had always felt as if something closed inside her mind, as if some inner shutter was pulled down. 'I need Paris and its pavements,' she told Goncourt, 'I need the *quais* at night, with all those lights . . .'[2] There are cities which hold the heart and symbolize aspirations, cities which summarize the past and seem to command the future, cities which exercise a lifelong, essential spell. Paris had always been such a city to Mathilde. Now she knew that she could not return to it in the predictable future.

The angry legend of Dieppe had died away; she was not mentioned, now, in the Press. She lived, discreetly and wretchedly, in a country which she found 'so sad, so sombre, so monotonous, that one dies there twice over'.[3] She spent a few days at The Hague, with the faithful Sophie, who received her more affectionately than ever, but the Dutch fogs only intensified her misery.[4] On 9 October she wrote in despair to her niece Caroline Murat:

I feel so overwhelmed in every way that I haven't the courage or the desire to make any plans . . . I haven't had a single letter from the Empress; I don't know her address, and I don't know if she would care to hear from me. I sometimes have news of the Emperor . . .[5]

A few days later, from Wilhelmshohe, where he was in captivity, he wrote to her:

My dear Cousin,
      As I know you've paid a visit to the Queen of Holland, I'm writing to be remembered to you, and to ask you to give her my respects. She has always shown me such sympathy that I'm sure she will commiserate with me in my misfortunes.
      I'm very sorry I'm so far from Holland, for otherwise I'd have asked you to come here on your way back. But the journey is too long and the weather too bad for me to encourage you to come . . .[6]

Mathilde must have been hurt and angry when, soon afterwards, Eugénie visited the Emperor. 'If it hadn't been for my journey to Wilhelmshohe, I should have answered your letter earlier,' she told Mathilde on 9 November. 'The Emperor asked me to thank you for offering to go and see him, he hopes you'll do so later . . .'[7] Mathilde did not go.

      Eugénie herself had escaped from Paris, after the fall of the Empire, with the help of her American dentist; she had sailed from Deauville to Ryde on an English yacht, and had soon been reunited with her son. Towards the end of September she had found a house in Kent which seemed a suitable permanent residence: Camden Place, Chislehurst. A great many of *le tout Paris* had followed her across the Channel.

      The thought of some other Chislehurst, of some solid house near London, in which she could live in comfort, had tempted Mathilde; and Caroline Murat had been trying to find one for her. By mid-October she had discovered one that seemed to be suitable.

Tell me what furniture the house is let with [answered Mathilde]. Is it clean? Are there kitchen utensils? Linen? Plate? Is it completely furnished, or ought one to see to all that for oneself?
      I shall be coming to London on Sunday[s], that's why I'd prefer the outskirts, but quite near, so that I can come into town for trifles, as easily as I did from Saint-Gratien. I shan't leave Mons until 15 November, and I've made no plans. I'm beginning to get anxious about it. Get me all the news you can; no one here knows anything. I only get *L'Indépendance* [belge] . . .

Don't tell anyone of my plan, before I've quite decided about it.[8]

By the time that Caroline sent details of the house, Mathilde had quite decided against it. Paris was now besieged by the Prussians; at Mons she felt closer to Paris, nearer to events. She was too despondent to make the journey to England, she dreaded the Channel crossing, especially in winter. Perhaps, even now, she could not overcome her aversion for the country. 'My dear Caro,' she answered, 'Thank you for your kind information, but it isn't any use to me. I don't want to go away, and, when Metz has fallen, I'll be waiting for the fall of Paris.'[9]

She continued, no doubt, to read *L'Indépendance belge*, with its wretched news of France; and, heartrending as any comments on the Prussian campaign were the more personal items of news. The corps of the Cent-Gardes, that symbol of Imperial France, had been disbanded.[10] And, on 5 September, the first day after the fall of the Second Empire, the Government of National Defence had dismissed Nieuwerkerke from his remaining offices.[11]

The dismissal of M. de Nieuwerkerke [said *L'Indépendance belge*] has been noted with satisfaction in *Le Journal officiel*. He is said to be interned and even to be kept under supervision until he has accounted for the pictures which he may have lent to friends . . . It was apparently for the same reason that Princess Mathilde was prevented from leaving Le Havre [sic], as people supposed that she had joined in these ready liberalities.[12]

The flamboyant comet had run its course. A quarter of a century after he had installed Mathilde in the rue de Courcelles, Nieuwerkerke was to disappear from France. He sold his *hôtel* in the rue Murillo, which he had hardly lived in, to an American by the name of Riggs. He sold his superb collection of armour and weapons for four hundred thousand francs to Sir Richard Wallace, the natural son of Lord Hertford, and in time it became part of the Wallace Collection in London. And then, 'overcome by disgust of Paris and France, he went and pitched his tent beside one of the most picturesque lakes in Northern Italy'.[13] He lived at the Villa Gattajola, near Lucca, for the rest of his life.[14]

In the autumn of 1870, Nieuwerkerke was only a reminder of disillusion and disappointment; but there were others who gave

Mathilde constant comfort, who eagerly acknowledged their friendship for her. Flaubert wrote to her from Croisset, where he was daily expecting Prussian troops. 'My hope lies in the day when I shall be able to come and see you. It will be the first use I make of my freedom.'[15]

The habit of the rue de Courcelles and Saint-Gratien had been a comfort and an inspiration. Now, suddenly deprived of his custom, of the refreshing presence of Mathilde, Flaubert had become aware of his need for them. Popelin sent him an account of Mathilde, and of their life in exile at Mons; and, in his answer, Flaubert expressed his love for *ma princesse*, the loyalty that bound him closer to her than ever. 'Ah, my dear Popelin, how far away the rue de Courcelles seems! What a dream it is! What an enchanted memory! Today the house appears to me like Paradise on earth. How I envy you, and the others who are near her!'[16]

Flaubert's loyalty was known, his love was understood and returned. Popelin answered: 'I can't predict the end of the drama in which we play such a lamentable part. But this I know: one day we'll embrace one another with delight, & you will be near *her*, among the best and best beloved of the faithful.'[17]

Gautier, like Flaubert, had been stunned by events. His own way of life, established with such labour, had instantly been destroyed. From Switzerland, where he was staying at the time of Sedan, he wrote to his friend and ghost-writer, Adolphe Bazin: 'Poor Emperor! What a lamentable end to a dazzling dream! And my dear Princess! What inconsolable grief! There it is, destroyed for ever, the Abbey of Theleme of Saint-Gratien! Shut like a tomb, that gracious Decameron, where so many sparkling conversations have been held! Where is she now, that beautiful, good creature, so loved and so understanding?'[18]

Before this last catastrophe, Mathilde had insisted that Gautier went abroad with his daughter. He had obeyed her, and taken Estelle to stay with her aunt, Carlotta Grisi, who was spending the summer at Montreux; and there, by telegram, he had learned of the Emperor's surrender. At first he thought it a Prussian invention; he had rushed to Geneva, where the truth was confirmed. And there he had read in a paper that Mathilde had been arrested and was being held as a prisoner in the Hôtel d'Angleterre at Dieppe. 'I left immediately for Paris,' he told her, later, 'in the hope of being useful to you in some way, or showing you, at least, that there was someone who belonged to you. You can imagine I didn't believe a word of the stupid story about the thirty-six cases and the fifty-one millions. At the rue de Courcelles they told me that Your Highness was safe and well . . . Though I can't contribute anything to the defence, I shall share the danger with the others.'[19] Gautier was far from well, and prematurely old, but an irresistible patriotism, a personal devotion drew him home.

The devotion was returned: on 8 September, from Mons, Mathilde sent him one of the first letters of her exile.

The agony of August has ended in the death of all I loved, of all that gave enchantment to my life . . .

I congratulate myself that I begged you to go away. It is one care less for me to know you are in a safe place which you love . . .[20]

The letter was sent to Gautier in Switzerland, but after many detours it arrived at last, in September, at the rue de Beaune in Paris, where he and his two unmarried, ageing sisters awaited the Siege.

Dear Princess [he answered],

I was moved to tears by your kind letter. To think that in such a disaster you could remember your most humble servant, your obscure friend, since you are willing to give me the title which will always be the greatest of my glories: I am moved to the most secret depths of my soul . . .[21]

September turned into October. Paris was besieged, and Napoleon III remained a prisoner at Wilhelmshohe: by some enormous irony, the castle had been the home of Jerome de Montfort when he was briefly King of Westphalia. Some time in October the Emperor was visited by Dr Evans, the dentist who had helped the Empress in her hurried escape from Paris. On his way back to England Dr Evans stopped for a few hours in Brussels, where he met Mathilde at the Hôtel de Bellevue. She talked to him freely about events, and told him that she would go to see the Empress the moment that the weather became more settled.[22]

Meanwhile, she returned to Mons. Events had left their physical effect on her. Sometimes her teeth became so clenched that she found it difficult to speak. Sometimes she wept on the benches in public parks. Physically she was in Belgium, emotionally she remained in Paris: so fixedly in Paris that often she imagined that she was waking up in the rue de Courcelles.[23]

Some of her friends no doubt displayed an emotional sympathy which made her own emotions more acute, and kept her in a state of nervous exhaustion. At times it seemed as if Mathilde had forgotten her true nature. For the first time in her life, she had lost her moral courage, her natural dignity, her sense of proportion. She had forgotten, so it seemed, the mainspring of her being, the unforgettable, splendid and inalienable fact that she was the niece of Napoleon. Overwhelmed by the fall of the Second Empire, she had forgotten that she herself remained a Bonaparte.

There was one friend who remembered it. For all his social errors, Dumas *fils* understood her essential nature. He saw her as the princess whose bronze bust by Carpeaux gave an imperial touch to his study. At Puys, where he was daily watching the degeneration of his father, he had no time for useless lamentations. The letters arrived from Mathilde, in Mons, more and more self-pitying and despondent. His reply was practical; his letter of advice, addressed to Popelin, showed his own concern and admiration for her. It was also a splendid, astringent proof – if the proof were needed – that the dramatist who had written *L'Ami des femmes* understood the reality of women.

Dear friend,

I had a letter from the Princess yesterday, she was more disheartened than ever. I hope she will get over it soon. It would not be right with her rank or blood to let herself be defeated like this. The times are hard, the test severe, but if she compares her own private griefs with the public sorrows, with the bereavements of daughters, wives and mothers, she will see that she is still among the privileged. She hardly has a right to complain when there are so many lamentations which are so well justified. Of course I know that other people's griefs in no way lessen our own, and that our misfortune always seems to be the greatest misfortune in existence, but the Princess is not just anyone, and her everyday way of life . . . should not be abandoned, especially in exile. She has broken with some pleasant customs, which held her by every fibre of her being, but she had some purely intellectual habits, and it was these which gave her her real worth among all the artificial values around her. She loved work, I should like to see her go back to it as soon as possible.

If France is to be re-opened to her, many things must happen. First of all, it must be closed to the Prussians, and for the moment it is they who are closing France to the French. They are besieging Paris. Perhaps they will come and die there. One never knows what Paris will do. One never knows what's boiling at the bottom of the great stock-pot. Paris may lie down under the Prussian like a Dubarry, or she may fight him like a Joan of Arc. Whatever happens, when peace is signed we shall have to witness the drama of '93 revived by third-class actors. I hope it will only be theatre and that the guillotine will be made of painted cardboard, but anyway this will be the formula.

All this will take time. The Princess can't spend this time in lamentations, she would wear herself out to no purpose. For her own sake, for her peace of mind and her outward appearance – for after all she is a Bonaparte, the truest Bonaparte that now exists – I should like her to assume, here and now, the attitude which suits her best as regards the present moment and I might even say as regards the future.

Princes – especially when they pass through a crisis such as this – should not count on the indifference of history. Nor should they accept its disdain. Their conduct in reverses is the eternal currency which they stamp with their own image, and there is always a truthful historian to put it into circulation. The Princess has no joint liability with the other members of her family. She was not responsible for the *coup-d'état*, she did not surrender Sedan. She did not, like the Empress, advise France to go to war, indeed just the opposite; she has no pretender to bring up, and her brother's defection does not in any way reflect on her. She is alone, with a few devoted friends, an independent fortune, nothing to expiate in the past, nothing to conquer for the future. She has only the present to fight. In my opinion all her politics can be summed up in three words – simplicity – work – beneficence. I'd like it if all that could be said of her were that she has settled down as an ordinary private person in a town in Belgium or Holland, that she is copying a fine Van Dyck or a noble Rembrandt and that she is doing good – in other words, that she's continuing abroad what she did at home. I should see that as an immediate consolation for her, and if she assumed that position at once it would protect her when she wanted to come back to France. It is for you, her friends, to guide her insensibly in this direction. I don't know if Mons, the capital of coal, is really compatible with such a plan. I can understand that she avoids Brussels – but Antwerp – Bruges – The Hague are not inconvenient. There are museums there, and private collections of pictures, opportunities for study and work. In short the Princess was very occupied a few months, even a few days ago, occupied with other people much more than herself, today she is inactive and this increases her depression. If you in particular could interest her in your special art, that would be a great step forward. Not to mention the fact that you would also become an artist again.

Well, I'm telling you my first idea just as it comes, because I've had a disheartened letter and I'm looking for the cure. If I were there, I feel I could help you, unfortunately I can't be. My father's here, he's growing worse and worse, and he's now completely unbalanced. We are threatened with a last disaster, and I almost want it when I see there's no longer any hope of saving a mind which is already scattered to the winds. What is left when that has gone? Dumas without his mind! He no longer even remembers about himself. He is as gentle as a child, he sleeps, or he plays with hundred-sou pieces, and he won't allow you to take them away from him. Luckily I have some here. If I hadn't, he would simply be reduced to the hospital. He never provided for anything in his life!

Good-bye, take courage. This is the moment when everybody needs it . . .[24]

Mathilde herself remained desperate for assurance and affection. Early in November, after several weeks of enquiries, she discovered that Lebrun was in Antibes,

and I'm not losing a minute [she wrote] in telling you how fondly I'm attached to you, and how I'm suffering from this separation . . .

If I am to go on living, still to take an interest in life, I must be able to hope that I'll see my dear Saint-Gratien again. It's there that I'd like to find my friends again, and live in obscurity. God knows, I have no regrets whatever for the official position. My independence of character puts me above such mean considerations. But what I regret are my friends, my country, my home, and the surroundings in which I lived without ambition, and with a gusto which to me was life itself . . .[25]

In a postscript to this *cri de coeur*, Mathilde announced that she was leaving Mons: from 15 November, Lebrun could write to her, under cover of Mme de Galbois, at 11, rue d'Arlon, Brussels.

It was, so Popelin's son would recall, a small *hôtel* on the corner of a square, near the Gare du Luxembourg. On the first floor were the salon and Mathilde's private apartments. On the second floor lived Mme de Galbois and young Marie Abbatucci. Marie's father, Charles Abbatucci, had been deputy for Corsica; he had recently died, and Mathilde had adopted the girl as a lady-in-waiting, and made herself responsible for her future. Eugène Giraud and Popelin shared a large room overlooking the square, and on the opposite side of the landing was a room which had been converted into a studio. It was there that they all spent the afternoon until it was time for the daily outing. After dinner they congregated in the salon. They followed the same routine as at Saint-Gratien.[1]

Gégé Primoli found Brussels suburban.[2] Mathilde must have found it provincial beside the remembered splendours of Paris. In the rue d'Arlon, with only Mme de Galbois and Marie Abbatucci to attend her, with only Giraud and Popelin for company, she must have been overcome by longing for the rue de Courcelles. 'Without me she would have died in Brussels,' Popelin told Goncourt, some years later. And, in a confidential moment which revealed his own conceit and vulgarity, he explained: 'I invented a new distraction for her every day. I read her entertaining books for three hours at a time, until she fell asleep. I rubbed her where she felt a pain . . . In fact I was reader, masseur, chiropodist, agent, lover and husband. If I hadn't obliged her to stay somewhere, I don't know what would have happened to her.'[3]

But no attentions could distract Mathilde from her obsession. She could think of nothing but Paris. Since September, the city had been cut off from the world; only balloonists and carrier-pigeons, high above the cannon-fire, could try to bring news in and out. On the last day of October, Gautier had recorded that they were eating horses and donkeys, and they would soon be eating rats and mice. The plan seemed to be to take Paris by famine, for there had still been no serious attack, and the Prussians did not even answer the fire from the fortifications. The city was melancholy, the cafés shut at half-past ten, the shops did not even open during the day; gas was rationed, and at night the rare passers-by felt their way furtively down the dim streets. There was not a carriage to be heard.[4]

In Brussels, almost in solitude, Mathilde continued to wait for news of Paris. 'I go out very little and see few people,' she told Caroline Murat late in November. '. . . I see that the animosity of the early days [against the Bonapartes] has gone, . . . and though the errors may be grave and we pay for them cruelly, the memory of eighteen years' prosperity cannot be erased. It's all *her* fault, they say . . .'[5]

A few weeks earlier, Mathilde had told Dr Evans that she would go to England to see the Empress; now she had spent oppressive hours in speculation. She was convinced that the Empress was to blame for every disaster. It was the Empress's fault that the Emperor had fought, that the war was lost, that the dynasty had fallen, that they were all in exile again. Sophie of Holland believed it: late in December she told Mathilde that the Empress was accusing herself in public. She had summoned the editor of the *Morning Post*, and told him, weeping, that she had been the cause of the war.[6] Mathilde must have speculated endlessly on the different course that history might have taken. Had it not been for the abortive *coup-d'état* at Strasbourg, the overwhelming charms of life with Nieuwerkerke, she herself might have been the Emperor's wife, and the Empire might have been whole. 'Had I been Empress,' she would say to Caroline Murat, 'we should not have lost Alsace and Lorraine.'[7] In her memoirs there is a passage which Gégé Primoli marked: 'Unfair and wrong – to be burnt.' It was Mathilde's assessment of Eugénie.

I shall prove [she wrote] what has come to be my profound conviction, that she was the principal Cause of our misfortunes. She took eighteen years to destroy the Emperor, and she wore him out. This woman, who is called virtuous because she had no lovers, ruined the best and most generous of men, and our poor country with him. She undermined our Society by her excessive luxury, by setting the example of boundless coquetry, by constantly giving more importance to the outward appearance of men and things than she did to their essential qualities . . .[8]

Mathilde's only pleasure, now, was receiving news of the people she loved, 'and the people who love me a little in return. I was very proud of the affection I'd inspired in you,' she told Lebrun, late in November. And she added:

When all's said and done, you will do me this justice: there was a great desire to do good and to be generous. One day, I reproached the poor prisoner of Wilhelmshohe for being harder to his friends than he was to his enemies. He said to me: 'It's very simple, my friends' wrongs are the only ones that touch me.'
Poor man, how he suffers, and what ingratitude they repay him with![9]

In Paris, the year 1871 began with the hundred and fifth day of siege and the Prussian bombardment of the city.
For Mathilde, in Brussels, the agony was intense. In despair she sought moral support from Lebrun.

I'm writing so that you don't forget me. I am in such a state that I can't be seen, I'm so upset by the bombardment of Paris. All that we loved will be destroyed. What's the use of living, if life is just to be regret and hate? Will no one have the courage to call for peace?
What ridiculous patriotism is this, destroying everything in the name of liberty? . . .
They say that your South of France is calm and in favour of peace. Shall we have it soon? That is my most ardent, heartfelt wish. I'd like to be with you: I'm sure your wisdom would calm me. You know that I'm only moved by the public misfortune.[10]

This was quite true. Mathilde did not regret the fall of the Empire because she herself lost wealth and prestige. She certainly did not regret the trappings of imperial life: what Flaubert had called her *corvées souveraines*. She regretted bitterly and profoundly the fall of the Bonapartes, the dissolution of a dream, the failure to maintain the Napoleonic legend. She had always been the most ardent Bonaparte of her generation, she had cared about the dynasty with an absolute devotion which far transcended the Emperor's own feelings. The Emperor loved his wife and son, he had wasted emotional energy on innumerable mistresses;

Mathilde had always given her deepest loyalties to Napoleon I
and his heirs. The tragedy which had overcome the Bonapartes,
now, was final. She knew that there could be no restoration.[11]
She also knew that they need not have suffered this immense and
irretrievable disgrace.

Napoleon III had been weak and irresponsible; Mathilde, for
all her childish political prejudices, for all her feminine weaknesses,
had shown a sense of responsibility to France. She had been
wholly against the war. She urged the Emperor, even now, to
speak to the French people. 'My ideas are completely in accord-
ance with yours,' he answered her from Wilhelmshohe. 'I
believe it's time to speak to the nation, and not to leave the field
open to those who so shamelessly oppress our poor country . . .
When my manifesto appears, everyone must try to ensure that it's
distributed in France . . .'[12]

The Emperor's proclamation was circulated in France on 8
February, the day that France elected a new government. The
Emperor said he had been 'betrayed by fortune,' he insisted that
he was still 'the proper representative' of France, and that any
other government was illegal. His proclamation had little effect;
and, by an ironic turn of fate, Mathilde's old acquaintance,
Adolphe Thiers, now seventy-three, became the head of the
Executive.

Mathilde herself was more than a Bonaparte: she was a patriot.
She cared more for her country than for her dynasty, and she
would undoubtedly have relinquished her rank if that had been
the means of ensuring that she spent the rest of her life in France.
In January, on her behalf, Charles Giraud, the former minister,
and professor at the École de Droit, had approached Thiers about
her return. 'I find Princess Mathilde's application perfectly
legitimate,' Thiers replied. 'You may assure her that on her return
to France she will find the welcome which she found there before
and will always find there.'[13]

Mathilde did not simply need France; she needed Paris and,
above all, she needed Saint-Gratien. Husbands and lovers might
be inconstant, but she must be sure of her daily routine, her
unchanging décor, and her friends. What she wanted to see,
above all, were her green cretonne-covered chairs, and her
faithful guests installed in them: she needed, as she said, *mes
perses et mes amis.*

Some of her friends, she began to see, now, had only been time-serving; and among them, to her regret, was Viollet-le-Duc. Years ago, by her good grace, he had decorated Notre-Dame for the Emperor's wedding. He had become the Emperor's architect, he had restored Pierrefonds and, had the Empire lasted, he would probably have restored Beauvais Cathedral. He had enjoyed an exceptional position in her own *salon*, where he had circulated his artistic theories, and shown a singular licence in his behaviour. Even the liberal Mathilde had at times been shocked, but she had attributed his conduct to his domestic troubles (Mme Viollet-le-Duc was notoriously unfaithful). She had found it all the easier to condone his free behaviour since he had seemed to be enamoured of her, and she had come to be extremely fond of him.

It was now February 1871, and she had heard nothing of him since the fall of the Empire. She wrote to him, and his answer seems to have been the last letter in their correspondence.[14] Perhaps Mathilde recognized formality where she had hoped to find sympathy, moral support and affection. Certainly she could not forgive him when he later published hostile comments on the Emperor and the Empire. She came to understand that his protestations of love had only been a means of exploiting her. In time she would laugh at her own stupidity, and say gaily: 'But Viollet-le-Duc always profited from his wife's liaisons.'[15]

Other friends continued to show their touching understanding. Dumas *fils* sent her, for New Year's Day, all the flowers that he could find in Dieppe.[16] Vimercati wrote to assure her that the furniture in the rue de Courcelles had been taken to safety (the *hôtel* was partly used as a hospital).[17] Sophie of Holland, who shared Mathilde's indignation and sorrow at events, wrote: 'I am suffering so much that I can't read the papers. But I have seen a poem by Théophile Gautier which did me good: O *Scapin Charlemagne*.'[18] Scapin-Charlemagne: it was a perfect phrase for a scurrilous, histrionic German emperor, a would-be hero. 'They say Scapin-Charlemagne really wants to make his entry into Paris,' added Sophie, a few days later; and again: 'Scapin-Charlemagne will spend five days at the Tuileries . . . I hope they blow him sky-high!'[19] Sophie was more French than German, and more Bonapartist than the Bonapartes. Years earlier she had sent the Emperor some salutary warnings, and predicted the disastrous course of events. Her letters had been found at the Tuileries after 4 September.[20]

On 18 February, Flaubert wrote. Dumas *fils* had told him how Mathilde was longing to come back to Paris. The two of them had discussed this wild yet understandable longing; but 'his advice is right,' said Flaubert. 'Don't try to come back to Paris now, it would be unwise . . . Patience and courage! Perhaps, in a few months, we'll talk about it all at the rue de Courcelles.'[21]

On 26 February, Thiers signed the shameful peace with Bismarck. On 1 March the Prussians entered Paris. Next day, well aware that Mathilde might take the law into her hands, and recklessly come home, Dumas *fils* implored her to wait:

I'm back from Paris [he explained], I wanted to see – I've seen . . . I went through the most aristocratic and the most plebeian districts, for the moment you can't live in either. The scum are everywhere. Excitement, anger, vice, laziness, drunkenness, rancour, . . . ignorance and ineptitude at the bottom, powerlessness at the top. The vulgar herd, with all its traditional passions, is spreading over everything and covering the city like tainted oil. A Bonaparte, man or woman, however they behaved, would not only be insulted, but massacred, and a woman would run other risks as well. Nothing can give you an idea of this scum which is rising up from the very depths of society, . . . and showing all its old instincts, all the talons and teeth of '93 . . . If you want to keep the memory of Paris and the need to see it again, stay where you are. If you want to rid yourself of the idea for ever, without regrets and lamentations, go and spend forty-eight hours there, incognito, and look about you. You will take away such an impression of this heartrending spectacle that you won't even think about it again . . .

Show a little courage, Princess.[22]

Mathilde needed courage. Her return was still to be delayed. On 18 March, incensed by Thiers' capitulation to the Prussians, the Commune seized power in Paris, and French troops were obliged to begin a second, far more bitter siege of the city.

Next morning, Sunday, 19 March, Napoleon III left Wilhelmshohe, and set out to join his wife and son in England. Escorted by a German general, he caught the train for Belgium. At Giessen they learned of the insurrection in Paris. At every station, on that sombre Sunday afternoon, they saw the banners hung out to greet the returning German troops, and inscribed with the names of German victories: Wissemberg and Woerth, Sedan and Metz. As they approached the Belgian frontier, their wretchedness grew more and more profound.

At Herbesthal, the frontier station, Mathilde was waiting for them. She burst into the Emperor's carriage, and clung to him. A German subaltern who was present recorded that she was hysterical. The Emperor remained impassible.

General de Monts was no doubt relieved to escape the situation and to bid farewell to his former prisoner. Napoleon III continued his journey to Verviers and Dover; and Mathilde returned to exile in Brussels.[23]

She was clearly on the verge of collapse. She was nearing her fifty-first birthday, and no doubt she felt the tensions of her age. In the last few years her private life had radically changed; and, though she was devoted to Popelin, she could not forget his precursor. Her family had been deposed and exiled, Paris and the rue de Courcelles were threatened with destruction, and she did not know if she would see Saint-Gratien again. It seemed as if all the foundations of her life had collapsed.

Late in March her exile was soothed by the renewal of friendship. Gautier's son arrived from London, and settled in the Place de la Couronne with his mother Eugénie Fort, his wife Élise and their infant son. On 25 March, Mme Fort went out to post a letter, and 'a few yards from the house,' she noted in her diary, 'I recognized Monsieur Popelin, whom I had seen at Neuilly, he was escorting a woman and coming towards No. 17. I came back to receive Princess Mathilde, who was amiable and gracious.'[24] Toto Gautier and his wife spent the following evening with Mathilde, and early next morning Élise burst into Mme Fort's room to announce 'that the Princess had asked to be godmother to Paul. She is very pleased,' noted Mme Fort. 'The godfather ought to be one of the two grandfathers. TG, of course.'[25]

Gautier himself had been driven by the Commune to Versailles, which was now the virtual capital of France. The thought of fratricidal war, of Frenchman fighting Frenchman, remained the most heartrending thought of all; to Mathilde it seemed the final humiliation. During the Siege she had wanted to stay in Belgium, because it seemed a reflection of France, because it was near Paris. Now she wanted to go to Italy, to escape the agony. As she had done more than once, in moments of profound depression, she unburdened herself to Lebrun.

What disturbs me is the cowardice, the atony of honest men and women, the defection I see everywhere, the utter lack of energy and courage! . . .
There isn't a prince who dares to present himself, to sacrifice himself, if need be, to save France! Where are the hearts of long ago, the spirit of the past, the love of country? There's nothing, nothing! Everything is crumbling. I'd like to go to Italy, I want to get away from it all. I'm wearing myself out with misery, waiting and hoping.[26]

Sometimes, after nine months of waiting, she could hardly bring herself to wait any longer. Once she told Marie Abbatucci to take a cab in secret and go and find out the times of the Paris trains. Only after two or three postponements did she finally decide not to set foot in Communard Paris.[27]

The only sense of security, the only alleviation of grief, came, now, from the correspondence and visits of friends. One new arrival in April was Gautier's friend and occasional ghost-writer, Olivier de Gourjault, who hastened to pay his respects to Mathilde. She welcomed him with her usual kindness.

She had just received a letter from Monsieur Soulié [Gourjault wrote to Gautier], saying that you were . . . weary after all the tribulations . . . I added, for my part, that among the privations which you had been unable to accept, that of no longer seeing her was the most painful and the most keenly felt. I told her about the conversations we had often had with you in the sinister days of the Siege. She instructed me to tell you how wrong you were not to come and instal yourself with her, your room was waiting for you, she asked me to say that she was surprised not to have seen you, etc., etc. In fact you are waited for, and hoped for . . .
Since Estelle is at Geneva, nothing prevents you from coming and settling here for a while.[28]

Next day Toto Gautier added his persuasion:

Dear father,
You should have received a letter from O. de Gourjault yesterday, telling you of his conversation with a Lady of your acquaintance, who would dearly like to see you in Brussels. You know that she means what she says, and that when she speaks you have only to obey her.

I suppose you must be worried about the question of money, if not for the journey, at least about what you must leave with the aunts; I have thought about it, too, and I've been to see Bérardi, the editor of *L'Indépendance* [*belge*]. Though literature is not in fashion at the moment, he received me very kindly, and I think that, if you talked to him, something would be contrived, so that you could send money from here to Versailles . . .

You would find many acquaintances here, and a good many hand-shakes are waiting for you. The aforementioned lady wants to be godmother to my baby, and, according to custom, you should be godfather; you would do well to learn your *credo* on the way . . .[29]

Gautier did not come at once. It was not lack of devotion that kept him from Brussels: it was physical and emotional exhaustion. But his son was far from tolerant of his absence.

Dear father [he wrote on 2 May],

Thanks to my connections, I have at last learned roughly what has happened to you, and I see with regret that you cannot spare a few days to come to Brussels, not for me, but for the Princess, who has offered you hospitality. All her old and loyal friends have written to her, and many have come *especially* to see her; you alone, who were one of the most favoured, have not come. However constantly she loves you, there will always be a cloud in her memory, after negligence like this, and I myself have come to be embarrassed about her. Besides, she wanted you to be godparent, with her, to my baby, and your absence will prevent this plan from being realized . . .

Greetings to all the friends of mine you see at Versailles, especially Soulié, thanks to whom the Princess and I occasionally have news of you . . .[30]

On 10 May, the Treaty of Frankfurt was signed, and the Franco-Prussian War was officially over. On 12 May Charles Giraud wrote from Versailles that he had twice mentioned Mathilde's return to 'the person concerned'. Thiers had listened attentively, even with affection. He wanted Mathilde to know that when the moment came 'she would find in him, once again, the friend of 1846'.[31]

On 17 May, Popelin arrived in Versailles; he had come for a warrant for Mathilde to use some of the rooms and furniture at Saint-Gratien.[32] Gustave Popelin, who had at last been brought from Puys to Brussels, remembered that one afternoon a messenger arrived at the rue d'Arlon. He had been sent by

H

William I – now Emperor of Germany – to assure Mathilde that she need not worry about Saint-Gratien. The Pavillon de Catinat would still be occupied, but the château itself would be evacuated.[33]

On 24 May, three days before Mathilde's birthday, there came the ultimate, most hideous disaster: the Communards set fire to Paris. It was in this nightmare, at Versailles, that Gautier wrote Mathilde her birthday sonnet.

> Paris brûle, la flamme à l'horizon s'élève;
> Cependant mai revient, mai rose et parfumé,
> Ramenant avec lui l'anniversaire aimé,
> Date chère où revit incessamment mon rêve.
>
> Le sang coule! . . . aux bourgeons monte la jeune sève,
> Et l'azur luit au ciel par la poudre enfumé;
> Les oiseaux ont repris leur chant accoutumé,
> Comme si le canon ne tonnait pas sans trêve.
>
> Et moi, je pense à vous à travers ma douleur;
> Saint-Gratien m'apparaît aux bosquets de Versailles:
> Du souvenir sacré rien ne distrait mon coeur.
>
> Mais mon humble jardin, dont croulent les murailles,
> N'a rien à vous offrir, tout criblé de mitrailles,
> Dans un éclat d'obus que cette pauvre fleur.[34]

On 28 May, after four days of fierce and wanton destruction, the Commune was overthrown, and Paris was free. On 16 June, Eugénie Fort wrote in her diary: 'TG leaves to-morrow for Brussels.'[35]

When Gautier reached Brussels, Mathilde had already gone. She had taken the Paris train and arrived, incognito, at the Gare du Nord.[36]

PART FIVE

The Third Republic

1871–1904

35

There was no carriage to take her home, and there was no cab to hire: all the horses had been slaughtered for food during the Siege of Paris. With her *femme de chambre*, the faithful Julie, stumbling behind her, Mathilde made her way on foot through the strangely silent, devastated city. Their footsteps rang on the broken roads as they passed the ruins of the Tuileries. There was a hole in the centre of the Place Vendôme, where the Column had recently been pulled down.

When they reached the rue de Courcelles, they sat down on a bench, exhausted. It was hot, and the air was dusty from the débris; Mathilde was thirsty, but she did not dare to enter a shop, and Julie went to fetch her a glass of gooseberry syrup from a wine-merchant's nearby.[1] Mathilde was grateful to see the façade of her *hôtel* intact, and yet she must have reflected bitterly on the ingratitude of some of her friends. It was a former guest at the rue de Courcelles who now, as a republican official, decided that the *hôtel* must remain closed.

She informed Thiers of her return. 'I think,' she wrote, 'that my past history should be a guarantee of my future behaviour. But as I don't want my conduct to be misinterpreted, through error or through malice, let me say now that I wish to keep clear of any intrigue and to remain outside politics. I feel sure that this frank statement will not leave the slightest doubt about the firm resolve I have taken.'[2]

Thiers had always respected Mathilde. 'Very dear Princess,' he had written, thirteen years ago, 'you know my old and constant affection for you, and you will see that time and difference of position haven't changed it.'[3] Now he accepted her *fait accompli*, and authorized her to take back the furniture which had been sequestered. Some of it was put into the small *hôtel* in the rue de Berry which her cousin, Princess Augusta, had sub-let to her.

As soon as her affairs in Paris were settled, she left for Saint-Gratien.

'You don't know what St Gratien is,' Gégé Primoli had said. 'Every tree reminds her of a moment in her life . . . It was there that she scattered her happiness around her. Is it not there, and there alone, that she should find it again?'[4]

The château was intact, but the Pavillon de Catinat was still occupied, and Mathilde could hardly conceal her anger at the sight of German soldiers passing her gates, and German ambulances lined up in the drive. Some of the summer-houses in the park were damaged, and much of the lawn had been trampled into mud. The boathouse by Lake Enghien had been burnt to the ground. Only the foundations remained; they stayed there for a long time, as a memorial to the enemy occupation.[5]

That evening the German headquarters staff asked to pay their respects. Mathilde received them, dressed in black. She acknowledged their civility, and withdrew.

She wrote immediately to Hébert, and told him that his room was waiting for him. He would have liked to come at once, to see her again 'in the corner of the earth you love the best, the only one where you feel happy'.[6] For the moment he had to stay in Rome. But Edmond de Goncourt arrived on 1 July. Mathilde grasped his hand, and drew him out into the familiar park, and began to talk about herself, and about her exile. He felt that she would have given up her title, any chance of the restoration of the Empire, in exchange for permission to live at home. They had a bourgeois dinner that evening, with Popelin, Giraud, Mme de Galbois, and Marie Abbatucci (Goncourt thought her childlike and charming).[7]

On 17 August, at Saint-Gratien, Goncourt met Gautier for the first time since the Siege. He found him serene and melancholy as ever. Mathilde herself watched him anxiously:

His health had been much worsened by the emotions and the countless privations he had suffered. I found him very weak; he walked with difficulty, and slept little, and he was often breathless. I was terrified by the progress of his heart trouble. His wit was still enchanting, he still shone through a cloud of melancholy which made him all the more endearing. His physical strength abandoned him. But he came nearly every week to spend a few days in the country with me. The sight of his suffering made him dearer to me. I was touched by his unchangeable serenity.[8]

Other friends were returning, too: Sacy, Augier and Octave Feuillet, who had been a protégé of the Tuileries. Lebrun, who had been such a solid comfort in the days of exile, called to find that Mathilde was not at home, but 'I expect you'll come and invite yourself to lunch or dinner when you go to the Institut,' she wrote. 'Promise me you will.'[9]

Mathilde was happy to see her friends reuniting round her, but she could not yet be sure of happiness. How long would they still see one another? Anxiety and uncertainty underlay everything. 'It is brave and good of her to come back,' George Sand wrote to Flaubert, 'at the risk of fresh upheavals.'[10] And in her round and generous hand George Sand wrote to Mathilde:

Madame,

I was very touched and proud to hear from my dear Flaubert that you sometimes think of me and ask for my news. I was worried when I heard that you'd come back to this troubled, unhappy country, which, alas! one loves none the less – this country where you surely have the right to continue to do good, since you have never done anything but that. Flaubert doesn't say where you are now – but, wherever you are, be sure that my thoughts are with you and my heart belongs to you.[11]

Mathilde was warmed by the warmth of George Sand, and wrote to her, freely, of her depression. George Sand answered from Nohant:

You speak of bad days, of the general atrophy, of a nation which wants to live and no longer knows which medicine to swallow. Yet these things are not so hard for those of us who work. You're a great artist, and art seems healthier than one could have hoped. Perhaps it will play a large part in our lives, a part which politics could not assume . . . Let us be artists, and work on for our moral resurrection.

You are always a good and beautiful star in my sky, and, wherever you are, you give light.[12]

In July 1871, in the studio at Saint-Gratien, Mathilde tried to soothe herself at her easel. Work, as she had told Sainte-Beuve, had always been her refuge from the harshness of life.[13] But it was only a month since the end of her exile, and her hand had not regained its assurance. Her thoughts were still disturbed.

Goncourt, visiting the château in mid August, found her still in a state of great irresolution; and for a woman of such decisive nature, such strong will, this uncertainty was almost painful. At the end of August, he stayed a night at Saint-Gratien, and found that the character of the place had changed. The conversation dragged, and there were awkward silences. There was so much which a tactful man was obliged not to discuss; and then Mathilde no longer had her old freedom of speech, she could no longer allow herself her brutal, trenchant comments, her eloquent outbursts, her original portraits of contemporaries. She was forced to restrain herself; and, sitting beside her, he sometimes felt, from a sudden physical reaction, that her indignation was rising, and ready to explode. And then, at once, she closed her eyes and seemed to lull her anger asleep.[14]

A few months earlier, when he was discussing Mathilde with Lavoix, Goncourt had deplored the fact that a woman of such distinction should have been susceptible to Popelin, that she should have compromised what remained of a noble life. It was the presence of Popelin in the rue d'Arlon which had prevented them from going to Brussels. His vulgarity embarrassed and angered them.[15]

Now, at Saint-Gratien, the aura of exile had grown pale, the idealism of absence had disappeared. Goncourt became aware that Mathilde was a fallible human being. As for Popelin, he seemed morose, despite the grandeur of his leading rôle; perhaps, at times, he found himself opposing a certain narrowness of mind, a certain stubborn, imperial and aggressive prejudice. Goncourt himself was influenced by the general sobriety and apprehension. As he strolled round the park that Sunday morning, he suddenly heard the clink of spurs, and came across a German officer.[16]

When Goncourt returned to Saint-Gratien, late in October, they discussed the Exhibition of 1867, and that gathering of all the kings who should have prevented disaster. Mathilde burst out:

Oh, there was only one sovereign who wanted to, who really wanted to, the Emperor of Russia. And I'm sure of that. The day of the gala dinner, the Russian Grand-Duchess came to me and said that the Emperor wanted to talk to my cousin before dinner, she asked me to let him know. I told her it was perfectly simple, and I went to find the Emperor. He came at once, and they began their tête-à-tête in a little salon. Then the Empress came in unexpectedly, and it all miscarried. I saw the Emperor leave the room at once, with a face as long as that![17]

Perhaps, for Mathilde, there still remained more personal regrets. On this visit, at the end of October, Goncourt slept 'in the huge bed which had once belonged to the huge Nieuwerkerke'. Until then the bed and the bedroom had been respected as those 'of a dead but unforgotten man. Today, it seems, they're given to the first comer'.[18] Mathilde had found it hard to discard this episode of the past. Now she was being practical, and perhaps she was glad to publicize her indifference. But the indifference may not have been complete.

'Your peaceful retreat is no longer saddened by the presence of the Prussians', Lebrun wrote in October. 'I have been thinking with delight of the moment when you ceased to be a prisoner, with those sentries at the gate of your park . . . What are your plans for the winter?'[19] Mathilde had planned to leave Saint-Gratien for Paris as soon as the winter weather began. She was to live at 18, rue de Berry, 'a dreadful little hole which Augusta had rented and which,' she told Lebrun in November, 'she has not been able to sub-let until now. Once upon a time I longed to be *home* again. I am profoundly sad that I can no longer be there, but in spite of that I do not and will not complain.'[20]

There was a poignant contrast between 24, rue de Courcelles and 18, rue de Berry. 'This apartment would be very fine for us,' Silvestre de Sacy told his daughter, 'but it seems very small and very mean for her . . . It is impossible not to be moved by this change of scene.'[21]

Edmond de Goncourt noticed a deeper and more regrettable change. The stars in the Mathildian sky were paling. As the new year opened, he lamented that there were no more intellectuals in her salon, just a flock of young girls, whom she rightly called her *minxes*. Only Gautier, tired and wan, roused himself at long intervals, and cast a firecracker into the waste of vapid femininity.[22]

In May, in the château on the shores of Lake Enghien, Gautier presented Émile Bergerat, his future son-in-law, to Mathilde.

Bergerat, a struggling young journalist of twenty-seven,

H*

arrived in a tailcoat borrowed from Armand Silvestre, a minor
Parnassian poet, and a white tie which had been given him by
Théodore Barrière, co-author of *La Vie de Bohème*. Mathilde
looked at Bergerat 'as her Uncle might have assessed a confidential messenger on a battlefield'. Then she gave him her hand to
kiss. He was terrified: the guests who arrived for dinner were so
distinguished 'that their very names, announced by the butler at
the door, gave me cramp in the calves of my legs'. [23]

Mathilde's account of Bergerat made Flaubert laugh aloud: he
said it had touches worthy of Saint-Simon.[24] Bergerat fell,
predictably, under the spell of Mathilde. 'She is the most interesting figure of the Second Empire, and whoever writes her life
will write the romance of that singular adventure.'[25]

It was Bergerat who recorded the evening in 1872 when
Gautier went to Saint-Gratien for almost the last time.

In that intellectual, sympathetic atmosphere, the peerless talker gave
himself entirely, just as certain flowers only give the essence of their
fragrance in a conservatory.

That evening [at Saint-Gratien], he shed the final perfumes of a
soul which would soon return to the garden of the gods.[26]

When he could no longer go to see her, he wrote in hope that
Mathilde did not forget him. 'No, I do not forget you,' she
answered. 'No one has taken your place . . . I love you with all
my heart, and my heart has not yet grown old.'[27]

Long ago, before the fall of the Empire, determined to take
care of him, she had sent her doctor to examine him. Le Helloco
had confirmed the weakness of Gautier's heart.[28] Mathilde had
no illusions, now, about his condition. When he could no longer
bear shoes on his swollen feet, she sent him a Persian carpet; and,
day after day, she came to sit with him until evening fell.
Gautier's republican friend, the writer Maurice Dreyfous, often
found her in the little house at Neuilly; and 'she seemed so good-
natured, so simply – forgive the expression – one of the family,
that I, who was one of the family, too, talked to her as if she was
a good friend'.[29]

On 22 October, Mathilde was told that Gautier was growing
worse and wanted to see her. 'I hastened to him,' she remembered.
'I found him dying, speechless, almost without breath. I grasped
his hand, and he returned the pressure.'[30]

He died next morning, in his sleep; and Renan wrote: 'Your Highness's friendship will have been the delight and recompense of a life which was otherwise so ill rewarded.'[31] Lebrun thought likewise. 'I deeply regret that Gautier should have died without the literary honours which he so well deserved. You did at least mitigate his ill fortune as much as you could, Princess. You gave him a charming sinecure, and you brought him closer to yourself: to a place where all the world might envy him.'[32]

ఎ 36 ఎ

In 1872 Mathilde left 18, rue de Berry and moved to a larger *hôtel*, no. 20 in the same street. She finally bought this *hôtel* in September 1879. Her civil list pension of five hundred thousand francs had ended with the Empire, and she was now entirely dependent on the annual allowance which the Demidoffs continued to make her. Yet two hundred thousand francs a year remained an imperial income; and while it may have seemed to Mathilde herself a noticeable restriction, it still enabled her to maintain Saint-Gratien and her new and handsome *hôtel* (today the Belgian Embassy) in Paris. 'As I haven't got a palace, I wanted to deck out a nest,' she explained to Gégé Primoli. At 20, rue de Berry, she re-created her décor, and resumed her famous receptions.

No one who went to the rue de Berry could doubt that they were visiting Mathilde. In the hall, where the walls were hung with red, stood marble busts of Napoleon III and Eugénie.[1] Through the door on the right one entered a sort of gallery formed by two consecutive salons. In the first, on pedestals, stood busts of Jerome de Montfort, Queen Hortense, and the Empress Josephine; on the white marble mantelpiece was a bust of Madame Mère, and, beside it, the triumphant bust of Mathilde by Carpeaux. In the second salon, which was divided by curtains from the first, was a big round table with a red silk cloth. Here, in immutable order, were the illustrated papers, the reviews, the books which had recently been presented, and the knick-knacks which Mathilde liked to toy with: her scent-bottles, her sweetmeat-boxes, and the work-basket which had belonged to her mother. It was here, at the end of a cherry-coloured sofa, that she used to sit, with her semicircle of intimates on her left, and chairs on the right for her visitors. On the walls, which were uniformly hung with red damask, the pictures almost touched one another; and from the dull gold frames there glowed the pale faces of princesses and kings.

In a third salon, which was parallel to the first two, there hung the Reynolds portrait of a woman which Mathilde bequeathed to the Louvre. This salon led into a huge room, some thirty feet wide and sixty feet long, which was roofed with glass. Four palm trees, growing in capacious oriental copper basins, gave it the appearance of a conservatory. Round the edge of the room, on console-tables, were superb Sèvres vases, and candelabra clustered with candles. Water-colour portraits were scattered on occasional tables, and displayed on miniature easels. A grand piano, and music-stands ornamented with gilt eagles, recalled the presence of Notre Dame des Arts. In the centre of the salon, on a tall grey marble column, like the genius of the place, the deity of the temple, stood the bronze statue of Napoleon.

This huge and bewildering salon led to the dining-room, which was lit from above, and could seat over twenty guests. The tapestries on the walls had been woven, on the orders of Pope Leo x, in the workrooms of Van Aalst: a riot of cherubs disported themselves, on golden yellow grounds, among garlands of fruit and flowers, brilliant birds and curious animals. Round the borders were crowns and feathers, the insignia of the Medici. At one end of the room stood a silver statue of the young Bonaparte at Brienne. In the middle of the table brooded a large golden eagle with half-folded wings.

On 9 January 1873, a telegram arrived from Pietri at Chislehurst. 'I regret to inform you that the Emperor died this morning.'[2]

The news was not unexpected. The Emperor was only sixty-four, but he had been in deplorable health for some years. Ever since he had gone into exile, he had been planning his return; now he had died – not like a Bonaparte, but like a common mortal, after an operation on his bladder. And, by the ultimate irony, he had died in England.

For the first time in more than thirty years, Mathilde brought herself to cross the Channel, to set foot in the country of Hudson Lowe. On her last visit she had come as Mathilde de Montfort, and met the sympathetic Thiers in London.[3] Now the bourgeois monarchy had gone, the Second Empire had come and gone, and Thiers was first President of the Third Republic. Mathilde must have felt great bitterness when, on 15 January, at St Mary's Church, Chislehurst, she attended her cousin's funeral.[4]

She was still not drawn to the Empress: 'the Spanish woman,' she called her – or, more briefly, *Elle*. Their incompatible characters had always kept them apart, and she still blamed Eugénie for the events of 1870. On 5 May, Sophie of Holland wrote to her, recalling that it was the anniversary of the great Napoleon's death, and the birthday of the Empress Eugénie: 'a day which is doubly disastrous for France'.[5] Mathilde must have agreed with all her heart.

And yet, whatever her instincts dictated, her duty impelled her to try to understand the Emperor's widow, to come closer to her in her loneliness. This was no moment to increase or publish family dissension. Plon-Plon was behaving despicably. He was fifty-one, impelled by ambition and years of frustration; he could not envisage the government of a nephew who had not even reached his majority. 'Napoleon is getting more and more beyond himself,' Mathilde wrote in March 1874. 'He has had an article published about the Prince's coming-of-age. It says, outright, that, until he's twenty-one, his nephew is only a schoolboy, while he himself is a man.'[6]

Mathilde must have watched political manoeuvres with distaste, and often with disdain. In the past few years she had learned how much the affection and loyalty of others depended on political success, on the vicissitudes of power. Girardin, who had once assured her of his respectful adoration, was now urging a rapprochement between France and Germany, and he was still disgustingly offensive about the Empire.[7] Saint-Victor, the critic, had once cultivated her friendship, but his feelings had changed since 1870. Perhaps he had never really been fond of her; perhaps, quite unjustly, he condemned her, as he condemned her cousin, for Sedan. In January 1875, Mathilde went to visit Goncourt, who was recovering from a long illness; her visit happened to coincide with that of Saint-Victor, who assumed that the meeting had been arranged. He left at once.[8]

Mathilde knew now, in the early months of 1874, why the visitors thronged to the rue de Berry. In 1873, Thiers had been removed from power by a coalition of the monarchist and conservative parties. Marshal MacMahon became the new President, but he represented no particular party. The Comte de

Chambord, the Legitimist claimant to the throne of France, had lost his chance of reigning because he refused to accept the tricolour flag instead of the white flag of the Bourbons ('I can easily console myself for that,' Mathilde had said, 'because the régime would have been too contrary to my instincts, and I should have gone back into exile').[9] The Orleanists were divided and powerless. The Prince Imperial was on the eve of his eighteenth birthday, his official majority; if he could only unite and lead his partisans, if he could gain and keep Prince Napoleon's support, he had a chance of regaining the throne. 'The Imperial régime has an excellent chance of being restored,' wrote Popelin. 'This [is announced] by an influx of new faces or rather old ones in the Salon . . .'[10]

Mathilde had sworn not to interfere in politics, and her presence in Republican France depended on her keeping her word. But while she received both Republicans and Bonapartists at the rue de Berry, she could not pretend to be impartial. On the eve of the Prince Imperial's birthday, she gave a dinner in his honour; on his birthday, 16 March, she gave a second dinner, and Popelin recorded that she 'made a little speech, the gist of which was as follows: "I drink a toast to the Prince whose majority makes him today the unique leader of us all. May our wishes soon bring him back among us and realize all our hopes." '[11] There could have been no clearer statement of her aspirations.

In her correspondence with the Prince, she recognized his title of pretender by addressing him with the formal *vous*. He asked her to return to their familiar ways. Mathilde, ever anxious to keep the family together, visited him and his mother at Arenenberg. Eugénie had assembled a house-party there after the celebration of his majority.

It was now nearly forty years since Mathilde had been to Arenenberg. She had left it as a girl, taking with her the turquoise forget-me-not ring, the symbol of her engagement to Louis-Napoleon. Now she returned, the only survivor, to the scene of that distant idyll. Instead of Hortense, animated and charming, exchanging confidences in her pink-and-white bedroom, there was the pale Eugénie in widow's weeds; instead of Louis-Napoleon there was his son, still dreaming of a Bonaparte restoration.

During the last few years, since Mathilde returned from exile, the décor of her life had been changing. In May 1873 had come the death of Lebrun, who had been her friend for a quarter of a century. Dumas *fils* was elected to Lebrun's Chair at the Académie, and Mathilde went to see his reception, to hear one loyal friend praise another. But Dumas was not, now, uncontested as the pre-eminent dramatist in her *salon:* Goncourt observed Victorien Sardou, the author of *Nos Intimes* and *La Famille Benoîton*, one day to be the author of Sarah Bernhardt's *Fédora*, and the *Tosca* which would inspire Puccini.

Augier and Labiche, Pailleron, Sardou and Dumas *fils:* this group of dramatists formed the basis of the *salon* in the mid 1870s. 'Dumas dined with the Princess yesterday,' Popelin once reported. 'It was the return of a prodigal son. . . I thought for a moment that Flaubert was going to knock the table over, he and Dumas almost came to blows over *le père Hugo*. Happily the Divinities which guard the hearth intervened, and all's well that ends well.'[12] Émile Augier, who had been a leader of the *école du bon sens*, delighted in discussing the theatre with a princess who shared his bourgeois principles.[13] Mathilde thought that Augier looked like a combination of François 1 and Henri IV, and she liked his opinions and his constancy. 'There is something frank and solid about him,' she wrote, when she drew his portrait, 'his wit is ever present and very responsive, he is full of bourgeois good sense . . . He is lazy by nature. Perhaps this is wise, because he doesn't want to outlive his celebrity. He has produced a good deal, and knows where to stop. He is a good friend, without ambition.'[14]

In 1876, she published an essay on Didi, one of her dogs, which had recently died; she sent a copy to Augier. He wrote a gallant letter of thanks to his literary colleague. 'Madame, it is full of grace, humour and kindness; it has the great charm of being very like you . . .'[15]

Goncourt, to whom she also gave a copy of *Didi*, considered that Mathilde was not a writer, but he showed his aesthetic sense and the familiarity of a friend who had known her for twenty years.

Princess,
I am going to ask a humble favour of you. During the last few days I've been thinking about the binding for *Didi*, trying to find something which didn't look (as Flaubert would say) like the binding of a *stinking*

bourgeois; and . . . I can't think of anything more appropriate than to
have the binding done by the author. Princess, you embroider like a
fairy colourist: some time this summer, would you find me a very
strong piece of dark silk, and cast two brilliant butterflies upon it . . .?
If you did, *le vieux* would be so grateful.[16]

Fastidious, devoted, observant, Goncourt was invited to
déjeuner at the rue de Berry to see Mathilde's personal treasures;
and, just as he had preserved in words her studio at Saint-Gratien,
so he now preserved her bedroom in Paris: a bedroom hung with
yellow silk, with a crucifix at the head of the bed, and a bust of
her beloved Mme de Reding. The dressing-room was all lit up
with the reflections of the sumptuous silver toilet set which
Catherine the Great had given to Potemkin.[17]

Whatever Goncourt's criticisms, the *salon* at the rue de Berry
remained the pre-eminent *salon* of Paris. A *salon* needed to have a
past; and, here, in the famous conservatory, memories could
stretch back to the early years of the century. Mathilde could
recall meeting Chateaubriand (who seemed to her unimpressive),
and dining with Balzac in 1848. 'She couldn't judge his intelligence as a conversationalist. . . All he did was repeat: "Oh, how
frightened I was! Oh, how frightened I was!" "It seemed very
odd to me," said the Princess.'[18] Other figures from the past still
appeared in her *salon*. On 18 April 1877, Goncourt saw Plon-
Plon dine at a *mercredi* for the first time, and thought him more
Napoleonic than ever; he still combined the irony of a Parisian
journalist with the lofty graciousness of a Roman prelate.
Alboni came quite often; she was now old and enormous, and
some said that her celebrated voice was 'stilled like that of a
nightingale after the spring'.[19] But she sang at the rue de Courcelles,
and Popelin declared: 'She enlivens us by her whole-hearted
laughter, and when she sings she enthrals us.'[20] Taine and Renan
still argued with one another under the palm trees. Chaix-d'Est-
Ange, the former *procureur impérial*, called at the rue de Berry and
talked with his familiar persuasiveness.[21]

And since Mathilde kept her old friends round her, and
recruited new ones, Heredia, the young Parnassian poet, sometimes made his appearance in the *salon*. 'I don't need to see [the
princess] to love her,' he told Popelin, 'but I find it delightful to
see her, all the same.'[22] And when he was prevented by gout

from paying his respects, he added: 'Would you be good enough to put me, metaphorically, at the Princess's feet? I should find it rather awkward to make the actual movement, though it is so natural to a man.'[23]

Gégé Primoli said that Mathilde had known most of the eminent Frenchmen of her time. They had been the ornament of her *salon*, but they had had no influence on her tastes. In literature and in art she remained what she was: an anti-snob with the courage to proclaim her convictions. Popelin considered that she owed her reputation for exceptional culture and intelligence largely to the circle she had chosen, to the friends whose love she had won. As he said, she was, above all, 'a woman of impressions'.[24]

Mathilde herself used the identical phrase when she talked to Gégé:

I'm a woman of impressions, . . . a smell, . . . a ray of sunlight . . . What do I care about the colour of something uninteresting? Like Goncourt with his Fragonard, Chardin, Watteau . . .? I don't see the need to appreciate the Flemish, they have dull, commonplace natures, I can't like them. My nature is all of a piece, I am an impressionable person . . .

'I like every dish at a dinner,' [said Gégé].

'I can't, I have my preferences.'[25]

Mathilde could not appreciate sophisticated writers. She was not, and would not have claimed to be, an intellectual; she could not understand the complexities of philosophy, the finer points of style. Long ago, at Saint-Gratien, Gautier had insisted on the peerless sublimity of Hugo, and 'Racine, Corneille and Molière, those poor dead dramatists, were sacrificed without mercy. Of course, in this case,' Mathilde told Sainte-Beuve, 'I didn't allow myself to make the slightest observation. Respect for the old costs me no more than sympathy for the young, and I'd rather have two admirations than one.'[26] Her silence was prudent, in every way: she lacked the Romanticism to understand Hugo, and the sense of style to appreciate classical dramatists. Sometimes, frustrated by the feeling that she missed intense satisfaction, she was carried away, and passed outrageous judgments. Years after Gautier had died, Goncourt wrote that she 'flatly denied his talent, according to her habit of denigrating her friends'.[27] It was on the evening of 20 September 1879. Gégé was present, and explained in his diary: 'There was a heated discussion between Goncourt and the Princess about Théo. The Princess, who regretted her lack of literary sense, grew even more impassioned than she intended. . . There are two phases in her judgment – in the first she only admires the talent of the people she loves, in the second she frets because she can't appreciate the talents of her friends. . . She is very artistic, but she lacks the sense of the picturesque.'[28]

No one had shown *le poète mathildien* more sympathy than Mathilde herself. But her appreciation had been given to the singer rather than the song. Like many women, she was more interested in an author than in his work. As Arsène Houssaye said, she would not be moved by the most powerful logic unless she was convinced by her heart. As Gégé wrote: 'She remains insensible to the finest lines in Leconte de Lisle, which she doesn't understand, but she will be moved by a *cri de cœur*.'[29] She wept when Gégé read her a poem which he had written her as a *collégien*, for it recalled a whole vanished epoch, and 'her heart . . . only understands the language with which it loved – and was loved'.[30] In music, too, Mathilde looked over her shoulder, towards the past. When, in her seventies, someone played Wagner to her, she shut her ears to the music of the future. Her Italian heart had woken to the airs of Bellini. These exclusive preferences did not prevent her from having piano lessons every Wednesday. They were an excuse for giving a salary to Sauzay, the old musician from the Conservatoire.[31]

Sometimes, unable to understand, or frankly disapproving, Mathilde found it hard to be Notre Dame des Arts. Years ago, she had told the Goncourts, bluntly, that their novel *Germinie* was nauseating.[32] In 1877, just after the publication of *La Fille Élisa*, Edmond went to dine at the rue de Berry. He was mortified that Mathilde did not mention his book. After dinner, as if she had suddenly woken from a daydream, she broke off a conversation and asked him: 'Goncourt, can you be prosecuted?' He was touched by her anxiety.[33] He did not know that she had been shocked by his novel of prostitution, murder and imbecility. 'What do you think of Goncourt's new book, *La Fille Élisa?*' she asked Gégé, two days later. 'I was painfully disappointed by it. I can scarcely believe that such a distinguished and faithful friend of ours has blundered in such a scurrilous manner.'[34]

Mathilde was capable of enjoying Turgenev's tales, and she invited their author to dinner; but she could not accustom herself to Naturalism. 'I only like novels,' she had said, 'when I'd like to be the heroine.' She dismissed Zola's *L'Assommoir* as 'ignoble';[35] she could hardly see herself as a drunken and finally imbecile working-class woman. She had never been able to keep her moral and aesthetic judgments apart. She relegated Thiers' *Histoire de la Révolution française* to the ante-room; she kept his *Histoire du consulat et de l'Empire* in her salon.[36]

And yet, when Goncourt, in a bitter moment, said that she enjoyed only Feydeau,[37] the comment was demonstrably untrue. She had read and re-read *Madame Bovary* soon after publication: not from affection for Flaubert, whom she did not know at the time, 'but out of admiration for such a true, sincere, naïve and living picture of provincial life. I confess,' she wrote, 'that I couldn't understand the *succès d'immoralité* of this book. If anything can make a person disgusted with vice, it is certainly the conduct of Madame Bovary.' She had found it harder to appreciate *Salammbô*: it did great honour, so she thought, to Flaubert's erudition, 'but its merit is less easily understood by the simple'. Simple herself, she was not attracted by the curious subject or the exuberant style. 'In this second book,' she added, 'one could already perceive the fault which occurs in all the author's works: little naturalness, and much exasperation, a desire to dazzle the public . . .'[38] The comments were honest and not unperceptive; when Mathilde made them, after Flaubert's death, she could claim to have known the author well.

But though she was not, by nature, the greatest admirer of his work, she recognized his quality and encouraged him. She recorded that he read her part of *Salammbô*, *La Tentation de Saint Antoine*, *L'Éducation sentimentale*, *Un Cœur simple*. Goncourt said that Flaubert also read her *Hérodias*.[39] Mme de Galbois insisted that he had read her *Bouvard*, if not *Pécuchet*.[40]

Some twenty years after the appearance of *Madame Bovary*, Mathilde tried to reconcile its author with another habitué of her salon: Ernest Pinard, who, as *procureur impérial* at Rouen, had attacked the novel at the famous trial. Flaubert had been acquitted of offences against public morals, but even Mathilde could not persuade him to forgive his prosecutor. In tones which were firm if not stentorian, Flaubert replied: '*Ça, Princesse, jamais!*'[41]

Legend says that it was Flaubert, standing on a table in the salon, who declaimed a description of the Armada by Heredia.[42] It was Flaubert to whom Mathilde confessed that she could not understand a word of Renan's *Prière de Minerve* '(I can quite believe it!' Flaubert told his niece).[43] It was Flaubert, momentarily forgetting *Bouvard et Pécuchet*, who did 'nothing, absolutely nothing,' at Saint-Gratien, and earned the absolute rest which he needed. 'I have the habit of spending a few days there every autumn,' he told a friend; perhaps it was only there that he forgot the unremitting labour of his writing.[44] Late in 1878, disturbed by his financial straits, Mathilde had suggested that he should have some situation; she told him that his friends were trying to get him a position worthy of him.[45] It was, perhaps, a little through her influence that Taine wrote to Flaubert in January 1879, saying that Silvestre de Sacy was dying, and that authority only asked to give him De Sacy's post as administrator of the Bibliothèque Mazarine. The sinecure carried a fine apartment and a salary of three thousand francs.[46]

Flaubert was tempted by the apartment, but he refused the offer. He found the idea of a sinecure humiliating.[47]

In the early months of 1879, he was less concerned with a sinecure for himself than with the future of Guy de Maupassant. He felt deep affection for this government clerk of twenty-seven, the nephew of his beloved Alfred le Poittevin; he also delighted in Maupassant's literary gifts, and had undertaken to guide him in his craft. Maupassant had now written *L'Histoire du vieux temps*, a one-act comedy in verse; and Flaubert had determined that it should be performed in the rue de Berry, with Madame Pasca in the leading part. Late in March, Mathilde promised Flaubert it would be performed the moment he returned to Paris. 'That day, of course, I'll present you,' Flaubert promised the aspiring dramatist.[48]

However, in April Mme Pasca was distraught by the end of a love-affair, and she could not bring herself to perform. 'Mme Pasca (between ourselves) nearly died of grief at her break with Ricard,' Maupassant explained to his mentor. 'She can think of nothing but her despair in love. Nom de Dieu, how stupid women are!'[49] 'Sacrée Pasca!' exploded Flaubert. 'Quelle dinde!'[50]

Three weeks later, Maupassant received an encouraging letter from Mathilde. She was eager to have his play performed, and she herself was asking Mme Pasca to choose her day and the person to act with her. 'I hope you'll come to the performance, and of course produce it,' wrote Mathilde. 'I shall certainly be delighted to meet you.'[51] 'What should I do?' wrote Maupassant in desperation to Flaubert. 'Write to her or call? In either case, will you please let me know the etiquette? When you write to her, what's the formula? . . . When you speak, do you say "Your Highness?" . . . I expect an answer from you at once.'[52]

Flaubert answered immediately. On 17 May, Maupassant addressed himself to Popelin:

Monsieur,

I hardly dare recall myself to you by reminding you of a very *daring* play which I performed before you, with a few friends, in the painter Becker's studio. But Flaubert tells me to use his name in asking you the following favour. This is a better recommendation.

Her Imperial Highness Princess Mathilde has been so extremely kind as to write and thank me for sending her a little comedy which I've written, and to ask me to dinner on Wednesday next. I am a complete stranger to the house, and I wonder if you'd be kind enough to present me? This would save me the difficulty of going in alone, and entirely unknown.

I hope, Monsieur, that I am not too indiscreet in asking for your patronage, and I hope you will agree to my request. If you do, I will come and call for you about seven o'clock, if that would be convenient . . .[53]

Mme Pasca finally agreed to act at the rue de Berry. Mathilde grew very fond of Maupassant; and in time Maupassant wrote to her: 'I very often imagine that I'm taking the five o'clock train to go and dine with Your Highness at Saint-Gratien.'[54]

Artists, like men of letters, came to the still imperial *salon*.

Édouard Detaille and Eugène Isabey (son of the miniaturist), Baudry, Boulanger and Carpeaux came to the rue de Berry as they had come to the rue de Courcelles during the Second Empire. Mathilde still entertained Jalabert, Philippe Rousseau and Bonnat. Anastasi, who had become blind, lived until his death in the Pavillon de Catinat; and once, when he came to the rue de Berry to see in the New Year, Mathilde said: 'You're dining with me to-morrow, I won't have you beginning the New Year all alone.'[55] Fromentin, with whom Mathilde had quarrelled in the latter days of the Empire, still sought her in the days of the Republic.

Some of her friends had never wavered in their devotion: Taine, accused of Bonapartist sympathies, presented himself at once in the famous conservatory. 'Faced with an accusation,' he said, 'one must rise to it.'[56] Coppée had been among the first to leave his card at the rue de Berry. Dumas *fils* came to dine soon after he became an Immortal, and tried, wrote Goncourt, acidly, 'to show himself a mere mortal, to crush his fellow-writers as little as possible . . .'[57]

It is in the Goncourt *Journal* that Mathilde is reflected most clearly in these early years of the republic. She gaily arrives for *déjeuner* with Edmond (princes, he says, enjoy themselves like children in the company of ordinary human beings). She invites Edmond to dinner on his fifty-second birthday, and after dinner they sketch out plans for an ideal *hôtel* which Mathilde will never build, 'but which she likes to build in imagination, with the imagination of her friends'. Sometimes the picture is less happy, and Mathilde is restless and preoccupied. Edmond, arriving unexpectedly at Saint-Gratien, once found her lying on a divan, 'having the sort of reflective siesta which she is accustomed to take at sunset'. Someone was reading her the latest Daudet: *Fromont jeune et Risler aîné*; but Mathilde was dozing. Then Popelin, ever inventive, had begun to marble paper with watercolours, Mathilde had snatched the paintbox from him and become completely absorbed in the childlike pleasure.

Next day, impulsively, at her suggestion, they had gone to Paris to buy antiques at Renard's. She had had an orgy of buying; but that evening, when they got home, Popelin had brought a number of tiny things out of his pocket: a screen, a glove-box, and a set of dolls'-house furniture. Mathilde demanded them; Popelin smiled as she became insistent, petulant, fierce, like a child. Then, as he intended, he gave them to her. 'Believe me, Goncourt,' he explained, later, 'one has to create an occasional scene with the Princess. That scene the other day, for example: it corresponded to certain things I knew . . . These scenes give her an outlet. Afterwards she is perfectly calm for a few days.' Goncourt admired such understanding. Mathilde, he reflected, always needed someone to find her distractions, baubles and even quarrels. She was a complex character: an amalgam of generosity, intelligence and vigour and childish weaknesses.[58]

Goncourt's assessment was partly true; but he was analysing the Mathilde of Republican days. Now she kept her Bonaparte convictions, but she was the hostage of politics. Now she kept the instincts which had made her Notre Dame des Arts, but she no longer had her influence. Now her complexion had lost its fineness, her figure had lost its shape, and her hair was thin; now, more than ever, she needed understanding and affection.

Popelin was not the lover whom Mathilde would have chosen in her youth, or in the high noon of the Second Empire; but in many ways he was a suitable companion for her in her middle age, in the days of exile and the Republic. He was only a shadow of Nieuwerkerke; but, unlike Nieuwerkerke, he took the trouble to understand her, to forestall and satisfy her needs. He spoke of her to Goncourt with a freedom which was distasteful; but his confidences, which were immediately noted in the *Journal*, presented Mathilde with absolute frankness and truth. Popelin was bourgeois; he saw the essential bourgeoise in the daughter of Catherine de Montfort. 'There is no woman more reserved in love,' he told Goncourt, 'and no woman who shows less imagination in pleasure. In fact, I don't know a woman who is so completely a bourgeois wife by nature. If her husband hadn't been violent to her, . . . I'm sure that she would never have had a lover . . . What she really likes, you know, is to feel herself surrounded by friends who are a little in love with her.'[1]

Mathilde's true nature was never seen with such clarity. Popelin himself was more like a bourgeois husband than a lover, and he bound himself to her in a thousand domestic ways. Gradually their liaison was being accepted as a virtual marriage; and outwardly there could not have been a more regular existence. Every morning, in Paris, Popelin left his *hôtel* at eleven and went to *déjeuner* at the rue de Berry. Every afternoon, at one, he went home again. Twice a week Mathilde had her painting lessons, once a week she had her music lesson. Twice a week she dealt with her affairs, and visited the Asile Mathilde at Neuilly. Every day at half-past six, 'my old, dear, faithful habit',[2] Popelin returned by cab, and they talked for half an hour; on the stroke of seven, she went to change for dinner. After dinner she settled down on her cherry-coloured sofa, and worked at her embroidery till eleven. Then she would rise, the guests would leave, and Popelin would walk home.

Often she went to visit him at the rue de Téhéran, and sometimes she would work in his studio. From time to time he organized festivities at his *hôtel.* 'We have inaugurated our winter season with a little dinner,' he told his father late in November 1873. 'It went off very gaily and we went to the theatre the same evening. We saw Sardou's famous *Oncle Sam* . . . On Thursday we went to the Gymnase, where Dumas' new play, *Monsieur Alphonse,* is having a huge success.'³ On Christmas Day, Mathilde and her intimate circle went to *déjeuner* at the rue de Téhéran, where Popelin had taken pains to please her. 'A Christmas tree was standing in the middle of the table. I'd covered it with multi-coloured favours and filled it with stuffed birds. It looked charming. There were different coloured ribbons hanging from the branches, and each of them led to someone's place, where there was a little present . . .'⁴ Shrove Tuesday, 1874, offered another chance for 'a little feast,' and

when the Princess came in, the drums beat on parade, the tricolour standard was lowered before Her, and the guards, commanded by an officer who saluted her with drawn sabre, presented arms to her with perfect precision. The drum and sabre and lance are all the most picturesque Japanese instruments. Two young girls, followed by the crowd of Ladies, presented Her Imperial Highness with a big basket full of violets, and, in a red robe, accompanied by Gustave, who bore the Key of the House on a Cushion, I myself advanced and, in a clear, firm voice, I delivered the following address . . .⁵

For all their domesticity, Popelin remembered that this 'bourgeois wife', this woman whose chief charms had always been her simplicity and good nature, was also the niece of Napoleon: a Bonaparte princess.

In 1875, he published *Cinq Octaves de Sonnets,* a collection of his poems dedicated to Gautier's memory. In an introductory letter, addressed to Mathilde, he recalled her poet at Saint-Gratien.⁶

Often, on mornings when they had both been staying at the château, Gautier had gone into Popelin's room, to read him what he had written in his hours of sleeplessness. Then he had copied it out for him in his fine microscopic hand. Among these poems was a sonnet written for Mathilde, one which did not find its way into *Un douzain de sonnets*. Gautier forgot its existence, and his bibliographer did not know of it, but Popelin preserved it among his papers:

A S. A. I. MADAME LA PRINCESSE MATHILDE
Au bord de l'Eurotas, Léda n'avait qu'un cygne.
Sur votre lac d'Enghien, lorsque vous paraissez,
Pour en faire accourir des essaims empressés,
Plus belle que la Grecque, il vous suffit d'un signe.

Ils sont là, tous rangés comme une flotte en ligne
L'aile ouverte, orgueilleux, leurs cols d'argent dressés,
Dédaignant les gâteaux pour être caressés
Par cette main dont seul Jupiter serait digne.

Et c'est un jeu charmant, Princesse, de les voir
Autour de vous, dans l'eau, palpiter et s'ébattre
Et s'élancer, émus d'un amoureux espoir;

Mais leur blancheur vantée il en faut bien rabattre;
Il semble, en approchant de votre main d'albâtre,
Que leur duvet neigeux se change on duvet noir![7]

Now, in the mid 1870s, Gautier had gone, and Mathilde had transferred some of her affection to François Coppée, his protégé. Now Sainte-Beuve had gone, and she had felt apprehensive when she learned that his letters to her would be published. Flaubert had made discreet enquiries, when the book was in proof, and reported that it was 'entirely in praise of the Empire and the Princess.'[8]

Over *déjeuner* at Saint-Gratien, in the presence of Popelin and Goncourt, Mathilde spoke warmly, now, of the man she had admired the most of all her habitués. Popelin, ferreting through her papers – presumably to help her write her memoirs – found her own account of Sainte-Beuve's first visit, a passage which expressed her exultation in the friendship of this 'superior man'. Popelin's vanity was hurt, his possessiveness was shaken. 'Sainte-Beuve was cunning,' he explained to Goncourt. 'He cultivated her as the *princesse supérieure* . . . You know the Princess as well as I do. Sainte-Beuve assessed her in five minutes, and found that, by paying this kind of court to her superiority, he could get all he wanted, without any trouble.'[9]

Goncourt, thinking aloud in his *Journal*, declared that Popelin was the ideal lover for Mathilde: a kind of painter-vassal, an artist of all work. And indeed Popelin showed her endearing attentiveness, imaginative sympathy; he was patient, gentle and firm. Yet Goncourt's earlier impression had not been entirely mistaken: Popelin sometimes asserted himself like a man who felt inferior to his surroundings. His repeated confidences about Mathilde's private life, about her personal papers, about her character, suggest a deplorable lack of integrity.

Mathilde herself was far from happy. Sometimes, on winter mornings, she would wake in anguish, as if she had committed a crime. Sometimes she must have contrasted Popelin with his precursor, and herself, in her mid-fifties, with the Imperial Highness of the Empire. Now she was compelled to take no part in politics, but there were moments when her regrets were too acute to hide. On 14 February 1876 came the *première* of *L'Étrangère*: the first acknowledged play by Dumas *fils* to be performed at the Théâtre-Français. Mathilde was present in a stage-box to honour her old friend; with her were Popelin and Giraud, and Goncourt, who no doubt recalled the tempestuous night of *Henriette Maréchal*. When Marshal MacMahon, the President of the Republic, entered the old Imperial box, he was greeted by an ovation. Mathilde stayed until the end of the play, but Goncourt saw that she wept.[10]

She did not only feel the despair of fallen dynasties. She still lived in uncertainty, in apprehension of another exile. She clung to her familiar surroundings, made more dear because it had once seemed that she might lose them. Every winter she grew melancholy at the thought of leaving Saint-Gratien, and yet there still remained only one city where she felt at ease. 'I haven't kept an unhappy memory of Brussels,' she wrote in 1876, 'but I don't think I could live anywhere except Paris . . .'[11] Again and again she told Goncourt how it hurt her to leave France:

It seems to me as if something shuts up in my head, it's like a shutter being closed . . . It's very strange, last time I went to Italy, I had a terrible headache at Toul, I had to lie down while the others were having dinner. Well, there, in bed, I really mean it, I was tempted to get up and slip off to the station, and let all my companions go on without me . . . I need Paris, I need its pavements . . . The *quais*, at night, with all those lights . . . You won't believe me, but there are days when I feel radiant at living here! I wanted to come here for so long . . . No, when I'm out of France, I feel a sort of restlessness . . . I can't wait to come back, to be here, to be among French people.[12]

Mathilde loved the grandeur and glory of France, its landscapes and horizons, the shades of meaning of its language, the character of its people. She could not understand the young generation, with their taste for travel. She had found her corner of the earth. With occasional brief exceptions, she spent her winters in Paris, and all her summers at Saint-Gratien.[13]

The way of life at Saint-Gratien was the simplest and most regular in the world. It was only broken by a weekly visit to Paris, and by a reception on Sundays. It did not go beyond the estate. Mathilde hardly left her domains even to pay a visit in the neighbourhood; excursions were few and far between, and a journey caused an upheaval. 'The greatest sacrifice she could make to her family,' said a friend, 'was to go to England, Switzerland or Italy. After three days, she was terrified that she might not be allowed home, and, after a fortnight, she was out of her mind with anxiety.'[14] 'I can see from here how you've spent today,' Lavoix told her in 1882. 'You've gone and greeted your trees and paid a visit to the farm; you have resumed your intimacy with all these things, which are your friends, and you have asked their forgiveness for your fortnight's infidelity.'[15] Mathilde had been on holiday at Deauville.

There were many who shared Mathilde's devotion to Saint-Gratien, who had fallen under the spell of her summer estate. Gégé, on a visit to the Empress at Camden Place, wrote to Popelin: 'I imagine my dear St Gratien where even the bad weather seems like sunshine . . .'[16] Popelin wrote to Gégé: 'St Gratien is a haven I don't need to praise to you. The place is greener than ever: green enough, if I may say so, to make Ireland blush . . .'[17] Gautier's son recalled Mathilde, in her brisk, almost military way, walking with her guests after *déjeuner*, talking with animation, summoning the terriers which had strayed among the trees: those groups of trees which 'gave the illusion of a Corot in the silver mists of the morning, and turned into a Claude Lorrain in the bright noons of summer'.[18] Edmond de

Goncourt had 'the habit' of getting out of the carriage at the little swing gate to the park, and taking his own familiar way to the château. And, in his *Journal*, which was often sharp and malicious, betraying his own frustrations and disappointments, he left an affectionate impression of the studio at Saint-Gratien,

> I want [he wrote] to leave a record of this room, which, under the Empire, was really the pleasant seat of government for art and literature, the benevolent Ministry of Graces. I want to leave a record which is like a painting and an auctioneer's inventory: something which, in future times, will let those who love the Princess's memory find her again . . .[19]

Goncourt brilliantly preserved the studio which had been the focal point of cultural life in the Second Empire. Frédéric Masson, whom he had presented to Mathilde, left one of the most complete accounts of Saint-Gratien in the Third Republic. Masson – 'un simpatico garçon', said Gégé[20] – was in his early twenties when the Republic began. He became a fanatical Bonapartist, and Mathilde adopted him as her family historian. It was Masson who now described the meals in that first-floor dining-room, walled on three sides by glass, which gave visitors the sensation of eating al fresco. But, as he politely expressed it,

> eating was the thing with which the Princess was least concerned. In the morning she drank tea, in the evening she drank water; on rare occasions she would take a mere sip from a glass of champagne, in which (as in her tea) she liked to crumble a biscuit. No one was simpler; like her brother, she paid no attention to the cooking. But he had an appetite, and she had none; and, except for banquets which were more imaginary than real, like Italian dishes or cheese, all she enjoyed were strawberries and cream, fruit and cakes. The menu set before her (which she read aloud to her guests) consisted of little at *déjeuner* except eggs, a fish dish, one or two meat dishes, and a cake. The cooking was no more elaborate at dinner. But if the gourmets were unsatisfied by these meals, what a feast of conversation! With a freedom tempered by respectful deference, among men all of whom were distinguished and most of whom were outstanding, the talk ranged over every topic in art and literature and history. The Princess did not have her seat in the audience, she took part in the performance. People did not speak in front of her, they spoke because of her; they were not courtiers, but it was to her that the words went like a homage . . .[21]

Mathilde had no time for empty flattery. She delighted in freedom of manner; and her own honesty of behaviour, her simple everyday clothes, her modest, familiar ways, attested, quite as much as her scorn of vulgarity, the exceptional distinction of her birth.

Early in 1879, from Chislehurst, the Empress wrote to Mathilde:
My dear Cousin,

My son has asked me to tell you that he has decided to go to the
Cape with the British Army. You will read [in the papers] about the
reasons which have led him to make this decision. I can only tell you
what he asks me to tell you, because he is very anxious that you
shouldn't learn it from the Press. I hope that Providence will bring
him back safe and sound . . .[1]

It must have hurt Mathilde profoundly that Napoleon's great-
nephew should have chosen to fight with those whom she still
considered Napoleon's jailers; and yet the decision was understandable. The Woolwich subaltern of twenty-three was tired of
an uneventful life. The prince who had been educated for responsibility, constantly instilled with a love of glory, was driven
by a longing to prove himself.

On 27 February he embarked for the Cape of Good Hope, to
join the British in the Zulu War. On 1 June he was killed in
Zululand.[2]

As the days passed, Mathilde became increasingly convinced that
Eugénie was to blame for the tragedy. Nine years ago, she had
driven the ailing Emperor into war with Prussia, she had hastened
the destruction of the Second Empire, and of the man who made
it. Now, as if she was bent on the immolation of the dynasty, she
had indirectly caused the death of her son. 'Her line of conduct is
just beginning to come to light,' Mathilde told Gégé on 4 July.
'She killed him just as she killed his father. He couldn't bear
living with her. She incited him to go to war. He went with his
strength spent and his spirit crushed! It's horrible! She is an
unnatural wife and mother!'[3]

Perhaps Mathilde's antipathy to the Empress led her to ascribe

(*Above left*) Portrait of Théophile Gautier.
From a watercolour by Princess Mathilde, 1870.

(*Above right*) Princess Mathilde. From a watercolour by Théophile Gautier, 1867.

Sonnet by Théophile Gautier, addressed to Princess Mathilde, July 1869.
It is published here for the first time.

A. S. A. I. madame la Princesse Mathilde

au bord de l'Eurotas, Léda n'avait qu'un cygne,
sur votre lac d'Enghien, lorsque vous paraissez,
pour en faire accourir des essaims empressés,
plus belle que la Grecque, il vous suffit d'un signe.

ils sont là, tous rangés comme une flotte en ligne
l'aile ouverte, orgueilleux, leurs cols d'argent dressés,
dédaignant les gateaux pour être caressés
par cette main dont seul Jupiter serait digne.

et c'est un jeu charmant, Princesse, de les voir
autour de vous, dans l'eau, palpiter et s'ébattre
et s'élancer, émus d'un amoureux espoir ;

mais leur blancheur vantée il en faut bien rabattre ;
il semble, en approchant de votre main d'albâtre
que leur duvet neigeux se change en duvet noir.

Theophile Gautier

St Gratien Juillet 1869

Anatole Demidoff,
husband of Mathilde.
From a photograph taken
in later life.

(*Above*) Princess Mathilde
in middle age.
From a photograph taken
in the last years of
the Second Empire.

(*Above left*) 'An eminent
mind, subtle, caustic,
indulgent out of goodness
of heart':
Charles-Augustin
Sainte-Beuve (1804–69).

Nieuwerkerke, towards
the end of his career.
From a photograph by
Reutlinger.

to her an influence which she no longer possessed. But, whatever her feelings for Eugénie, Mathilde had loved her nephew, and she went to England for his funeral. On 12 July, with her brother and his sons, she waited at Camden Place to receive Queen Victoria. Twenty-four years earlier, just before the Prince's birth, Mathilde had received the Queen on her state visit to Paris. Now, at his funeral, she led her into the *chapelle ardente*. The Queen laid a large wreath on the coffin; Princess Beatrice laid a purple crystal cross, garlanded with violets, and they knelt for a moment in prayer. Napoleon – now the head of the family – thanked the Queen for all her kindness; Mathilde repeated her gratitude, and said, impulsively: 'He rushed forward – he must have been out of his mind.' The Queen said that he had only had the natural wish to distinguish himself.[4]

In 'a spirit of sacrifice', with the thought that she was obeying the Prince Imperial's wish, Eugénie had said that she would receive Mathilde, Napoleon and his sons, after they returned from the funeral service. Mathilde came to see her. Napoleon ordered his carriage and, without a word of excuse, drove back to London.[5]

Three days later, at Saint-Gratien, Mathilde told Goncourt:

Yes, I saw [the Empress], but she didn't say anything to me . . . The room was quite dark, you couldn't see . . . So I don't know if she was crying or if she just didn't want to speak . . . Yes, I mean it, she didn't say anything . . . Though I think she might have found a word, at a moment like that, . . . something nice for the sake of our future relations . . . Oh, yes! She said to me: 'You know, all his wounds are in front.' . . .

In fact, they were all thunderstruck to see us; it put their plans out . . . The Duchesse de Mouchy wanted to stop me from receiving the Queen of England . . . I was obliged to say to her that I knew what to do, I didn't have to be taught my profession . . . As for the Queen of England herself, she was excellent and behaved with perfect dignity.[6]

Queen Victoria had found Mathilde 'very little altered'.[7] Yet, though to some she seemed to have kept remarkably young, Mathilde must at times have felt the burden of her fifty-nine years, the burden of increasing unhappiness. Goncourt said that she complained about the protracted mourning for her nephew.

I

But Goncourt could hardly have been deluded: the indifference and even the irritation hid profound emotions. Mathilde was much afflicted by the violent, primitive death of the Prince Imperial: by the death of all the hopes of the dynasty.

For she had no illusions, now, about the restoration of the Empire. The Prince Imperial had been a natural, unchallenged leader, educated for an imperial future. There would never be a united party round her wild, vindictive, middle-aged brother. The codicil to the Prince's will was already a subject of discord. This codicil, inspired by Rouher, expressed the wish that he should be succeeded not by Prince Napoleon, but by Prince Victor, his son.

Napoleon did not begin what he knew would be a losing contest with Victor. He pretended to support the Third Republic. Both his sons were studying in Paris. Mathilde preferred Louis, who was her godson; he was only fifteen, but he already showed himself hardworking and serious. However, she invited Victor to the rue de Berry, and did all she could to prepare him for his future. 'The two young princes are charming,' Renan wrote at the end of the year, 'and Princess Mathilde is very occupied with them; her two nephews are taking an increasingly important place in her life.'[8]

Soon after the Prince Imperial's death, Gégé Primoli noted that relations had always been strained between Chislehurst and Saint-Gratien. He said that Eugénie and Mathilde still detested one another, and he considered that they were both to blame. And yet Eugénie's letters to Mathilde were not merely formal; they suggested that she was willing to be friends. The disunity in the family seemed to demand some dignified understanding between the two ageing women; tragedy and dissension seemed to give them a new common ground.

More than once, Mathilde was obliged to smooth over difficulties between her brother and his family and the Empress. In December 1880, Eugénie wrote:

I have just read an attack on my son's policy in [*Le Napoléon*], the paper which is said to be inspired and subsidized by your brother. It accuses him 'of having disregarded Napoleonic policy' since the death of the Emperor Napoleon III. Since the Prince Imperial reached his political majority, I have stood aside. I hate crude aggression, and I think there's nothing to be gained by descending into the arena. But if *someone* means to criticize my son's conduct all the time, without respect for the past, I should suppress my grief, and I shouldn't hesitate to join in the contest any longer . . .[9]

Eugénie had apparently been blinded by emotion. Mathilde replied that she could see nothing in *Le Napoléon* which might have troubled her. There was no mention of the Prince Imperial, and she was sure that her brother would never attack the young man whose death had been a public loss.[10] In 1881, Eugénie was hurt that Mathilde, Napoleon and his sons were not attending a memorial service for the Prince Imperial at Saint-Augustin. Mathilde replied that she still mourned her nephew, but political demonstrations were not to her taste. She and her brother would attend a mass at Saint-Gratien.[11]

The Empress was not the only source of anxiety to Mathilde. The Bonapartists begged Victor to accept the title of pretender which the codicil had conferred upon him. Napoleon drafted a letter of renunciation for him. Just as Victor was about to sign and destroy all hopes for the future, a group of Bonapartists urged him to oppose his father. 'It would be suicidal to sign,' Frédéric Masson wrote to Mathilde, 'but not to sign would mean a break with his father. We must write another letter. There are two sentences which are particularly terrible: one about the Prince Imperial's will, and another about the Bonapartist party.'[12]

Napoleon's behaviour horrified Mathilde, and she did not spare her criticism. But all she wanted now was peace, and her only political ambition was to see the past respected. Among her dearest treasures were two which Eugénie had sent her. One was the paper-knife which had been on the Prince Imperial's desk; he had asked that if he died it should be given to her. The other was the Grand Cordon of the Légion-d'honneur which Napoleon had worn on St Helena.[13]

In September 1879, Flaubert had paid a visit to Saint-Gratien. Mathilde had urged him to stay longer, but he was harassed by the proofs of *L'Éducation sentimentale*, and he was anxious to resume his labours on *Bouvard et Pécuchet*. It was his last autumn visit. He was tired from constant overwork and from financial worries; his health had long been indifferent. On 8 May 1880, very suddenly, he died. 'The time for laurels is over,' he had written to Mathilde, 'and for me the time for roses, too.'[14]

December 1881 brought the death of Eugène Giraud. He had been her friend even before her cousin came to power. Now he died, unexpectedly, of a stroke in his studio. 'I'm broken-hearted!' Mathilde told Gégé. 'For thirty-four years we had lived the same life, and he was an . . . essential part of mine . . . To-morrow I shall go with him to his resting-place.'[15] Next day, at the funeral, Goncourt saw her, 'superb in her grief.' The old guard of the *mercredis* was passing, and he and Dumas *fils* remained the last. Only they would understand, now, when Mathilde recalled the Wednesday dinner at the rue de Courcelles which the Tuileries had called *le dîner des bêtes.*[16]

She herself knew that she must draw a new generation to the rue de Berry: that sometimes, in these Republican days, she would have to go and seek them out. Late in November 1881, Mme Alphonse Daudet recorded: 'The other evening I saw a corner of the Empire: Princess Mathilde, her nephew Victor Bonaparte, and her suite: . . . a whole little Court, white-haired, and ageing, and declining, a Court which seems to be seeking pastures new, a revival of youth. It was in the studio of a well-known painter, and the Princess was partly there, it was clear, out of curiosity about some artists whom she doesn't see in her *salon* and had to come and find on neutral ground.'[17]

It was soon after this chance encounter that Goncourt set about introducing the Daudets to the *salon*. He needed all his diplomacy, for the Massons 'never stopped repeating that, if Daudet was received, he would write a novel called *La Princesse Bathilde*, in which Mathilde would be disgracefully treated.'[18] At last, however, on 7 March 1882, Mme Daudet recorded: 'The other evening we were received in Princess Mathilde's *salon* for the first time.'[19]

Soon afterwards, she added that she had seen Mathilde again: 'Superior in tone . . . I find it easier to understand the group she formed around her; and what a pretty décor, that huge glassed-in salon! . . . But, in spite of the Princess's liberal mind and inclinations, the air of a Court hovers about it; little intrigues are spun round her personality . . .'[20]

Some of the 'little intrigues' which Mme Daudet had in mind may have been those of the Massons; certainly, when her son, Léon Daudet, the violent Right-wing journalist, came to write his book on the modern *salon*, he made a determined attack on Masson, who, he said, was 'detested for his odious character'.[21]

Léon Daudet was hardly more charitable in his account of the rue de Berry:

Everything at Princess Mathilde's was imperial in style. She worked at her embroidery all the evening, and the evening was usually very dreary. It is true that I saw these things towards the end: 'when the rats were leaving', as Goncourt said. But according to the accounts I was given, it had always been the same.[22]

The Massons' warnings to Goncourt were realized all too faithfully. Daudet and his son were to prove themselves about the most scurrilous guests in the later days of the *salon*.

The year which brought *le ménage Daudet* to the rue de Berry also reminded Mathilde of a scurrilous guest of long ago. It was now eighteen years since Viel-Castel had died, embittered and disgraced. He had left his mistress, Mme Évremond de Bérard, all the little black books, prefaced and ended by his signature, in which, for thirteen years, he had recorded the sins of the Second Empire. Mme Évremond de Bérard had now found a Swiss publisher for the six volumes of memoirs.[23]

On 13 December, at the rue de Berry, Goncourt and Lavoix found Mathilde in a state of apprehension. They sensibly advised her to wait until she had seen the first volume before she judged it. They told her not to advertise Viel-Castel by refuting his statements in the Press. Mathilde dismissed them as cowards, and cried out to her assembled guests: 'It's horrible, these days: you have to let yourself be insulted without even replying.'[24]

Ten days later *Le Gaulois* announced that the first volume of the *Mémoires* had been seized. The *Mémoires* were nonetheless published in 1883. The sixth and last volume had hardly appeared before a new edition was in preparation, and a Brussels publisher was being sued for piracy.

ᴣᴐ 39 ᴄᴧ

On the last day of 1882, Gambetta died. He had been instrumental, with Thiers, in founding the Third Republic, and though he had retired from politics some time earlier, there were people who saw his death as a political watershed. Goncourt declared that, if the Prince Imperial were alive, the Republic would have ended within a fortnight.

Prince Napoleon was sixty; but he still kept his intense and frustrated longing for power. He felt that the death of Gambetta had given him his chance.[1] On 16 January 1883, he had posters published in which he demanded a plebiscite.

It was an ill-conceived action; Duclerc, the President of the Council, had the posters destroyed, and Napoleon was arrested and imprisoned in the Conciergerie. Charles Floquet, the popular radical who had recently been Prefect of the Seine, seized the occasion to attack the Bourbon and Bonaparte dynasties: he proposed exile for the members of families which had reigned in France. Goncourt, reading the morning papers on 17 January, learned of the arrest and of the debate in the Chamber. That afternoon he presented himself at the rue de Berry. Mathilde made some pretence of serenity, but in her eyes he detected the terror of exile.[2]

He was not the only friend who was anxious about her future. A few days later, Édouard Behaine, the diplomat, mentioned it to President Grévy. Grévy seemed to have little sympathy for Mathilde, and he believed that she was working for the Bonaparte restoration; but he told Behaine that the Republic would not think of distressing a woman. She could be assured that all would be well. The message gave Mathilde some relief, but she was still disturbed. Her disturbance was not lessened by the fact that Popelin had decided to leave for Italy with his son.[3]

There must have been times when Popelin wanted to make his son amends for a childhood which had been very insecure. Gustave had enjoyed little family life. His mother had died when he was ten; within a year or so of her death, his father had been drawn into a liaison with Mathilde, and the child could hardly have been unaware of this new preoccupation. Then the war had come, and he had been left with the Dumas, near Puys. After the War, he had been sent as a boarder to the Collège Rollin in Paris. Whatever the wisdom of these decisions, he must have felt that he was pushed aside.

Mathilde was very conscious of this, and she tried, touchingly hard, to give him some maternal affection. When he was at the Collège Rollin she asked him to the rue de Berry on Sundays, and Popelin fetched him in time for *déjeuner*. When he was living at the rue de Téhéran, she sent an eager injunction: 'I hope you mean to come and dine on Wednesdays. But that isn't enough: I'm so fond of you that I want more than that. Come *when you want* and without being asked: I'll take that as a proof of your affection, which means a great deal to me. *My house is yours*.'[4]

She did all she could to draw Popelin's son into her innermost circle, she wrote to him as a mother might write to a recalcitrant son, a child who seemed unwilling to come home. She sometimes gave him errands to do, for it was a means of ensuring that he remembered her, it was a way of keeping in touch. She asked him to choose her a palette in Paris.[5] She asked him to go to Saint-Gratien and have one of Giraud's portraits removed from the salon and sent to her, she asked him to take down the portrait of Mme Defly from her bathroom, and to have it wrapped up and despatched.[6] When she and Popelin went to Deauville, she reported to Gustave: 'Your Father is bathing, he is well and everybody misses you.'[7] In 1880, when Popelin was ill at Saint-Gratien, she dashed off a daily bulletin to the rue de Téhéran.[8] Her affection was eager and genuine; but the handful of little notes, some on pale blue paper, some on white embossed with the golden crown and imperial bee, gives a marked impression that Mathilde needed Gustave's love much more than he needed hers. His affection would bind her still closer to his father.

After he left the Collège Rollin, Gustave had gone to the École des Beaux-Arts, where he learnt painting from Bonnat and Ferrier. In 1882 he had won the Premier Grand Prix de Rome, which entitled him to four years at the French School at the Villa Médicis.[9] Gégé Primoli, who had also been at the Collège Rollin, promised to look after him in Rome. 'I'm touched to the heart by the brotherly friendship you promise my young Gustave,' Popelin told Gégé. 'You seem to me his tutelary genius and I find that a very sweet and comforting feeling. You know how dearly I love the child. I love him so much that I'm constantly forcing myself not to express it, I'm afraid of overwhelming him with it. Sometimes I find myself envying the freedom that mothers can show . . .'[10]

Mathilde knew Popelin's unbounded love for his son. She must have understood that he wanted to take Gustave to Rome. Yet she could not bear to let Popelin out of her sight, and she was afraid that he might settle in Italy. Now, on the eve of his departure, her brother had caused a political crisis; she needed Popelin's presence, his comforting support, more than ever. He himself was well aware how much she needed it.

Before I do anything else, I should like to reassure you about your poor aunt's morale [he wrote to Gégé on 20 January]. Her morale is excellent, as good as it can be considering these unfortunate events. I'm really vexed to be leaving her at a moment like this. But she has a great many people round her, & there's a great coming & going, which will help her to bear my absence a little . . .

Can you get me a good Room with a fire? I should be so grateful . . .[11]

Eight days later, Gégé installed him at the Hôtel de Londres in Rome. He stayed until 21 February. 'Popelin left at two o'clock,' Gégé wrote that day in his diary. 'I put him on the train, and then his son came back to the house with me. It's the first time that he's left his father [sic], and, not being expansive like most motherless children, he must suffer twice over.'[12]

Gustave was not only depressed, he was unwell; he developed such a fever that on 9 March Popelin returned to Rome.[13] Mathilde, acutely anxious, sent telegrams and letters, and was angry that they would not let her come. On 28 March Gustave set off, with his father, for the restorative 'natal air' of Paris.[14] In May, Mathilde reported to Gégé that Gustave was well, 'and more authoritative with his Father than ever'.[15]

Late in September, Goncourt stayed at Saint-Gratien. He was writing a new novel, *Chérie*, and he read some of it aloud. He had protested more than once that Mathilde did not appreciate his work; and she listened to him, now, with a certain lack of sympathy. 'He read us several chapters with unremitting feeling,' she told Gégé. 'It's the life of a young girl up to the age of 29 – her passions and her loves. It's all descriptions . . . When he reads, he beats time with his left hand to emphasize the balance of the phrases. He is very well – gay and charming *apart from his work*.'[16]

On 12 October, Gégé's friend, Charles Grandjean, who had met Popelin in Rome, had *déjeuner* at Saint-Gratien for the first time. He was touched by the welcome he received, especially as Mathilde was 'moved to tears by the departure of Gustave, who's going back to Italy tomorrow. The farewells were painful . . .' In December Grandjean added that she had received a joint letter from Gustave and Gégé. This letter, and her pleasure in Gustave's evident good humour, 'had made her radiant . . . I have never seen her so happy'.[17]

Mathilde was not happy about her family. In January, during the crisis over her brother, she had behaved with restraint and circumspection. The Empress, too, had shown dignity and self-control. As soon as she heard of Napoleon's imprisonment, she had written to Mathilde, announcing her imminent arrival in Paris. 'When I heard of his arrest,' she said, 'I remembered only one thing: that he bears the same name as I do. There are times when differences must give way to unity.'[18]

There was little unity in the family. Soon afterwards, the Bonapartists persuaded Victor to promise to bring an action against his father, as the counter-pretender. A pro-Victor group was formed within the party, and it gained support by repeating that the Empress was in Victor's favour. Eugénie was disturbed, because she had made peace with Napoleon. In May 1884 she asked Mathilde to make her neutrality known. 'I feel sorry, my dear cousin, to know that you are involved in these painful discussions.'[19] Mathilde also found the discussions painful; Popelin reported her deep depression. Victor had now left his father's house and was living with the Benedettis at Fontainebleau, where his supporters were inciting him to action. 'I haven't the strength to forgive you for your unforgivable behaviour,' wrote Mathilde in June. 'It is very painful for me, since I've loved you so much

I*

in your youth, to be compelled to blame you when I wanted you to be beyond reproach.'[20]

Victor himself was in no mood for reproofs. The Prince Imperial had expressed a wish that he should be his heir; no one could now oblige him to abandon his position. Victor's relations with his father steadily grew worse, and on 19 June 1885 an article appeared in *Le Figaro* and *Le Matin* which made the break complete.

A few days later, on 2 July 1885, a law was passed which decreed exile for all the heads of families which had reigned over France, and for their direct heirs; the law also gave the Government the right to exile other members of these families if necessary.

There was clearly no future, now, for the Bonapartes. France was on the eve of a new political interest: Boulangism.

And so Mathilde and her brother were more vulnerable than, perhaps, they had ever been, and fiercer in the defence of their dynasty. Plon-Plon, in Switzerland, set to work on a book, *Napoléon et ses détracteurs;* and Mathilde, who had dismissed Sainte-Beuve for what she thought a personal betrayal, now dropped Taine for his comments on her ancestors.

Taine was working on his historical study, *Les Origines de la France contemporaine.* The first volume had appeared in 1875, the sixth and last would appear nineteen years later, and his fame as a historian would rest on this massive work, a survey of France from pre-Revolution days to the post-Napoleonic era. On 15 February 1887, Taine published the first of a series of articles on Napoleon in *La Revue des Deux Mondes.* He had tried to get Mathilde's approval for the publication. She had answered, politely, that she trusted to his tact, and that she had no authorization to give. It is said that Taine had also asked advice from Renan. 'You find me very embarrassed, my dear Renan: if I publish my work on Bonaparte I shall quarrel with a great lady who has always shown me constant kindness.' 'My dear Taine, when I published my life of Jesus, I didn't hesitate to quarrel with a far greater lady who had brought me up: the Church.'[21]

Taine, like Sainte-Beuve, cared more about his integrity of mind than he did about pleasing Mathilde; but there were still times when Mathilde refused to acknowledge intellectual honesty.

Two days after his article appeared, she wrote to him.[22] Her letter was much more vehement than his two 'mis-statements' warranted; but Mathilde was not merely correcting Taine, she was expressing her loyalty to her family. Taine's comments touched the Napoleonic legend.

Mathilde wrote as a Bonaparte. Taine answered as an historian. 'I regret all the more,' he ended, 'that I should have shocked you because, in my second article, I am probably going to shock you more.'[23]

It was not Taine's second article, but his third, which ended all communication. Mathilde then sent him a visiting card on which, for once, her hand was very plain. She had written three capital letters: P.P.C. They stood for *Pour prendre congé:* to take leave.

Taine ceased to go to the rue de Berry, but Renan was still found there. Renan was a close friend of Plon-Plon's, but he still felt his position insecure. In August 1887, Plon-Plon wrote in astonishment to Mathilde: 'I was very painfully surprised to read in [Renan's] history of the people of Israel, page 415, à propos of Saul: "As Bonaparte was, so was David." ' It seemed a clear allusion to Napoleon's ruthless execution of the Duc d'Enghien.

Plon-Plon was painfully surprised, Mathilde was furious. Renan was alarmed when he heard what havoc he had caused. He had mentioned Napoleon simply because he was a recent ruler and he should mean something to his readers.

I have always said that Napoleon is one of the four or five greatest men in history [he explained to Mathilde]. He accomplished his extraordinary work with the minimum of crimes which poor humanity demands for great successes. If I am now obliged to maintain that he was a little saint, a sensitive soul, a fastidious man – oh, I don't understand any more . . . From the heights on which one must stand to write history, one doesn't see such finical details.[24]

Renan returned to the rue de Berry. Mathilde felt no resentment, but she had been reminded that she belonged to another epoch, an historical epoch in which she had had imperial rights. Now she was a Bonaparte in the Third Republic.

She was already being presented as an historical figure. In 1883, when an exhibition, *Portraits du Siècle*, opened at the École des

Beaux-Arts, Winterhalter's portrait of the Empress hung eloquently next to Hébert's portrait of Mathilde;[25] and in 1885, in
his *Confessions*, Arsène Houssaye wrote touchingly: 'Princess
Mathilde would have been the best of empresses, because of her
grand manner and because of her greatness of heart.'[26] Banville,
in his *Camées parisiens*, movingly recalled Mathilde in her imperial
days: the brow that was made for diadems, the strong profile
which suggested candour and joy, 'and affirmed a mind artistic
enough to understand the splendours of Art and the splendours
of Life'.[27]

Some of her old habitués made less generous observations. In
1882–3, Maxime du Camp, who had left the rue de Courcelles
under a cloud, published his *Souvenirs littéraires*, and made unforgivable, unsubstantiated comments on Mathilde's private life.[28]
In 1886, Goncourt published passages from his *Journal* in *Le
Figaro*, and he earned angry complaints from her. The first
volume of the *Journal* appeared in March 1887, and that October,
when he had read the second, Taine assured a friend: 'If I still
dined in town, I should now find out in advance if he'd be going,
and, if he was, I should refuse the dinner. I think that his close
friends and Princess Mathilde herself must feel about it as I do.'[29]

ꙮ 40 ꙮ

Edmond de Goncourt might well have seen Mathilde as a subject
for a realistic novel. Had he been less attached to her, had he not
exhausted his own reflections by noting them in his *Journal*, he
might have analysed her as coolly as he did la Fille Élisa.

As it was, he recorded her unsettled moods, her moments of
loneliness. Now, in her sixties, as she ceased to know the loving
admiration of those around her, she had moods of bitterness, and
moods of despondency. One day in January 1882 (it was just
after the death of Eugène Giraud), she had suddenly begun to cry;
she said that she didn't know what to do, she wanted something
which would take her a little out of her grief. 'She needed her
friends *to adopt her a little*.' Goncourt had been touched by this
warmth of heart.[1] That September, at Saint-Gratien, she had
accused him and Popelin of ignoring her. 'If it had been a pretty
young girl, of course you'd have noticed her, but I am only an
old woman now!' She seemed to have some 'vague jealousy of
the young people in the house.'[2]

A few days later, still at Saint-Gratien, she had drawn Goncourt
aside, and, walking on until they could no longer be overheard,
she had talked to him about Popelin. She had looked at Goncourt
piercingly, to ascertain his feelings, and asked him if he
had noticed anything. She spoke doubtfully, anxiously, about
Popelin's affection; and suddenly she burst out: 'Does he love
me? . . . Does he love me? . . . Look, Goncourt, I can feel it, it's
as if he was doing his duty!' Goncourt replied that Popelin was
worried about his own ill-health, and about his son. Mathilde
did not listen. 'It's strange,' she went on, 'when his son was quite
small, a child, he wasn't like that. Now that the boy's grown up,
he is occupied, preoccupied with him. Look at him, now, when
he has to go to Paris, look at him with his gloves on ready, his
coat over his arm, consulting his watch all the time, look how

worried he is that the carriage will be late. You'd think he had a
rendezvous, wouldn't you?' Goncourt suggested that Popelin was
absorbed by his new book: his translation of *Le Songe de Poliphile*.
Mathilde ignored the arguments. 'He ran about a good deal, six
years ago. He's recently been seeing some dreadful women again,
Mme Feydeau, Mme Dardenne de la Grangerie . . .' Goncourt
protested that Popelin loved Mathilde completely. In a tone of
voice which expressed a multitude of things, she answered: 'Oh,
Goncourt, he does so little for me now. He doesn't speak to me
any more, he doesn't tell me anything. Oh, he's very strange!' She
added, crying silently: 'A month ago, I imagined things, and my
imagination goes a long way . . . But let him go and settle in
Italy with his son, I shan't try to stop it . . . I know what men are
like about affections which are growing old. I got used to having
my heart broken long ago . . . But I still want to rise above it.'[3]

Dumas *fils* declared that Mathilde had not forgotten Nieuwerkerke; in her mind, he said, le Surintendant still surpassed Popelin
in every way. In September 1884, Mathilde herself told Gégé that
Popelin and Nieuwerkerke had met the previous day. 'She said
that if she met him it would have no effect on her. But I can't
believe,' wrote Gégé, 'that one kills one's emotions like that.'[4]

Yet in the years since Nieuwerkerke's defection, Popelin had
earned not only acceptance but admiration. Masson saw him as a
Renaissance figure at a Medici Court: 'The universal artist who
conceives everything well, says everything well and does everything well.'[5] Grandjean found him 'omniscient, admirably
gifted, endowed with remarkable good sense, and full of feeling
and generosity.'[6] Goncourt had come to record his respect for
Popelin's understanding of Mathilde: for his tact, his patience, his
inventiveness.[7] Hébert had sometimes been slightly jealous of
this quasi-official relationship, for 'the antique passion,' he told
Mathilde, 'still survives under the ashes of the years'.[8] But in 1887
Hébert himself told Popelin: 'You are her good shield and buckler
against the blows of Fate; your lofty, philosophic reason must
give her calm. We need calm in all conditions of life, but we need
it even more if, like her, we are on the heights where one is most
exposed to the storm.'[9]

Popelin, unlike any other man in her life, gave Mathilde
tranquillity, the steady domesticity which she had always needed.

Marriage, he said to Gégé, 'should be repose, serenity and peace.'
He brought serenity and peace into their life together. 'We are,'
he said, 'like those nations with no history: very happy.'[10] In *Un
Livre de Sonnets*, which appeared in 1888, some nineteen years
after their 'marriage'. he suggested their dependence on one
another. In his sonnet *En Voyage*, he described the anxieties of
separation; and the letter which the traveller receives at the inn
recalls that bundle of travellers' telegrams, that record of care and
constancy, which he himself preserved among his papers.[11] As for
Mathilde, she had come to be absorbed in Popelin. His ill-health
only brought him closer to her, for it made him seem more
dependent on her. She looked after him with the love of a girl. 'I
do not lack friends,' she wrote, years later, 'but he alone was
necessary to me – he had absorbed my life.'[12]

On 19 July 1888, Gégé Primoli arrived at Saint-Gratien. Mathilde
had been sending him such unhappy letters, she had asked him
so often to raise her morale, that he had come from Rome to visit
her. 'I did well to come,' he noted, 'but I shall only be able to give
her moments of forgetfulness. I shan't be able to raise her morale,
it is too deeply affected.' Last time he saw her, she had seemed a
woman of forty-five; today she seemed – as in fact she was – well
over sixty. 'The Princess was Life and Health when I left her,
two years ago; now she is the embodiment of Anguish and
Despair.'[13]

The cause of her anguish and despair was Popelin. He had been
mysteriously ill for six months. Angina had been mentioned.
The local doctor at Enghien said that his general condition was
poor, he had 'disturbing symptoms and a touch of pleurisy as
well. They had not noticed the pleurisy, and, when they detected
it, it was very late. This seemed to be the reason for the last
crisis.' Popelin was better, now, but he was so weak that he could
not eat at table, and, as soon as he moved, he had a fit of giddiness.
He was overwhelmed with attentions, but he was not recovering,
no one could think what to do, and there was talk of sending him
to the South of France. Mathilde, whose life depended on habit,
was disturbed at the prospect.[14]

Besides, as Gégé Primoli observed, in this summer of 1888,
there were two other clouds on the horizon. The first, which
grew more ominous every day, was Gustave Popelin. Gustave,

unsociable and distrustful, could not hide his aversion for Mathilde. Popelin spent his time protecting Mathilde and Gustave from each other, and putting ointment on their respective wounds.[15]

The other cloud which Gégé noticed was Marie Abbatucci, 'a nice girl of about forty'. She was the daughter of Charles Abbatucci, who had been the Deputy for Corsica during the Second Empire. Marie later remembered how she had been brought up at the Ministry of Justice, where her grandfather Abbatucci was Minister. Gégé Primoli told a different story. Marie's father, so he said, had been such a fanatical Bonapartist that he had ruined his family in the cause. He had been so concerned with politics that he had had no time for anything else. His wife had been slightly unbalanced: she had never left the house, and she had never seen beyond her casserole. The household had not been enlivened by the presence of Marie's idiot sister. Marie herself had not even had a bed: she had slept on top of a pile of books, in an alcove. Sometimes she used to go out with her father, and her greatest pleasure had been to visit the Primolis in the rue de Varenne. One evening Charlotte Primoli had taken her to visit Mathilde.

Mathilde had met her again in Brussels, and she had taken her under her protection. Mathilde was always sensitive to other people's misfortunes, and Marie had not only lost both her parents, she had now been deserted by her fiancé. On the eve of their wedding, he had left her in order to marry the well-endowed daughter of Mme Alexandre Dumas.[16]

Mathilde had gradually made Marie into her lady-in-waiting. Popelin had shown her a father's kindness. Indeed, he had sometimes shown concern that she was still unmarried: 'There's a new marriage in prospect, Valentine de la Tour's,' he had written to Gégé in 1877. 'Marie is certainly better than any young girl we know, and she isn't married even so . . .'[17] He watched over her protectively. 'Have you heard of General Abbatucci's death?' he asked Gégé early in 1878. 'It was a great loss for his family and especially for poor Marie.'[18] It was not surprising that Marie became increasingly devoted to Popelin; in her mind, perhaps, he took the place of the father and uncle she had lost. He showed her more constant kindness than the young fiancé who had abandoned her.

Mathilde was naturally aware of Marie's devotion. Nieuwer-kerke had left her, years ago, for a young girl; she did not mean to be a victim a second time. Gégé recorded that, when they went on their summer holiday, 'it would have been ridiculous, had it not been profoundly touching', to see Mathilde leaning out of her window, watching anxiously as Popelin and Marie bathed together. When Popelin fell ill, Marie would not leave his bedside. Mathilde observed her with mistrust, with hatred – and yet, at times, with gratitude for her placid, constant attentions.[19]

Now, on 20 July 1888, Popelin came down to the salon at Saint-Gratien. Pale and weak, he took Mathilde's arm, and they walked together in the sun, in the kitchen-garden. Gégé took photographs of them. 'The one I like best, the one which gives me the best impression of reality, is the one where the invalid is leaning on the Princess, and they are followed by a dog. You see the couple from behind, but you would know them anywhere, ... they touch the heart like a glimpse of Philemon and Baucis.'[20] The photograph held all the comfortable security to which Mathilde aspired. In another photograph, she and Popelin are coming down the path towards the camera. Marie Abbatucci, smiling, walks behind them.

At this moment of acute anxiety for Mathilde, there appeared a novel which resurrected the great personal deception of her past. The Massons had never stopped repeating that if Alphonse Daudet was received at the rue de Berry, 'he would write a novel called *La Princesse Bathilde*, in which Mathilde would be disgracefully treated'.[21] Goncourt had brushed aside their warning, and ensured that the Daudets were accepted. Early in 1882 they had been invited to the *salon*.

Six years later, Alphonse put Mathilde into *L'Immortel*. In this novel, which revolved round the Forty Immortals of the Académie, he did not show her with respect or even with compassion. He presented Maria-Antonia, Duchess Padovani, as a bluff, imposing Corsican, passionate, and afraid of middle age, deserted by her lover, Samy, the worthless Prince d'Athis, whom she had given years of her life and countless undeserved distinctions.

He was a hollow bell, this Samy . . . And she had raised him high, very high, she had told him what to say and, more important, what

not to say, she had prompted his movements and actions until the day
he saw he had reached the top and kicked away the now superfluous
ladder.[22]

There, surely, was Nieuwerkerke in 1869; and, as if to make
the allusion clearer, the abandoned Duchess sought relief at
Mousseaux, the country estate on which she spent a part of every
summer. The Lake of Enghien had been replaced by a river, but
otherwise the retreat bore a striking likeness to Saint-Gratien.

Nothing, wrote Daudet, had outwardly changed in the life of
the Duchess.

She did not countermand the invitations which she had sent out
for the season . . .
Hour after hour, the visitors continued to arrive, from Blois, from
Onzain (Mousseaux was half-way between the two stations); and the
landau, the calèche and two big breaks set them down at the steps in
the main courtyard . . . There were distinguished familiar visitors
from the rue de Poitiers, Academicians and diplomats . . . And then
life organized itself again as it had always done. In the mornings there
was visiting, or working in one's room, meals, more sociability, and
siestas; then, in the cool of the day, there were long carriage drives
through the woods, or expeditions on the river in the light flotilla
anchored at the end of the park . . .
Really, if he could have seen her, the Prince d'Athis, the treacherous
Samy (everyone was thinking about him, but no one mentioned him),
his pride would have suffered. It would have suffered to see how small
a void he had left in this woman's life, and indeed in this royal house.
Mousseaux was humming and buzzing with activity, and, in the
whole of the long façade, only three shutters were closed, in what
was called the prince's pavilion . . .[23]

The fullness of the social round belied the emptiness of heart.
Maria-Antonia's life seemed devastated at an age when it was
hard to begin again. She could still see the prince's furtive look,
'his false and painful smile' at their last meeting. His desertion lent
her an aura: made her, once again, the object of the daydreams
of her guests; and she was ready, with a desperate readiness which
somehow surprised her, to become the mistress of Paul Astier, a
man almost young enough to have been her son. She was hurt
enough and blind enough to marry him.

When *L'Immortel* appeared in 1888, it caused a sensation. It was
the first novel to present the Academic world. It also satirized a

famous forgery case which had occurred at the end of the Second Empire: the case in which Vrain-Lucas, a gardener's son, had imposed some seven thousand forged letters on Michel Chasles, the eminent mathematician. Yet the novel was largely interesting for its sharp, unkind portrayal of Mathilde and Nieuwerkerke. On 1 August, Gégé Primoli noted in his diary that all Paris had recognized the Duchess as 'my poor dear Princess.' Gégé, disturbed and disgusted, spoke to Goncourt: the great friend of Daudet, and the only person who could have given certain details to him. Goncourt swore by all that was sacred that he had not noticed any likeness; and yet he was obliged to agree that Daudet had been wrong to describe the Duchess walking in her park with her little dogs, and that he had been wrong to make her Corsican. Gégé replied that happily Mathilde suspected nothing, he had found the book on her table with only the first pages cut. He had put it among the other books in her library to spare her this new vexation. Possibly Goncourt understood: some people were astonished that Mathilde still received him after the publication of his *Journal*.[24]

On 27 August, Gégé returned to Paris and had *déjeuner* with Popelin at the rue de Téhéran. He was drawn to 'the excellent Poliphile'. 'His sweet serenity, his long silky beard which smells of violets, his blue eyes which reflect the skies of Greece and Italy': all gave Gégé a perfect idea of the philosopher of classical times.[25]

Popelin still suffered from an inexplicable lassitude, and it was still a cause of anxiety. A few days later, the doctors decided that he should go to Arcachon, near Bordeaux.[26] Arcachon was renowned for its bathing; if he could not bathe, he could at least enjoy the bracing air of the Atlantic coast.

It never occurred to Mathilde that she would not go there with him. She was obliged to visit Turin for the marriage of her niece, Laetitia, on 11 September. When she came back, she and Popelin would set off for Arcachon together. Popelin told her that he and Gustave meant to go to Arcachon without her; on her return from Italy she could join them.

Driven into a corner [wrote Gégé], he finally confessed that his son detested her, and was jealous of her. He had told him that he wouldn't even come and see him if he found him living with her again . . .

The poor woman was stupefied . . . And she told me everything that she'd borne for the past year.

'Every morning this winter, at 7 o'clock, whatever the weather, at the age of sixty-eight, . . . I went to ask Gustave for news . . . He never seemed to show any gratitude for the care I took of his father . . . And he didn't bother with the poor man! . . . Sometimes it was snowing, it was raining in torrents, it was cold, and he didn't ask me once to stay for *déjeuner* though he always asked Marie in front of me . . . It was he, in his hatred, who thought of putting Marie between us . . . And she used to stay while I came home alone . . .'[27]

Gégé discreetly advised Marie to make Popelin wait for Mathilde, and not to seem to hurry his departure. Next morning, while he was still in bed, Mathilde came in to tell him that Popelin had promised to wait for her. 'Poor woman!' he wrote. 'This concession gives her back her serenity – but it makes me terrified for her peace of mind. It shows me the influence of Marie.'[28]

That evening, with Gégé and Mme de Galbois, Mathilde was to set off for Turin. Before they left, they dined with Popelin. Gégé was still convinced that Mathilde had not read *L'Immortel* – or, at least, that she had not recognized herself in it. Suddenly, at table, he heard her say, 'without anger, but with deep grief and what seemed to be a gentle reproach for ingratitude: "She hadn't done anything to him, that Corsican woman . . ." '[29]

During the marriage celebrations at Turin, Mathilde had only one thought in mind: to return to Popelin in Paris. When she reached Paris, she did not even go to the rue de Berry: she had herself driven directly to the rue de Téhéran. Marie was installed there; and, going round the *hôtel*, Mathilde discovered her dressing-gown and slippers.[30]

> Viens près de moi, tout près, tout près, plus près encor,
> Viens, je veux respirer ton haleine fleurie,
> Et je veux appuyer ma tête endolorie
> Sur le soyeux tissu de tes beaux cheveux d'or.
>
> Je veux, comme un avare enterre son trésor,
> Tenir ta douce main dans ma main amaigrie,
> Et je veux me bercer en une rêverie
> Où mon âme se livre à son nouvel essor.
>
> Car de l'être alangui, plus subtile et plus pure

Elle s'envolera d'une plus libre allure,
Vers le ressouvenir d'un paradis perdu.

J'en saurai goûter mieux les suprêmes délices
Quand la santé, m'ayant fait boire à ses calices,
Me l'aura, dans la force et la gaîté, rendu.[31]

Somehow, Popelin and Marie contrived to calm Mathilde, and they left, all three, for Arcachon.

I have been here for a fortnight [Mathilde told Gégé, on 6 October] . . . We are in a perpetual squall of rain, wind and hail – one can only just take a step or two outside between the downpours. You can imagine my feelings.

People say that the country here is wonderful – it's terrible . . . I think that in another three weeks my miseries will be over, and I'll bring my dear invalid back in good form . . .[1]

Charles Grandjean saw Popelin the day after his return. 'He seemed to me transfigured,' he told Gégé. 'He looks like he used to do, his voice is firm, and he really seems to be strong. He still complains of minor troubles: fits of giddiness, for example. But let me say that Potin, the great heart specialist, burst out laughing when he was told of Dieulafoy's diagnosis. In his opinion, Popelin had pleurisy after his rheumatism, and, if the pleurisy had been attended to in time, there would probably have been no complication.'[2]

On the return from Arcachon, the storm finally burst. Mathilde and Marie were no longer the princess and the lady-in-waiting, the employer and the employed, the mother and the adopted daughter. Henceforward, they were simply two women who watched one another with hatred. Marie twice gave in her resignation; Popelin twice persuaded her to withdraw it. She wrote a third letter of resignation, on the eve of his departure for Cannes. This time she did not return to the household.[3]

It was, apparently, in December that Popelin went to Cannes. Mathilde wanted to join him. He sent her a telegram to say that, if she arrived, he would leave the same day. He also wrote that he felt responsible for Marie's reputation. He would not return to Mathilde unless she received her.[4]

'Your letter worries me,' Plon-Plon told Mathilde on 7 December. 'I feel you're unhappy. Take heart. Where's Monsieur Popelin going? How is he? If you went somewhere where I could join you, it would be a great pleasure for me – I [could go] to Naples or Palermo – I'd be very happy to be with you for a while, you're almost *the only* person I have left.'[5] Mathilde would have liked to talk to him; she wrote to him twice. 'Thank you for your two letters of the 13th,' he replied. 'I'm very sorry to hear you're *suffering* so, *open your heart*, it will do you good, it will relieve you, no one loves you more than I do . . .'[6]

For some months Popelin did not appear in the rue de Berry, and Marie went to see him every day. Mathilde, who had been the embodiment of health, could no longer sleep; and, at four or five in the morning, she would get out of bed and roam in misery round her *hôtel*.

She did not only have Marie watched; she used to hire a cab, and stop it at the corner of the rue de Téhéran. Through the little window in the back, she could see the entrance to Popelin's *hôtel*. She saw Marie go in every day, but she did not always see her leave. Once she saw her arrive, all radiant, her carriage filled with flowers.

Mathilde attempted to show that she was not defeated by age; and she received her guests as if nothing had happened. They came to the rue de Berry to show their respectful compassion: even people who had not come for years came to show their sympathy.[7]

Mathilde said later that her agony had really begun in January 1889.[8] It was, no doubt, early that month that Charles Grandjean wrote to Gégé:

Must I tell you of a rumour which is going round Paris? There is no indiscretion in revealing it, for the least informed people know about it, the people who are least familiar with the Princess. They say . . . that she has half broken with Popelin because of Mlle A. This is definitely said. I know absolutely nothing. But, even if one eliminates all the hearsay, one is tempted to believe there's some truth in it.[9]

Late in January, Plon-Plon wrote again to Mathilde.

I'm very worried about your situation. But I don't see the remedy.

I can't bear to feel that you're so unhappy and so far away. I think
that deep down I can guess the reason for your grief, but I don't know
anything positive. I've heard a vague rumour of an incredible
marriage! It's odious, as far as you're concerned – and almost grotesque
in the eyes of society! . . . Is someone still in the South of France? . . .
If you don't feel inclined to write, ask Benedetti or Masson. I'm
anxious to hear your news.[10]

Mathilde could not bring herself to write. On 10 February
Plon-Plon announced: 'Adelon should arrive the day after to-
morrow; he's good, devoted and discreet, and I'm waiting with
great interest to hear what he has to tell me of your affairs.'[11] He
was astounded by what he heard. 'The information he gave me is
inexplicable! I can understand your misery . . . I see no solution
except with time . . .'[12]

Popelin had sworn that he would not come back to the rue de
Berry without Marie. Some time in the first half of the year –
possibly in March – he appeared again.[13] Perhaps he understood
that opinion was against him; perhaps (thought Gégé) he hoped
to deceive people by his presence. Whatever the reason, he came
back for *déjeuner* and dinner once a week, and in the morning 'he
deigned to pay a visit of a few minutes – a doctor's visit to a poor
invalid. He alleged that he had neglected his son too much for the
past nineteen years, and that he could not desert his hearth and
home. And beside his hearth,' added Gégé, 'the young lady
warmed her feet and waited for him.' From time to time Mathilde
rebelled in fury at the thought of sharing him, and she wanted to
make him choose between them. But she was too afraid of his
choice. She contented herself with the hope that one day he would
cease to see Marie; and she despised herself for her cowardice.[14]

In June, Gégé took rooms at 14, rue de Berry, to be near her.
He found her cruelly changed. 'If you'd come five minutes
earlier,' she said, when he arrived, 'you'd have found Popelin
here. He's just gone.' Gégé understood, from her manner, what
she must have suffered to have Popelin back; and then, walking
up and down the long gallery, she told him, simply and honestly,
what certain letters and indiscretions had already half suggested to
him.

For nearly twenty years, her liaison with Popelin had been
accepted as a virtual marriage, and he had gradually been accepted
by her family. When he met her, he had been a man with a good

talent and a sizeable fortune; she had given him social standing, and satisfied his vanity. In 1879, their physical relationship had suddenly been 'cut, *cut*, as if by a knife'. Though she still wanted it, she had said nothing; her dignity had prevented her from complaining, or from running after him. He had said that he was ill, absorbed by his literary work. Whatever the real reason, his love had been platonic for ten years.

Last year, when he had his mysterious illness, Mathilde had gone every morning, throughout the winter, to visit him at the rue de Téhéran. She was there at seven o'clock, but she usually found that Marie was there before her. At Saint-Gratien, Marie had continued to look after Popelin, to perform the most intimate tasks which she might have left to a servant. As soon as dinner was over, she had gone to his bedside, while Mathilde, in misery, had been kept in the salon by her social duties. Sometimes, unable to bear the strain, she had followed her upstairs, and there had been scenes and explanations. Mathilde was worn by anxiety over Popelin's health and by the betrayal she suspected. Dr Potin had been called in, and, seeing Popelin's weakness, he had asked him if he had made any exertion. Popelin had proclaimed what the most insensitive of men never admits. He told the doctor: 'I haven't had relations with the Princess for nine years.' Gégé thought that Mathilde did not mind the confession of their liaison; she resented, bitterly, that Popelin had told the doctor that it was over. Soon afterwards, on her return from Turin, she had found Marie installed in his *hôtel*.[15]

Now, on 12 June 1889, when most of her Wednesday guests had gone, and only a few intimates remained in the salon, Mathilde abandoned her social pose, and talked with freedom, passion and eloquence. The scene, recorded in Gégé's diary in the small hours of the morning, sometimes recalls the scene of twenty years earlier, when she had told the Goncourts of her break with Sainte-Beuve.

She began to pace up and down the lighted empty salon, superb in her ample grey silk dress, with her admirable pearls round her neck, and a ruby drop falling on her breast like a little drop of blood . . . And she grew animated, she talked, fire and tears lit up her eyes, her voice was trembling with grief and indignation, her heart overflowed in words . . . 'I'm ashamed of my cowardice,' she said, 'my lack of dignity . . . One night he came in to me, ten years ago, he made me make my will, he asked me to leave a sum to Marie, and I left her 100,000 francs; it's infamous! . . . And at Arcachon, under the table, they were pressing one another's feet, and looking at me, and saying: "You're not eating anything, Princess, you're not well, what's the matter?" The wretches! . . . And now, when he comes, when he looks at me, I feel he's looking avidly to see if I have another wrinkle, another white hair. And he reproaches me for not knowing how to grow old . . . My misfortune is to have kept too young a heart . . . And I'm not saying all this as recrimination, because I'm ready to forgive and forget . . . But let him stop seeing her, or at least let him give me some vague hope that one day he will stop seeing my most mortal enemy . . .'16

Late in June, Popelin came to Saint-Gratien, and he occupied his usual room; but he looked like a man condemned to death. He would not speak to Mme de Galbois, because he accused her of having informed against him. They looked at one another with hatred. Early on 1 July, Mathilde came into Gégé's room to say that Popelin had just left for Paris. 'And he was all scented!' she said. 'But he wasn't yesterday . . . Can you understand it? He's writing verse, and I can't write a line!'17

Popelin had decided to take the waters at Uriage, in the Isère. Gustave was to go with him, and Mathilde was tortured by the thought that Marie might go, too. She asked advice from Hébert, for they still kept a kind of emotional intimacy. Hébert knew a local doctor; she begged him to ask his friend to watch Popelin.

Dear Princess [wrote Hébert on 25 July],
    I'm writing by this post to my friend and doctor in Uriage to ask him to tell me if the young lady comes to Uriage during these Gentlemen's stay. To tell you the truth, dear Princess, I don't believe she will, even though Gustave begs her to do so – always in his capacity as best friend . . .
    Certainly if she came and joined these Gentlemen, it could and would get on your nerves, but it wouldn't answer the question, because one can come and meet friends in a popular spa without it's absolutely proving an intimate liaison with one of them. No, I think the important thing would be to know what's going on in Popelin's mind. Is he disturbed and depressed about the rumour of this affair which he would like to see forgotten by you and everyone? That is what he maintains and what I still believe. Or does he want you to

force a rupture . . .? Frankly, in the latter case, I don't see what he'd gain, so I prefer to believe in the first theory. And it is with this hope that I beg you not to rush anything, dear Princess, letters may be better than appearances, try to be trusting and affectionate in your own . . . Keep me informed, write to me often, I'll reply at once . . .[18]

Mathilde needed no encouragement. A week later, Hébert wrote to acknowledge 'her last letters'. They had been less hopeful than the one she had sent him on the eve of Popelin's departure.

One of these days [said Hébert] I'll write Popelin a friendly letter, trusting in his words of affection for you. I think he'll reply and confirm what he said: deep grief at the disturbance created by this affair, which is only a tissue of stupid calumnies, . . . his wish to find serenity again, and, above all, his devotion to the Princess – for the rest of his life. There, I'm sure, is the summary of the answer he will send me. If I were you, dear Princess, I should take what I was given and I shouldn't try to find out what is said or done beyond what I was told. That would be the best and most sensible way to end this long agony; but would you be calm enough to take it? You are still too young and too loving to be so indulgent and so philosophic.[19]

Hébert's advice was rational and well-meant, but it almost confirmed Mathilde's worst fears.

A week later, on 8 August, Gégé Primoli recorded that she was still in misery. She showed him the letters that Popelin sent her: they were, he thought, correct and dry, but Popelin addressed her as *tu*. Gégé was revolted by this cold familiarity: one addressed a woman as *tu* to tell her that one loved her, not to tell her about one's colds and cascara. Mathilde said that Popelin had never called her *tu*, even when he loved her most. Gégé felt that this sudden intimacy was meant to prevent Mathilde from showing his letters. She answered with touching, passionate letters worthy of Mlle de Lespinasse: 'You reproach me for not growing old. Well, you needn't worry, I'm growing old if growing old means detaching oneself from everything.' And again: 'You regret you can't find any more subjects for verse, I envy you for regretting only that.' Nothing showed more clearly than these letters the chasm between Popelin and Mathilde. They spoke different languages. Popelin wrote fine, empty phrases, and Mathilde struggled to find some feeling behind the expressions, and answered with a cry from the heart.[20]

It was about now that Gégé took Mathilde to the haberdasher's in Enghien. He was petrified by a snatch of conversation between the haberdasher and the princess. 'Ah, Princess, you're back again?' 'Yes, I've been back a month.' 'How is Mr Popelin?' 'Very well.' 'And Mlle Abbatucci?' Mathilde, very coldly: 'She's dead.' 'Dead! She can't be.' 'Why not? Why can't she die like anyone else?' 'What a dreadful thing! Do you hear that, *mes-demoiselles?* You remember Mlle Abbatucci? She used to come in every morning with Mr Popelin? She's dead! . . . And where did she die, Princess?' 'I don't know, in Spain or Italy . . . Show me some veils.'[21]

Gégé left Saint-Gratien on 19 August. He was so concerned about Mathilde that he himself wrote to Popelin. His diplomatic letter brought a comforting reply.

My dear Friend [Gégé wrote again on 8 September],
    Although your letter is an answer it gave me so much pleasure that I must thank you for it with all my heart. The frankness with which you immediately [opened] your heart convinces me of your good faith . . . So don't let's talk about it any more, don't let any mis-understanding remain between us.
    I hope that the waters at Uriage will finally have cured you and that you'll find the rest and tranquillity which you need for your health and work at Saint-Gratien. As for me, I'm very well at Ariccia . . . I should be delighted to do you the honours of it, and you should certainly persuade my aunt to come and prolong her summer in Rome before she goes back to Paris. But I've been making this wish for nineteen years and it hasn't been realized!
    Please remember me to Gustave and believe me your most affectionate

                                                    JOSEPH PRIMOLI.[22]

Since Gégé's departure, Mathilde had turned to another confidant, Charles Grandjean, a recent friend of whom she had grown very fond. Grandjean, an Inspector-General of Historic Monuments, had married Claire du Locle, the daughter of the director of the Opéra-Comique. Mathilde was delighted with them both. She found them soothing, sane, reliable in her moments of crisis. Now, in August 1889, she sent Grandjean a letter which reflected her pitiful attempts to see reason, to find the truth among her conflicting, besetting thoughts.

If a man says he is wrongly accused of a love-affair, if he denies he has been a woman's lover, what should he do to prove his innocence?

Shouldn't he break off all relations with her?

If on the contrary he protests in words and continues his relationship with this woman, doesn't he confirm his guilt?

In what does Mr Pop[elin]'s compromised honour consist? In
having deceived me for ten years under my own roof with Mlle
Abba[tucci]. How can he prove to the world that this is a *calumny*?
By continuing to invite her to his house all the time? By declaring
himself her protector and her friend?

He comes back to me and thus deceives the woman he wants to
rehabilitate and support. Is this either logical or loyal? This new
betrayal of two people, calculated to deceive and to hide his relationship with her?

What is this relationship? I don't know.

The simple friendship which he declares he feels for this woman
would be more free than this. She clearly has an aim in mind, she is
thinking of marriage. If he goes on and compromises her even further,
he's playing her game and claiming that he's honourable to the person
he's compromising.

I'd like you to make Gus[tave] aware of this double betrayal . . .
He is cold and cruel and under the woman's influence.

Speak loud and clear to him, try to drive some sense into him, he's
so unbalanced.

I want honesty, I don't get it from the father or the son.

Why don't they choose the side that suits them best? But at least
choose one.

Forgive me for boring you, but I count on your friendship . . .[23]

It was impossible for anyone to judge for her, or advise her.
Faced with her unsolicited confidences, her desperate appeals, her
friends only wanted to escape. If they withdrew, in time the
storm might pass. For the moment, in the autumn of 1889, it was
easier to escape Popelin than Mathilde; and Frédéric Masson, the
Bonaparte historian, the habitué of the rue de Berry, avoided him
with cold deliberation. Popelin wrote to ask if he had forgotten
their long friendship. On 7 October, Masson answered:

No, my dear friend, I haven't forgotten anything. – Anything. –
and if you accuse me of indifference or forgetfulness, it would be
unjust, because I have suffered more than you can think from no
longer seeing you. I have suffered from it even more this hard summer
than I did that last sad winter. But I have been involved in spite of
myself, and whatever I said, in what seemed to me an inextricable
situation. I have been honoured with confidences which I certainly did

not seek, and I was aware of their danger. All I could do, as an honest man, was to take the path I've taken, and I have tried to keep away, and to do my duty, though by doing so I should appear ungrateful for friendships which were the honour & charm of my life. I felt such conduct cruelly. I couldn't and shouldn't have acted otherwise. I hadn't the right to take sides . . .[24]

Popelin remained hurt. Five months later, in March 1890, he wrote again, asking why Masson had abandoned him. Masson continued to play for safety: 'You ask me why I abandon you . . . I thought that the solution, whatever it was, could only be the result of free and personal decisions, and I always hoped that it would be such that life would begin again for you. There are my reasons. The day all this is over, you know that I shall hasten to see you . . .'[25] In a desperate attempt to ensure his friendship, Popelin sent him 'a Napoleonic bowl': a present which was calculated to touch his historian's heart. Masson returned it to him at once.[26]

Mathilde herself remained in misery.

I think of nothing except my present situation. I want to get out of it at any price – even by death. That is what they really want, and what he desires. They would be free – and I have had my day! Oh, they're infamous! *She* and the son are villainous . . . And he's so weak! . . . He writes poems and he's consoled – he has no preoccupations. He says that he doesn't think or feel any more, he says he's fond of me! A nice farce, which doesn't deceive a soul![27]

Early in 1890 she seems to have asked Ernest Lavisse to demand the truth from Popelin; then she felt the request was ill-timed, and hastily withdrew it. On 6 February she sent Lavisse a tel-egram:'If you haven't yet paid the visit to the rue de Téhéran, don't do so until you've seen me.'[28]

Sixteen years ago, in his *Journal*, Goncourt had recorded 'the little Abbatucci' brooding in the salon, her eyes betraying 'the dark trouble of a sea before the storm.' Ironically, he had added: 'I go to bed, reflecting that Popelin is the ideal lover whom the Princess might dream of . . .'[29]

Goncourt had recorded that judgment in 1874. Now, in 1890, Popelin was still beloved, he was still the man who had given her most happiness. Nieuwerkerke's infidelities had meant less to her by their very number, their very ostentation. If Popelin had deceived her, he had done so in a deeper, much more dangerous, far more hurtful fashion. Mathilde had never been able to feel that Nieuwerkerke belonged to her; she had always believed that Popelin was her virtual husband, that he loved her as completely as she loved him. Now she saw that this belief might have been mere delusion. Sharing him would mean that she accepted his duplicity.

She continued to share him.

The situation is fundamentally unchanged [recorded Gégé], but the acute condition has become a chronic illness. The Princess, who does not admit half-measures, . . . wants Popelin, to whom she has given herself for life. Popelin wants the young lady, who finds herself compromised because of him by the Princess's outbursts. He divides his life in two. He comes to the Princess's in the country from Saturday evening to Monday morning – from Wednesday evening to Friday morning. The rest of the time he stays at home in Paris to receive Marie. This sharing exasperates the Princess, but she must certainly resign herself to it if she wants him. From time to time, she rebels, bursts out, and sends him a very dignified letter of dismissal. But the next morning . . . he appears at the usual time . . . And, as usual, he goes into the Princess's room an hour before dinner, lies on the green chaise-longue, says he isn't well, and asks her to stroke his head with her little ungloved hand . . . And – to flatter her – he tells her she does him good . . . And she's happy![30]

In July 1890, Mathilde appeared to have broken finally with Popelin, and Charles Grandjean tried to mediate between them.

Thank you [she answered], I shall never forget your proof of friendship, your kind intervention, but I despair of ever seeing my affection restored. After eighteen months of real agony, one finds oneself very much changed. It seems that I am the one who has been in the wrong, and they make me expiate it.

Innocence is suffering. Mr Popelin is unscathed, so is Mlle. The son is supporting them. The whole trio want to get rid of me – which they have done, . . . and [now[Mr Popelin asks me what he can do for me!

Is it for me to beg for a return to a state of things which he cannot grant me? I am at the end of my strength, my courage and my hope. Nothing changes – on the contrary!

I've had my day, they are making me brutally aware of it, it is my fault, my fault, my very great fault. My mistake was that I believed and hoped, time doesn't change anything.

It was I who made the concessions, now there's nothing more to demand . . .[31]

But the affair was not over yet, it continued and it seemed insoluble, though more than one of Mathilde's friends tried to solve it. In September, 1890, from Baden, Lavisse wrote to say how he wanted to win Mathilde some belated peace. 'But I'm afraid I shouldn't be any more successful than the others, though I'm convinced that *he's* suffering, too, very cruelly – and that is at least a proof that he's kept the affection he should feel for you . . .'[32]

Mathilde agreed. She was convinced that if Popelin had not been bullied and harassed by Gustave and Marie, all would have been forgotten long ago. On 27 September she told Gégé that Popelin was prolonging his stay at Saint-Gratien. Marie was away at Tréport, where Popelin had rented a villa for her, but 'we shall see when she comes back if she continues her assiduities'.[33]

For some time, now, Popelin had come to see Mathilde more often, and their relationship had almost returned to its old state. He was good-humoured, he seemed to want to resume his familiar habits. He was unhappy at the rue de Téhéran, she wanted to give him back his calm and his security. Early in October she felt that Gustave would also like to return; but she made no gesture towards him, she could not forget what he had said to her. On 11 October she recorded that she and Popelin had been to Marly.[34]

But she remained unsure of herself, profoundly depressed. Early in November she told Gégé: 'I shall fight to the end – but without being deceived . . . It is my fault, my fault, my very great fault! I only blame myself . . .'[35] She had chosen to adopt Marie as a daughter, she had made herself responsible for her future, she had given her a home for nineteen years. And perhaps for eleven years, now, Marie had been Popelin's mistress. Looking back, Mathilde saw that she had innocently fostered disaster. When Gégé asked to write her life, she said: 'Of course! But what a sad subject! . . . I have discovered rather late, as dear Gautier used to say: "Nothing is any use, and anyway nothing exists." '[36]

Gégé saw Mathilde as the subject for a biography. Daudet, who had put her into his novel, *L'Immortel*, saw her, now, as the subject of a play. *La Lutte pour la vie* was, he wrote, 'in a sense, the continuation and the consequence' of *L'Immortel*. In this some-

A group at Saint-Gratien. Popelin is standing on the right, next to Mathilde. Marie Abbatucci is sitting, hatless, on the steps.

Mathilde and Popelin at Saint-Gratien, 20 July 1888.
From photographs by Joseph Primoli. 'The one which gives me the best impression of reality,' wrote Primoli, 'is the one of the invalid leaning on the Princess, and followed by a dog [sic]. You see the couple from behind, but you would know them anywhere, and they touch the heart like a glimpse of Philemon and Baucis.'
Marie Abbatucci appears on the right in the other photograph.

Saint-Gratien, Mathilde's summer residence. It was, as Hébert told her,
'the corner of the earth you love the best, the only one where you feel happy'.

(*Above*) Mathilde, in later
life, with Charles Gounod.
She had ensured his first success
in the theatre, and she remained
his 'constant, sure, devoted friend'.

(*Left*) Mathilde with a
gardener at Saint-Gratien.
From a photograph by
Joseph Primoli.

times touching melodrama, which was performed at the Gymnase, Mme Pasca, who had known the rue de Courcelles, played the Duchess Padovani, now the ageing Mme Astier, deserted for a young woman she had befriended. Gégé saw the play on 11 December, and it was, he wrote,

all the more poignant for me as I was seeing my poor Duchess Padovani in flesh and blood. Paul Astier is P[opelin], more than blackened: it isn't the weak and honest man I know, but the Duchess is undoubtedly Her . . . The novelist is always something of a seer, and he describes the scenes that are to come. Having tried to get under the Princess's skin, he thought: 'What would she do if she thought, or knew, that her lover had deceived her with a young girl who owed her everything?' – and he guessed right.[37]

Early in March 1891 Mathilde learned that her brother was ill in Rome, and that he was not expected to live.

She took the train for Rome at once. Napoleon was dying, in much pain, at the Hôtel de Russie. The doctors could do nothing for him; Clotilde was praying, but she could not talk to him, now, any more than she had been able to talk to him during the thirty-two years of their loveless marriage. Mathilde was the only person who dared to approach him, to help him to go in peace. Longing for family unity, she tried to reconcile him with the son whom he had disowned, and she brought Victor to him. The Bonapartes were a violent and an unforgiving race; Napoleon ordered him from the room, and the doctors, waiting in the passage, blamed her for hastening her brother's death. He died next day, 17 March 1891. He was sixty-eight.

Mathilde had lost a confidant, but her misery continued. At one moment it seemed as if there might be some *rapprochement* with Popelin. 'Gustave came to ask me to *déjeuner*,' she told Grandjean. 'The poor Father is glad of this convention, and so am I. If only I could see the end of my unhappiness at last!'[38]

Popelin himself longed to be reconciled. Writing to Hébert, he revealed his profound dejection. Hébert answered: 'The glimpse you give me of your state of mind proves that the unhappy situation is still the same and perhaps always will be. You have taken a conciliating line, but it is bristling with difficulties. Let us hope that this trial will end in the peace which you deserve, the

K

great tranquillity of soul which everyone so needs.'[39] '*She* and
Gust. are as one,' Mathilde told Gégé. 'The poor Father isn't
happy. He doesn't hesitate to say so, but he can't change anything.'[40] She was convinced that Gustave was largely responsible for
the whole crisis. He had threatened to leave his father if his father
stopped seeing Marie. He was not only moved by his resentment
of Mathilde: he was moved by gratitude to Marie, who had
arranged his marriage to her friend, Henriette Doumerc.[41] It was
natural that Marie should come to the rue de Téhéran.

Mathilde herself, in misery, sent for her old friend Gabriel
Daubrée, the geologist, and poured out her soul to him. 'I have
never seen or heard anything more touching,' he remembered.
'She was superb in her sincerity, her naturalness, her poignant
humanity ... Suddenly she drew herself up, as if she had exhausted
her tears, her stock of indignation, and pulled herself together:
"That's enough of that for today, we'll drive round the Bois, and
talk of something else." Almost at once, her face, which was more
obedient than her heart, resumed its proud serenity, and the trace
of tears was effaced.'[42]

Her serenity did not last. Late in August she told Gégé that since
he had gone she had had no moments of happiness.[43] The day after
she had written to him, her mood had abruptly changed; Gustave
had invited himself to Saint-Gratien with his father. He had been
charming, and Popelin had been delighted to see him there. 'So
the situation has improved,' Mathilde explained to Gégé, 'and as a
consequence I am serene . . .'[44] A few days later, her peace of mind
had gone again, and she declared that, since her brother's death,
she had been haunted by the thought of dying. 'What can one do
about it? Live and suffer, and gradually fade away – and complain
as little as possible.'[45]

On 19 January 1892, a brief obituary appeared in *The Times*.
Alfred-Émilien de Nieuwerkerke, 'a sculptor, and Director of the
Fine Arts under Napoleon III,' had died in Lucca at the age of
eighty-two.[46]

It is doubtful whether Mathilde felt any grief at his death. She
had not seen him for more than twenty years. He belonged to a
world that must have seemed unreal to her. Now there was only
one man in her mind, one man with whom she was vulnerable.

On 17 May, at about three o'clock in the morning, she was

woken and told that Popelin was dead. He had spent the previous evening with his son and Marie. At ten o'clock Gustave had gone to see his fiancée. When he came back at midnight, Popelin had asked him to take Marie home. Two hours later, he died in his chair. Mathilde had been informed immediately.

She went to the rue de Téhéran, and, as she entered the room, she said that someone else must be told. Gustave replied that Marie knew. She was in the next room. He brought her in. Perhaps he hoped that there would be a reconciliation. There was none.[47]

↔ 42 ↔

That day Mathilde had a telegram sent to Gégé Primoli.[1] He went to see her, and to take the burden of her grief and her regrets. For four years, she said, there had not been a day when she had not wept. At Saint-Gratien, where she had lived with Popelin, her grief was more acute than ever. 'Of course I have often thought of the terrible effect which the return to Saint-Gratien must have had on you,' Lavisse wrote in July. 'Be brave, dear Princess. Don't believe that you have no more purpose in life. You must remember those who have gone, and love those who love you. And to these, believe me, you are essential. I'm afraid that you may doubt it in your desolation and despondency. But it's true, it's absolutely true . . .'[2] Mathilde greatly needed to be assured that she still had a purpose, that she was still essential to her friends. She wrote to Lavisse of her insignificance, and he answered with robust indignation: 'Nobody is more significant than you.'[3]

In the first weeks after Popelin's death, Mathilde suffered bitterly. 'Yesterday, when her mind was wandering,' Gégé wrote in his diary, 'she said to her *femme de chambre:* "Where is he? What's become of him? I can't live like this!" And she burst into tears. To-day she told me: "I'll end by blowing my brains out." She meant it when she said it, but she won't do it, and she will suffer for years from the love that was stolen from her and from the strong right arm that she has lost.'[4]

Even now, it was clear to Gégé that she did not only suffer from her bereavement: she suffered also from the thought of Popelin's betrayal. She found a thousand traces of the liaison all about her: traces which seemed palpable proofs of guilt. Here was an enamel of Marie which he had painted, there was a photograph in which he and Marie were exchanging glances. And when, at the end of the day, she sat alone on her sofa, beside the big armchair he had always sat in, she wept not only with misery, but with anger. She had changed her life for Popelin, aged herself by twenty years to harmonize her existence with his own; and now she believed that his lassitude had been a sign of his supreme betrayal.

But still she was not sure.

According to all I see and hear the general conviction is *that he deceived me* for the sake of his self-esteem – that I was his dupe and am now his victim! No one dares to tell me so – everybody thinks so! Do you think so, too [she wrote to Gégé]? In that case why shouldn't I try to forget him and fortify my heart and mind? Could I do it? Should I be better for doing it? Or is it wiser to drown in the tide of griefs and regrets? Gégé, you must tell me the truth. I ask you to. I must get out of my rut.

Dumas is going to see Gust[ave] and talk to him loud and clear . . .[5]

No doubt the death of his father had roused all Gustave's dormant aversion for Mathilde; besides, he had recently married and he did not want to be disturbed by legal formalities.[6] Whatever the reason, he had given no sign of life since his marriage. He said nothing about his father's will, and he made no move to return Mathilde's correspondence to her. She rejected the thought of a lawsuit, for it would show Popelin's blameworthy conduct all too clearly.[7] 'You mustn't judge her condition by what she writes to you,' Grandjean had told Gégé in mid July. 'She is sad, profoundly sad, but she isn't incurably wounded, as we might have feared. She is gradually getting better. She even seems to me better than she was last winter or the winter before. At the moment, there's only one thing which really torments her, and that is Gustave's stubborn refusal to return the letters. It isn't that he's positively refused to return them. But his attitude is worse than a refusal.'[8]

Gégé sent her wise advice, but Mathilde could not take it.

Everything you say is right, but I can't apply it. I'm deeply wounded – everything reminds me of him, and the wound bleeds as soon as it's touched by memory . . . I miss him at every moment – I looked after him like a child, he was my concern, my only concern – everything was concentrated in him . . .

No news yet about returning my letters, and nothing about the legacy which was left to my incurables. He doesn't reply to *anything* or anyone. I will keep you informed. You're a great consolation to me – and I count on you to console me.

Doucet often comes – he's very good to me. Grandjean is a faithful friend . . .[9]

Grandjean was an excellent friend. He did not merely listen to Mathilde's regrets, he persuaded her to use her energy. In July he encouraged her to put her papers in order.[10] In August he suggested that she should continue to write her memoirs. She was spurred into activity. She thought of compiling a book on Popelin: a series of appreciations by those who had known him best.[11]

She also decided to organize an exhibition of Popelin's work. Some might have thought the gesture humiliating, a public confession that she had been unjust. Mathilde was glad of a task which allowed her to dwell on her memories, and to foster his fame. But the exhibition had to be quickly arranged, while Popelin's death was still remembered in the world of art; and Mathilde had lost her confidence and her energy. Early in September, after some moment of particular melancholy, she told Grandjean:

. . . Though you've had enough of my prose, I must write to you this morning to say how much I regret the bad moments I gave you yesterday . . . Another thing which adds to my grief – shall I have time to arrange this exhibition properly? Shouldn't I do better to hide in some corner where the world would forget me, and rid my friends of my sad self? I'm no good for anything any more, I'm living a life which is bad for myself and for others . . .

All that I can expect of life is to have my grief alleviated and to lose interest in many things – that is why I am trying to find out what can give me most pain, so that I shall come to have less regret. This struggle between my heart laid bare and my mind, which continues to reason, doesn't give me a moment's peace. However, I'll do everything you advise me. I want to keep you with me as long as possible. Scold me, get angry with me, I shall be grateful to you all the same . . .[12]

She was so lonely, so in need of companionship, that she added, two days later: 'Isn't it better to escape one's real friends when one's pain is too great? One has to live. But why, since there can be no consolation? Forgive me, I'm having one of my worst days . . .'[13] 'I feel the weight of my grief more than ever,' she added on 18 September. 'I only cling now to the friends who knew him, loved him and appreciated him . . .'[14] At one moment she seems to have felt too ill to continue arranging the exhibition. 'It would certainly have been a great grief for me if I had been forced to give up,' she told Grandjean at the end of the month. 'I won't say more about it today, for the past three days I have been rather unwell, and this inaction is bad for me. My head gets tired. I go backwards instead of forwards . . . My pain is deep and incurable, believe me. And my age adds much to my despair. Why should one force oneself to go on living when one is near the end? . . .'[15]

Everything was food for her distress. One day Toto Gautier found some negatives on top of a cupboard. He recognized them as pictures of Popelin and he had them developed. They had been taken at the time when Mathilde still trusted Popelin. She looked at them for a long while, and then the memory came back to her, and, with it, the perpetual doubt, and the fact of his death. She wept, and wandered into the park at Saint-Gratien, to escape her guests. 'I feel death in my soul,' she told Grandjean, 'and I no longer hope for anything. In one of the photographs he is with her. I have torn it up, and smashed the negative.'[16]

For the past four years, since her return from Turin, the visit to Arcachon, something seemed to have died in her. 'For the past four years,' she told Gégé, 'I haven't lived . . . I had and still have a fixed idea of him – Him, always him – or rather the ideal that I had created.'[17] There, unconsciously, in a phrase, she had revealed herself, the bitterness of her disillusionment. She had regretted the end of her physical relationship with Popelin,[18] yet her love had perhaps been all the more intense when it was platonic. She had felt a new spiritual freedom, she thought she had established a relationship which she had not known with Anatole or Nieuwerkerke: a relationship of complete and mutual trust, the perfect relationship which she had always needed. For the third time she had created an ideal of a man, only to see it destroyed.

And since, again, she had concentrated all her emotions on the man she loved, she felt lost without her exclusive preoccupation. 'I still hope to find him again,' she wrote in August. 'I look for him everywhere! I miss him every moment – I used to tell him everything, to open my heart. And now I'm choking . . .'[19] At times she even missed the last four wretched years, for 'they were still very happy, because he was there.'[20]

She was still working at the exhibition, but Gustave was so

unwilling to lend his father's enamels that Dumas *fils* and other friends were obliged to intervene. Gustave judged Mathilde harshly. 'He is more and more against me,' she had told Lavisse.[21] He delayed a long time before he carried out his father's wish about a legacy to her incurables; Mathilde had looked after the home at Neuilly for many years, and it had suffered badly during the war. She had to ask Benedetti to write to him about it.

Gustave found a more personal way of expressing his antipathy: he still insisted on keeping her letters to his father. Mathilde was convinced that Marie was withholding some of them. 'Even if I gave back mine,' she told Grandjean in October, 'she would keep the ones that she's stolen . . .'[22] Gustave laid down conditions for the return of the letters, and again Dumas *fils* had to intercede.[23]

In January 1893, when Mathilde had waited for nine months, when she thought that everything was over, the steadfast Dumas handed her the packet of sealed letters. She was sure that some of them were missing. 'I'm sure that someone has made a selection; I haven't found a single letter, either before or after '88, referring to the betrayal of which I was the victim, the betrayal which brought tumult into my life . . . I am overwhelmed, very unhappy, may God and my friends have pity on me . . .'[24] She felt more despondent than ever.

The following month the whole unhappy episode of the correspondence was settled. 'My affairs with Gust. have ended for the best,' Mathilde assured Gégé. 'He brought his wife to see me . . . I gave her a bracelet – he was moved by my behaviour. But I did it for the sake of the poor Father.'[25] On 24 April, after *déjeuner*, Gustave suddenly arrived at Saint-Gratien. Perhaps he had come to apologize for his past bitterness, to assure Mathilde that his resentment and hostility had gone; perhaps he had come to ask her a favour. Yet he left without explaining his visit. 'I don't know why he came,' she told Claire Grandjean, 'but his visit surprised me and disturbed me very much . . .'[26] Just before Christmas, he brought her some photographs of his father's bedroom and study.[27] Gégé noted that she had been refused access to Popelin's vault at Père-Lachaise, and that she had written impassioned letters, and pushed them through the grille.[28] Possibly Gégé exaggerated; but among Mathilde's papers is a note which might be ascribed to 1893:

Dear Princess,
Here is the key to the vault at Père-Lachaise, which you asked me for last year – you remember I didn't have it at the time.

I should have liked to bring it to you myself, and to assure you of all my tender and respectful affection.

GUSTAVE POPELIN.[29]

In May 1897, on the eve of her seventy-seventh birthday, Gustave wrote to Grandjean: 'I'd be very glad to talk to you for a minute. Nothing very serious: it's about the Princess's book-plate. It must be ready before she leaves for St Gratien . . .'[30] Perhaps she had asked him to design a book-plate for the volumes which Gautier, her librarian, had chosen. Perhaps it was Gustave's birthday present, a confirmation that Popelin's son was finally her friend.

K*

༄ 43 ༅

Since the crisis over Popelin, Mathilde had probably understood the importance of her relationship with Gégé. As a boy he had admired her, as a youth of seventeen he had been enamoured of her; now, as a man, he felt for her that intense, understanding affection, that delicate love which is summarized in the word *tendresse*.

Gégé was one of her family, he understood her impulsive manner, her passionate outbursts, her single-mindedness, her inability to compromise. As a Bonaparte, he appreciated her historical creed. Sociable, imaginative and highly intelligent, he too enjoyed the company of writers, artists, actors and intellectuals; like Mathilde, he had had small time for empty pomp and circumstance, for the ceremonial which she dismissed as *chinoiseries*.

Like Mathilde, he was also an unrelenting idealist: as a *collégien*, he had expressed his scorn of *un beau mariage*, of marriage for material benefits. He had decided not to marry unless he was in love. He had been much taken with Jeannine, the daughter of Dumas *fils*. Mathilde had wanted the marriage, Dumas *fils* would have been delighted, and Jeannine confessed her affection for him. But Gégé would not commit himself. Probably he was prevented by his overwhelming love for his mother; indeed, he felt such devotion for her that it is hard to see how he could have chosen any 'conflicting' relationship. When his mother died in 1901, he was a confirmed and lonely bachelor of fifty.

His relationship with Mathilde did not conflict with his love for his mother: indeed, it seems to have been an extension of it. 'The thought of seeing you again,' he wrote to her, 'of being held in your maternal embrace, has decided me to leave Rome . . . My dear aunt, let us hold each other close, let us make our two solitudes into society: I depend on you – on you alone!'[1] That undated letter, probably written after his mother's death, suggested the significance of the relationship. 'When I stop escaping from myself,' he explained to Mathilde, 'I am overcome by sadness . . . Only your *tendresse* may, perhaps, at times alleviate it.'[2]

The letter was sent from Naples, where Gégé was cruising with the Empress. She, too, after the death of her son, was comforted by this lonely man who understood the filial relationship so well. But Gégé could hardly have felt for her the sympathy he had always felt for Mathilde. Eugénie was cold; Mathilde was warm, so responsive that their letters always crossed and their thoughts perpetually coincided. A boxful of correspondence shows how Gégé loved and understood her, and another shows how she returned his immense affection. He thought of her constantly: he sent her a postcard of the memorial to Napoleon III in Milan;[3] he sent her a card gay with violets, the Bonaparte flowers, and a message in Italian: 'The first violet has bloomed in my grateful heart at the sweet memory of Saint-Gratien.'[4] 'I come to you,' Mathilde told Gégé, 'when my heart is overflowing with grief.'[5] When he stayed with her, the year after Popelin's death, she used to come to his room every morning, and sit, weeping, at the foot of his bed.[6] 'It's only when you're here,' she wrote, 'when I know you're in the room over mine, that I don't wake up crying at night.'[7] All her regrets were summarized in the single name Popelin; all her plans were made so that Gégé could be with her.[8] When he left her after a visit in 1894, she was 'all disorientated.'[9] He was very moved by her need of him.

Long ago, years before the crisis over Popelin, Gégé had escorted her to a dinner-party. He had come solemnly down the stairs at the rue de Berry. 'She was in full evening dress, *décolletée*, and I was wearing a white tie and tails. We both burst out laughing, and our good humour has continued more or less ever since.'[10] Gégé had always shared her humour, he had always been able to entertain her; and nothing, in her later years, restored Mathilde's morale like his bracing and devoted love.

Don't think I'm coming to Paris to entertain you, my dear Aunt [this on 12 October 1893]. *You're* going to entertain *me*! *You'll take me* to see Sardou's play about the Empire, [and] Sarah Bernhardt, . . . one wet day *you'll take me* to the museum at Versailles, another to the

Louvre (the museum) and another to the Louvre (the shop). In fact,
I intend to *tire you out*, so that when I go you'll say: 'Thank God, now
I can have a rest!'[11]

For all her desolation, Mathilde had never ceased to be 'the
Princess,' or to be – as Sainte-Beuve had called her – Notre Dame
des Arts. From time to time, she would suddenly say: 'Read me
a story by that foul Maupassant'; she found his writing astringent,
a tonic in her moments of depression. Even after she had suspected Popelin of infidelity, she had asked him to make an enamel
portrait of Maupassant, and she had attended the sittings. She
was fond of Maupassant: he had been the protégé of Flaubert,
he had been presented to her by Popelin, and she liked him for
his lack of inhibition. She had no doubt been delighted when,
one summer evening in 1887, he had sailed in a balloon over
Saint-Gratien – so low that he could hear her guests in conversation on the verandah. He had sent her dates from Tunis as a
New Year present, and told her of his visit to Carthage, where,
as he visited the ruins of the aqueduct, he had seemed to hear
'the sonorous voice of Flaubert crying out his admiration. The
place I stopped at is in fact one of those he visited (I met people
who had been his guides), and . . . there I thought of him
and of all those who loved the great, good and simple
man . . .'[12] Among them was Mathilde; and, on his return from
Africa, Maupassant had a letter from her which gave him a
sudden vision of the rue de Berry, 'and I caught a glimpse of the
Princess,' he told her, 'with her gracious smile, receiving her
guests. If travel gave us nothing but the pleasure of coming back
and rediscovering, that would still be a great deal.'[13]

Years earlier, Mathilde had seen Jules de Goncourt slowly
degenerating from syphilis. Now it was clear that syphilis and
continual overwork had destroyed Maupassant's health, and,
since 1890, she had watched unhappily as his reason had begun to
fail. 'I had Mr de Maupassant to *déjeuner* this morning,' she
wrote to Grandjean from Saint-Gratien, on 17 October 1891.
'How changed he is! It upset me very much, he stammers when
he talks, he exaggerates the smallest things, and he thinks he's
cured . . .'[14] Two months later, Maupassant attempted suicide.
'He's calm and very melancholy,' wrote Mathilde in an undated
letter to Mme Strauss. 'His wound has healed. God grant that he

will recover.'[15] 'What sad news you give me of Maupassant,' she wrote, later, to the same correspondent, 'and how can he get better? He wanted to so much, and you wanted it, too. He is very alone if he is to be properly looked after . . . If you see him again, talk to him about me . . .'[16] It was at the rue de Berry, soon afterwards, that Maupassant finally became deranged: he could no longer control his ideas or connect his sentences, he talked wildly throughout dinner, and assured Admiral Duperré that he could command a fleet himself. The next day Dr Blanche sent him to an asylum; he died there, hopelessly insane, eighteen months later.

Mathilde, who could not bear white hair, or leafless trees in winter, who was troubled by the thought of old age, the passing of time, was forced, now, to accept the deaths of some of her dearest friends. Thirty-five years earlier, she had set Gounod on his career. In June 1893, he came to spend the day at Saint-Gratien and Gégé declared that, since Gautier's death, he was one of the four greatest charmers in Paris.[17] That October, Gounod died. It was a terrible shock for Mathilde, Grandjean wrote to Gégé,

for nowadays the death of a contemporary is a stunning blow for her, and how many of them have died in the past year, from Lavoix to Blanche and Gounod! It has come to the point where I tax my ingenuity to find old men of eighty who are well so that I can 'casually' mention them to her.

I cannot see her depressed like this, because I feel that, with her robust health, she still has several good years to live. It's only her morale which is affected, and it isn't incurable . . .

And, believe me, it isn't grief that's killing her. Her grief is immense, but it's the kind of grief she can live with. What's killing her is that she is destroying herself by her irritation with everything around her. She is still immensely energetic, and she's only using her energy to fret herself, to create herself subjects for exasperation. So she must be distracted, prevented from having time to get worked up about everything. It's difficult, but not impossible.[18]

Mathilde's own letters to the Grandjeans reflected her constant, painful longing for peace of mind. 'I feel so worn, so discouraged by life, so uninterested in everything, that I don't dare to hope for anything any more . . .'[19] 'What can I say about myself? There's still the same emptiness, the same regrets. I can't get used to it and I'm getting so sad; I feel myself growing old so unhappily.'[20] 'I am in a bad state of mind. Everything that reminds me of my past life breaks my heart. Would you both like to come and dine next Wednesday? That will give me courage . . .'[21]

As the 1890s continued, the Grandjeans grew increasingly close to her. Claire encouraged her in her plans for improving Saint-Gratien; the young woman, in the early, happy years of her marriage, brought her moments of stability. 'It gave me a great pang to see her go,' Mathilde told Charles Grandjean, one day in 1893. 'She was such a comfort to me with her affection and her even temper . . .'[22] Claire Grandjean was an understanding, loyal listener: Mathilde could speak to her of her grief without fear of indifference or betrayal.

She could not talk to a friend without opening her heart; and sometimes, in her desperate need to recall the past, to justify herself, to think aloud, she had confided in false friends. Once, at least, she learned that she had misplaced her trust, and she bitterly reproached herself for degrading Popelin's memory. She was so upset by the thought that she had nervous spasms and found her hands ice-cold.[23]

You'll tell me I'm mad [she wrote to Grandjean], perhaps I am – but I feel so acutely that I can only suffer . . .

I had a nice visit from Doucet yesterday morning, it did me good. I worked hard [at my painting] with him. It gave me courage to go on, and in those few hours I found real relief.

. . . I am grateful for the good friendship which you both give me. You have adopted me with my great grief! I understand all the kindness and the sacrifice which that involves. I think I shall go to Paris after *déjeuner* – I must think about my return.[24]

Even her return to Paris, every autumn, brought her moments of depression. She clung to Saint-Gratien, where she had lived, now, for more than forty years, the château which had been her most constant home. She was reluctant to leave the studio which Goncourt had preserved, in his *Journal*, for posterity, the verandah where Gautier had composed his sonnets, the salon where Flaubert had wanted to make his declaration of love. She had planned Saint-Gratien with Nieuwerkerke, she had lived there for years with Popelin: she felt she was nearer to him there than she was in Paris. 'I am too old to travel,' she told

Grandjean on 11 September 1894, 'It seems to me that I should be leaving my dear departed once again. Nothing can distract me and nothing should.'[25] A few days later she added:

Doucet is here – he's trying my portrait. It will be a sad memento to leave to you and to all my friends – and another acknowledgment which I owed him . . .

I shall still have some bad moments to undergo – like the moment when I leave St Gratien. Who knows if I shall come back to it?[26]

I understand your need of calm and tranquillity [she wrote to him one autumn: probably in 1895]. If only one could find it! What wouldn't one do! We can do nothing – we can't even order our lives as we wish. For three years the mainspring inside me has been broken. I'm struggling, but I'm not growing used to it. I am more than ever overwhelmed by my grief – but I've talked enough about myself.[27]

Mathilde had always had a gift for friendship, she had known how to express her touching need of her friends. Now she showed her dependence increasingly; and, telling some friends how much she missed them, she added:'But if you're both happy where you are, . . . I'd be wrong to complain. One must love people for themselves – I shall never be an egoist – my affection is wholly one of devotion.'[28] 'Do you think you'll come and see me in the country like you did last year?' she asked Joseph Reinach, the politician. 'I cannot give up the very great pleasure of seeing those I love, and I'm grateful for what I'm given . . .'[29]

And to Ernest Lavisse, the historian, she expressed herself in a phrase which seems to hold her essential nature, to summarize the purpose of her life. 'I want to leave in the hearts and minds of those who have loved me an impression of truth, and of gratitude for friendship – that is my one ambition.'[30]

She herself remained a militant friend. Late in 1889, when she was in despair about Popelin, she was campaigning for Lavisse, who was anxious to be elected to the Académie. 'Yes, of course I'll do all I can,' she promised him on 4 December. '. . . Go on, and don't give up your place. Come and invite yourself to dinner on Monday if you can.'[31] 'Bertrand and Halévy are *secured* for you,' she added, a fortnight later. 'Come and dine with me next Monday with Bertrand, who'd like to meet you . . . You should see [the Duc d'Aumale] – I'm sure you'd get him.'[32]

Lavisse had to try a second time for his election; but one summer day in 1892, just after Popelin's death, Mathilde went to the Institut to hear the result just as she had gone, years ago, for Gautier. As she stood in the courtyard, in the rain, Lavisse appeared at a window, and cried out: 'We may have won!' She blew him a kiss. 'I cannot tell you how touched and grateful I am, dear Princess,' the new Academician wrote, 'when I think of the interest you showed in me.'[33] For Mathilde herself, his election was not only a triumph but a tonic.

In 1895, when Anatole France was campaigning for a seat among the Forty, Mathilde invited him to dine and secure the vote of the Duc d'Aumale. The Duc talked all the evening; when he left, Mathilde whispered a word to him about her candidate. The Duc shook hands with him 'in a meaningful way ... It was understood that in this handshake he granted him his vote. France had hardly been able to speak, but he had listened to his future colleague; this sympathetic attention had been more eloquent than the finest of speeches.'[34] On 20 December 1896, Anatole France took Ferdinand de Lesseps' seat among the Immortals.

Mathilde had no prestige with the Republican Government, but she still endeavoured, through her friends, to see that due decorations were bestowed. Her correspondence with the dramatist Georges de Porto-Riche reflects the old, familiar eagerness: 'The Fourteenth of July is approaching,' goes a letter dated simply 30 June. 'As you know the Minister, do talk to him about the cross [of the Légion-d'honneur] for Doucet. I surely have no need to plead Doucet's cause to you...'[35] Doucet was her drawing-master; Mathilde was as anxious as ever to gain recognition for her friends. She asked Porto-Riche himself to dine and discuss a private performance of one of his plays, and Porto-Riche knew how to respond. He was aware of her frivolous tastes – a telegram from her goes simply; 'Sweets received delicious thanks and remembrances – Mathilde.' He also knew, like all of the world, of her overriding passion for her dynasty. 'Thank you a thousand times for your kind thought,' she scribbled on a card, 'translated into two bunches of violets.'[36]

The passing of years, the desolation in her private life, had not weakened her worship of her uncle. When one of her friends was looking through the *Almanach de Gotha,* and counting all the kings among her relatives, Mathilde interrupted: 'That's all very well, but what is it worth compared with being the niece of Napoleon?' One day, a small child was brought by its mother to the rue de Berry; and, while the mother was engrossed in conversation, the child examined the treasures in the salon. Suddenly it noticed a statue, pulled at its mother's sleeve, and cried excitedly: 'Maman, it's *him!*' The *him* touched Mathilde to the heart. Lavisse recalled that she spoke fondly of Napoleon's beauty when he was First Consul. 'One day she grew scarlet with rage when an elderly scholar contested this beauty. As the elderly scholar was very plain, she did not fail to tell him so; then, as he was also an old friend, she regretted her quick temper.'[37]

Sardou was only the latest friend to learn the penalty for *lèse-majesté.* Mathilde often visited the dramatist at his splendid house at Marly. She was enthralled by his conversation. On 27 October 1893 she attended the première of his historical comedy, *Madame Sans-Gêne.* The play was set in the days of Napoleon, and the heroine was the laundress who married Lefebvre – the miller's son who became a Marshal of France. Gégé, who was with Mathilde, noted in his diary:

She felt terribly put out at seeing her aunts insulted on stage, and especially at feeling that every eye in the audience was upon her . . . I had some difficulty in making her stay. However, at the end of the act, as I was afraid of the Emperor's appearance, . . . I took her out by the stage door . . . The poor Princess was all flustered and upset, and, in the heat of the moment, she vowed she would tell Sardou what she thought of him.[38]

Even Sardou took a little while to compose an answer to her letter; but among his papers is a draft of his reply. 'Princess,' he ended, 'I have never thought that the profound respect I feel for you imposed an obligation on me to revere all your family...'[39]

It was some years before Mathilde would accept his argument, but finally her anger was forgotten. Sardou, more fortunate than Taine, was observed again escorting her round the splendours of Marly.

Her friends were taken from her, all too soon, by death; she could not afford to dismiss them. On 27 November 1895, at a

Wednesday at the rue de Berry, a telegram arrived with the news that Dumas *fils* had died. He had been brash in his younger days, perhaps he had been too eager and too confident, too clumsy in his expressions of devotion; but she had long since known him to be one of her most loyal friends. He had proclaimed his faithfulness when the Empire fell, he had sent her letters of wisdom and solace in her exile, he had helped her in her despair over Popelin, interceded with Gustave for her letters. It seemed that he had always been there, at the crises in her life. 'I know only too well,' wrote Joseph Reinach, 'that new friendships do not and could not ever replace those which have come to be part of life itself.'[40] She answered: 'I am very upset and distressed by the death of Dumas. He was an old and faithful friend. At my age every loss you suffer hurts you more deeply – but it doesn't make you insensible to those who hold out their hands.'[41]

Goncourt remained, now, the only survivor of the great generation of writers. Henri Lavedan, the dramatist, remembered her visits to Goncourt's Grenier: the *salon* which *le Maréchal des Lettres* had opened in 1885 in his house at Auteuil.

She was always delighted by these visits to the Grenier, which took her out of her usual surroundings, and the following Sunday the master of the house would bring us the echo of the pleasure which – with a touch of happy surprise – she had found there.
'But my dear, how nice your young friends are! How kind! Polite! Delightful!'[42]

Goncourt died on 16 July 1896: thirty-four years, almost to the day, since he had first visited Saint-Gratien. 'I greatly regret poor Goncourt,' Mathilde told Reinach, 'he had only little faults, but he had great qualities . . . Alas, those who live long suffer much.'[43] To Gégé she wrote: 'He was one of my old friends, often unbearable – but he was there, full of good intentions. It is a new shock and a new grief . . . I keep on seeing poor Goncourt's face. And his poor house, what will become of it?'[44] She was both astonished and indignant to learn that, in his will, he had founded the Académie Goncourt. It was not, presumably, that she disapproved of a society established to encourage young writers, but she deplored the jury who would award the prizes. She knew nothing of Céard and Huysmans, and she thought Zola 'filthy'.[45]

And yet it could not be said that Mathilde had grown rigidly conservative in her old age. Paul Bourget, the novelist, who had been the star of the Grenier, also shone in the rue de Berry; Anatole France, the lion of Mme de Caillavet's *salon*, was welcomed as a lion by Mathilde. Under the palms, beneath the statue of Napoleon, Maurice Barrès talked to the granddaughter of Rostopchine, the man who in 1812 had set light to Moscow; and he talked to Lavisse, who had recently refused the Embassy in Berlin, because, he said, there was nothing to be done.[46] Mathilde gave a dinner in honour of Adelaide Ristori, the *grande dame* of dramatic art, now in her seventies, and she invited Mounet-Sully to meet her.[47] The derelict tomb of Mlle Mars at Père-Lachaise impelled her to complain to the Comédie-Française.[48] She not only showed respect for the past, she showed interest in the present: she invited Réjane and La Duse to the rue de Berry. As a girl, she had known Jules Janin; now she entertained the critic Jules Lemaître. Once she had met Chateaubriand, who had made an indifferent impression;[49] now she earned the devotion of Proust.

Proust had hardly left the *lycée* when he began to frequent the rue de Berry; and, with the confident impulse of youth, he asked Mathilde to dictate her memoirs to him. He was so young that she did not take him seriously; and by her refusal posterity lost one of the most remarkable books of the century. No one would resurrect the past as Proust would do; and no one had a richer or more complex past than Mathilde. As it was, Proust tried to read the vicissitudes of her thoughts in the changing expression of her eyes.

I remember how the charming eyes of Princess Mathilde took on a different beauty as they rested on some or other image left on her retina and in her memory by some great men, some great sights of the beginning of the century, and it is that image, emanated from them, which she saw and we shall never see. I had a feeling of the supernatural when, at such moments as this, I met her gaze: that gaze which, in a short and mysterious line, in an action of resurrection, joined the present to the past.[50]

Inevitably, he put Mathilde into his great novel. He put her in without disguise, a sturdy, factual figure: speaking exactly as she spoke, looking precisely as she looked, surrounded by the familiar anecdotes he had heard. Only the historian would recognize Mathilde as the Duchess in Daudet's *L'Immortel*; no one could fail to recognize her in *À l'ombre des jeunes filles en fleurs*.

The day when we went to see the Cynghalais, as we were coming back, we caught sight of an elderly but still beautiful woman; she was coming in our direction, followed by two other women who appeared to be escorting her, she was wrapped up in a dark cloak and wearing a little bonnet tied under the chin with two ribbons, 'Ah! there's someone who'll interest you,' Swann said to me. The old lady was now a few feet away, and smiled with caressing sweetness. Swann took off his hat, Mme Swann dropped a low curtsey, and wanted to kiss her hand, but the woman, who looked like a Winterhalter portrait, raised her up and kissed her. 'Come on, now, put on your hat,' she said to Swann in a deep, rather gruff voice, like an old friend. 'I'm going to present you to Her Imperial Highness,' Mme Swann said to me. Swann drew me aside for a moment while Mme Swann talked to Her Highness about the fine weather and the animals which had just arrived at the Jardin d'Acclimatation. 'It's Princess Mathilde,' he said to me. 'You know: the friend of Flaubert, Sainte-Beuve and Dumas. Just think, she's the niece of Napoleon I. She was asked in marriage by Napoleon III and by the Emperor of Russia [sic]. Talk to her a little. But I don't want her to keep us standing for an hour.'[51]

In his novel, which was at times so factual, Proust recalled the break with Taine, the patriotism which Mathilde expressed with an honest Wurtemberg bluntness. He contrasted her slightly masculine frankness with her languorous Italian smile. Like Mme Daudet, like Masson, he noticed her Second Empire style of dress; but, unlike them, he saw, perhaps, why she chose to wear it. 'Although no doubt the Princess wore it from affection for the fashions she had liked, she seemed to have meant not to make an error in historical colour, and to satisfy those who expected her to evoke another age.'[52]

Mme Swann made another curtsey, and the old lady smiled at them all

with a heavenly smile which she seemed to bring back from the past, from the graces of her youth, from the *soirées* at Compiègne, a smile which flowed, sweet and pure, across a face which had been sullen not so long ago; and then she went off followed by her two ladies-in-waiting . . . 'You should go and leave your name at her *hôtel* one day this week,' Mme Swann said to me. 'You don't turn down the corner of your card for all these *royalties*, as the English call them, but she will invite you if you have your name put down.'[53]

There was another novelist, a friend of Gégé Primoli, who left his impressions of the *salon*. Somewhere about the turn of the century, Abel Hermant was presented to Mathilde, and invited to 'the realm of the rue de Berry.'[54]

Mathilde was sitting facing the door as Hermant entered the *salon:* and she gave the very ordinary chair the appearance of a throne.

It was the Princess whom I saw first, and she took such imperious possession of my gaze that I, who was usually interested in décors, noticed almost literally nothing of her surroundings . . .

She was nearly eighty, but she could show her shoulders in full evening dress, and wear no jewels except a single strand of great black pearls. All the essentials of the mask remained. She was like a medallion, undefaced.[55]

As the century drew to its close, Mathilde's life seemed at last to come full circle, to attain a new, historic dignity. It was now, when her old friends were dying, that a figure from the bourgeois monarchy returned, quite unexpectedly, to the scene.

The Duc d'Aumale, the fourth son of Louis-Philippe, had not only distinguished himself as a general; he was also a noted historian, the author of an *Histoire des Princes de Condé*, and a member of the Académie-Française. He was a bibliophile and an art-collector (he would one day leave the château of Chantilly and his collections to the Institut). He was a Maecenas among princes, just as Mathilde was Notre Dame des Arts. One day, in Bonnat's studio, where he was sitting for his portrait, the conversation turned to Mathilde; and warmed, perhaps, by the artist (who was one of her habitués), the Duc felt a sudden wish to see her again. He was a patriot like Mathilde; he had offered to fight for France in 1870. He, too, set his country above politics. Now he had assured the Government of his political neutrality, and he had come back to end his life at Chantilly. Mathilde had given the Republic the identical assurance, so that she could spend the rest of her days in France.

The Duc invited Mathilde to Chantilly. Bonnat remembered how he waited, impatiently, for her, on the steps of the château. 'Here came the carriage: at the window, framed in a little black velvet bonnet with white feathers, appeared the Princess's kind and smiling face. The Duc took off his hat and balanced it on his cane; he offered her his gouty hand, trying to disguise it under his pearl-grey glove.' She tactfully pretended not to see his embarrassment, and barely touched his hand as she got out of her carriage. Bonnat observed, with a painter's eye, how she picked up her violet poult-de-soie skirt, revealing a billow of lace, a small reddish-brown half-boot, and a pink cashmere stocking. She had never been able to accept black stockings, any more than she had accepted tailored suits. 'She used to say that she didn't like women disguised as men: she kept to silk and lace.'

The Duc complimented her on her taste, and gave her his arm, 'and the royal couple went to the dining-room, followed by the two courts which merged into one variegated procession. One had the vision of some golden wedding in a fairy-tale . . .' After that first visit, Mathilde went to *déjeuner* every spring at Chantilly, and the Duc came to dine every winter at the rue de Berry. Matilde gave him the place of honour in the middle of the table, a concession she had only made for the Empress. She herself sat on his right. They were served simultaneously.[56]

In 1901, in *Mes Cahiers*, Maurice Barrès wrote that all the Bonapartes had the same point of view: they were all against party politics, they were waiting for a general state of mind which would make them necessary, which would bring them once again to power. Mathilde, at least, had no illusions that her dynasty would be restored. She would not criticize the Republic which had allowed her to come back to France.[57] One day in 1894, as she left the Russian Church after a memorial service for Alexander III, she caught sight of the President's wife, and she stood aside to let her pass. 'Madame la présidente,' said Mathilde, 'you should go first. I am glad to have the chance of being introduced.' 'Madame,' replied Mme Casimir-Périer, 'there was no need for an introduction; no one can fail to know you.' 'Madame la présidente, I am really glad to have been introduced. I hope you will give the President my sincere good wishes.' The two women shook hands. Someone whispered to Mathilde that she had just crossed the Rubicon. 'No', she said, 'but I did not want to cross the bounds of politeness. It was my duty.'[58] If, in her salon, someone ventured to criticize the President, Mathilde said simply: 'He represents France.'

She was aware of her obligations, and she was aware of her value as an historical figure. She understood, like Gautier's son, 'that everyone tried, instinctively, to be asked to the rue de Berry as if it was a Museum of Memories'.[59] She understood that they found her *salon* a refuge from the plebeian present. 'Your Highness,' Renan had written to her, on the death of the Prince Imperial, 'still stands erect amidst these disasters, personifying the good that we have dreamed of.'[60] Now the century of the Bonapartes was over; but people came to see Mathilde: to sense the majestic past.

Mathilde, in her eighties, was indeed a venerable figure. Proust, as he entered her salon, was dazzled by the thought of his precursors. 'When one thinks,' he wrote in 1903, 'that this *salon* . . . was a focal-point of literature in the second half of the nineteenth century, . . . one cannot help believing that certain worldly powers may have a fecund influence on literary history, and that few women used such powers so nobly as the Princess."[1]

The long picture gallery at Mathilde's duly became the décor for the Princesse de Parme. Much of the etiquette at the Princess de Guermantes' receptions was taken from the etiquette at the rue de Berry. Proust did not waste his experience of the imperial *salon*: indeed, he used Madame de Galbois as a lady-in waiting to the Princesse de Parme; and perhaps the Princesse de Parme took her title from the violets which were the Bonaparte flowers.[2]

It was a Bonaparte princess, in her extreme old age, who supported Frédéric Masson, the Bonaparte historian, when he stood for the Académie-Française. It was a Bonaparte princess who opposed Edmond Rostand as a candidate: she resented his *L'Aiglon* as a travesty of her family legend. When the play burst on Paris in March 1900, thirty years after Sedan, it stirred the national pride in Napoleon and his dynasty. Mathilde refused to see Sarah Bernhardt impersonating her cousin the King of Rome. She was still 'the Princess of Taine's P.P.C. and the exit from *Madame Sans-Gêne*'.[3]

It was a Bonaparte princess, militant in her eighties, who still showed her respect for the French army. 'If, on her way back from the Bois, at the Arc de Triomphe, she met an infantry regiment, drums beating, she would get out of her coupé, out of courtesy to the flag, and she used to say she was tempted to follow the band.'[4] Once, as she walked along the boulevards, a pedlar brushed past her, hawking some obscene publication. She could not refrain from asking him how he could sell such filth. He stopped, astounded, doffed his cap, and muttered: 'I'm sorry, Princess, I used to be in the Garde Impériale . . . But what can I do? I have to earn my living.' 'Of course, but you could sell something else.' And she slipped a coin into his hand.[5]

Gautier's son, who told the story, said that Mathilde had many friends among the humble. She knew all the keepers at the Bois de Boulogne (most of them had been there during the Empire). Even now, when it might be imprudent to acknowledge a Bonaparte, they saluted her, and found some pretext to approach her for a friendly word. The gate-keepers told her their bits of news, they sometimes told her their troubles, and she gave them practical sympathy. She was a familiar figure in Paris, and cab-drivers, asked to go to 20, rue de Berry, always smiled and said: 'Ah, chez la Princesse!'

She herself adored Paris, as she had done even before she had known it. She adored its life, its people, and its vitality, the rattle of its cabs and omnibuses. Nearly every day she drove towards the Madeleine, and got out of her carriage at the boulevard des Capucines; and then, recalled Toto Gautier,

accompanied by her lady-in-waiting or by someone else she had invited on the expedition, she would walk delightedly, briskly, along the *asphalte adoré*.

If she happened to meet a man she knew, she would take his arm and lead him to the rue de la Paix. She was at home there: she knew all the principal jewellers, all the leading sellers of feathers and flowers. She stopped at their shops, and sat down at the counter, resting on it a marvellously suède-gloved hand. She was received with respectful familiarity, without the obsequious eagerness which is accorded to millionaires. Everyone showed her his latest creations, sure of getting a word of praise or judicious criticism, or a word of advice dictated by a true and constant feeling for art.

For years she had been a friend of Worth, the couturier. Once he had added splendour to the Tuileries and Compiègne; now he dressed the great ladies of the Republic. At least once a year Mathilde would go to his country house at Suresnes, 'as simply and humanly as any bourgeoise,' and inspect the latest improvements.[6] She showed great appreciation of him and of his work, and she often went to the shop in the rue de la Paix, just because the spirit moved her. She was a faithful client until the day of her death.[7] Worth had long since understood that Mathilde would not have fashion imposed on her. People who ventured to suggest: '*Everyone's* wearing this,' received the brisk response: 'I'm not *everyone*, and I dress as I please!'[8] Life might be increasingly uniform, but Mathilde was not banal in anything.

Even in her eighties, she had a horror of idleness, and of mental inactivity. She supervised her household accounts down to the last detail. In the mornings, said Toto Gautier, she would put on a silk apron and follow her valets round the *hôtel* in the rue de Berry, dusting the ornaments, putting every object, every piece of furniture, in place. On evenings when there was no reception, she sat on the little cherry-coloured sofa, the folds of her silk dress spread around her, and her face suggesting a drawing by Ingres. Under the turquoise celadon lamp, she stitched away at her embroidery, watched her ladies-in-waiting at their own, from time to time took charge of their work, or painted flowers on fans.[9] François Coppée recalled that no event, happy or unhappy, occured in the lives of her friends without Mathilde showing her pleasure or bringing her consolation. 'Which of us, artist or writer, has not received the sign of her watchful interest on the morning after a success? Even in her last years, despite her great age, did she not hurry, with touching haste, to the bedside of a sick friend? So it was that we came to call her by one name alone – the Good Princess.'[10] When Gégé asked her what she most missed about the Second Empire, she said at once: 'The good that I could do.'[11] As Lavedan wrote, she was good to perfection.[12]

Mathilde's unceasing activity, her constant acts of kindness, could not save her from her deepening despondency. In the summer of 1902 she told Hébert that she was sad at heart, and that life was gently ebbing from her. 'This last thought did not please us at all,' he answered with loving astringency.

... You are surrounded by more respect and devoted affection than anyone else in this country. We will not allow a noble being, tempered as you are, to be gently drawn towards that bourn from which no traveller returns.

You must look after yourself, ... keep your morale high and unshaken, and *work*. Yes, dear Princess, you must work, the result is unimportant, the essential thing is to set oneself a task and fulfil it properly . . .[13]

But Mathilde felt lonely, irremediably sad. Her letters and telegrams to Gégé reflected her despair. 'Dear beloved Gégé, I'm still waiting for you, don't make me wait too long. I am alone and unhappy, and I don't believe in life.' 'Come and make me go on living.'[14] Mathilde was incapable of fine phrases; such words came from her heart. And in her sadness she even turned to the Empress whom she had so often condemned, the woman who had been brought closer to her by age and tragedy. In May 1903, from the Villa Cyrnos, at Cap Martin, Eugénie wrote: 'I'm so sorry . . . that you're sad and dispirited. I can understand that your solitude weighs upon you . . . Griefs . . . seem heavier as one grows older. I wish with all my heart that I could be with you more often, but, alas, my destiny has condemned me to a life of wandering.'[15]

On 3 July 1903, at Saint-Gratien, as Mathilde was coming down the spiral stairs from her bedroom to the studio, she caught her foot in her skirt, and fell. She had fractured her femur. She was very old and tired, and she had no overwhelming wish to live. She recognized that this would be the end. By some extraordinary chance, she would die from the same injury as Madame Mère.

Three days later, Gégé and the Empress arrived in Venice, on board the *Thistle*. A gondola drew alongside the yacht, bringing the mail, and Gégé noticed a number of telegrams. So it was that he learned of the accident, and learned that he was summoned to Saint-Gratien.[16]

About a fortnight after her fall, Professor Berger, her doctor, allowed Mathilde to move from her bedroom on to the terrace outside; and there Toto Gautier saw her, lying back, almost recumbent, in her armchair. She was resting her feet on a foot-stool, and she was swathed in white: in white woollen shawls, white lace and white muslin.

She was emaciated by lack of food, and by the immobility which was imposed on her by the apparatus round her leg. Her cheeks were hollow, her nose had shrunk, her hands – those wonderfully fine hands – had become almost impalpable. She looked like Vela's Napoleon (the statue at Versailles), and she looked even more like the mask which Antommarchi cast from Napoleon's face at St Helena. That day, she had a singular vivacity in her glance; and her eyes, grown large in her thin face, looked round with a childlike, touching expression, delighted once again to see the beloved, familiar outlines of the great clumps of trees, lit up by the sunlight of a limpid afternoon . . .[1]

Far away, in Hendaye, in the Basses-Pyrénées, Pierre Loti wrote to Gégé. He confessed that since his youth he had been drawn to Mathilde, to this woman who was so vital, intelligent and good. He had wanted a picture of her, he had looked for one, in vain, in the rue de Rivoli. 'If you could possibly get me the smallest photograph, you can't imagine how pleased I should be; but I realize I'm very bold to ask. In ten days or so I'm setting off for my beloved Orient again . . .'[2] He sailed on the *Vautour* for the Levant with a signed photograph of *la bonne princesse*.[3]

Her family, like her friends, were moved by affection. The Empress prolonged her visits to Saint-Gratien. Clotilde came, in her habitual black woollen dress, her silver-white hair drawn tightly back (Gégé noticed how her sensual mouth contrasted with her spiritual smile).[4] She offered Mathilde an invalid chair; but Mathilde disliked the thought of such contrivances, she preferred her own favourite chair, which had been fitted with wheels.[5] Lavisse begged her not to resent ill-health. 'All you need now, dear Princess, is a little patience. Let time do its work. Eat properly. I hope you're making heavy demands on your cows and hens. Milk, eggs, sunshine, and the care of those who love you: that's the régime you need. It's enough to make one want to be ill . . .'[6]

No one could have cared for her more lovingly than Gégé. He knew from the doctors that she was not expected to walk again, and no doubt he knew her true condition. He had decided to devote himself to her completely. When Clotilde had come and gone, and Louis had returned to Tiflis, Gégé stayed on, alone, at Saint-Gratien. Only in April he had seen Mathilde *décolletée*, doing the honours of her *salon*. Now she had suddenly become her age, her face had become the face of a woman of eighty. She herself was bitterly aware of the change. 'The Princess had a horror of everything which spoke of old age and death,' wrote Gégé on 22 September. 'She didn't like the country in winter, she was saddened by the leafless trees . . . And now, when she becomes aware of her state and her age, she has fits of despondency which nothing can appease . . . The Princess cannot eat any more . . . She has grown so weak that I can see her waste away . . . She is also suffering from acute rheumatism in her poor legs, which have been immobilized for nearly three months.'[7]

Mathilde, aware of Gégé's tenderness, gave him tangible signs of gratitude: the bust which Nieuwerkerke had sculpted of her; a cast of her hand; some bouquet-holders which she had used at the Tuileries. But nothing, he wrote, 'is worth the look and the gentle smile with which she thanked me for having stayed with her, for giving her the comfort of knowing that she is not alone'.[8]

Winter was approaching, but she could not bring herself to leave Saint-Gratien. It was Gégé who finally made arrangements for her to go. On Thursday, 1 October, wearing a violet dressing-gown and a little white cambric nightcap, she was carried down to the waiting coupé. It was Gégé who arranged for the stretcher to be disguised by a blue silk counterpane which he had brought her from Rome; it was Gégé who walked beside her, holding her hand as they went down the stairs. The ambulance-coupé opened at the back. He had a vision of a coffin being lifted into a hearse, and he tried to hide it from her by getting into the coupé first, to receive her.

I sat down beside her with Dr Berger . . . She looked at her park, she had a greeting for the gardeners, and for the woman at the lodge who asked in tears, as she opened the gates: 'Will she ever come back to this dear Saint-Gratien which she has created?' All the way to Paris, the little street urchins were crying out gaily: 'There's the ambulance!' and trying, with cruel curiosity, to have a look at the invalid. She held my hand convulsively . . . We were shaken and tossed about, the journey had never seemed so long to me . . . She was not in pain, but she was apprehensive, in anguish. The motor-cars, the bicycles, the railway, the big waggons . . . Everything alarmed her.

They reached Paris at last, and, by the Avenue de la Grande Armée, they reached the Arc de Triomphe. She saw it, and blew it a kiss.[9] The kiss held all that she had felt when, sixty-two years earlier, as a young bride coming out of exile, as the Emperor's niece coming home at last, she had kissed the soldier on the frontiers of France.

Coppée came to see Mathilde, and left in distress.[10] Three of her incurables from the Asile Mathilde brought her artificial flowers; she took the young girls to her and embraced them. On 9 October, Toto Gautier came to the upstairs salon where she was lying on her chaise longue. 'She has grown very small and very thin,' he told his wife. 'She speaks slowly and with difficulty, but she knows quite well what she wants to say.'[11] Late in November, *L'Éclair* reported that her friends were alarmed by her weakness. She no longer had the papers read to her.[12]

Yet the same correspondent in *L'Éclair* wrote that her mind was still alert. And she had clearly not lost her interest in politics. Ernest Lavisse saw that she remained despondent about the future. 'She felt that many of the things she loved were being thrown away, and she did not know to what purpose . . .' When he was about to leave her, after a brief visit, she motioned to him to sit down; and, almost inaudibly, she asked him: 'How are public affairs?'

I told her [he remembered] that public affairs were not going too well, but that as an old professor of history I knew that they had never gone well, and that not going well seemed to me to be natural in politics. I told her that politics had always pleased some people and displeased others, and that the discontented had always predicted the end of the world, but that the world was still there, and would probably be there for a long while yet. It was my function to reassure her, but I could never convey my own confidence to her. As the Princess approached her end, her mind took refuge in the distant past – the past of which this troubled woman was the splendid relic.[13]

'She lived as long as she could,' wrote Toto Gautier. 'It seemed as if, by this tenacity, she wanted to show that she belonged to a race of bronze: as if, proud of her origins, she wanted to remain as witness and as proof of an epoch. It was an epoch so fabulous, even now, that if one had not seen the living, almost direct descendant, one might have thought it had been invented by legend.'[14]

Mathilde told her beads as she had always done before she went to sleep, but she still could not accept all the demands of the Catholic faith. As Lavisse recalled, she was tolerant in religious matters, and she had a religion of her own. From her early childhood, she had always said her prayers, morning and evening, before a crucifix and a picture of the Virgin, and she had asked that the crucifix should be buried with her, with a rose and a carnation, her favourite flowers, and a medallion of Napoleon. But, at heart, Mathilde remained sceptical, she hesitated at 'the great Perhaps'; and Lavisse had the impression that she hoped for life everlasting, but that she could not really believe in it. She had turned to him, recently, since he was a scholar, hoping for some satisfying answer; and then she had reproached him for being no wiser than the rest.[15]

The Abbé Laine, who was more of a friend than a priest, came to see her, now, and so did the curé of her parish church, Saint-Philippe-du-Roule. Mathilde received them politely, but she was not convinced by what they said. She had asked the Abbé Jeannier, the curé of Saint-Gratien, to continue the visits which he usually paid her in the country, and it was he who prepared her for the unknown. She was very fond of him: he was the grandson of a hero of the Grande Armée, he represented a little of the legend which had been the passion of her life.

On 2 December she asked for her chaise longue to be drawn close to the window. There was a pale sun over Paris, and she said, smiling: 'The sun of Austerlitz.'[16]

She had always done good, she had always tried to relieve

misfortune, and her last intelligible words were words of charity, and perhaps an expression of regret for charities which had been left unperformed. 'I have work to finish,' she said; and then: 'Il faut être bon. One must be good.'[17] Then she grew increasingly paralysed, and she no longer spoke.

On 1 January, Gégé wrote that she was growing weaker every hour. She could hardly move her lips to kiss him. She had now lost the power of speech for nearly a week. And yet her mind was still alert: when he brought her the red carnations which Masson had sent her for the New Year, her face had glowed with sudden admiration. She had been given morphia to alleviate her pain; when she came out of her sleep, Gégé gave her a single, long-stemmed rose. The petals fell on her hands, and he recalled how, in her youth, men could not distinguish a rose-petal from her cheek.[18]

On 2 January, Clotilde asked to have the last sacraments administered. Gégé sent for the curé of Saint-Gratien. He arrived at ten o'clock. Mathilde was barely conscious, but her eyes were open. Gégé leant over her bed and smiled at her, holding her attention, so that she was not aware of the dismal formalities.[19] All the pain that he had suffered on his mother's death he suffered once again, and his love was delicate and touching. Only Proust, perhaps, was capable of understanding his grief, of appreciating his *tendresse*; and Proust wrote to him now:

If the Princess is aware of her state – and I profoundly hope that this is spared her – how it must hurt her to think that she must leave you. She loved you so much that when I close my eyes and try to find, in memory, the most gracious image of the Princess, the one most full of charm, of smiling love, of tenderness, I think of her at the moment when she spoke your name, your *petit nom*, and said that you would be returning soon.[20]

On 2 January, when the last sacraments had been administered, she fell into a coma, and Gégé sent for certain friends who wanted to kiss her hand for the last time.

The day was drawing to a close [remembered François Coppée], and, in the half-shadow, I saw the bed, and round the bed Princess Clotilde, the nuns, and a few other people. I heard the death-rattle of the dying woman, and I saw her emaciated hand lying on the edge of the bed. I went to her softly, and kissed it. It was already cold.

I prayed for a moment; then I rose and looked around me. The door of the little salon was half open: the little salon full of carefully chosen *objets d'art*, where she had had herself carried when she could still leave her bed. But I saw a vision: the Empress was there, exhausted by so many emotions and unwilling, still, to go away.[21]

She went away briefly, at half-past six. Mathilde died at seven o'clock. She was eighty-three.

On 4 January, in a letter to Gégé, Proust wrote the epilogue:

Let me just tell you that I weep bitterly with you, because I loved the Princess with infinite respect – and because it hurts me so much to think that you are so unhappy ... You have at least the comfort of ... knowing that you were the delight – the profound delight, the happiness – and also the charming gaiety, the perpetual entertainment – in the Princess's life. No one made her feel, as you did, the worth of gaiety and the charm of tenderness.[22]

That day, Gégé fulfilled her wishes, and found a carnation and a rose to be buried with her. He chose the rose 'La France', as a symbol of the country she had greatly loved. Kneeling by her coffin, he laid them on her heart, with her crucifix and a medallion of the Emperor.[23]

Yet, even now, the past intervened, the dynasty made itself sadly remembered. Émile Combes, who had recently become Président du Conseil, was afraid that the funeral might inspire an imperialist demonstration. It was a mean, irrational fear: perhaps it only covered his own hatred of the Catholic faith, his own detestation of the Bonapartes. However, he refused to allow the service to be held at Mathilde's church in Paris, Saint-Philippe-du-Roule, and he refused to allow her nephew, Louis, to be chief mourner. Maurice Paléologue, the diplomat, was instructed to tell the Imperial Family that the funeral must be held at Saint-Gratien, and that Louis must not attend it. Only on these conditions would the Government permit Mathilde to be buried in the church at Saint-Gratien. The Government would also authorize a service in Paris, provided that the Empress, Princess Clotilde and her daughter, the Duchess of Aosta, were not present.

The Third Republic showed a meanness of spirit which would have roused Mathilde to Bonaparte anger. And yet she would have recognized that there was a singular rightness in holding her funeral service at Saint-Gratien: in the little village whose name had come to be inseparable from her own.

Saint-Gratien, the rue de Courcelles and the rue de Berry had made a contribution to French civilization. Indeed, it might be said that they had brought the tradition of the *salon* as near as possible to perfection.

In the seventeenth century, the Marquise de Rambouillet had presided over the first intellectual *salon*. The eighteenth century had seen the *salons* of high society, the *salons* of the great financiers, and those where art and intellect held sway. Napoleon had been aware that such institutions fostered civilized manners, and he had encouraged his officers' wives to open them. Mme de

Staël's *salon* during the Restoration had reflected the history of the time, and Mme Ancelot's, which began in the Restoration and continued into the Second Empire, was sometimes called an entrance to the Académie-Française. During the reign of Louis-Philippe, Mme Émile de Girardin had drawn men of letters and journalists, poets and politicians, to her *hôtel* in the rue Saint-Georges. During the Second Empire, Mme Xavier de Ricard had entertained the later Parnassian poets; and Mme Sabatier, la Présidente, had inspired the supreme Bohemian *salon*, earned the devotion of Gautier, Flaubert and Meissonier, and become the *Vénus blanche* of Baudelaire. These *salons*, and innumerable others, had fostered social graces, and encouraged learning and the arts. But none of them had given France so much as the *salon* of *la bonne princesse*. 'This *salon*,' wrote the Goncourts, 'is the true *salon* of the nineteenth century, and the mistress of the house is the perfect type of the modern woman.'[1]

Though Mathilde was no musician, she had eased the début of Saint-Saëns, and she had ensured Gounod his first success in the theatre. She had been the friend of Bizet and Auber, Liszt and Rossini. She had befriended most of the eminent writers of the day. She had given Sainte-Beuve his seat in the Senate. She had fought to win Gautier a Chair in the Académie, she had made him her librarian and she had inspired him to become *le poète mathildien*. She had given Flaubert his Légion-d'honneur, and her fond and faithful encouragement. She had secured the cross of chevalier for Edmond de Goncourt, and warmed him with her friendship until his death, she had watched over Jules with compassion, and she had persuaded the Comédie-Française to perform *Henriette Maréchal*. She had earned the devotion of George Sand and the vivacious friendship of Mérimée. She had received the Daudets, and been disloyally portrayed in *L'Immortel* and *La Lutte pour la vie*. She had sponsored Maupassant and inspired Proust. She had invited Musset to read his work in her *salon*; she had looked after the delicate Coppée, found him a sinecure, and arranged for his plays to be performed. She had won the admiration of Banville and Heredia. She had entertained Dumas *père*, she had been the close friend of Dumas *fils*, she had applauded and encouraged Augier and Ponsard and Sardou. She had helped to give Anatole France his place among the Immortals. She had been the friend of Taine and the liberal friend of Renan. The

princess who had earned the deep affection of Thiers had lived
to sponsor historians like Lavisse and Masson.

'She loved the Comédie-Française,' wrote Jules Claretie, on
her death, 'as she loved everything which brought lustre to
France.'[2] Mathilde had campaigned to restore the tomb of Mlle
Mars, she had staged an early performance by Sarah Bernhardt,
she had set Mme Agar on her career, befriended Mme Pasca,
Réjane and Mounet-Sully, and 'good God', she cried to the
Goncourts, 'I should certainly have received Rachel!'

As for the world of art, she had always shown it particular
affection, for, whatever the merit of her paintings, she was an
artist, too. Admittedly she had sometimes revealed unfortunate
prejudice. She had refused to recognize Delacroix, and none of the
Impressions had found their way to the rue de Courcelles. But
she had appreciated Ingres, Meissonier and Vernet, she had
fought to help Gavarni, and she had sat, triumphantly, to
Carpeaux. Her visitors' book included the names of most of
the eminent artists of the time.

She had given her moral support to Pasteur at a time of public
controversy; she had campaigned for Robin and befriended
Berthelot. Few Frenchmen of distinction had failed to come to
her *salon*: Ferdinand de Lesseps, 'the cutter of canals', Émile de
Girardin, who established the cheap Press, Viollet-le-Duc, who
restored the château of Pierrefonds, Baron Haussmann, the
formidable Préfet de la Seine who created Second Empire Paris.
At the *hôtel* in the rue de Courcelles, which the Emperor had
given her, Mathilde received royalty and ambassadors from
every country in Europe, and from many countries far beyond;
she greeted politicians of all parties. In the rue de Berry, in the
Third Republic, her liberal principles remained unchanged.
Only the Dreyfus Affair could create a temporary difference.

In 1848, when her cousin was standing for the Presidency,
Mathilde had assembled in her *salon* all those who might serve
his cause. In the days of his presidency, her *salon* had shown its
clear support for the Second Empire which was to come. During
the Second Empire, it had reflected Mathilde's political views:
her love of Russia, her longing for the unification of Italy. And
yet, in her *salon*, politics still remained of secondary importance.
As Henry Houssaye emphasized, 'they did not make or unmake
ministries [at the rue de Courcelles]. They made Senators at

thirty thousand francs, professors at the Collège de France, librarians, laureates at exhibitions, knights and commanders of the Légion-d'honneur, members of the Académie-Française and the Académie des Beaux-Arts.' And, assessing Mathilde's achievement, Houssaye added: 'It was she who made Court and Society familiar with the ideas of art. She was the august and all-powerful intermediary between the studio and the palace. She accustomed the first people in the State to dine at her table side by side with painters, scholars, poets and sculptors who were already known to the world but unknown to them. She made herself the patron of every man of talent who could add a pearl or a fleuron to the Crown of France.'3

Her guests admired her liberalism and her absolute loyalty. They were impressed by her clear, frank, personal views of people and events, by her picturesque, Saint-Simonian way of expressing them. Above all, they were touched by her kindness. 'Let me tell you,' she wrote to a friend, 'that I am never happier than when I can do some service – especially to the people I love. And when it's only a question of opening a purse, it's so natural to me that you mustn't thank me . . .'4 If Society called her Notre Dame des Arts, everybody knew her, and with reason, as *la bonne princesse*.

Mathilde was kindness in person, but she was more than kind: she understood the nature of friendship. She did not merely entertain the celebrities of the time, she did not only give them honours and material security. For all her intellectual and aesthetic limitations, her moods, her moments of prejudice, she was a woman of constant warmth and delicate understanding. Her achievement was to draw to herself nearly all her great compatriots, over half a century, through all political turmoils, and to give them her affection, a sense of appreciation. The assurance of her interest, the certainty of her friendship, gave them an incomparable refuge, it gave them pleasure, confidence, ambition. It helped to create the climate for achievement.

They in turn gave their devotion to an extremely feminine woman.

If I were in the mood for writing poetry [Hébert told her, during the Third Republic], . . . I should tell you, discreetly, about the respectful passion which you inspired in so many of us, and especially in me.

. . . And I'd tell you what you already know: that it was your feminine charm and not your imperial diadem which, in the brilliant years of the Empire, conquered and held those neurotic, unsociable, fierce, wild, ill-mannered creatures known as artists. You tamed them and they lived together, peacefully, at your feet. Dear Princess, the woman who had that power, the woman who, for all that adoration, has remained true to herself and faithful to her word is one of those . . . whom one loves all one's life.[5]

Mathilde was proud of such admiration, delighted by such protestations of love. In the vicissitudes of her private life, she herself needed constant reassurance, she needed to be essential, to draw men to her.

Yet, though their devotion was genuine, it remained impossible for them to forget that she was a princess. Mathilde was an Imperial Highness, the cousin of Napoleon III. She was, above all, the niece of Napoleon; and this transcendent relationship gave her a prestige which no other woman could attain. It gave her *salon* pre-eminence in the Second Empire (beside Mathilde, the Empress was a *parvenue*); and, in the humiliation and sadness of the Third Republic, when the demagogues were levelling and destroying, when French society was in decline, it made the rue de Berry a world apart, an independent world in the heart of Paris, a world still radiant with the Napoleonic legend.

Mathilde had lived all her life in the legend. She had been born in exile, she had sat, as a child, at the feet of Madame Mère, she had spent her early years in a palace which was a museum to the Emperor's memory. Since her marriage, she had worn the seven strings of pearls which Napoleon had given to her mother; in her salon she sat beneath his statue, like a worshipper at the feet of her deity. She had been ready to break with friends who criticized and attacked him, like a believer discarding infidels. Her devotion was uncritical, some said it was fanatical, but it was still magnificent, and it was a touching sign of her need. Napoleon was her constant, necessary religion, the god to whom she had dedicated all her active existence. He was the only hero who remained to her, the only man who had not disillusioned her.

Her face recalled that of the prodigious Uncle whom she had never known; and perhaps, unconsciously, she had modelled her character and behaviour on his own. 'When you heard her speak,' wrote Gautier's son, 'when you saw her walk or make a gesture, when you watched her enthusiasm and her tempers – oftened feigned and quickly appeased – when you heard her opinions, so clear, . . . so fair, always marked by an incisive word, you found the traces of the Napoleonic spirit.'[6] And Henry Houssaye added:

Contemporaries of Napoleon said that he had a charm without parallel when he wished to please. Princess Mathilde always wanted to please. This gift of charm was not the only resemblance between the uncle and the niece. In her firm, decisive, almost virile cast of mind, in her clear and definite and imperious ideas, in her powerful, vivid, sweeping impressions, . . . the Emperor's historians rediscovered him.[7]

These tributes, published on her death, echoed the opinion which Sainte-Beuve had published, four decades earlier.

And, by an ultimate paradox, it was her Bonaparte nature which set Mathilde above politics, which made her *salon* imperial, made it a world apart. 'She was a princess by the beauty of her face and the beauty of her soul,' wrote Henry Houssaye, 'just as she was a princess by her birth. But she was more than a princess, she was a Bonaparte, and she was more than a Bonaparte, she was French.'[8] For her, as for Napoleon, her country stood above politics. She loved it with a single-minded passion. In her *salon*, quite simply, one found oneself in France.

Notes

MU *Le Moniteur universel*   RDDM *La Revue des Deux Mondes*
RDP *La Revue de Paris*

PART ONE
The First Exile
1820-40

1

1 Princess Mathilde: *Souvenirs des années d'exil. I*. RDDM, 15 December 1927, 721 sqq.
2 Ilchester (ed.): *The Journal of the Hon. H. E. Fox*, 299
3 *Mémoires et correspondance du Roi Jérôme* . . . VII, 418–21
4 Ilchester, op. cit., 262
5 *Mémoires . . . du Roi Jérôme*, loc. cit.
6 Princess Mathilde, op. cit., 732
7 Princess Mathilde, op. cit., 734
8 Ilchester, op. cit., 267
9 Princess Mathilde, op. cit., 729
10 Princess Sophie to Princess Mathilde, 20 October 1841 (Popelin)
11 Princess Mathilde, op. cit., 729–30
12 Primoli Diary, 22 June 1893 (Primoli)
13 Princess Mathilde, op. cit., 730
14 Ibid., 722–3
15 Ilchester, op. cit., 267
16 Countess of Blessington: *The Idler in Italy*, 392
17 Ibid.
18 Ibid., 405–6
19 Ibid., 407
20 Ibid., 406
21 Princess Mathilde, op. cit., 738

2

1 Blessington, op. cit., 209–10
2 Princess Mathilde, op. cit., 744
3 Joseph Méry: *Scènes de la vie italienne*, I, 119, 120–1, 122
4 The Prince de Montfort to Princess Mathilde, 6 July 1833. Copy in the Popelin Collection
5 Princess Sophie to Princess Mathilde (Popelin)
6 Princess Sophie to Princess Mathilde (Popelin)
7 Princess Mathilde, op. cit., 752
8 Princess Mathilde: *Souvenirs des années d'exil. II*. RDDM, 1 January 1928, 76 sqq.

3

1 Note pour S. M. l'Empereur. Situation de S. A. I. la Princesse Mathilde vis à vis du Prince Jérôme (Primoli)
2 J.-N. Primoli: *Autour du Mariage de l'Impératrice*. RDDM, 1 November 1924, 71
3 Princess Mathilde, op. cit., 81–2
4 Ibid.
5 Princess Mathilde, memoirs (Popelin)

6 Ibid., 28–9
7 Ibid., 31
8 Ibid., 31–2
9 Letter of 9 March 1840 (Popelin)
10 Princess Mathilde, memoirs (Popelin)
11 Ibid., 35
12 Valérie Masuyer: *Mémoires, Lettres et Papiers,* 291–2
13 Princess Mathilde, memoirs (Popelin)
14 Ibid.
15 Masuyer, op. cit., 307
16 Princess Mathilde, memoirs (Popelin)
17 Masuyer, op. cit., 315–6
18 Princess Mathilde, memoirs (Popelin)
19 Masuyer, op. cit., 317–8
20 Princess Mathilde, memoirs (Popelin)
21 11 September 1836; RDDM, 1 November 1924, pp. 71–2
22 Ibid., 72
23 RDDM, 1 November 1924, p. 72
24 Princess Mathilde in RDDM, 1 January 1928, 89–90
25 RDDM, 1 November 1924, p. 72

4

1 Princess Mathilde, loc. cit., 97–8
2 J.-N. Primoli: *La Princesse Mathilde et le Duc d'Aumale.* RDP, 1 August 1922, 466–7
3 Letter of 17 July 1838; quoted by

Kühn: *Prinzessin Mathilde Bonaparte,* 328–9
4 Letter of 13 September 1838; quoted by Kühn, 329
5 Jules Janin: *Voyage en Italie,* 206–7
6 Princess Mathilde, RDDM, 1 January 1928, 101 sqq.
7 Ibid.
8 Undated letter to Hélène Villamil (Popelin)
9 Popelin Collection
10 Ibid.
11 Ibid.
12 11 August 1838 (Popelin)
13 Popelin Collection
14 Ibid.
15 Ibid.
16 27 December 1838 (Popelin)
17 Ibid.
18 Ibid.
19 Letter to Hélène Villamil, 22 March 1839 (Popelin)
20 Letter of 1 May 1839 (Popelin)
21 Letter of 26 May 1839 (Popelin)
22 Typescript copy of letter (Primoli)
23 Duchesse de Dino: *Chronique,* II, 377, 399
24 Note pour S. M. l'Empereur. Situation de S. A. I. la Princesse Mathilde vis à vis du Prince Jérôme (Primoli)
25 Princess Mathilde, RDDM, loc. cit.
26 Princess Caroline Murat: *My Memoirs,* 108
27 Ibid.

PART TWO
The Interregnum
1840–52

5

1 André Gayot: *Une ancienne muscadine,* 98

2 Dino, op. cit., II, 427
3 *Correspondance de Liszt et de la Comtesse d'Agoult,* II; 9 December 1840

4 Princess Mathilde in RDDM, 15 January 1928, 359–63
5 Ibid., 363–83
6 Ibid., 384–6

6

1 Princess Mathilde, memoirs (Popelin)
2 Ibid.
3 Ibid.
4 Ibid.
5 Ibid.
6 Ibid.
7 Ibid.
8 Ibid.
9 Dino, op. cit., III, 128.
10 Gayot, op. cit., 122
11 Letter of 25 June 1842 (Popelin)
12 Princess Mathilde, letter to Hohenlohe (quoted by Castillon du Perron, 85)

7

1 Princess Mathilde to Mme Villamil, 23 January 1845 (Popelin)
2 Princess Mathilde, memoirs (Primoli)
3 Primoli Diary, November 1893: Primoli Diary, 1879, p. 106 (Primoli). The man in question was said to be 'the Comte de S.'
4 Ernest Hébert to Princess Mathilde, 26 October [1874]. (Primoli)

8

1 *Le Curieux*, 15 October 1883, pp. 9–10, gives what is said to be Nieuwerkerke's birth certificate, 'the original of which no longer exists'. According to this he was born at 8 a.m. on 16 April 1811, the son of Alexandrine-Aimée-Louise-Albertine Devassan, wife of Sieur Charles O'Hara de Nieuwerkerke, 'propriétaire, de présent [sic] en voyage.' Charles de Nieuwerkerke is said to have died at 9, rue des Écuries d'Artois, in Paris, on 20 or 21 March 1864, at the age of 75, and to be buried on his estate at Villiers (Aisne)
2 Princess Mathilde, memoirs
3 Primoli Diary
4 Undated draft petition in Princess Mathilde's hand (Primoli)
5 Comte Rodolphe Apponyi: *Vingt-cinq ans à Paris*, IV, 441
6 Kühn, op. cit., 352–3
7 Letter of 11 October 1846 (Primoli)

9

1 Maréchal de Castellane, *Journal*, IV, 100–1
2 Germain Bapst: *Le Maréchal Canrobert*, I, 501–2
3 Castellane, loc. cit., IV, 102
4 Ibid., IV, 117–8
5 Extract of letter dated only '1848' (Popelin)
6 Henri Malo: *Mémoires de Madame Dosne*, II, 18. 11 December 1848
7 Ibid., II, 66; 25 December 1848
8 Ibid., II, 82; 30 December 1848
9 Ibid., II, 98–9; 16 January 1849
10 Apponyi, op. cit., IV, 277–8

10

1 Bapst, op. cit., I, 499
2 Malo, op. cit.
3 Murat, op. cit., 78
4 Apponyi, op. cit., IV, 309
5 Bapst, loc. cit.
6 Comte H. de Viel-Castel: *Mémoires sur le règne de Napoléon III*, I, pp. 33 sqq.
7 Ibid., I, 65 sqq.
8 Ibid.
9 Letter to Pierre Lebrun, 10 March 1851. *Revue bleue*, 4 January 1913, 1–2
10 Viel-Castel, op. cit., 148–9; 1 June 1852

11 For Mathilde's first visit to
Saint-Gratien, see Murat, op. cit.,
60–1
12 Viel-Castel, op. cit., I, 155;
23 June 1852
13 Ibid., I, 135–6; 28 April 1852

14 Letter of 25 January [1852].
(Popelin)
15 Apponyi, op. cit., IV, 414–7
16 Murat, op. cit., 98–9
17 Viel-Castel, op. cit.; Bapst, op.
cit., II, 48–9

PART THREE
The Second Empire
1852–70

11

1 The actual figures were 7,839,000
against 256,000. There were 206,300
abstentions
2 Princess Mathilde, memoirs
(Popelin)
3 Viel-Castel, op. cit.
4 H. Bouchot: *Les Élégances du
Second Empire*, 203–4
5 Princess Mathilde, memoirs
(Primoli)
6 Impératrice Eugénie: *Lettres
familières*, I, 23 and p. 236, note
7 Viel-Castel, op. cit., II, 121–2
8 Bapst, op. cit., II, 48–9; Castellane, op. cit., IV, 403–4
9 Mérimée: *Lettres à Viollet-le-
Duc*, 18–19; Bouchot, op. cit., 21–2
10 RDDM, 1 November 1924, 98;
and Princess Mathilde, memoirs
(Primoli)
11 RDDM, loc. cit., 102
12 Maxime du Camp: *Souvenirs*, I,
152
13 Princess Mathilde, memoirs
(Primoli)

12

1 Viel-Castel, op. cit., II, 188
2 Mme Jules Baroche: *Le Second
Empire. Notes et Souvenirs*, 59
3 Prosper Mérimée: *Correspondance générale*, I, 44–5

4 Baroche, op. cit., 44–5
5 A. Varloy: *Gustave Nadaud*, 47–8
6 Primoli Diary, 1879, 43–4
(Primoli). Presumably Primoli refers
to *Le Songe d'Auguste*
7 Viel-Castel, op. cit., III, 157–8
8 M. Thiébaut: *Edmond About*, 80
9 12 November 1859 (Primoli)
10 Thiébaut, 127, 130
11 Viel-Castel, loc. cit.
12 Mérimée: *Lettres à Viollet-le-Duc*,
43
13 J. Bonnerot: *C. Saint-Saëns*, 83,
43–44
14 6 January 1891 (Primoli); J.-G.
Prod'homme and A. Dandelot:
Gounod, I, 193–4
15 Comte de Hübner: *Neuf ans de
Souvenirs*, I, 108
16 Viel-Castel, op. cit., 285–6
17 Ibid., 287–9
18 Ferdinand Bac, quoted by
Castillon du Perron, 145
19 Viel-Castel, op. cit., III, 287
20 Ibid., 299

13

1 Primoli papers. Quoted by H.
Houssaye, *L'Écho de Paris*, 5 January
1904
2 Viel-Castel, op. cit., III, 14
3 Ibid., 61
4 Primoli papers

5 Viel-Castel, op. cit., III, 117–8
6 Undated note (Primoli)
7 Viel-Castel, op. cit., III, 151
8 Queen Sophie to Princess
Mathilde, 14 June 1855 (Popelin)
9 Viel-Castel, op. cit., III, 213
10 Undated note (Primoli)
11 Undated note (Primoli)
12 Note dated 'samedi' (Primoli)
13 Goncourt *Journal*, VI, 14
14 Viel-Castel, op. cit., III, 214
15 Undated letter (Primoli)
16 Prince Imperial to Princess
Mathilde, 15 March 1869 (Primoli);
Primoli Diary, 17 March 1869 (ibid)
17 Bouchot, op. cit., 95
18 Baroche, op. cit., 200
19 Barrès: *Mes Cahiers*, III, 111
20 For the alleged daughter of
Mathilde and Nieuwerkerke, see
Chapter 33, note 14

14

1 *Saint-Gratien.* Chapter by Émile
de Girardin in *Enghien et ses Environs*,
44–6; Murat, 60–1
2 Manuscript note by Théophile
Gautier *fils* (Gautier)
3 F. Masson, *La Princesse Mathilde
après la guerre. La Revue hebdomadaire*,
30 March 1912, 609 sqq.
4 Ibid.
5 Typescript note by Théophile
Gautier *fils* (Gautier)
6 Masson, loc. cit.
7 Girardin, loc. cit.
8 Ibid.
9 Ibid.

15

1 Goncourt: *Journal*, VIII, 61–2
2 Ibid., XI, 215
3 Claretie: *La Vie à Paris, 1904*,
6–7; Primoli Diary, 22 July 1888
(Primoli)
4 RDP, 15 January 1904, 419–22

5 Primoli Diary, loc. cit.
6 Masson, loc. cit.
7 Queen Sophie to Princess
Mathilde, 24 April 1849 (Popelin)
8 Queen Sophie to Princess
Mathilde, 3 October 1852 (Popelin);
among the other extracts from her
letters, in Popelin's hand, is one
dated 11 July 1856, Maison du Bois:
'Apropos, Mons. Demidoff menace
de venir ici; je lui ai fait signifier que
je ne pouvai pas lui interdire l'entrée
du pays, mais que je ne le reverrai
jamais. Comme il est menteur avant
tout, il est capable de débiter autre
chose.'
9 Viel-Castel, op. cit., IV, 280–2.
10 Amiral de La Roncière Le
Noury: *Correspondance intime*, I, 81
11 Princess Mathilde, memoirs
(Primoli)
12 Ibid.
13 Viel-Castel, op. cit., IV, 53
14 Ibid., IV, 53, 55 sqq., 59–60,
64
15 11 February 1859 (Popelin)
16 Viel-Castel, op. cit., V, 29–30
17 27 July 1860 (Popelin)
18 Goncourt: *Journal*, VI, 8–9
19 Princess Mathilde, memoirs
(Primoli)
20 Viel-Castel, op. cit., V, 74
21 Mérimée: *Corr. gén.*, V, 142–3

16

1 *L'Artiste*, 1 February 1860, p.
48
2 Mérimée: *Corr. gén.*, III, 470
3 Baroche, op. cit., 150
4 Earl of Malmesbury: *Memoirs of
an ex-Minister*, II, 226
5 Draft letter, 19 November 1885
(Primoli)
6 Lord Malmesbury to Princess
Mathilde (Primoli)
7 Quoted by Castillon du Perron,
158

8 Note pour S. M. l'Empereur. Situation de la Princess Mathilde vis à vis du Prince Jérôme (Primoli)

9 Queen Sophie to Princess Mathilde, 27 July 1860 (Popelin)

10 MU, 23 November 1860; Viel-Castel, op. cit., VI, 99–100

11 Viel-Castel, op. cit., VI, 133–5

12 Bonnerot, op. cit., 40

13 The story recalls Primoli's observation in his diary for 1870: 'Moi, je préfère une rose à une rosette. Ça sent mieux et ça suppose moins d'intrigues: tout au plus une intrigue de cœur.'

14 23 May 1861; RDDM, 1 November 1925, pp. 59–60. In January 1853, Mathilde had expressed her regret that she could not secure the post of Inspector of Fine Arts for Gautier (ibid.)

15 RDDM, loc. cit.

16 MU, 5 July 1861

17 For Gautier and Princess Mathilde, see Joanna Richardson: *Théophile Gautier, His Life and Times,* 193–6 and passim

18 Delacroix: *Journal,* II, 179, note

19 F. Masson, loc. cit.

20 For an account of Princess Mathilde's art collections, see Serge Grandjean: *Les intérieurs et les collections de la Princesse Mathilde*

17

1 Princess Mathilde: manuscript memoirs (Popelin)

2 Princess Mathilde: portrait of Sainte-Beuve (Primoli). In an unpublished passage on Sainte-Beuve, among the Primoli papers, she writes: 'J'ai beaucoup connu Sainte-Beuve et j'ai rarement rencontré dans ma vie un homme plus aimable faisant mieux causer les autres et sachant mieux tirer parti des hommes ...

Lorsque je l'ai connu il n'était plus jeune ni de corps ni d'esprit. Il était souvent malade, incommodé, ... mais toujours et malgré tout vaillant au travail, bien faisant à l'[-], sans morgue, sans affectation d'aucun genre – l'esprit constamment ouvert, curieux, encourageant pour les jeunes et les petits, et plein de ce charme aimable qui contribue à plaire et à vous faire croire qu'on lui plaisait ... '

3 Princess Mathilde, portrait of Sainte-Beuve (Primoli)

4 Ibid.

5 Ibid.

6 Amédée Achard, MU, 15 October 1869

7 20 June 1861; Sainte-Beuve: *Corr. gén.,* XII, 132

8 16 November 1861: ibid., XII, 203–4

9 August 1862 (Primoli)

10 [21 November 1861]; Sainte-Beuve, op. cit., XII, 245

11 25 November 1861 (Primoli)

12 *L'Artiste,* 15 March 1862, p. 135

13 14 June 1862 (Primoli)

14 21 July 1862 (Primoli)

15 [2 July 1862]; Sainte-Beuve, op. cit., 377–8 and 378, note

16 J. de la Faye: *La Princesse Mathilde,* 213–5

17 Ibid., 216.

18 14 June 1862 (Primoli)

19 Sainte-Beuve: *Lettres à la Princesse,* 231

20 22 [August] 1862; Sainte-Beuve: *Corr. gén.,* XII, 387. The letter in the correspondence is tentatively dated July, but this could not be correct.

21 Princess Mathilde: portrait of Renan (Primoli)

22 16 August 1862; Goncourt: *Journal,* V, 147–50

23 MU, 6 September 1861

24 13 September 1862 (Primoli)

25 15 September 1862; Sainte-Beuve, op. cit., XII, 416–8

26 12 November 1862; Sainte-Beuve: *Corr. gén.*, XII, 467–8.
27 12 November 1862 (Primoli)
28 21 November 1862 (Primoli)
29 Primoli Diary, 16 September 1880 (Primoli)
30 Ibid.
31 19 December 1862; Sainte-Beuve, op. cit., XII, 500
32 1 January 1863; Sainte-Beuve; op. cit., XIII, 37
33 12 January 1863; Sainte-Beuve, op. cit., XIII, 51
34 22 January 1863 (Primoli)

18

1 Letter to Princess Mathilde (Primoli)
2 Hegermann-Lindencrone: *In the Courts of Memory*, 28
3 *La Presse*, 23 January 1863
4 Goncourt: *Journal*, VI, 12 and 14
5 Writing to his niece on 22 May 1864 (*Corr.*, V, 143), Flaubert says: 'Ce soir je vais aller, pour la prèmiere fois, chez la princesse Mathilde.' Possibly this was the first occasion on which he dined there.
6 Princess Mathilde, portrait of Gustave Flaubert (Primoli)
7 Goncourt: *Journal*, VI, 17–18
8 *La Presse*, 16, 17 July 1867
9 Pasteur: *Correspondance*, IV, 391–2
10 Ibid., II, 358–9
11 Mérimée: *Corr. gén.*, VIII, 286–7
12 Ibid., VIII, 306–8
13 Viel-Castel, op. cit., VI, 185–6
14 Ibid., 197 sqq.
15 Ibid., 201
16 Ibid., 202–3
17 Ibid., 209–10
18 Ibid.
19 Viel-Castel, op. cit., VI, 331–2
20 Letters of 28 November and 1 December 1882 (Primoli)
21 Viel-Castel, op. cit., III, 48

19

1 *La Presse*, 13, 15 March, 13 May 1863
2 Ibid., 9 April 1863
3 Ibid., 7 May 1863
4 Ibid., 26 May 1863
5 Goncourt: *Journal*, VI, 73
6 26 March 1863 (Primoli)
7 *La Presse*, 30 May, 4 June 1863
8 Goncourt: *Journal*, VI, 68
9 [30 May 1863]; Sainte-Beuve: *Corr. gén.*, XIII, 171–2
10 28 May 1863 (Primoli)
11 16 July 1863 (Primoli)
12 Sainte-Beuve: *Corr. gén.*, XIII, 239
13 Goncourt: *Journal*, VI, 78–9
14 Ibid., 92
15 *La Presse*, 26 August 1863
16 6 August 1863; *Revue bleue*, 4 January 1913, p. 3
17 *L'Artiste*, 1 May 1863; p. 196
18 *La Presse*, 4 June 1863
19 Undated letters (Primoli)
20 Letter to Princess Mathilde, dated only '13 Dé[cembre]' (Primoli)
21 *L'Artiste*, 15 July 1863, 45
22 M. du Camp: *Souvenirs*, I, 218–23; *La Presse*, 29 December 1867
23 Sainte-Beuve: *Corr. gén.*, XIII, 414
24 Ibid.
25 Du Camp, loc. cit.; in *Letters and Recollections of Julius and Mary Mohl*, p. 201, Mme Mohl writes to Mrs Simpson: 'There has been much noise about the minister taking into his hands the School of Art [l'École des Beaux-Arts], appointing Neukerke as head of all. He got hissed by the students, who ran after him across the Pont des Arts, and sang, 'O Mathilde, idole de mon âme' . . . (Excuse all this scratching; I think it safest.)'
26 J. Abbot: *La Princesse Mathilde*, 30
27 Théodore de Banville: *La*

Lanterne Magique. Camées parisiens,
297–8
28 A. Houssaye: *Confessions,* IV,
256
29 *La Vie parisienne,* 6 July 1867
30 E. Reinaud: *Charles Jalabert,* 235
31 M. Silver: *Jules Sandeau,* 178.
However, on 21 January 1867 *La
Presse* quoted Mathilde's letter of
condolence to Mme Ingres, on the
death of her husband: 'La mort de
M. Ingres est une perte publique:
mais, plus heureux que bien d'autres,
il laisse après lui, dans ses œuvres,
une impérissable mémoire.'
32 Sainte-Beuve: *Corr. gén.,* XIII,
295; Goncourt: *Journal,* VI, 128–9.
33 Sainte-Beuve: *Corr. gén.,* XIII,
335, 492
34 *La Presse,* 1 March 1864
35 Ibid., 29 February, 2 March 1864;
M.-L. Pailleron, *François Buloz et ses
Amis. Les Derniers Romantiques,* 147
36 *La Presse,* 7 March 1864
37 Ibid., 29 March 1864
38 Ibid., 1 April 1864
39 *L'Artiste,* 15 April 1864, p. 189
40 *La Presse,* 10 May 1864
41 Ibid., 1 June 1864
42 Ibid., 26 May 1864
43 *Le Journal des Débats,* 10 June
1864
44 Sainte-Beuve: *Corr. gén.,* XIII,
524 and 526
45 11 June 1864 (Primoli)
46 Sainte-Beuve, op. cit., XIII, 516
and note; *La Presse,* 13 June, 6
October 1864. Sometimes Mathilde
herself felt apprehensive about her
brother's freedom of speech. Among
her papers is a note which she sent
Sainte-Beuve on 21 July: 'My
brother's dining here with me on
Tuesday the 26th – would you make
the effort to come too – to stand up
to him – it would be such a relief for
me. I'm inviting Taine.'
47 30 October 1855 (Primoli)

48 22 November 1864 (Primoli)
49 Malmesbury: *Memoirs of an ex-
Minister,* II, 87
50 J. Claretie: *Souvenirs du Dîner
Bixio,* 170–1
51 *L'Éclair,* 22 November 1903
52 Malo, op. cit., II, 281
53 Goncourt: *Journal,* VIII, 31
54 Ibid., VIII, 102–3
55 Ibid., VIII, 146
56 Primoli Diary, 2 October 1867
(Primoli)
57 J. Abbot: *La Princesse Mathilde*
58 Ibid.
59 *La Presse,* 2 August 1864
60 Primoli Diary, 1864 (Primoli)
61 Ibid., pp. 3–4, 37–40 (Primoli)
62 Ibid., 37–40
63 *La Presse,* 11, 12 August 1864
64 Ibid., 12 August 1864
65 14 August 1864 (Primoli)
66 17 August 1864 (Primoli)
67 14 August [1864]; *Revue bleue,*
4 January 1913, p. 4
68 Sainte-Beuve: *Corr. gén.,* XIII,
623–4
69 13 October 1864 (Primoli)
70 Primoli Papers
71 14 October 1864; *Revue bleue,*
loc. cit.
72 Nieuwerkerke's nomination to
the Senate brought a fulsome tribute
from *La Presse* on 10 October

20

1 *L'Artiste,* 1 February 1865, p. 72
2 Sainte-Beuve: *Corr. gén.,* XIV,
41–2, and note
3 Ibid., XIV, 63–4
4 31 January 1865 (Primoli)
5 31 January [1865]; Sainte-Beuve,
op. cit., XIV, 68
6 Ibid., XIV, 73–4
7 21 March 1865 (Primoli)
8 Sainte-Beuve: *Lettres à la
Princesse,* 144–5
9 *La Presse,* 15 January, 21, 27

April 1865; *La Vie Parisienne*, 22 April 1865; *La Petite Revue*, 2 September, 1865

10 *La Petite Revue*, 6 May 1865, p. 174

11 *La Presse*, 21 May 1865; *L'Artiste*, 15 May 1865. Claudius Popelin was also awarded a medal this year in the paintings and drawings section.

12 Hegermann-Lindencrone, op. cit., 67–71

13 Jules de Goncourt: *Lettres*, 253–4

14 Ibid., 254

15 Sainte-Beuve: *Corr. gén.*, XIV, 169

16 30 April [1865] (Primoli)

17 Quoted in Sainte-Beuve: *Corr. gén.*, XIV, 170

18 Sainte-Beuve, op. cit., XIV, 174–5

19 Goncourt: *Journal*, VII, 101–2

20 Ibid: VII, 104–5; see also Jules de Goncourt: *Lettres*, 258–9

21 Goncourt: *Journal*, VII, 110–11

22 Ibid., VII, 123

23 Sainte-Beuve: *Corr. gén.*, XIV, 342

24 Ibid., XIV, 324–5

25 5 September 1866; *Revue bleue*, 11 January 1913, p. 37; quoted in Sainte-Beuve: *Corr. gén.*, XIV, 325

26 Ibid.

27 Pasteur: *Correspondance*, II, 214

28 His rival had been the zoologist Henri-Félix de Lacaze-Duthiers

29 *L'Illustration*, 15 April 1865; quoted in Sainte-Beuve, *Corr. gén.*, XIV, 152

30 Flaubert: *Corr.*, V, 187

31 Rochefort in *Le Figaro*; quoted by Le Meur: *L'Adolescence et la Jeunesse d'E.-M. de Vogüé*, 25–6

32 Got: *Journal*, II, 46–7

33 Pipe-en-Bois: *Ce que je pense d'Henriette Maréchal*, 19, 26

34 Flaubert: *Lettres inédites à la Princesse Mathilde*, 8

35 Concourt: *Journal*, VII, 149

36 J. de Goncourt: *Lettres*, 264–5

37 Goncourt: *Journal*, V, 147–50

38 Ibid., V, 223–4

39 Ibid., VIII, 44–5

40 Ibid., VIII, 79

41 Ibid., VIII, 146–7

42 Jules de Goncourt: *Lettres*, 348, note

21

1 Whitehurst: *Court and Social Life in France under Napoleon III.* I, 153–4

2 Sainte-Beuve: *Lettres à la Princesse*, 203–4, 207, 217

3 M.-L. Pailleron: *François Buloz et ses Amis. Les Derniers Romantiques*, 93

4 6 March 1866 (Primoli)

5 17 January [1867]. (Primoli)

6 18 May [1868]. (Primoli). See also Goncourt: *Journal*, VIII, 202

7 Ms portrait in Claudius Popelin's writing (Primoli)

8 Fleury et Sonolet: *La Société du Second Empire*, III, 138–9

9 Apponyi, op. cit., IV, 274

10 Primoli Diary, 21 October 1879 (Primoli)

11 Mme O. Feuillet, loc. cit.

12 Some of Mathilde's correspondence with Mme Strauss may be found at the Bibliothèque Nationale, N.A. Fr. 13209

13 Goncourt: *Journal*, 13 December, 1862

14 Portrait of Gustave Flaubert (Primoli)

15 Goncourt: *Journal*, VII, 183–4

16 13 August 1866 (Primoli)

17 14 August 1866 (Primoli)

18 *Lettres inédites à la Princesse Mathilde*, 16–18

19 Ibid., 18–19

20 *Corr.*, V, 220

21 *Lettres inédites à la Princesse Mathilde* 21

22 *Lettres à la Princesse*, 236–8

M

23 13 September 1866 (Primoli)
24 Ibid.
25 20 September [1866]; *Revue bleue*, 11 January 1913, pp. 37–8
26 23 September 1866. Typescript of letter (Primoli)
27 *La Presse*, 24 September 1866; on 31 January 1862 the same paper had reported: 'M. le vicomte de Païva, envoyé extraordinaire et ministre plénipotentiaire de S. M. le roi de Portugal et des Algarves, a eu l'honneur d'être reçu en audience particulière par S. A. I. Mme la princesse Mathilde et de lui remettre une lettre autographe du roi don Louis Ier; ainsi que le diplôme et les insignes de l'ordre royal de Sainte-Élisabeth.'
28 Goncourt: *Journal*, VII, 209
29 Ibid., 204–5
30 *La Presse*, 31 October 1866
31 *Lettres inédites à la Princesse Mathilde*, 22–3
32 *La Presse*, 19 October 1866
33 Ibid., 6 December 1866
34 Ibid., 13 December 1866

22

1 Flaubert: *Corr.*, V, 298
2 *Revue bleue*, 11 January 1913, p. 38
3 Typescript of letter of 19 April 1867 (Primoli)
4 Whitehurst, op. cit., I, 289–90
5 Hegermann-Lindencrone, op. cit., 166–9
6 *La Presse*, 3 June 1867; *La Vie parisienne*, 8 June 1867, p. 398
7 *La Presse*, 13 June 1867
8 Ibid., 14 June 1867
9 *La Vie parisienne*, 8, 15 June 1867
10 Got, op. cit., II, 69–70
11 8 May 1866 (Popelin)
12 5 April 1867 (Popelin)

23

1 Goncourt: *Journal*, VIII, 44–5
2 RDDM, 1 November 1925, pp. 73–4
3 Primoli Diary, 1867 (Primoli)
4 Ibid.
5 Ibid.
6 RDDM, loc. cit., 82–4
7 Princess Mathilde: portrait of Gautier (Primoli)
8 RDDM, loc. cit., 77
9 Undated note (Primoli)
10 RDDM, 1 November 1925, 79
11 Note dated 1862 (Primoli)
12 Undated note (Primoli)
13 6 May [1866]. (Primoli)
14 2 March 1867 (Primoli)
15 7 March 1867 (Primoli)
16 Goncourt: *Journal*, VIII, 44
17 Fromentin, *Correspondance et Fragments inédits*, 205–7
18 *La Presse*, 15 August 1869
19 Peladan: *Ernest Hébert*, 151–2, 196
20 28 December 1868 (Primoli)
21 14 December 1868 (Primoli)
22 5 [?] February [1869]. Primoli
23 Primoli Diary, 13 December 1880 (Primoli)
24 Goncourt: *Journal*, VII, 113–4
25 Goncourt: *Journal*, VIII, 51
26 On 20 October 1867, *La Presse* announced: '*L'Étendard* annonce un prochain mouvement dans le personnel des sous-préfets . . . Dans ce mouvement figure le nom de M. Théophile Gautier *fils*, rédacteur du *Moniteur*, qui serait appelé à la sous-préfecture de Valognes.' On 10 November 1868, announcing Gautier's own appointment as Mathilde's librarian, the paper added the curious statement: 'Son gendre, M. Catulle Mendès, est sous-bibliothécaire de la princesse depuis quelques années.' On 24 December 1868 *La Presse* announced the appointment of

Théophile Gautier *fils* as chief of the Press department at the Ministry of the Interior.
27 Sainte-Beuve: *Lettres à la Princesse*, 311 and 316–7
28 Primoli Diary, May–October 1867, pp. 125–6 (Primoli)

24

1 *Lettres à la Princesse*, 329
2 *La Presse*, 11 July 1868
3 *Lettres inédites à la Princesse Mathilde*, 50
4 On 11 May *La Gazette des Étrangers* recorded that Nieuwerkerke had left for Spain two days earlier, with Alfred Arago and Giraud; on 28 May the paper announced his return.
5 Goncourt: *Journal*, VIII, 110–1
6 Ibid., VIII, 122
7 Mérimée: *Corr. gén.*, VIII, 251
8 Primoli Diary, 14 October 1868 (Primoli)
9 Primoli Diary, October–December 1868, 26 sqq. (Primoli)
10 Hegermann-Lindencrone, op. cit., 207–8
11 Goncourt: *Journal*, VIII, 127
12 *Lettres inédites à la Princesse Mathilde*, 60
13 Mérimée's sitting is described by Primoli, in his diary for 1868, 74–5 (Primoli)
14 For Gautier's conversation, see Richardson, op. cit., 240, 264–5
15 Goncourt: *Journal*, VIII, 125–6
16 Richardson, op. cit., 219
17 Ibid., 224–5
18 Ibid., 225
19 Ibid.
20 Ibid.
21 Ibid., 226
22 Ibid.
23 27 October 1868 (Primoli)
24 *La Presse*, 10 November 1868

25 9 November 1868; RDDM, 1 May 1953, pp. 145–6
26 10 November 1868 (Primoli)
27 Richardson, op. cit., 227

25

1 Troubat: *Souvenirs du dernier secrétaire de Sainte-Beuve*, 349–50
2 Sainte-Beuve: *Lettres à la Princesse*, 361
3 Troubat, loc. cit., 350
4 Ibid., 350–2
5 Goncourt: *Journal*, 6 January 1869
6 Ibid., VII, 65–6
7 RDDM, 1 May 1953, 150
8 13 September 1862 (Primoli)
9 Sainte-Beuve: *Lettres à la Princesse*, 365–7
10 18 January 1869; RDDM, 1 May 1953, 149
11 Troubat, loc. cit., 352

26

1 Mérimée: *Corr. gén.*, VIII, 476–7
2 27 April 1869 (Henriot)
3 Ibid.
4 4 May 1869 (Henriot)
5 Ibid.
6 Goncourt: *Journal*, VIII, 199–200
7 Claretie: *La Vie à Paris, 1895*, 324: François Coppée: *Le Gaulois*, 3 January 1904
8 MU, 7, 8, 11 June 1869; *La Presse*, 9 June 1869
9 20 April 1866 (Popelin)
10 MU, 7 June 1869
11 *La Presse*, 29 July 1869
12 For Mme de Galbois, see: Dominique [i.e. Marcel Proust]: *Un Salon historique. Le Figaro*, 25 February 1903. See also Chapter 45, note 20

27

1 Apponyi, op. cit., IV, 441

2 By an imperial decree of 30 January 1861, recorded in the MU on 3 February, Nieuwerkerke, who was then Directeur-général des Musées impériaux, intendant des beaux-arts de la Maison de l'Empereur, had been appointed to the Council of the Imperial Household.
3 Viel-Castel, op. cit., VI, 278–9
4 *La Presse*, 1 January 1869
5 Goncourt: *Journal*, VIII, 164
6 *La Presse*, 17 February 1869; Goncourt: *Journal*, VIII, 60, note. On 19 February *La Presse* announced that employees from the Louvre had fetched the pictures from the Cercle impérial
7 Goncourt: *Journal*, VIII, 159–60, note; 170–1, note; 171
8 Ibid., VIII, 159
9 Ibid., VIII, 175–6
10 Ibid., VIII, 186–7
11 Ibid., VIII, 220
12 Popelin Collection
13 Mérimée: *Corr. gén.*, VIII, 683
14 Ibid., VIII, 694
15 Primoli Diary, VII, 120 (Primoli)
16 Primoli Diary, 5 August 1884, 19 July 1888 (Primoli)
17 Primoli Diary, 19 July 1888 (Primoli)
18 Primoli: *Notes intimes. Fragmens quotidiens.* 15 July – 7 September 1888 (Primoli)
19 Primoli: *Notes intimes.* February – June 1870, 124–5 (Primoli)
20 25 October [1890]. (Primoli)

6 Princess Mathilde. *Mr Coppée* (Primoli)
7 Coppée: *Souvenirs*, 111–3
8 *Corr.*, VI, 20–1
9 *Lettres inédites à la Princesse Mathilde*, 56
10 For the best assessment of Flaubert's character, see Enid Starkie: *Flaubert. The Making of the Master*
11 Introduction to Flaubert: *Lettres inédites à la Princesse Mathilde*, pp. x–xi
12 Album of Charlotte Primoli (mother of Gégé Primoli). Primoli Papers
13 Jules de Goncourt: *Lettres*, 308, note
14 Quoted by Primoli, loc. cit., 342–3
15 Quoted by Richardson; *Théophile Gautier*, 233
16 MU, 15 October 1869
17 Troubat, op. cit. 352, note
18 *Lettres à la Princesse*; Troubat, op. cit., 352, note
19 For appreciations of Sainte-Beuve, and accounts of his death and funeral, see *La Presse*, 15 October 1869; MU, 15, 17 October 1869
20 23 October 1869; *Revue bleue*, 11 January 1913, p. 39
21 Ibid.
22 This is clear from the Primoli papers. In a note of October 1869, Charles Giraud also writes: 'Troubat vous va faire envoyer le buste qui avait été fait il y a six mois ...' (Primoli)

28

1 Coppée: *Lettres à sa Mère et à sa Sœur*, 26–7
2 Coppée: *Souvenirs d'un Parisien*, 105
3 Coppée: *Lettres*, loc. cit.
4 Ibid., 28
5 Coppée: *Souvenirs*, 105–7

29

1 Mérimée: *Corr. gén.*, IX, 9. *La Presse*, 4, 7 January 1870
2 Joseph Primoli: *Notes on Princess Mathilde* [1892] (Primoli)
3 Marquis de Belleval: *Souvenirs...*, 305
4 *La Presse*, 10 January 1870

5 *The Times*, 7, 8 January 1870
6 MU, 11 January 1870
7 For Mathilde's alleged marriage with Popelin, see note 20
8 Information from M. Claude Popelin
9 Ibrovac: *Heredia*, 263–5. For an appreciation of Popelin as writer and craftsman, see P. de Bouchaud: *Claudius Popelin. Peintre, Émailleur et Poète*
10 Goncourt: *Journal*, VIII, 90
11 *La Presse*, 4 November 1864
12 Arsène Houssaye: *Confessions*, IV, 256
13 *La Presse*, 15 August 1869; Goncourt: *Journal*, VIII, 215
14 Abbot: *La Princesse Mathilde*. The pamphlet was both unkind and unsympathetic; but while at times it suggested a caricature, it had a certain seriousness of purpose. The author suggested that Mathilde could influence the Emperor, stabilize the Second Empire and the future of France
15 Princess Mathilde: *Comment il faudrait vieillir* (Primoli)
16 Primoli Diary, 19 July 1888 (Primoli); but in the dedicatory letter of *Cinq Octaves de Sonnets* (1875), Popelin says: 'Depuis plus de dix années je ne travaille que par le désir de vous plaire.'
17 Information from M. Claude Popelin; see also *Le Curieux*, June 1887, p. 253
18 20 February 1869 (Popelin)
19 28 May 1869 (Popelin)
20 Goncourt: *Journal*, VIII, 229. In 1879, the *Almanach de Gotha* announced that Mathilde was married to Popelin. The statement was strangely irresponsible; Popelin believed that Nieuwerkerke had made it out of malice. But Nieuwerkerke had no reason to do so, for he had long been indifferent to

Mathilde; nor would his statement have been enough without her corroboration. Mathilde was distressed by the announcement: Marie Abbatucci told Goncourt that she had been 'in a terrible state, . . . that her exasperation had been really comic; and one day, when she had been complaining excessively about it, poor Claudius had been obliged to say: "Do you think I'm very happy about it myself?" '
Mathilde denied the statement in the press (and Gégé Primoli recorded his disbelief in his diary), but the legend persisted. In *Le Curieux*, June 1887, p. 253, Popelin is described as 'le second mari de la princesse Mathilde'. No date, however, is given for the marriage. In his *Souvenirs d'un Enfant de Paris*, 1911, Émile Bergerat mentioned the alleged marriage. M. Claude Popelin, grandson of Claudius, believes that a *mariage de conscience* was solemnized by a young priest called Baudrillart, who later became Archbishop of Paris. But on her death certificate, Mathilde was described as the widow of Demidoff. This statement – and all that is known of her character – precludes any second marriage.

30

1 Undated letter (Henriot)
2 *La Presse*, 28 January 1870
3 *La Presse*, 25 May 1870
4 Primoli Diary, VII, 22 (Primoli)
5 Ibid.
6 Claretie: *La Vie à Paris, 1908*, 182
7 Coppée: *Lettres*, 37
8 *L'Artiste*, 1 April 1870; see also *La Presse* and MU, 31 March 1870
9 Primoli Diary, VII, 125
10 Eugène Sue et Félix Pyat: *Mathilde*, II, iv.
11 *La Presse* recorded on 1 May

that the six sales had brought in a
total of 4,863,031 francs
12 *La Presse*, 1 May 1870
13 Ibid.
14 MU, 1 May 1870
15 Whitehurst, op. cit., II, 330
16 Unidentified cutting (Primoli)
17 Dr P. Ménière: *Journal*, 290
18 *La Presse* and MU, 21 May 1870
19 Whitehurst, op. cit., II, 341–2,
345
20 Goncourt: *Journal*, VIII, 219
21 *La Presse*, 22 June 1870
22 Primoli Diary, 2 March 1870
(Primoli)
23 J. de La Faye, op. cit., 245
24 22 June 1870 (Henriot)
25 Edmond de Goncourt to
Théophile Gautier, 23 June 1870

31

1 14 July 1870 (Henriot)
2 MU, 16 July 1870
3 Ibid.
4 Renan: *Corr.*, I., 347; Goncourt:
Journal, IX, 211–2; MU, 24 July 1870
5 MU, 29 July 1870
6 *La Presse*, 31 July 1870
7 Bapst, op. cit., IV, 208
8 Ibid., 235–6
9 Ibid.
10 Goncourt: *Journal*, IX, 18–19
11 12 August 1870 (Henriot)
12 *La Presse*, 3 August 1870
13 14 August 1870 (Henriot)
14 Note dated '1870, samedi';
quoted by Primoli, loc. cit., 356
15 La Roncière Le Noury, II, 174
16 Goncourt: *Journal*, IX, 26–7
17 *The Times*, 5, 6 September 1870:
MU, 5, 6 September 1870

PART FOUR
The Second Exile
1870-1

32

1 Primoli: *Politique et Voyages*,
1870. Mons, 12 September (Primoli)
2 Gustave Popelin. Letter to
Charles Grandjean, 1926 (Popelin).
In a letter of 1870, also in the Popelin
Collection, he wrote to his father
from Puys: 'I am very happy and I
am beginning to work with madame
Dumas ... I wish you would tell me
about your travels after you left
Dieppe and especially why you did
not say goodbye to me when you
went ...'
3 Primoli: *Politique et Voyages*, loc.
cit.; in his diary for 1894 however, he
wrote that she went to Rouen, where

she was met by Dumas *fils* and
Flaubert.
4 Gustave Popelin, loc. cit.
5 Primoli Diary, 19 July 1888
(Primoli)
6 Gustave Popelin, loc. cit.
7 9 September 1882; Goncourt:
Journal, XII, 190–1
8 Primoli, *Politique et Voyages*, loc.
cit.
9 *La Presse*, 10 September 1870
10 *The Times*, 8 September 1870
11 Ibid., 9 September 1870
12 *L'Indépendance belge*, 8 September
1870
13 Ibid., 9 September 1870
14 Théophile Gautier to Estelle
Gautier, 9 September 1870; *Mercure*

de France, 15 May 1929, 128–9
15 MU, 10 September 1870
16 Ibid., see also *L'Indépendance belge*, 12 September 1870
17 MU, 11 September 1870
18 *La Presse*, 14 September 1870
19 Undated letter (Popelin)
20 Letter dated 'mercredi soir' (Popelin). See: Joanna Richardson: *Unpublished Letters of Flaubert. The Times Literary Supplement*, 13 June 1968
21 Primoli: *Politique et Voyages*, loc. cit., quoting letter from Princess Mathilde, 12 October 1870
22 Princess Mathilde to Primoli, 14 September 1870, quoted in *Politique et Voyages*
23 12 September 1870 (Primoli)
24 14 September 1870 (Primoli)

33

1 Princess Mathilde: *Souvenirs des années d'exil, II*. RDDM, 1 January 1928, 89–90
2 Goncourt: *Journal*, XI, 174
3 Letter of 14 September 1870, quoted in Primoli, *Politique et Voyages*, 1870 (Primoli)
4 Letter of 12 October 1870, quoted in Primoli, *Politique et Voyages*, 1870 (Primoli)
5 Murat, op. cit., 222–3
6 12 October 1870 (Primoli)
7 9 November 1870 (Primoli)
8 17 October 1870; Murat, 224–5
9 28 October 1870; ibid., 225–6
10 *L'Indépendance belge*, 10 September 1870
11 Decree of 5 September 1870, quoted in MU, 7 September 1870
12 *L'Indépendance belge*, 7 September 1870
13 Marquis de Belleval: *Souvenirs de ma jeunesse*, 278, 305
14 In her *Mémoires* (1899, p. 45), Mme de la Ferronays mentioned that

in this new retreat 'M. de Nieuwerkerke, now old, but ever gallant, . . . organized a very elaborate life for himself, and great mystery has always hung over it'.

Lady Paget, the wife of the British Ambassador to Rome, solved some of the mystery in the summer of 1874. The Pagets had taken a villa near Lucca, on Lake Garda, and among their neighbours were Nieuwerkerke and two ladies who lived with him at that fascinating place Gattajuola, which with great artistic knowledge they had made perfect. The ladies, who were looked upon with suspicion by the Lucchese nobility, were an old, very bourgeois Princess Cantacuzène and her very sympathetic adopted daughter, Olga, the authoress of many charming novels . . . She painted and played exquisitely, in fact there was nothing she could not do. She might then have been twenty-five. Nieuwerkerke, who was an old man, called her *ma chère enfant*. She married a year later, much to the world's astonishment, Don Lorenzo Altieri, a clever and cultivated Roman who had known the family intimately for several years.'

Lady Paget 'found out', she said, that Olga Cantacuzène was the daughter of Nieuwerkerke and Mathilde; they had 'found this good dull little Princess Cantacuzène and induced her to adopt the child'.

It is hardly credible that Mathilde had had a child by Nieuwerkerke after she had been his mistress for thirteen years, and that she had contrived to hide the birth at the height of the Second Empire. Nor can one believe that she would have failed to acknowledge her child, or that she would have had her adopted or let her live with her father. It is much more probable that the girl was Nieuwerkerke's daughter by some other woman (perhaps Princess Cantacuzène); it is just possible that she was his mistress.

As for Nieuwerkerke (whom Lady Paget considered 'very agreeable'), his visits to France grew increasingly rare. He was in touch with Dumas *fils* as late as 1888 (Bib. Nat. N. A. Fr. 24639, ff 10–11). He died at the Villa Gattajola in January 1892

15 *Lettres inédites à la Princesse Mathilde*, 94–5

16 Undated letter [November 1870] (Popelin). See also Richardson: *Unpublished Letters of Flaubert. The Times Literary Supplement*, 13 June 1968

17 29 November 1870 (Popelin)

18 Quoted by Richardson: *Théophile Gautier*, 248

19 Ibid., 250

20 Ibid., 248–9

21 Ibid., 250–1

22 Edward Crane (ed.): *The Memoirs of Dr. Thomas W. Evans*, II, 512

23 Goncourt: *Journal*, X, 38–9, 22–3

24 Undated letter (late 1870). (Popelin)

25 8 October 1870: *Revue bleue*, 11 January 1913, p. 40

34

1 Letter to Charles Grandjean, 1926 (Popelin)

2 Primoli: *Politique et Voyages*, 1870. Brussels, 8–15 September

3 Goncourt: *Journal*, XII, 198–9

4 Letter to Carlotta Grisi, 31 October 1870 (Henriot)

5 Murat, op. cit., 226–7

6 Queen Sophie to Princess Mathilde, 27 December 1870 (Popelin)

7 Murat, op. cit., loc. cit.

8 Princess Mathilde, memoirs (Primoli)

9 *Revue bleue*, 18 January 1913, p. 70

10 Letter of 18 January 1871; ibid., p. 71

11 This appears to be confirmed by Ernest Daudet, in his pamphlet *La France et les Bonaparte*, which was published in 1871.

12 4 February 1871 (Primoli)

13 Telegram of 10 January 1871; quoted, but wrongly dated, by Bouniols, *Thiers au pouvoid*, 290

14 Viollet-le-Duc: *Lettres inédites*, 100–1, and note

15 Goncourt: *Journal*, X, 219

16 Undated letter from Dumas *fils* to Popelin (Popelin)

17 Ottaviano [Vimercati] to Princess Mathilde, 27 January 1871 (Popelin)

18 Queen Sophie to Princess Mathilde, 2 February 1871 (Popelin). The poem is not recorded by Spoelberch de Lovenjoul in his *Histoire des Œuvres de Théophile Gautier*

19 Queen Sophie to Princess Mathilde, 5, 12 February 1871 (Popelin)

20 Primoli Diary X, 1871, p. 127

Among the Popelin papers are extracts, in Popelin's hand, from Sophie's correspondence with Mathilde. On 8 February 1861 Sophie wrote: 'The Emperor's strength abroad lies in the disunity and the cowardice of his enemies, their fear of his incomparable army; at home, his strength lies in the people, their faith in him and in his name. *She* [the Empress] isolates herself from her real friends . . . from thoughtlessness, and from total ignorance of the facts. Poor, gracious & beautiful woman, nature did not fit her for the cares of her high position.'

'She should have adored him instead of trying to drag him to his perdition . . .

'The other day the British Minister,

Lord Napier, left us to become Ambassador to St Petersburg. He said to me: "Can I do anything for you?" "Yes," I replied, "promise me never to do any harm to the Emperor Napoleon." He reflected for a moment. Then he said: "I promise." . . .'

It was a remarkable answer from Queen Victoria's envoy, but perhaps it was the only one which a diplomat could give. A few weeks later, on 16 April, Sophie wrote to Mathilde about the Empress: 'I understand every detail of what you tell me about *Her*. One has to bear her . . . He is too sensible not to distinguish in his own mind those who are really and sincerely devoted to him.' The Empress felt it her duty to oppose the 'Italian' line in the Empire's foreign policy; when Cavour, the chief architect of Italian unity, died in the summer of 1861, Sophie told Mathilde (16 June): 'I know we both feel the same about the death of Cavour. The loss is immense, and it will be increasingly felt. The chariot which he sped on its way will still roll on, at first, but when incidents arise, what will happen? They say *She* showed her joy at his death! The blindness is incredible.' Late in 1861, after consultations between Mathilde and the Emperor, William of Holland was asked to Compiègne. Sophie insisted that he should go, because, as she explained on 9 October, 'now he will be bursting with longing to go back to Paris & he knows quite well that he wouldn't dare to go back, if he showed himself hostile.' The King returned enchanted with his visit to France. 'He adores each and every one of you,' Sophie reported on 5 November. 'He alone understands the Emperor's politics, his most secret intentions. He admired the

Empress. Poor Clotilde is the only one in disgrace.' Sophie felt small regret when, in December 1861, the Prince Consort died. 'I remain convinced that, politically, Albert's death is not a misfortune. He detested the Emperor so' (4 January 1862). As a Wurtemberg princess and as a lover of France, Sophie was sharply conscious of the growing threat to France from across the Rhine. 'You have forged arrows against the Emperor Napoleon,' she said bluntly to a German diplomat. 'No,' he replied, '*not arrows, yet*, but a shield' (11 September 1863). On 8 May 1866, Sophie warned Mathilde of the imminent Austro-Prussian War. 'I believe there will be a war, & I'm very unhappy. Forgive me for being *Austrian* in Germany, I'm not Austrian in Italy.' Sophie's letters to Mathilde also reflect her own disastrous marriage to William III, and the pernicious influence of his mistress, Mme Musard. On 28 November 1865 she wrote: 'He is completely under the influence of that horrible woman . . . She rouses him against the Emperor & his government, he's become very hostile to them, which is a real grief to me.'

21 *Lettres inédites à la Princesse Mathilde*, 101

22 2 March 1871 (Popelin)

23 Henri Welschinger: *La Captivité de Napoléon III à Wilhelmshohe*, RDDM, 15 April 1910, 924–5

24 Diary of Eugénie Fort (Gautier)

25 Ibid.

26 1 April 1871; *Revue bleue*, 18 January 1913, 7

27 Goncourt: *Journal*, X, 38–9

28 21 April 1871 (Gautier)

29 22 April 1871 (Gautier)

30 1 May 1871 (Gautier)

31 12 May [1871] (Primoli)

32 Eugénie Fort, in her diary, records his arrival

33 Gustave Popelin to Charles Grandjean, 1926 (Popelin). In an undated note to Claudius Popelin, among the Popelin papers, Dumas *fils* writes: 'Je partirai samedi pour Bruxelles, escorté du jeune Gustave ... Flaubert m'accompagnera très probablement.'

34 *Le Vingt-Sept Mai. Œuvres de Théophile Gautier. Poésies,* 271

35 Diary of Eugénie Fort (Gautier)

36 In an undated letter to Mathilde, probably written in late May or early June 1870, Charles Giraud says: 'Si vous venez à Paris, Samedi, ayez la bonté de me le marquer j'irai vous joindre rue de Berry et vous mettrai au courant' (Primoli)

PART FIVE
The Third Republic
1871–1904

35

1 Goncourt: *Journal,* XII, 196

2 Quoted by Castillon du Perron, 218

3 Letter dated 'avril 1858' (Primoli)

4 Primoli Diary, October–December 1868, p. 88 (Primoli)

5 Gustave Popelin to Charles Grandjean 1926 (Popelin)

6 Hébert to Princess Mathilde, 29 June [1871] (Primoli)

7 Goncourt: *Journal,* X, 22–3

8 RDDM, 15 November 1925, p. 361

9 *Revue bleue,* 18 January 1913, p. 71

10 *Correspondance entre George Sand et Gustave Flaubert,* 281–2

11 8 September 1871 (Primoli)

12 21 June 1872 (Primoli)

13 24 October 1863 (Primoli)

14 Goncourt: *Journal,* X, 29

15 Ibid., IX, 221–2

16 Ibid., X, 30

17 Ibid., X, 36–7

18 Ibid.

19 4 October 1871. Typescript (Primoli)

20 *Revue bleue,* 18 January 1913, p. 72

21 RDDM, 19 November 1926, 428–9

22 Goncourt: *Journal,* X, 56, 77

23 Bergerat: *Souvenirs d'un Enfant de Paris,* I, 345, 346–8

24 *Lettres inédites à la Princesse Mathilde,* 127

25 Bergerat, op. cit., 350

26 Ibid., 355–6

27 Richardson, op. cit., 266

28 Goncourt: *Journal,* VIII, 152–3

29 Dreyfous: *Ce que je tiens à dire,* 166, 322–4

30 RDDM, 15 November 1925, p. 365

31 Renan: *Corr.,* II, 32–3

32 24 October 1872. Typescript (Primoli)

36

1 F. Masson: *La Princesse Mathilde après la Guerre. La Revue hebdomadaire,* 30 March 1912, 623 sqq.

2 The telegram is among the Popelin papers

3 Kühn, op. cit., 351

4 Crane, op. cit., II, 613

5 Queen Sophie to Princess Mathilde, 5 May 1873 (Popelin)

6 6 March 1874 (Primoli)

7 Popelin to Primoli, 2 March 1877 (Primoli)

8 Goncourt: *Journal*, X, 231: Delzant, *Paul de Saint-Victor*, 137–8

9 Princess Mathilde to Lebrun, 14 July [1871]; *Revue bleue*, 18 January 1913, 71

10 Popelin to his father, 14 February 1874 (Popelin)

11 Popelin to his father, 17 March 1874 (Popelin). Among the Primoli papers is a letter from Ernest Lavisse to Princess Mathilde, 30 December 1878; 'Je sais que Votre Altesse ne désire rien de plus au monde, si ce n'est le bonheur de ses neveux d'Angleterre et de France, qui grandissent pour nous commander, nous sauver et nous venger. Il reviendra bien des jours heureux, Princesse!'

12 Popelin to Primoli (Primoli)

13 Augier to Princess Mathilde, 1876 [?] (Popelin)

14 Ms. portrait in Popelin's handwriting (Primoli)

15 Letter of 1876 (Popelin)

16 24 May 1876 (Popelin)

17 Goncourt: *Journal*, X, 223

18 Théophile Gautier *fils*, *Le Figaro*, 3 January 1904

19 Mme Alphonse Daudet, op. cit., 73–7

20 Popelin to Primoli, 28 April 1877 (Primoli)

21 Popelin to Primoli, 20 December 1876 (Primoli). Popelin writes: 'Nous avons eu les obsèques de ce bon & spirituel Chaix-d'Est-Ange ... La Princesse a été très-affectée de cette catastrophe; elle avait dîné chez lui, 8 jours avant, avec la reine Sophie, &, depuis, il était venu passer une heure rue de Berry, causant avec le charme qui lui était particulier. Votre tante assistait au service funèbre ...'

22 Letter of 1888 (Popelin)

23 Undated letter (Popelin)

24 Primoli Diary, 1880 (Primoli)

25 Ibid.

26 RDDM, 1 November 1925, p. 80

27 Goncourt: *Journal*, XII, 48

28 Primoli Diary, 21 September 1879 (Primoli)

29 Houssaye: *Confessions*, IV, 159; Primoli Diary, 30 November 1893 (Primoli)

30 Primoli Diary, loc. cit.

31 Primoli: *La Princesse Mathilde et le maestro Sauzay. Revue hebdomadaire*, 6 October 1917

32 Goncourt: *Journal*, VII, 100

33 Ibid., XI, 135

34 30 March 1877 (Primoli)

35 Writing to Sainte-Beuve on 16 June 1867, Mathilde says: 'La brochure Zola est si folle que ma colère me tombe; dans une société bien organisée un homme qui [-] le public pr. de pareilles ordures sans respect pr. l'art devrait être enfermé.' (Primoli)

36 Primoli Diary, 1880 (Primoli)

37 Goncourt: *Journal*, VIII, 74

38 Portrait of Gustave Flaubert (Primoli)

39 Goncourt: *Journal*, XI, 127

40 [Proust]: *Un Salon historique. Le Figaro*, 25 February 1903

41 Dreyfous: *Ce qu'il me reste à dire*, 272

42 Ibrovac: *Heredia*, 156

43 *Corr.*, VII, 374

44 *Corr.*, VIII, 138

45 *Corr.*, VIII, 215

46 Ibid.

47 Ibid., and *Corr.*, VIII, 174

48 *Corr.*, VIII, 243

49 G. de Maupassant: *Lettres inédites à Gustave Flaubert*, 84

50 Ibid.

51 Ibid., 85–7

52 Ibid.

53 17 May 1879 (Popelin)

54 Undated letter (Primoli). In 1885, Mathilde was trying to help Mme Pasca. Among the Popelin papers is a letter of 11 December in which Octave Feuillet tells Popelin: 'La Princesse a bien voulu me charger d'une petite commission relative à Mme Pasca. J'ai vu suivant le désir qu'elle m'avait exprimé, MM. Claretie et Delauney [sic]. Je voudrais rendre compte à Son Altesse du résultat, assez médiocre, hélas! de mon double démarche.'

55 Goncourt: *Journal*, X, 155

56 *H. Taine, sa vie et sa correspondance*, III, 261

57 Goncourt: *Journal*, X, 239

58 Ibid., 27 September 1882

37

1 Primoli Diary, 1888 (Primoli)

2 Popelin to Primoli, 28 April 1877 (Primoli)

3 29 November 1873 (Popelin)

4 26 December 1873 (Popelin)

5 20 February 1874 (Popelin)

6 *Cinq Octaves de Sonnets. Épître dédicatoire*, 18–21, 23–4, 27–8

7 The unpublished sonnet, in Gautier's hand, is dated 'St Gratien Juillet 1869.'

8 Letter of [1873] (Popelin). See also: Richardson: *Unpublished Flaubert Letters. The Times Literary Supplement*, 13 June 1968

9 Goncourt: *Journal*, X, 219

10 Ibid., XI, 76; *Soirées parisiennes*, 1876, 50–1

11 Princess Mathilde to Joseph Ratomski, 29 May 1876 (Popelin)

12 Goncourt: *Journal*, XI, 174

13 F. Masson in *Le Temps*, 5 January 1904. Louis Ganderax, ibid.

14 F. Masson in *La Revue hebdomadaire*, loc. cit.

15 Letter of 1882 (Primoli)

16 16 July 1877 (Popelin)

17 22 July 1877 (Primoli)

18 Unpublished typescript of article (Gautier)

19 Goncourt: *Journal*, X, 211–5

20 Primoli Diary, September 1880 (Primoli)

21 F. Masson in *La Revue hebdomadaire*, loc. cit.

38

1 Letter of 1879 (no other date given) (Primoli)

2 Goncourt: *Journal*, XII, 32

3 4 July 1879 (Primoli)

4 *The Letters of Queen Victoria*, Vol. III, 30–2; Murat, op. cit., 332–3

5 *Impératrice Eugénie: Lettres familières*, II, 104

6 Goncourt: *Journal*, XII, 36–7

7 *The Letters of Queen Victoria*, III, 30–1

8 *Corr.*, II, 190

9 14 [?] December 1880 (Primoli)

10 Princess Mathilde to the Empress Eugénie [December 1880] (Primoli)

11 Princess Mathilde to the Empress Eugénie, 31 May 1881 (Primoli)

12 June 1882 (Primoli)

13 Goncourt: *Journal*, XII, 49–50

14 [22 April 1880] *Lettres inédites à la Princesse Mathilde*, 236

15 30 December 1881 (Primoli)

16 Goncourt: *Journal*, XII, 140, 141

17 Mme A. Daudet. *Souvenirs . . .*, 100–1

18 Goncourt: *Journal*, XII, 147–8

19 Mme A. Daudet, op. cit., 106–9

20 Ibid., 108–9

21 Léon Daudet: *Salons et Milieux littéraires de 1880 à nos jours*, 249–50

22 Ibid.

23 *Le Gaulois*, 23 December 1882; *Gil Blas*, 4 August 1883; *Le Figaro*, 6 March 1885

24 Goncourt: *Journal*, XII, 213

39

1 In his *Journal* for 1 January 1883, Goncourt recorded the Prince's 'strange excitement' at Gambetta's death
2 Goncourt: *Journal*, XII, 227–8
3 Ibid., XII, 229–30
4 Note dated '15 novembre' (Popelin)
5 Note dated '1 juillet' (Popelin)
6 Note dated 'vendredi' (Popelin)
7 Note dated '19 août', postmarked '82' (Popelin)
8 These notes are kept among the Popelin papers
9 Information from M. Claude Popelin
10 10 November 1882 (Primoli)
11 20 January 1883 (Primoli)
12 Primoli Diary, 21 February 1883 (Primoli)
13 Primoli Diary, 8 March 1883 (Primoli)
14 Primoli Diary, 28 March 1883 (Primoli)
15 15 May 1883 (Primoli)
16 28 September 1883 (Primoli)
17 13 October, 7 December 1883 (Primoli)
18 20 February 1883 (Primoli)
19 23 May 1884 (Primoli)
20 25 June 1884 (Primoli)
21 Primoli Diary, 9 March 1893 (Primoli)
22 *H. Taine: sa vie et sa correspondance*, IV, 227–8, note
23 Ibid., 227–30
24 *Corr.*, II, 321–2
25 Claretie: *La Vie à Paris, 1883,* 206
26 Houssaye: *Confessions*, IV, 162
27 Banville: *Camées parisiens*, 243
28 M. du Camp: *Souvenirs littéraires*, I, 217–8
29 *H. Taine: sa vie et sa correspondance*, IV, 257

40

1 Goncourt: *Journal*, XII, 142
2 Ibid., XII, 197–8
3 Ibid., XII, 200–1; Feydeau had once asked Mathilde to intervene to save his wife who had been accused of shoplifting (Primoli Diary, September 1880)
4 Primoli Diary, 13 September 1884
5 24 July 1880 (Primoli)
6 Letter to Primoli, 18n October 1883 (Primoli)
7 Goncourt: *Journal*, X, 199–201, 205–6
8 Hébert to Princess Mathilde [1878] (Primoli)
9 23 July 1887 (Popelin)
10 Primoli Diary, September 1880
11 *Un Livre de Sonnets*, 63. Some of the telegrams are still among the Popelin papers
12 Letter to Primoli, 15 August [1892] (Primoli)
13 Primoli Diary, 19 July 1888 (Primoli)
14 Grandjean to Primoli, 11 July 1888 (Primoli)
15 Primoli Diary, 1888 (Primoli)
16 Ibid.
17 8 July 1877 (Primoli)
18 31 January 1878 (Primoli)
19 Primoli Diary, loc. cit. (Primoli)
20 Primoli Diary, 20 July 1888 (Primoli)
21 Goncourt: *Journal*, XII, 147–8
22 A. Daudet, *L'Immortel*, 235–6
23 Ibid., 273, 277–9
24 Primoli Diary, 1, 29 August 1888 (Primoli)
25 Ibid., 28 August 1888
26 Ibid., 7 September 1888
27 Ibid.
28 Ibid., 8 September 1888
29 Ibid.
30 Primoli Diary, 1889, 37 sqq (Primoli)

31   *Convalescence*. Claudius Popelin: *Poésies complètes*, 269

41

1   Letter dated 'Arcachon', 6 octobre' [1888] (Primoli)
2   9 November 1888 (Primoli)
3   Primoli Diary, 1889, 37 sqq. (Primoli)
4   Ibid.
5   7 December [1888] (Primoli)
6   15 December [1888] (Primoli)
7   Primoli Diary, 1889, loc. cit.
8   Letter to Charles Grandjean, 20 July 1890: 'Après dix-huit mois de véritable agonie . . .' (Primoli)
9   Undated letter (Primoli)
10   23 January 1889 (Primoli)
11   10 February 1889 (Primoli)
12   19 February 1889 (Primoli)
13   Popelin was staying at Saint-Gratien in June. On 18 March, however, Prince Napoleon told Mathilde he had heard she was better (Primoli)
14   Primoli Diary, 1889, 37 sqq. (Primoli)
15   Ibid.
16   Primoli Diary, 1889, 65–6 (Primoli)
17   Primoli Diary, 1889, 85 (Primoli)
18   25 July [1889] (Primoli)
19   1 August [1889] (Primoli)
20   Primoli Diary, 1889, 137–8 (Primoli)
21   Primoli Diary, 8 August 1889 (Primoli)
22   8 September 1889 (Popelin)
23   Letter to Charles Grandjean, 1889 (Grandjean)
24   Masson to Popelin, 7 October 1889 (Popelin)
25   Masson to Popelin, 11 March [1890] (Popelin)
26   Masson to Popelin, 14 March [1890] (Popelin)
27   30 January [1890] (Primoli)
28   Bib. Nat. N.A. Fr. 25168 f 267

29   Goncourt: *Journal*, X, 210
30   Primoli Diary, 1890 (Primoli)
31   20 July 1890 (Primoli)
32   13 September 1890 (Primoli)
33   20, 27 September 1890 (Primoli)
34   11 October 1890 (Primoli)
35   2 November [1890] (Primoli)
36   25 October [1890] (Primoli)
37   A. Daudet: *La Lutte pour la Vie;* preface, p. x; Primoli Diary, 11 December 1890 (Primoli)
38   Letter dated '25 mardi' [1891] (Grandjean)
39   5 January 1891 (Popelin)
40   3 December [1891] (Primoli)
41   Mathilde to Primoli, 27 December [1890 or '91]. Information from M. Claude Popelin
42   Victor Du Bled, *La Société française*, 227–8
43   26 August [1891] (Primoli)
44   27 August [1891] (Primoli)
45   4 September [1891] (Primoli)
46   *The Times*, 19 January 1892
47   On 8 June 1892 the Empress wrote to Mathilde from Farnborough: 'Au moment de mon départ du Cap Martin j'ai appris que vous aviez eu le chagrin de perdre un vieil ami dont la mort devait vous causer un vrai chagrin . . . J'ai tant souffert moi-même que je prends part à toutes les souffrances . . .' (Primoli)

42

1   'Princesse me charge douloureuse mission de t'apprendre la mort subite de Monsieur Popelin – Doucet' (Primoli)
2   23 July 1892 (Primoli)
3   24 August 1892 (Primoli)
4   Primoli Diary, 1892 (Primoli)
5   22 August 1892 (Primoli)
6   'Mon père épousa en 1892 (bref, deux ou trois mois après le décès de Claudius, favorable à ce

mariage organisé par Marie Abbatucci) Henriette Doumerc, fille d'un avocat à la Cour d'Appel de Paris.' M. Claude Popelin, in a letter to the author, 10 July 1967

7 Mathilde to Primoli, 26 July [1892] (Primoli)
8 15 July 1892
9 20 July 1892 (Primoli)
10 15 July 1892 (Primoli)
11 Letter to Primoli, 15 August 1892 (Primoli)
12 8 September [1892] (Grandjean)
13 10 September [1892] (Grandjean)
14 18 September [1892] (Grandjean)
15 28 September [1892] (Grandjean)
16 Letter of 1892 (Grandjean)
17 7 August 1892 (Primoli)
18 Primoli Diary, 1889, p. 82
19 15 August 1892 (Primoli)
20 19 August 1892 (Primoli)
21 Letter dated '17 septembre' (Bib. Nat. N.A. Fr. 25168 ff 283–5)
22 14 October [1892] (Grandjean)
23 Undated letter (Popelin). In a letter to Dumas *fils*, dated '13 octobre', Mathilde writes: '. . . d'après ce que vous m'avez dit hier G[ustave] voudrait effacer toute trace des 25 années passées auprès de moi.' This letter is kept in the Bibliothèque Nationale (N. A. Fr. 24636, ff 405–6). It was probably written in 1892. If Mathilde's statement is correct, she had therefore known Popelin since 1867.
24 26 [January 1893]. Grandjean. And see also letter to Primoli, dated 26 [January 1893] (Primoli)
25 12 February 1893 (Primoli)
26 24 April 1893 (Grandjean)
27 Princess Mathilde to Primoli, 22 December 1893 (Primoli)
28 Primoli Diary, November 1893 (Primoli)
29 Undated note (Primoli)
30 19 May 1897 (Grandjean). Among the Popelin papers is a note

from Prince Louis-Napoleon, nephew of Mathilde, dated 20 January 1904, acknowledging Gustave Popelin's letter of condolence on her death

43

1 Letter on black-edged paper, dated '7 Xbre' (Primoli)
2 Letter dated only '29 mai' (Primoli)
3 Primoli papers
4 Ibid.
5 12 February 1893 (Primoli)
6 Primoli Diary, 1893 (Primoli)
7 Primoli. Notes, 1895 (Primoli)
8 Primoli Diary, 25 June 1893
9 22 December 1894 (Primoli)
10 Primoli Diary, 1 December 1880 (Primoli)
11 12 October 1893 (Primoli)
12 26 December 1888 (Primoli)
13 Undated letter from Cannes, written on Maupassant's return from Africa (Primoli)
14 17 October 1891 (Grandjean)
15 Bib. Nat. N. A. Fr. 13209 f 127
16 Ibid., ff 132–3
17 Primoli Diary, 22 June 1893 (Primoli)
18 19 October [1893] (Primoli)
19 Letter dated '5 avril' (Grandjean)
20 Letter dated '23 avril' (Grandjean)
21 Letter dated 'Dimanche' (Grandjean)
22 Letter dated '19' [1893] (Grandjean)
23 11 October 1893 (Grandjean)
24 Ibid.
25 11 September [1894] (Grandjean)
26 24 September [1894] (Grandjean)
27 Letter dated '10 octobre' (Grandjean)
28 Letter dated 'dimanche 5 avril' (Bib. Nat. N. A. Fr. 13209 ff 9–10)

29 Letter dated '13 juin' (Bib. Nat. N. A. Fr. 13564 ff 131–2)
30 Letter dated '18 avril' (Bib. Nat. N. A. Fr 25168 ff 298–9)
31 Letter dated '4 décembre' (Bib. Nat. N. A. Fr. 25168 ff 288–9)
32 Telegram dated '18 décembre 1889' (Bib. Nat. N. A. Fr. 25168 f 266)
33 8 June 1892 (Primoli)
34 RDP, 1 August 1922, 479–81
35 Bib. Nat. N. A. Fr. 24966 ff 61–2
36 Ibid., ff 51, 74
37 RDP, 15 January 1904, 419–22
38 Primoli Diary, 1893 (Primoli)
39 Mouly: *La Vie Prodigieuse de Victorien Sardou*, 258–60
40 Letter of 1895 (Primoli)
41 Bib. Nat. N. A. Fr. 13564 ff 125–6. 29 [November 1895]
42 Lavedan: *Avant l'Oubli*, II, 228–9
43 Bib. Nat. N. A. Fr. 13564 ff 133–4
44 Among the Popelin papers is a note from Charles Grandjean to Gustave Popelin dated, 'samedi', he writes: 'Lundi, si on enterre Goncourt, la Princesse ira à la cérémonie'
45 Primoli papers
46 Barrès: *Mes Cahiers*, I, 118–9, 120–1
47 Claretie: *La Vie à Paris, 1895*, 343
48 Claretie: *La Vie à Paris, 1897*, 362–3; ibid., 1898, 36
49 *Le Figaro*, 3 January 1904
50 RDDM, 1 November 1925, 75. See also Joanna Richardson: *Proust and the Princess, The Times Literary Supplement*, 17 October, 1968
51 Proust: *À la recherche du temps perdu*, III, 142–3
52 Ibid., 143
53 Ibid., 145–6
54 A. Hermant: *Souvenirs . . .*, 171 sqq.
55 Ibid.
56 *La Princesse Mathilde et le Duc*

d'Aumale. RDP, 1 August 1922, 479–81
57 M. Barrès: *Mes Cahiers*, II, 206
58 *L'Éclair*, 22 November 1903
59 Unpublished typescript passage of article on Princess Mathilde (Gautier)
60 *Corr.*, II, 174

44

1 *Un Salon Historique. Le Salon de S. A. I. la Princesse Mathilde. Le Figaro*, 25 February 1903. The article is signed 'Dominique'.
2 Ibid., and D. Leon: *Introduction to Proust*, 29–30, 217. See also Joanna Richardson: *Proust and the Princess. The Times Literary Supplement*, 17 October, 1968
3 Leslie, op. cit., 65; letter of 3 August 1900 (Primoli)
4 Emile Gebhart: *Le Journal des Débats*, 4 January 1904
5 This, and the following anecdotes, are taken from *Mort de la Princesse Mathilde*, the article by Théophile Gautier *fils* in *Le Figaro*, 3 January 1904
6 In 1882 she took Goncourt, who described Suresnes in his *Journal*, XII, 191–2
7 J.-P. Worth: *A Century of Fashion*, 97–9
8 Théophile Gautier *fils*, loc. cit.
9 Article by Lavedan from an unidentified paper, May 1904 (Primoli)
10 François Coppée: *La Princesse Mathilde. Le Gaulois*, 3 January 1904
11 Undated note (Primoli)
12 Levedan, loc. cit.
13 26 August [1902] (Primoli)
14 Primoli Diary, 3 December 1902 (Primoli)
15 9 May 1903 (Primoli)
16 Primoli notes

45

1   *Le Figaro*, 3 January 1904
2   21 August [1903] (Primoli)
3   Undated letter, and letter of 11
January [1904] addressed to Primoli;
letter of 25 August [1903] addressed
to Princess Mathilde (Primoli)
4   Primoli Diary, 17 July 1888
(Primoli)
5   Typescript passage of published
article by Théophile Gautier *fils*
(Gautier)
6   4 September 1903 (Primoli)
7   Primoli Diary, 22 September
1903 (Primoli)
8   22 September 1903. Notes.
*Dernière maladie de la Princesse
Mathilde* (Primoli). *The Times*
reported her fortune as some 2m.
francs (5 January 1904). She left her
papers to Primoli, and her fortune to
her godson Louis.
9   Primoli Diary, 1 October 1903
(Primoli)
10   According to Castillon du Perron,
La Princesse Mathilde, 296, where the
year is wrongly given as 1904
11   9 October 1903 (Gautier)
12   *L'Éclair*, 22 November 1903
13   RDP, 15 January 1904, 419–22
14   *Le Figaro*, 3 January 1904
15   RDP, loc. cit.

16   La Faye, 342
17   RDP, loc. cit.
18   Primoli Diary, 1 January 1904
(Primoli)
19   Ibid., 2 January 1904
20   This letter, on black-edged paper,
is dated only 'mardi', and it is among
the Primoli papers. See Joanna
Richardson: *Proust and the Princess*.
The Times Literary Supplement, 17
October, 1968
21   La Faye, 344
22   This letter, also on black-edged
paper, is among the Primoli papers.
It is dated simply 'Lundi', but it was
certainly written on 4 January 1904.
See Joanna Richardson: loc. cit.
23   Primoli Diary, 4 January 1904
(Primoli)

46

1   Goncourt: *Journal*, 13 December
1862
2   Claretie: *La Vie à Paris, 1904*,
6–7
3   *L'Écho de Paris*, 5 January 1904
4   Undated letter to an unknown
correspondent (Popelin)
5   14 April [1875] (Primoli)
6   *Le Figaro*, 3 January 1904
7   *L'Écho de Paris*, loc. cit.
8   Ibid.

Selected Bibliography

The following are among the books consulted. English books are published in London, French books in Paris, unless otherwise stated.

ABBOT, J., *La Princesse Mathilde (Demidoff-Bonaparte)* (Londres et Bruxelles. 1870)

APPONYI, Comte Rodolphe, *Vingt-cinq ans à Paris (1826–1852)*. Journal du Comte Rodolphe Apponyi, attaché de l'Ambassade d'Autriche à Paris. Publié par Ernest Daudet. IV. 1844–1852 (Plon. 1926)

AUGUSTIN-THIERRY, A., *La Princesse Mathilde, Notre-Dame des Arts* (Éditions Albin Michel. 1950)

BAC, Ferdinand, *Intimités de la IIIᵉ République, II* (Hachette. 1935)
La Princesse Mathilde. Sa vie et ses amis (Hachette. 1928)

BALDICK, Robert, (tr. and ed.) *Pages from the Goncourt Journal* (Oxford University Press. 1962)

BANVILLE, Théodore de, *La Lanterne magique. Camées Parisiens. La Comédie-Française* (Charpentier. 1882)

BAPST, Germain, *Le Maréchal Canrobert. Souvenirs d'un siècle* (Plon, Nourrit. 1898–1913)

BAROCHE, Mme Jules, *Second Empire. Notes and Souvenirs*. Préface de M. Frédéric Masson (Crès. 1921)

BARRÈS, Maurice, *Mes Cahiers* (Plon. 1929–1933)

BEAUMONT-VASSY, Vte de, *Histoire intime du Second Empire* (Librairie Sartorius. 1874)

BELLEVAL, Marquis de, *Souvenirs de ma jeunesse* (Émile Lechevalier. 1895)

BERGERAT, Émile, *Souvenirs d'un Enfant de Paris. I. Les Années de Bohème* (Charpentier/Fasquelle. 1911)

BLESSINGTON, Countess of, *The Idler in Italy* (Paris. Galignani. 1839)

BONNEROT, Jean, *C. Saint-Saëns. Sa Vie and son Œuvre* (Durand. 1914)

BOUCHAUD, Pierre de, *Claudius Popelin. Peintre, Émailleur et Poète* (Lemerre. 1894)

BOUCHOT, Henri, *Les Élégances du Second Empire* (Librairie illustrée. 1896)

BOUNIOLS, G., *Thiers au pouvoir, 1871–1873* (Delagrave. 1921)

CASTELLANE, Maréchal de, *Journal, 1804–1862* (Plon. 1895–1897)

CASTILLON DU PERRON, Marguerite, *La Princesse Mathilde* (Librairie Académique Perrin. 1963)

CLARETIE, Jules, *La Vie à Paris, 1883* (Havard. 1884)
La Vie à Paris, 1895 (Charpentier. 1896)

La Vie à Paris, 1897 (Charpentier, 1898)
La Vie à Paris, 1898 (Charpentier, 1899)
La Vie à Paris, 1904 (Charpentier, 1905)
La Vie à Paris, 1906 (Charpentier, 1907)
La Vie à Paris, 1908 (Charpentier. 1909)
Souvenirs du Dîner Bixio (Charpentier. 1924)
COPPÉE, François, *Lettres à sa Mère et à sa Sœur, 1862–1908*. Publiées par Jean Monval (Lemerre. 1914)
Souvenirs d'un Parisien (Lemerre. 1910)
CRANE, Edward A. (ed.), *The Memoirs of Dr. Thomas W. Evans. Recollections of the Second French Empire* (Fisher Unwin. 1905)
DAUDET, Alphonse, *L'Immortel. Mœurs parisiennes* (Lemerre. 1888)
La Lutte pour la Vie (Calmann-Lévy. 1890)
DAUDET, Mme Alphonse, *Souvenirs autour d'un groupe littéraire* (Charpentier. 1910)
DAUDET, Ernest, *La France and les Bonaparte* (France et Belgique. Chez tous les libraires. 1871)
DAUDET, Léon, *Études et Milieux littéraires de 1880 à nos jours* (Bernard Grasset. 1927)
DELACROIX, Eugène, *Journal* (Plon. 1893–1895)
DE LA FAYE, Jacques, *La Princesse Mathilde. Une nièce de Napoléon* (Emile-Paul. 1928)
DELZANT, Alidor, *Paul de Saint-Victor* (Calmann-Lévy. 1886)
DINO, Duchesse de, *Chronique de 1831 à 1862* (Plon. 1909–1910)
DREYFOUS, Maurice, *Ce que je tiens à dire. Un demi-siècle de choses vues et entendues. I. 1862–1872* (Ollendorff. 1912)
Ce qu'il me reste à dire (Ollendorff. 1913)
DU BLED, Victor, *La Société française depuis cent ans. Quelques salons du Second Empire* (Bloud & Gay. 1923)
DU CAMP, Maxime, *Souvenirs littéraires* (Hachette. 1882–1883)
EUGÉNIE, Impératrice, *Lettres familières* (Le Divan. 1935)
FEUILLET Mme Octave, *Quelques Années de ma Vie* (Calmann-Lévy 1894)
Souvenirs et Correspondances (Calmann-Lévy. 1896)
FLAUBERT, Gustave, *Correspondance*. Nouvelle édition augmentée (Conard. 1926–1930)
Correspondance entre George Sand et Gustave Flaubert. Préface de Henri Amic (Calmann-Lévy. 1904)
Lettres inédites à la Princesse Mathilde. Préface de M. le Comte Joseph Primoli Étude de Madame la Princesse Mathilde (Conard. 1927)
Lettres inédites à Tourguéneff. Presentation et notes par Gérard Gailly (Monaco. Éditions du Rocher. 1946)
FLEURY, General Cte, *Souvenirs* (Plon-Nourrit. 1897–1898)
FLEURY, Comte, et SONOLET, Louis, *La Société du Second Empire. T. III. 1863–1867*. (Albin Michel, n.d.)
FROMENTIN, Eugène, *Correspondance et Fragments inédits*. Biographie et notes par Pierre Blanchon (Plon-Nourrit. 1912)
FUCHS, Max, *Théodore de Banville, 1823–1891* (Cornély. 1912)
GAUTIER, Théophile, *Poésies complètes* (Lemerre. 1890)

GAYOT, André, *Une ancienne muscadine. Fortunée Hamelin. Lettres inédites, 1839–1851* (Émile-Paul. 1911)

GIRARDIN, Émile de [and others], *Enghien et ses environs* (Michel Lévy. 1862)

GONCOURT, Edmond and Jules de, *Journal. Mémoires de la Vie littéraire* (Monaco. Les Éditions de l'Imprimerie nationale. 1956–)

GONCOURT, Jules de, *Lettres*. Introduction d'Henry Céard (Flammarion. Fasquelle. 1930)

GOT, Edmond, *Journal* (Plon-Nourrit. 1910)

GOUNOD, Charles, *Mémoires d'un Artiste* (Calmann-Lévy. 1896)

HALÉVY, Ludovic, *Carnets*. Publiés avec une introduction et des notes par Daniel Halévy (Calmann-Lévy. 1935)

HALPÉRINE-KAMINSKY, E., *Ivan Tourguéneff d'après sa correspondance avec ses amis français* (Charpentier. 1901)

HEGERMANN-LINDENCRONE, L. de, *In the Courts of Memory, 1858–1875*. From contemporary letters (New York. Harper & Brothers. 1912)

HERMANT, Abel, *Souvenirs de la Vie mondaine* (Plon. 1935)

HOUSSAYE, Arsène, *Les Confessions. Souvenirs d'un demi-siècle, 1830–1880* Dentu. 1885–1891)

HÜBNER, Comte de, *Neuf ans de souvenirs d'un ambassadeur d'Autriche à Paris sous le Second Empire, 1851–1859* (Plon. 1904)

IBROVAC, Miodrag, *José-Maria de Heredia. Sa Vie – son Œuvre* (Les Presses Françaises. 1923)

ILCHESTER, Earl of [ed]., *The Journal of the Hon. Henry Edward Fox (afterwards fourth and last Lord Holland) 1818–1830* (Thornton Butterworth. 1923)

JANIN, Jules, *Voyage en Italie* (Bourdin. 1839)

JEROME, King, *Mémoires et correspondance du Roi Jérôme et de la Reine Catherine* (Dentu. 1861–1866)

JOLLIVET, Gaston, *Souvenirs d'un Parisien* (Tallandier. 1928)

KÜHN, Joachim, *Prinzessin Mathilde Bonaparte* (Berlin, Deutsche Verlagsgesellschaft für Politik und Geschichte. 1929)

KURTZ, Harold, *The Empress Eugénie* (Hamish Hamilton. 1964)

LA RONCIÈRE LE NOURY, L'Amiral de, *Correspondance intime (1855–1871)* (Honoré Champion. 1928)

LAVEDAN, Henri, *Avant l'Oubli. II. Écrire* (Plon. 1934)

LEON, Derrick, *Introduction to Proust* (Kegan Paul. 1940)

LISZT, F., *Correspondance de Liszt et de la Comtesse d'Agoult, 1840–1864* (Grasset. 1934)

MALMESBURY, Earl of, *Memoirs of an ex-Minister. An Autobiography* (Longmans, Green. 1884)

MALO, Henri, *Mémoires de Madame Dosne, l'Égérie de M. Thiers* (Plon. 1928)

MASUYER, Valérie, *Mémoires, Lettres et Papiers*. Avec une introduction et des notes par Jean Bourguignon (Plon. 1937)

MAUPASSANT, Guy de, *Lettres inédites à Gustave Flaubert*. Publiés par Pierre Borel (Éditions des Portiques. 1929)

MÉNIÈRE, Prosper, *Journal* (Plon. 1903)

MÉRIMÉE, Prosper, *Correspondance générale*. Établie et annotée par Maurice Parturier (Toulouse. Édouard Privat. 1953–)
Lettres de Prosper Mérimée à la Comtesse de Montijo (Edition privée. 1930)

Lettres à Viollet-de-Duc (*documents inédits*) *1839–1870* (Champion. 1927)
MÉRY, [Joseph], *Scènes de la vie italienne* (Dumont. 1837)
MEYER, Arthur, *Ce que je peux dire* (Plon. 1912)
MORTIER, A., *Les Soirées parisiennes*. Par un monsieur de l'orchestre (Dentu. 1875–1884)
MOULY, Georges, *La Vie Prodigieuse de Victorien Sardou (1831–1908.)* D'après des documents inédits (Albin Michel. 1931)
MURAT, Princess Caroline, *My Memoirs* (Eveleigh Nash. 1910)
NAUROY, Charles, *Le Curieux* (N.p. 1883–1888)
PAGET, Walburga, Lady, *The Linings of Life* (Hurst & Blackett. 1928)
PAILLERON, Marie-Louise, *François Buloz et ses Amis. Les Derniers Romantiques* (Librarie académique Perrin. 1923)
Le Paradis Perdu. Souvenirs d'Enfance (Albin Michel. 1947)
PASTEUR, Louis, *Correspondance, 1840–1895*. Réunie et annotée par Pasteur Valléry-Radot (Librairie Bernard Grasset. Flammarion. 1940–1951)
PELADAN, *Ernest Hébert. Son Œuvre et son Temps* (Ch. Delagrave. 1910)
PINARD, Ernest, *Mon Journal* (Dentu. 1892)
PIPE-EN-BOIS, *Ce que je pense d'Henriette Maréchal, de sa préface et du théâtre de mon temps* (Librairie Centrale. 1866)
POPELIN, Claudius, *Cinq Octaves de Sonnets* (Lemerre. 1875)
Un Livre de Sonnets (Charpentier. 1888)
Poésies complètes (Charpentier. 1889)
PROD'HOMME, J.-G. and DANDELOT, A., *Gounod (1818–1893). Sa Vie et ses Œuvres, d'après des documents inédits* (Delagrave. 1911)
PROUST, Marcel, *À la recherche du temps perdu. III. À L'ombre des jeunes filles en fleurs* (Gallimard. 1949)
QUERLIN, Marise, *La Princesse Mathilde* (Lausanne. Éditions Recontre. 1966)
RECLUS, Maurice, *Émile de Girardin. Le Créateur de la Presse Moderne* (Hachette. 1934)
REINAUD, Émile, *Charles Jalabert, l'homme, l'artiste, d'après sa correspondance* (Hachette. 1903)
RENAN, Ernest, *Correspondance. 1846–1892* (Calmann-Lévy. 1926, 1928)
RICHARDSON, Joanna, *Théophile Gautier. His Life and Times* (Reinhardt. 1958)
Sarah Bernhardt (Reinhardt. 1959)
Rachel (Reinhardt. 1956)
SAINTE-BEUVE, Charles-Augustin, *Correspondance générale*. Recueillie, classée et annotée par Jean Bonnerot (Stock. Privat Didier. 1935–)
Lettres à la Princesse (Michel Lévy. 1873)
Souvenirs et Indiscrétions. Le dîner du Vendredi saint. Publiés par son dernier secrétaire (Michel Lévy. 1872)
SILVER, Mabel, *Jules Sandeau* (Boivin. 1936)
SIMPSON, M. C. M., *Letters and Recollections of Julius and Mary Mohl* (Kegan Paul. 1887)
SPAZIANI, Marcello (ed.), *Joseph-Napoléon Primoli. Pages inédites* (Rome. Edizioni di storia e Letteratura. 1959)
Gli amici della Principessa Matilde (Rome. Edizioni di Storia e Letteratura. 1960)
STARKIE, Enid, *Flaubert. The Making of the Master* (Weidenfeld & Nicolson. 1967)

SUE, Eugène, and PYAT, Félix, *Mathilde. Drame en 5 actes. Tiré des Mémoires d'une jeune femme* (Tresse. 1847)

[TAINE, H.], *H. Taine, Sa vie et sa correspondance.* Tomes III & IV (Hachette. 1905, 1907)

THIÉBAUT, Marcel, *Edmond About* (Gallimard 1936)

TROUBAT, Jules, *Souvenirs du dernier secrétaire de Sainte-Beuve* (Calmann-Lévy. 1890)

VARLOY, A., *Gustave Nadaud. Sa Vie and ses Œuvres (1820–1893).* (Daragon. 1910)

VENTO, Claude, *Les Salons de Paris en 1889* (Dentu. 1891)

VICTORIA, Queen, *The Letters of Queen Victoria.* Second series . . . Edited by G. E. Buckle. Vol. III, 1879–1885 (Murray. 1928)

VIEL-CASTEL, Comte H. de, *Mémoires sur le règne de Napoléon III (1851–1864).* Avec une préface par L. Léouzon le Duc (Chez tous les libraires. 1883)

VILLEMESSANT, H. de, *Mémoires d'un journaliste.* 3e série (Dentu. 1873)

VILLEMOT, Auguste, *La Vie à Paris.* Chroniques du Figaro. Ire et 2e séries (Michel Lévy. 1858)

VIOLLET-LE-DUC, E. E., *Lettres inédites.* Recueillies et annotées par son fils (Librairies-Imprimeries Réunies. 1902)

WHITEHURST, Felix M., *Court and Social Life in France under Napoleon III* (Tinsley Bros. 1873)

WORTH, Jean-Philippe, *A Century of Fashion.* Translated by Ruth Scott Miller (Boston. Little, Brown & Co. 1928)

The following are among the articles consulted:

BONNEFON, Paul, *Princess Mathilde. Lettres et billets inédits. Revue bleue,* 4, 11, 18 January 1913.

CHAUMEIX, André, *Le Comte Primoli.* RDDM, 1 July 1927, 223 sqq.

COPPÉE, François, *La Princesse Mathilde. Le Gaulois,* 3 January 1904.

DE SACY, Silvestre, *Lettres à ma fille. I. (1862–1871). II. (1871–1878).* RDDM, 1, 15 November 1926.

D'OCAGNE, Maurice, *La Princesse Mathilde au temps de sa jeunesse et sous l'Empire.* (Reprinted from *La Revue hebdomadaire,* 9 October 1926.) *Les dernières années de la Princess Mathilde. (La Revue hebdomadaire,* 8 August 1925.)

DOMINIQUE [i.e. Marcel Proust], *Un Salon historique. Le Salon de S.A.I. la Princess Mathilde. Le Figaro,* 25 February 1903.

GANDERAX, Louis, *Une Princesse française. Le Temps,* 5 January 1904.

GAUTIER, Théophile (*fils*), *Mort de la Princesse Mathilde. Le Figaro,* 3 January 1904.

GEBHART, Émile, *La Princesse Mathilde. Le Journal des Débats,* 4 January 1904.

GRANDJEAN, Serge, *Les intérieurs et les collections de la Princesse Mathilde.* Communication à la Société d'Études d'Avallon (Yonne). 1967.

HOUSSAYE, Henry, *La Princesse Mathilde. L'Echo de Paris,* 5 January 1904.

JOLLIVET, G. [?], *La Maladie de la Princesse Mathilde. L'Éclair,* 22 November 1903.

LAVISSE, Ernest, *La Princesse Mathilde. La Revue de Paris,* 15 January 1904.

MASSON, Frédéric, *La Nièce de l'Empereur. Le Temps*, 5 January 1904.
La Princesse Mathilde après la guerre. La Revue hebdomadaire, 30 March 1912, 609 sqq.
MATHILDE, Princess, *Souvenirs des années d'exil*.
   I. Rome et Florence. RDDM, 15 December 1927, 721 sqq.
   II. Autour du Mariage. RDDM, 1 January 1928, 76 sqq.
   III. À la Cour de Nicolas Ier. RDDM, 15 January 1928, 359 sqq.
PRIMOLI, J.-N., *La Princesse Mathilde et le maestro Sauzay. La Revue hebdomadaire*, 6 October 1917.
Autour du Mariage de l'Impératrice. RDDM, 1 November 1924, 64 sqq.
La Princesse Mathilde et Théophile Gautier. RDDM, 1, 15 November 1925.
La Princess Mathilde et le Duc d'Aumale. RDP, 1 August 1922.
RICHARDSON, Joanna, *Unpublished Letters of Flaubert. The Times Literary Supplement*, 13 June 1968.
Proust and the Princess. The Times Literary Supplement, 17 October 1968.
WELSCHINGER, Henri, *La Captivité de Napoléon III à Wilhelmshohe*. RDDM, 15 April 1910, 901 sqq.

PERIODICALS

The following are among the periodicals consulted.

L'Artiste (1860–1870)
L'Indépendance belge (1870–1871)
Le Moniteur universel (1855–1868)
La Petite Revue (1863–1866)
La Presse (1862–1870)
La Revue de Paris (1864)
La Vie Parisienne (1863–)
The Times (*passim*)

Index

DATE DUE

GAYLORD   PRINTED IN U.S.A.